Photoshop® CS3 for Nature Photographers

A Workshop in a Book

Ellen Anon

Tim Grey

BICENTENNIAL
1807
WILEY
2007
BICENTENNIAL

WILEY PUBLISHING, INC.

Acquisitions Editor and Development Editor: Pete Gaughan
Technical Editor: TK
Production Editor: Christine O'Connor
Copy Editor: Kim Wimpsett
Production Manager: Tim Tate
Vice President and Executive Group Publisher: Richard Swadley
Vice President and Executive Publisher: Joseph B. Wikert
Vice President and Publisher: Neil Edde
Media Project Supervisor: Laura Atkinson
Media Development Specialist: Kit Malone
Media Quality Assurance: Angie Denny
Book Designers: Franz Baumhackl and Lori Barra
Compositor: Franz Baumhackl
Proofreader: Rachel Gunn
Indexer: Ted Laux
Anniversary Logo Design: Richard Pacifico
Cover Designer: Ryan Sneed
Cover Image: Ellen Anon

For general information on our other products and services or to obtain technical support, please contact our Customer Care Department within the U.S. at (800) 762-2974, outside the U.S. at (317) 572-3993 or fax (317) 572-4002.

Wiley also publishes its books in a variety of electronic formats. Some content that appears in print may not be available in electronic books.

Library of Congress Cataloging-in-Publication Data is available from the publisher.

Dear Reader,

Thank you for choosing *Photoshop CS3 for Nature Photographers, A Workshop in a Book*. This book is part of a family of premium-quality Sybex graphics books, all written by outstanding authors who combine practical experience with a gift for teaching.

Sybex was founded in 1976. Now, more than 30 years later, we're still committed to producing consistently exceptional books. With each of our graphics titles we're working hard to set a new standard for the industry. From the paper we print on to the writers and CAD professionals we work with, our goal is to bring you the best books available.

I hope you see all that reflected in these pages. I'm very interested to hear your comments and get your feedback on how we're doing. To let us know what you think about this or any other Sybex book, please send me an email at sybex_publisher@ wiley.com. Please also visit us at www.sybex.com to learn more about the rest of our growing graphics line.

Best regards,

NEIL EDDE
Vice President and Publisher
Sybex, an Imprint of Wiley

To my husband, Jack, and sons, Josh and Seth—thanks for sharing the passion; and to my parents for planting a love of nature and photography within me.
—Ellen Anon

To Mom. Thanks for taking me camping, for encouraging me to dream big, and for everything.
—Tim Grey

Acknowledgments

Ellen Anon   First, I want to thank my family, especially my husband, for their patience with me when I am away taking photos or teaching workshops or when I'm holed up in my study working; I appreciate your support and the extra burdens I sometimes place on you. And special thanks to Josh for working out the technical details involved in recording the training materials.

Second, I realize how fortunate I am to have so many friends in the field who have gone out of their way to further my career. Peter Burian is a good friend and colleague who continually shares opportunities with me and offers support along the way. Arthur Morris was a close friend and mentor for years who opened doors for me that have had major impacts on my life. Joe and Mary Ann McDonald took a risk and hired me to teach at their digital institute (www.hoothollow.com) before even meeting me. Teaching with them is an honor, and the bonus is that they have become friends. Rick Holt, who teaches workshops with me at Hoothollow and at the Art Wolfe Digital Institute, is my buddy. Freeman Patterson and Art Becker are friends, mentors, and sources of inspiration. Michael Nadler provides support and a good word at just the right moment to just the right people. Of course I want to thank Tim, my co-author, for collaborating on this project. Thank you all.

I am extremely grateful to our contributors, who were incredibly generous with their time, writing, and images: Fabiola Alcazar, Josh Anon, Peter Burian, Greg Downing, André Gallant, Charles Glatzer, Darrell Gulin, Rick Holt, Lewis Kemper, Joe McDonald, Arthur Morris, Michael Reichmann, John Shaw, and Tony Sweet. All are busy professionals, yet they made time to help us. Thank you!

Of course, I am thankful to the folks at Wiley for seeing the value in this project. Some authors have horror stories to tell about their editors. I feel extremely lucky that our team has been absolutely wonderful. Pete Gaughan served as the acquisitions editor as well as the development editor. Pete is an amazing man who somehow knows exactly what to say to keep me on track. He's quite gifted, and I'm quite grateful! Al Ward, our technical editor, did a great job of making certain everything is accurate and offered insightful suggestions as well as an excellent sidebar. As you, the reader, can tell, our production editors, compositors, and proofreaders also did an excellent job.

Thank you also to the Adobe prerelease team, especially John Nack and Jeff Chien, as well as forum members who were always responsive to questions and who made learning CS3 a pleasure.

Last, I want to thank my personal friends (you know who you are—at least I certainly hope that you do!) for your support and encouragement. And a special thank you to those readers who purchased the first edition of this book and thereby made this edition possible!

Tim Grey   It seems these days that every book which bears my name comes at a crossroads of many projects with competing deadlines and significant time requirements. Thank goodness I love my work, as I'm fortunate enough to not have any shortage there. Of course, for this particular project, that meant my co-author, Ellen Anon, got the job of updating the vast majority of the content. Thank you, Ellen, for helping make sure this revision is much better than the original.

I also want to thank the many photographers who have inspired me with their own work and even in some cases provided images or text for us to include in this book. These include John Shaw, Art Wolfe, George Lepp, Dewitt Jones, Arthur Morris, Jeff Greene, Ira Meyer, Alice Cahill, and the many amateur photographers whose images I've had the pleasure of seeing at various presentations and workshops. I'm fortunate to be able to see so many incredible images from so many excellent photographers.

I'd also like to add a special thanks to Pete Gaughan at Wiley. He has proven time and again with many book projects (how many have we worked on together now?) that he has the patience of a saint and the kindness to go with it. I am fortunate to have someone I enjoy working with so much to help make my books the best they can be.

Finally, to all my friends and family who have stood by me and encouraged me, thank you. You know who you are, and I hope you know how much I appreciate you.

About the Authors

Ellen Anon

Ellen got her start with photography at age five, but for years it remained a hobby as she took a very long fork in the road, eventually earning a Ph.D. in clinical psychology. Finally in 1997 a broken foot forced her to take a break from work as a psychologist, and she used the time to study John Shaw's photography tapes. (*Thank you, John, for starting me on the road to photography as a career.—Ellen*) She debated briefly between building a traditional darkroom in her home and creating a digital darkroom. because she's not fond of being closed up in small, dark spaces with strong smells of funky chemicals, she opted for the latter. Ever since, photography has been a two-part process for her. Making the image in the field is step one, and optimizing it in the digital darkroom is step two. Being creative with it is the icing on the cake!

Ellen is now a freelance photographer and writer who specializes in expressive photography. Ellen's images, based on nature, are sometimes realistic and sometimes abstract but are always designed to elicit emotional reactions from the viewer. Her goal with her photographs is to go beyond the ordinary in ways that she hopes stimulate others to pause and appreciate some of the beauty and wonder of our earth. Ellen's images are included in collections in several countries. She is represented by several stock agencies, and her photos have been showcased in galleries and used in numerous publications (including Sierra Club's *Mother Earth* and Inner Reflections 2007 calendar). She is an Apple V.I.P. Pro Photographer and an Apple Certified Trainer for Aperture.

In addition to *Photoshop CS3 for Nature Photographers: A Workshop in a Book*, Ellen is the coauthor of *Aperture Exposed: The Mac Photographer's Guide to Taming the Workflow* (Sybex, 2006) with her son Josh Anon and has contributed chapters to several other books. Ellen leads both photographic- and digital darkroom–oriented workshops for Santa Fe Workshops, Art Wolfe Digital Photography Center, and the McDonald Digital Wildlife Institute. She is a featured speaker at various events and is also a frequent contributor to a variety of photography magazines. Ellen is an active member of the North American Nature Photography Association (NANPA) and is an instructor for its high-school scholarship program. She is also a member of the National Association of Photoshop Professionals (NAPP) and the American Society of Media Photographers (ASMP).

Photography has taken Ellen to locations from Hawaii to South Africa to Japan and has paved the way for her to meet all sorts of wonderful people. Her husband and two sons, all of whom are quite skilled with cameras, sometimes travel with her. Fortunately, they adapt to her crazy schedule and willingly plan vacations around her photographic destinations.

Tim Grey

A lifetime of working with computers and a love of photography combine as the perfect passion for Tim Grey. He got started with computers at the age of ten and took his first photography class in high school. In college, he started tinkering with Photoshop, helping others learn how to use the software. Since then his passion for all things related to photography and digital imaging has grown exponentially.

Tim loves learning as much as he possibly can about digital imaging, and he loves sharing that information even more. He does so through his writing and speaking appearances. His articles have been published in *Outdoor Photographer*, *PC Photo*, and *Digital Photo Pro* magazines, among others. He is the author or co-author of more than a dozen books on digital imaging and photography, including *Color Confidence: The Digital Photographer's Guide to Color Management* and *Photoshop CS3 Workflow: The Digital Photographer's Guide*. He also presents seminars and workshops at a variety of industry trade shows and other venues.

Tim publishes a regular "Digital Darkroom Questions" email list, where he answers questions related to digital imaging for photographers. To add your email address to the list, visit www.timgrey.com.

When he isn't working to meet deadlines on his latest book, Tim enjoys venturing out with his digital SLR to find new subjects. When traveling on business around the country and the world, he capitalizes on any "downtime" to go out walking with camera in hand capturing whatever catches his eye, which typically includes urban subjects. He also often ventures out to find nature subjects around his home near Seattle, Washington.

Foreword

Adobe Photoshop has changed the world of photography immeasurably. It is an amazing, powerful tool, now at the hands of nearly every photographer. I don't claim to be an expert in the program, but that doesn't change my admiration for its depth, its scope, or what talented artists can create with it.

For nature photographers, the biggest reason for excitement is being in control of your process. Shooting with digital equipment means that the artist controls every step, from being in the field to "processing" using your digital darkroom and even to printing. With the artist in control of these steps, the final product—your art—will more closely reflect your vision.

Digital's convenience allows new opportunities beyond Photoshop. I'm able to shoot in India and nearly instantaneously send photos back to the office in Seattle, Washington, for posting on my website. Once when I was giving a talk in Asheville, North Carolina, my laptop was stolen, along with the slide show I was to give. If these had been slide carousels, my only choice would have been to cancel my talk; there would have been no way to get replacement slides picked, processed, and sent to me quickly enough from my office in Seattle—and that's assuming the slides weren't originals and lost forever. In this day and age, though, it was a minor setback. My office managed to upload new files for me to a web server, and I borrowed a laptop to make the presentation, all within eighteen hours.

But digital's most important benefit for me is that it enables me to view a photo in the field just after I've shot it, instead of having to wait weeks until I'm back home and had the film processed. It has opened my work up to new possibilities, and it allows me to be more spontaneous and take risks that are impossible with film, thanks to instantaneous feedback.

Digital photography isn't necessarily more convenient than traditional film photography, at least not yet. Instead of hauling bricks of film across the world, I'm hauling USB external hard drives for redundant backups, and I'm hauling solar-powered chargers for batteries to power my laptop.

But the smart photographer knows that comparing today's digital equipment with today's film equipment is a losing game. The true revolution of digital is in its infancy. You may not be quite ready to switch your entire photographic workflow over to digital right now, but there will come a time when it will be much more convenient and much less expensive, and in the end, you, the artist, will have much stronger control over the final product by shooting digitally.

This is exactly why *Photoshop CS3 for Nature Photographers: A Workshop in a Book* is so timely. Every evolution in the technology of photography—and I think it's worth remembering that photography in any era has always been concerned with the newest technology—comes with a learning curve. I'm very impressed with the scope of the work in this book, the depth of the knowledge, and the clear instruction. Ellen and Tim do a fantastic job of guiding the reader through the technical maze of digital photography. This is a book for all levels of photographers—from those who have shot for years on film and are transitioning to those who are at the beginning of their craft and starting out using digital cameras. It's a book about digital workflow and related issues, but first and foremost it's a book about photography.

In the end, that's the most important thing: the photograph. The rest is a means to an end; my true love—and I suspect yours as well—is not the technology or the tools but the image. What really matters is looking at the photos we take and being reminded with awe of the beauty and fragility of our natural world.

—ART WOLFE
World-renowned nature photographer, artist, and author; recipient of numerous photography honors; and publisher of award-winning books

Contents

Chapter 4   **Foundations**   95

Chapter 5   **Workflows and First Steps**   145

Introduction

Photoshop and nature photography are a logical marriage. Although there are some people who regard Photoshop as an evil that degrades the purity of nature photography, in reality nature photography has long been a two-step process. The first step involves making the best possible picture in the field. The second is creating the best possible output from that capture. Ansel Adams is widely acclaimed as one of the greatest black-and-white nature photographers of all time. Yet if you had a chance to view some of his prints before he optimized them in his traditional darkroom, you might not have looked twice at them. Although he was an excellent photographer, he was truly a master of the darkroom. Today, Photoshop enables many more people to become masters of the darkroom—the digital darkroom.

Becoming a master of the digital darkroom can be a daunting task. Trying to learn the program by trial and error is a most time-consuming—and frustrating—approach. Finding the time and money to spend a week at a workshop devoted to Photoshop for photographers involves a major time commitment, to say nothing of the significant expense involved.

You'll find lots of Photoshop how-to books on the bookstore shelves, but many address the needs of graphic artists more than those of photographers. Graphic artists need to use vector tools such as the Pen tool or Shape tool, which aren't of much use to most photographers. And although some Photoshop books do target photographers, few specifically address the unique needs of nature photographers. Many of these books focus on areas unimportant to nature photographers. For example, they may spend many pages dealing with retouching portraits or repairing scans of old photos.

Most nature photographers need to know how to take their images off memory cards and into the computer and then how to use Photoshop to edit and optimize them. They need a straightforward workflow that pertains to nature photography and that's easy and efficient to follow. That's the goal of *Photoshop CS3 for Nature Photographers: A Workshop in a Book*.

Further, this book addresses some of the unique concerns nature photographers experience, such as white balance and color correction. Of course, all photographers deal with white balance, but many are concerned with making their images truly neutral. As nature photographers, we often get up before dawn to capture the beautiful early morning light. That light that we go to great lengths to capture is far from neutral. In fact, it's the warmth of it that makes so many of our images. If they were portrayed as neutral, many would lose their impact.

Photoshop offers a multitude of ways to accomplish almost every task. Which method is the best to use in a specific situation often depends on the type of image you are modifying. Throughout the book we bear in mind that your subjects are nature and gear the techniques to those that are likely to give you the best results the most easily.

We want this book to be easy to use and have organized it to follow the basic workflow. Each chapter lays a foundation for the following chapters. You'll also notice that we incorporate an element called Try It! in this book.

Try It! These sections offer a chance to take a break from reading and to practice the techniques that have just been covered using your own images or those that we provide on the companion CD. Reading about a technique is one thing, but for most people, it doesn't sink in until you actually do it. By providing you with images to practice on, we hope to make this book more like a workshop.

You'll notice that most of the book is written in the first-person plural, meaning that both Ellen and Tim recommend the technique or approach that is being described. Occasionally, we break into third-person singular when one of us is describing a personal experience or preference. Although generally we provide you with clear guidance for how to proceed, sometimes Tim prefers one approach while Ellen favors another. We have opted to present both approaches to you because both are viable options; it's not that one is right and the other wrong. It's simply a matter of each of us having certain preferences based on the types of images we regularly work with. You too may find one or the other approach more useful with your images. By providing both, we offer you the best of our joint experience.

Who Should Use This Book

Every nature photographer who wants people to look at their pictures and say "Wow!" should use this book.

Photoshop CS3 for Nature Photographers: A Workshop in a Book is designed for nature photographers who want a straightforward workflow customized to make their images have the most impact. If you are new to Photoshop, you'll find that we start off with the basics and gently build your abilities. We give you plenty of opportunities to practice what you're learning using images we provide as well as your own. We write in an informal, casual, but clear way, providing lots of examples and color illustrations to help you develop your skills.

If you already have some familiarity with Photoshop and want to update your workflow to take advantage of the new features in Photoshop CS3, we'll show you how. If you've found in the past that you don't always get the best results or that your workflow is inconsistent, we'll help you hone your skills. We'll provide techniques that will allow you to optimize your images efficiently. And if you'd like to get some ideas of how to be creative with your images, this is the book for you! We cover a variety of ways of compositing (combining) images as well as creating various digital montages, filter effects, and even digital multiple exposures.

If you take other types of photographs as well as nature photographs, our workflow and techniques will still work well for you. You'll gain the tools and abilities you need to make your pictures come alive.

Note: Although Photoshop is available in Standard and Extended configurations in CS3, every technique that we describe can be done using the Standard version. The Extended version of Photoshop contains additional features that are of particular benefit when working with 3D, motion, architecture, and construction, as well as comprehensive image analysis such as a forensics expect might need to do. It's one of the few times that we nature photographers actually get to buy the less expensive version of something!

What's Inside

The organization of this book follows the general workflow that we recommend. Here is a glance at what's in each chapter:

Chapter 1: Thinking Digitally discusses the photographic techniques you need to use in-camera to get the best results. It covers choosing RAW versus JPEG, understanding exposure, understanding the various types of histograms, setting white balance, and shooting for composites, as well as ethical considerations.

Chapter 2: Bridge explains how to customize and use Adobe Bridge to download, view, compare, loupe, sort, and edit your images. You'll learn how to streamline this process and organize your images so you can easily find them.

Chapter 3: Adobe Camera Raw covers using the raw converter to make most of the global changes to your images, even TIFF and JPEG files. The adjustments you make here are the foundation of your workflow and will help you create the best possible image.

Chapter 4: Foundations lays the foundation to make Photoshop work in a predictable way for you, including color management issues as well as setting the Preferences. It also covers using some of the basic selection and brush tools you'll be using later in Photoshop.

Chapter 5: Workflows and First Steps describes how to create a flexible workflow using Smart Objects and Smart Filters as well as the traditional workflow. It also covers cropping, rotating, and image cleanup in Photoshop and introduces the concept of layers.

Chapter 6: Exposure Adjustments introduces you to using layer masks and guides you through making various tonal adjustments including Levels, Curves, and Shadow/Highlight.

Chapter 7: Color Adjustments continues the use of adjustment layers to help you fine-tune the color in your image using Hue/Saturation, Selective Color, and Color Balance.

Chapter 8: Composites covers a variety of ways to combine images to create effects not possible in a single image, including creating panoramas, replacing skies, using an extended depth of field, using an extended exposure latitude (including using Merge to HDR to create 32-bit images), and combining parts of various pictures into a single image.

Chapter 9: Creative Effects presents ways to become more expressive with your images, including converting to black and white or partially colorized images, using various filters, creating digital montages, and even making digital multiple exposures.

Chapter 10: Output covers the workflow after you have created your master file in order to resize, reduce noise, and sharpen your images for print or the Web.

Chapter 11: Time-Savers presents ways to become more efficient, including actions and batch processing. It also covers ways to create watermarks and copyright brushes.

What's on the CD

The companion CD contains a series of training videos to augment the materials in the book. The training videos cover many of the new features introduced in Photoshop CS3 as well as instruction on some basic techniques such as using layer masks.

The CD also provides sample images for you to use to practice the techniques in the book. Use them to follow along with the instructions and to try each new technique as it is presented. Taking the time to use these images will reinforce what you're reading.

How to Contact the Authors

Both of us welcome feedback from you about this book or about books you'd like to see from us in the future. You can reach Ellen by writing to ellenanon@aol.com or Tim by writing to tim@timgrey.com. For more information about Ellen's workshops and photography, visit her website at www.sunbearphoto.com. To learn more about Tim's writing and appearances, visit www.timgrey.com.

Sybex strives to keep you supplied with the latest tools and information you need for your work. Please check its website at www.sybex.com for additional content and updates that supplement this book. Type **photoshop and nature** in the search box (or enter the book's ISBN, 978-0-470-11989-1), and click Search to get to the book's update page.

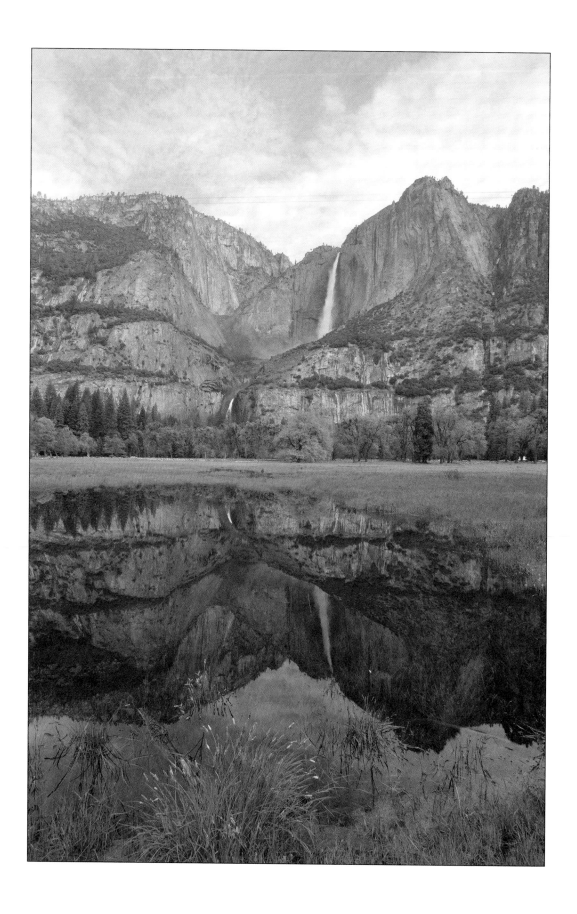

Thinking Digitally

The first step in digital photography is to create the best possible picture in the field. The second step is to optimize that capture and use software to present the final image in the best possible way. Digital photography requires embracing some new concepts and choosing the best tools to get the job done. The better your photographic techniques and the more efficient your workflow, the less time you'll spend on the computer doing mundane tasks and fixing mistakes. That will leave more time for photography itself as well as creative interpretations of the images using Photoshop.

This chapter covers some of the concepts you need to consider in the field and other choices you may face.

1

Chapter Contents

Photographic Techniques

It really doesn't matter whether you are using film or digital to capture your images—the basics remain the same. Digital photography and Photoshop are not excuses to be sloppy. You still have to do everything possible to take the best pictures you can in the field. That way, the time you spend at your computer will be devoted to optimizing images, being creative, and perhaps other business, rather than trying to compensate for mistakes you made while taking the pictures.

With digital capture you still need to use most of your photographic tools to help create the best images possible, including tripods, mirror lockup, and cable releases when appropriate. Although we claim to sharpen images in a raw converter or Photoshop using the Unsharp Mask or Smart Sharpen filter (techniques described in Chapter 10, "Output"), this sharpening is not designed to fix an out-of-focus picture. Rather, its intent is to compensate for the slight softening that occurs in the digital process.

Focus carefully and accurately so that you capture the sharpest picture you can. Use a tripod whenever it's reasonable. In fact, using a tripod is essential when you want to combine images to expand exposure latitude, and it's highly recommended when you intend to create a panorama by stitching together several individual photographs. If you don't use a tripod when taking several pictures at various exposure settings in order to create an exposure latitude composite, then when you try to combine them into a single image (discussed in Chapter 8, "Composites"), the images won't combine properly; in fact, they may not merge at all. If you try to shoot a panorama without a tripod, you're likely to encounter all sorts of complications when you try to stitch them together, a topic also covered in Chapter 8.

You need to use a polarizer or split neutral-density filter when appropriate, even though it's essentially possible to digitally create a custom neutral-density filter by combining exposures or by using adjustment layers and layer masks, all of which are covered later in this book. If the scene lends itself to using a split neutral-density filter, as in Figure 1.1, it will save you time and effort later, so use it!

Similarly, you need to choose your camera settings such as Aperture Priority, Shutter Priority, or Manual to create the type of image you have in mind. Planning to use Photoshop is not an excuse to suddenly rely on the fully automatic shooting modes. Many nature photographers shoot in Aperture Priority or Manual because controlling the depth of field is their primary concern. If you envision a picture with a shallow depth of field, photograph it that way using a wide aperture to begin with rather than relying on one of the blur filters within Photoshop. Use a filter later to accentuate the effect if desired. Occasionally, nature photographers may choose to use Shutter Priority for a specific need such as to create a blur of birds in flight (like the ones shown in Figure 1.2) or to create a pleasing softness to moving water. Although you can create motion blurs in Photoshop, planning your image ahead of time (for example, using a slow shutter speed combined with panning) enables you to capture images with motion effects that would require a lot more time to make digitally. In some cases, you can capture motion effects that would be nearly impossible to re-create in Photoshop, because objects closer to you blur more than objects that are farther away.

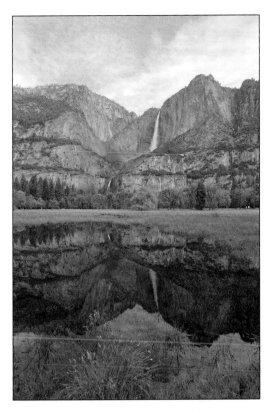

Figure 1.1
Use good photographic techniques, including tripods, cable releases, and even split neutral-density filters, when appropriate, to capture the best images possible and then optimize them in Photoshop for impact. (Photo by Ellen Anon.)

Figure 1.2
It is doubtful you could re-create this blur effect in Photoshop. (Photo by Ellen Anon.)

Compose carefully. Of course you can crop the image later, but that means you will be cropping away pixels, leaving fewer pixels. With fewer pixels your final image will have less detail and may not be able to be printed as large as you had hoped. Take the time to create a pleasing composition so you can use all the pixels your camera is capable of capturing.

Careful metering is as important as ever, even though you now have histograms to give you immediate feedback as to whether the exposure is correct. Meter as you always have, but make it a habit to check the histogram, at least for the first image in a series, to see whether you need to tweak your exposure.

Throughout this book, we've asked some of the top nature photographers in the world to share some of their insights and favorite tips for using Photoshop effectively. Here, in the first of these "pro" sidebars, Charles Glatzer, M. Photog., briefly shares some thoughts about shooting digitally. Glatzer, a professional photographer and teacher for more than 20 years, hosts "Shoot the Light" instructional photographic workshops throughout the United States and abroad. His images are recognized internationally for their lighting, composition, and attention to detail.

Getting It Right in the Camera

by Charles Glatzer

© Charles Glatzer, www.shootthelight.com

Consistency is key to my livelihood. When capturing images in the field, I eliminate as many variables as possible.

To consistently transpose the images we see in our mind to the capture medium, it is necessary to previsualize the result. Previsualization is possible when one has gained technical proficiency. Knowing the photographic fundamentals and being able to see and understand light, its quality and quantity, its physical properties, etc., and how they relate to your subject and capture medium will allow you to take control of your imagery.

And, although Photoshop affords me the ability to apply levels, curves, contrast, and saturation adjustments while tweaking exposure and color balance to an image, I prefer to get it right in the camera. In doing so, my workflow is now faster and more productive, allowing me to transpose the image I captured on my CF card to the printed page more efficiently.

Translation: I can spend more time in the field.

Choosing RAW versus JPEG

It's funny how this has become such an emotionally charged topic for some, almost akin to the classic "which is better?" debates, such as Nikon versus Canon or Apple versus Microsoft. The truth is both formats have advantages and disadvantages, which we'll discuss. However, the evolution in software to convert raw images has made it just as easy, and in some cases more efficient, to use raw files rather than JPEGs.

Before considering the benefits of each format, we'll define what each one is. RAW is actually a pseudoformat used to refer to a lot of camera manufacturer proprietary formats: Canon CR2 and CRW, Nikon NEF, Olympus ORF, Fuji RAF, and more. It's a category of files rather than a specific file format like JPEG and TIFF. raw files are similar to film negatives. They're files containing all the information about the amount of light that was captured by each sensor. Parameters such as color space, white balance, sharpening, saturation, contrast, and so on, are recorded as metadata or tags, but they're not applied to the image in-camera. You can still readily modify all these parameters at the time of conversion.

JPEG is a file format that uses lossy compression each time you resave your file in order to decrease the file size. This means as the pixels are compressed, data is thrown away, even the initial time when the camera first writes the image. Each time thereafter that you resave your image, it is recompressed, and more data is lost. Although you may not notice any problem with the initial image, if you resave an image often, you are likely to see some degradation in image quality. Figure 1.3 presents sections of the same image at 100 percent magnification. The first image was a raw file saved as a TIFF file; the second image was resaved numerous times as a JPEG to illustrate the potential image degradation that can occur.

Figure 1.3 A section of an image originally captured as a raw file and the same section after being resaved multiple times as a JPEG. (Photo by Ellen Anon.)

TIFF is a generic file format people often use to save their raw files after conversion or to save images that were initially shot as JPEGs. TIFF files can be compressed, but they use lossless compression, so you can resave your files with no loss of image quality. TIFF files are larger than JPEG files, meaning that they require more space on a hard drive.

Another difference among these formats has to do with something called *bit depth*. Many nature photographers start to feel over their heads when computerese slips into the discussion, but bit depth isn't very complicated. In simple terms, a *bit* is the smallest unit of information that can be recorded digitally—either a 1 or a 0—and it refers to black or white (even in a color image). In an 8-bit image, each color channel (red, green, and blue) contains 2^8, or 256, possible tonal values. Since each channel has 256 possible tonal values, each pixel has 16.7 million (256×256×256) possible color values, as shown in Table 1.1.

Table 1.1 Colors and Bit Depths

Bit Depth	Typical Format	Possible Colors per Component	Possible Colors per Pixel
8 bits	JPEG	256	16.7 million
12 bits	raw	4,096	68.7 billion
16 bits	PSD, TIFF	65,536	281 trillion

Now, 16 million may seem like more than enough, but in reality, at times the transitions between tones in an 8-bit image are not smooth, which is called *posterization* or *banding*. Twelve-bit images, which is what most cameras can capture in raw, have 4,096 tonal values for each color channel, which means a choice of 68.7 billion (4096×4096×4096) possible colors. Tonal gradations are much smoother with so many possible values for each pixel.

JPEG images are limited to 8 bits, so some JPEG images may demonstrate posterization. Although not a problem for many images, some images, particularly those requiring smooth gradual transitions of color and tone, such as sunset pictures, may show evidence of banding. Clearly, more detail can be accurately conveyed the higher the bit depth. Eight-bit color files used to be common, but 16-bit images are now the standard for most photographers. Even 32-bit files are starting to emerge and can be created using Photoshop's Merge to HDR, which we'll cover in Chapter 8. (HDR stands for *high dynamic range.*)

It can seem confusing initially that in Photoshop you have options to use 8-bit or 16-bit images (even 32-bit if you've created an HDR image). If you have a JPEG image, it is clearly an 8-bit image. When you convert a raw file, which is usually a 12-bit file, you can convert it as either an 8-bit file or a 16-bit file. Converting into an 8-bit file results in a smaller file in which you have discarded 3,840 possible tonal values per color channel. That's a lot to throw away!

When you convert a raw file that is initially 12 bits into 16-bit space, you retain all your original data. You can use the additional tonal values as you make adjustments to the image. In other words, as you tweak the color and tonal values within the image, the adjustments can take advantage of the additional tonal options. Way back in Photoshop 7, there was minimal support for 16-bit images, but Photoshop CS, CS2, and CS3 all offer considerable support, making it logical to convert into 16-bit space.

What's So Great About RAW?

A lot of things! As just described, you have many more possible tonal values, which offer the possibility of more accurate detail in your photos and smoother tonal transitions. But raw has other advantages as well. For example, you can "expose to the right" (as we'll described shortly) and then correct the exposure in the raw converter to optimize the signal-to-noise ratio and have the most accurate tonal information with the least problems from noise.

More important, all the information captured by the sensor is available, and during the conversion process, you get to determine how it appears. A tremendous amount of flexibility and control is available to you as to how to present the information you captured on the sensor, as you can see in Figure 1.4. The raw capture (top) was converted with settings that revealed significantly more color than was captured in the JPEG version (bottom) of the same image. No pixels have been damaged, and yet the image is significantly more dramatic.

Figure 1.4 The raw capture (top) was converted with settings that revealed significantly more color than was captured in the JPEG version (bottom) of the same image. No pixels have been damaged, and yet the image is significantly more dramatic. (Photo by Ellen Anon.)

You can modify the exposure of raw files after the fact, making the image lighter or darker, sometimes significantly lighter or darker. In most cases, you can tweak the exposure in the raw converter such that there is rarely a need to bracket exposures by a third of a stop in the camera anymore, except when you are in danger of clipping your highlights. *Clipping highlights* means you have overexposed your image and captured no detail in the highlights. Although you can instruct the converter to distribute the information the sensor captured in ways that will maximize the contrast, decrease it, or change the white balance, and so on, what you can't do is to re-create information that isn't there. So if you have highlights with no information or shadows with no information, you may be able to lighten or darken them, but you won't be able to re-create detail within them.

That may make it seem that you would be wise to underexpose rather than overexpose, but the fact is that more noise may become visible in the image when it is lightened, as shown in Figure 1.5. For the best results, try to limit lightening in a raw converter to one stop or less. We'll talk more about this issue later in this chapter when we discuss exposing to the right.

In addition to being able to make final decisions about parameters such as exposure, contrast, white balance, color saturation, and more in the raw converter, you can even select the color space there. Usually you will want Adobe RGB (1998), which is a wide color space that correlates well to the colors most ink-jet printers can print. When capturing as JPEG files, most cameras use the sRGB color space, which has fewer colors available. sRGB is particularly suited for web use and projection use. We'll talk more about color spaces in Chapter 5, "First Steps."

Note: If your camera allows you to select a color space, Adobe RGB (1998) is a good choice for nature photographers.

RAW also offers you the ability to easily fix some problems that occur in some images, such as noise reduction for images taken using higher ISOs, chromatic aberration that occurs with some lenses resulting in fringing, and vignetting. We'll explain how to identify these potential problems and how to easily minimize or eliminate these issues using Adobe Camera raw in Chapter 3.

It used to be that the downside of all this flexibility and capability was that in order to use raw images you had to convert them. Although you still have to convert a raw file before final output, new software such as Aperture and Lightroom make it as easy to work with raw files as with JPEGs. We'll talk more about those programs later in this chapter. Photoshop CS2 offered a feature called *smart objects*, which allowed you to place a raw image in your PS file and adjust it at will. The technology was new enough then and had some limitations, so we didn't adopt it as part of our regular workflow at that time. In CS3, Smart Object technology has been improved to make it practical to incorporate raw files right into our PS documents. We'll cover this more extensively in Chapter 5.

Figure 1.5 Lightening the rocks revealed considerable color noise—the magenta, green, and blue blobs on areas of the rocks that should be shades of gray. (Photo by Ellen Anon.)

Many people are happy using the converter in Photoshop called Adobe Camera raw, noting the ease of workflow with Adobe's Bridge program. (We'll look more closely at using Bridge—which replaced the File Browser used in versions of Photoshop prior to CS2—in Chapter 2 and at AdobeCamera raw in Chapter 3.) Some users prefer a separate raw converter program, whether developed by third-party software makers (for example, Capture One, Bibble, or BreezeBrowser) or supplied by camera manufacturers. As mentioned, other people are using Aperture or Lightroom, which incorporate the converter into the image-editing program.

The one remaining notable downside of shooting in RAW is you will need a lot more storage space, both in your camera and on your computer, when you capture in raw than if you use JPEG.

Advantages and Disadvantages of Taking JPEGs

Taking JPEGs does offer some conveniences. For example, capturing in even high-resolution JPEG means you need less storage space; a 1GB compact flash card will make you feel like you can shoot forever. Also convenient is that JPEG images are ready for you to edit or resize and show others in slide shows, emails, or whatever you desire (although programs such as Aperture offer these same conveniences for raw files).

But JPEGs have two *huge* downsides. One is that whatever your camera settings are, including color space, contrast, sharpening, white balance, exposure, and saturation, they are applied to your image at the moment of capture. Any changes must be done within Photoshop itself to this 8-bit image and will result in some destruction of pixels and therefore image degradation. In reality, this may often be so slight that it's not noticeable, but it's there. And, sometimes the differences may be huge. For example, if you accidentally use the wrong white balance, a JPEG image may seem nearly useless at first and at best may require extensive corrections in Photoshop. But the extent of the exposure corrections you'll be able to make will be less because you'll have only an 8-bit image to work with, and extensive Photoshop corrections may result in posterization or noise. Furthermore, as discussed earlier, a JPEG file is compressed lossy, which means that even when you first open it on your computer, it has already thrown away some information the sensor captured when you took the picture. Sometimes this is not noticeable, but at other times it can result in banding and other strange artifacts.

Which is right for you, JPEG or RAW? For most serious amateur and professional photographers, RAW is the way to go. If you make large prints and want the best images you can get, RAW is without a doubt the way to go. If time and convenience are your priorities and if you primarily post your images on the Web, email them to friends, and make only an occasional tiny print, then JPEG may be for you. If you plan on selling your images or entering contests, check with your intended clients or the contest rules, because some will require you to provide the original raw file as well as the converted image.

Try It! Shoot a series of images in raw and in JPEG. Expose them to the best of your ability in JPEG and then use the same settings for the raw version. Then shoot one set with an incorrect white balance setting. Capture a variety of scenes, including some with shadow areas, some with significant highlight areas, and some more average-toned scenes. See whether you can detect a difference in the optimized versions. You may have to wait until you finish a few more chapters so you can optimize both versions of the pictures to their maximum potential for your final decision.

Understanding Histograms

Without a doubt one of the most important advantages of shooting digitally is the ability to check the histogram to ensure you are exposing your images correctly. In the old days—that is, just a few years ago, before digital was so common in the field—wherever there was a group of photographers shooting similar subject matter, you'd inevitably hear someone ask, "What are you shooting at?" People felt comfortable with their compositions but always worried about setting the exposure correctly, knowing that as little as 1/3 stop difference could mean the difference between an awesome image and a throwaway.

With digital cameras you can review your shots on the small LCD screen on the back of the camera. Although this may be somewhat helpful for double-checking your composition and to a certain extent to check for sharpness, the real value lies in displaying the histogram. Get in the habit of checking the histogram in the LCD on the camera back (like the one shown in Figure 1.6). In addition, if your camera has a flashing highlight overexposure alert feature, be sure to enable it. The alert will cause the area of the picture that appears to have clipped highlights to blink or have marching ants. That way you'll know immediately what areas may not have highlight detail, and you can decide whether you need to modify your exposures.

Figure 1.6
The major value of the LCD screen on your camera back is the chance to review the histogram and double-check your exposure.

What is a histogram? A *histogram* is simply a bar graph showing the distribution of the tonalities (lightness/darkness) of the pixels you captured in the image. Each pixel not only describes a color value but also a brightness value. The tonal range extends from pure black on the far left to pure white on the far right, with the different tonalities in between. This means that dark tones are toward the left, middle tones are in the middle, and light tones are toward the right. The higher the peak corresponding to any particular value, the more pixels there are of that particular tonality within the image.

Types of Histograms

All histograms are not the same. Many cameras display an RGB histogram that is a combination of the pixel values in each of the three channels. This is different from a luminosity or brightness histogram that other cameras use. The data in a luminosity histogram is a weighted combination of the values in each channel. Still other histograms show each channel individually. Each type of histogram has advantages and disadvantages.

Luminosity histograms are easier to use to determine if you have areas within your image that are pure white or pure black, lacking detail. The only time a pixel will register against the far-right or far-left side of a luminosity histogram is when all three channels have a value of 0 or all three have a value of 255. With a luminosity histogram, there is no question that if you have a spike of data on either edge, you have pure black and/or pure white areas in your image, as shown in Figure 1.7.

Figure 1.7 When a luminosity histogram has a spike on one or both edges, you can be certain that the image has areas that are pure white or pure black, like the windows in this image. (Photo by Ellen Anon)

RGB histograms sometimes look very similar to their luminosity counterparts, while at other times they differ substantially. An RGB histogram presents all the data from each channel, so if just one channel has a value of 0 or 255, you will see data peaking against the edges of the histogram. It will appear that you could have highlights or shadows without detail when in fact that may not be the case, as shown in Figure 1.8.

Figure 1.8 If your image contains very saturated colors, the RGB histogram may indicate potential blown-out and/or blocked-up areas, whereas a luminosity histogram will clearly indicate that these areas are not close to being pure white or pure black. (Photo by Ellen Anon.)

RGB histograms may have spikes on the edges when there are no white or black areas because some colors legitimately have one or more channels with values of 0 or 255. For example, pure red is represented by RGB values of 255, 0, 0; pure green would be 0, 255, 0; and pure blue would be 0, 0, 255. Similarly, cyan is 0, 255, 255; magenta is 255, 0, 255; and yellow is 255, 255, 0. But those are not the only colors that use the extreme values of 0 and 255.

Any color that has a value of 0 or 255 in a single channel will contribute to a spike on the edge of an RGB histogram. For example, the purple in Figure 1.9 has a color value of 132,0,189. In an RGB histogram any pixel that shade of purple will contribute to a spike in the shadows, making it appear as if there are blocked-up shadows when there may not be. That same shade of purple will be represented by data at the point corresponding to a tonal value of 60 in a luminosity histogram...far away from either end of the histogram.

Figure 1.9 Checking the histogram for a color such as this shade of purple that has RGB values of 132,0,189 clearly indicates how an RGB histogram differs from a luminosity histogram.

Checking the histogram for a color such as this shade of purple that has RGB values of 132,0,189 clearly indicates how an RGB histogram differs from a luminosity histogram.

That may make it seem like it would always be easier to use a luminosity histogram. The issue is that if you have a subject with very saturated colors, such as a poppy or a bright red cardinal, in reality the colors vary slightly to allow you to perceive detail in the flower petals or the bird's feathers. So, you need to have the tonal values varying. If a lot of the pixels are values that contain 0 or 255, the chances are that you don't have as much detail in those colors as you may need. A luminosity histogram would give you no indication of any potential trouble, whereas an RGB histogram would be clearly indicating overexposure and/or underexposure. By adding or subtracting light from an exposure, you may be able to capture those areas of the flower or bird with more detail.

Which type histogram should you use? That depends. Many cameras offer only one or the other type of histogram, while some of the newer models offer a choice. What's most important is to be aware of what type of histogram your camera uses so you will understand precisely what the data is saying.

Interpreting Histograms

Some people mistakenly think that an ideal histogram would be a bell-shaped distribution of pixels. *In fact, there's not a single ideal histogram for all images.* Rather, the ideal histogram for an image is one that captures all the data within that particular image. Let's look at a series of pictures and their histograms.

Figure 1.10 shows a good histogram for an average scene with a full range of tonalities. Note that the pixels extend across the entire histogram, but there are no spikes at either end. Spikes at the ends would mean you have pixels that are overexposed and/or underexposed and therefore areas with no detail. Since all the pixels fall within the bounds of the histogram, this picture will have detail throughout.

Figure1.10 This is an ideal histogram for a scene with a full range of tonalities. (Photo by Ellen Anon.)

Figure 1.11 shows an underexposed picture. All the pixels are in the left portion of the histogram, indicating no light tones. Since you know that the pelican is in fact white, a proper exposure would have the pixel distribution moved to the right. If you are shooting a subject with a large light area and see a histogram that looks like Figure 1.11, you need to add light to your exposure.

Figure1.11 This picture is underexposed. Note that all the data in the histogram is skewed toward the left and there are no light tonalities. (Photo by Ellen Anon.)

Compare the image and histogram in Figure 1.11 with those of Figure 1.12. The latter is a well-exposed picture with an ideal histogram of an overall dark scene with a few bright areas. If the exposure had been any brighter, the whites would have been *blown out* and lost their feather detail. *Blown-out highlights* means that no detail has been captured in the brightest areas of the picture. It's another way of referring to clipping. Although the darker portions of the picture may need to be lightened in the raw converter or in Photoshop, this is the ideal in-camera capture because it captures all the detail information in both the highlights and the shadows. Don't get confused between an ideal in-camera histogram for the capture and the final histogram of the optimized image, which may be noticeably different. The goal in-camera is to capture all, or at least as much, information as possible. Once you have the information, you can modify it as you tweak the image, but information you don't capture in the first place is not going to be there no matter what!

Figure1.12 Overall dark scenes with small bright areas will have histograms that look like this. This is not underexposed, even though the data is skewed toward the left, as in Figure 1.11. (Photo by Ellen Anon.)

Figure 1.13 shows an overexposed image. Note the spike on the right side of the histogram indicating blown-out highlights. Unfortunately, no amount of Photoshop magic can restore data that was not captured. Checking your camera's histogram regularly, and using the highlight alert feature in your camera, can avoid the frustration of taking an entire series of pictures like this.

Figure1.13 The whites in this image are blown out, as indicated by the spike on the right side of the histogram.
(Photo by Ellen Anon.)

Now compare the histogram and picture in Figure 1.13 with those in Figure 1.14. This picture of white birds on a nearly white sky is not overexposed, although most of the pixel data is skewed toward the right. This is the type of histogram you want in this type of situation—light background and light subject with minimal dark areas.

Figure 1.15 shows a histogram of a high-contrast scene. It has a spike on the left side of the histogram, although the data extends through the tonalities all the way toward the right of the histogram. There is no way to capture this shot at this time of day without losing either some highlight detail or some shadow detail. Ordinarily it's better to preserve the highlights and sacrifice some shadow detail, as was done in this image. An alternative appropriate for some situations, which we will discuss later, is to shoot multiple exposures and combine them in one image.

Figure1.14 A light subject with a light background will have a histogram that is skewed toward the right. (Photo by Ellen Anon.)

Figure1.15 This scene has too much contrast to capture in a single shot. The spike on the far left of the histogram shows that there is some loss of information in the shadows, but the highlights have been preserved. (Note that the small spike on the right is just before the end of the histogram.) (Photo by Ellen Anon.)

Finally, let's look at the histogram of a silhouette in Figure 1.16. As you may expect, the far-left side of the histogram shows a spike, but in this case it doesn't mean the image is underexposed. On the contrary, we want silhouettes to be pure black! Sometimes when you shoot a silhouette, the spike won't be all the way toward the left. The reason for this is you will need to expose the image so that you capture the most detail possible in the rest of the image. This will mean exposing to the right (which we'll discuss later in this chapter) even if the silhouette is then too bright. It's a simple matter to darken the silhouette in the raw converter or in Photoshop. By exposing to the right and then darkening part of the image, the darkest tones will have less noise.

Figure1.16 Silhouettes will often have histograms that have a spike on the left side indicating areas of pure black. (Photo by Ellen Anon.)

The bottom line is that there is no single ideal histogram for every situation. You have to think about the tonalities in your image and where they should fall on the histogram to know what is ideal for any particular situation. It's important to make sure you don't have spikes at the extreme ends of the graph, since that could mean shadow or highlight areas without detail. However, when the lighting has so much contrast that you can't avoid spikes on one or both ends of the histogram, you must consider the tonalities of your subject and preserve as much detail as possible in the subject. If necessary, you can forgo some detail in the background. Normally the order of priorities is to preserve detail in the subject; don't clip the highlights, even in the background; and maintain shadow detail including in the background. If your subject has a very dark area and the background has bright areas—such as bright clouds— you may opt to maintain the detail in the dark areas of your subject, at the expense of the detail in the clouds.

Of course, if you are shooting a silhouette, a spike at the left side of the histogram indicating blacks for the silhouettes is acceptable, while any specular highlights may be fine as pure white. But for most images, in order to capture detail in both the shadows and the highlights, you want the tonalities to fall within the boundaries of the histogram.

Note: Some photographers new to digital and Photoshop think they don't have to worry about exposure anymore because they can "fix it later" in Photoshop. The harsh reality is if you blow out the highlights or totally block up the shadows, the only "fix" will be to clone in pixels from other areas. Photoshop gives you lots of ways to tweak the exposure, which we'll explain in Chapter 6, "Exposure Adjustments," but if the data isn't there because of overexposure or underexposure, Photoshop isn't going to create it for you.

Exposure

If you check the histogram and see that you have a spike at the far right and room on the left side, you need to modify your exposure to have less light. If you are shooting in Aperture Priority, you may choose to put in some minus exposure compensation, or if you are using manual mode, either use a smaller aperture or increase your shutter speed. Because you're shooting digitally, you have a third option—to switch to a slower ISO. Although you still need to set the correct exposure compensation, you can use the same depth of field/aperture setting as you originally wanted (perhaps in an effort to keep the background out of focus) and the same shutter speed (perhaps in an attempt to blur your subject).

Similarly, if the histogram is indicating a spike at the black end and has room on the right side, you'll want to add light via plus exposure compensation, slower shutter speeds, wider apertures, and/or possibly a faster ISO to allow you to use the desired apertures and shutter speeds. Faster ISOs—those with the larger numbers—mean that less light is required to hit the sensor to achieve the proper exposure. The problem with this is that the faster the ISO, the more noise the picture may have. Some cameras have less noise while using higher ISOs than do other cameras. Test your own camera to determine the highest ISO you can use without noise becoming an issue. When using a higher ISO, be extra careful not to underexpose your image. In general, use the slowest (smallest number) ISO that you can.

Note: Usually, the lower the ISO, the less noise you will encounter. Noise is in many ways the digital equivalent of film grain, except that it tends to be more evident in darker shadow areas. It appears as variations in color and tonality in areas that should be smooth.

Technically, the ideal histogram for a raw image should not only contain all the pixels with no spikes at the ends, but also it should be exposed as far to the right as possible with no blown-out highlights. This is to obtain the best signal-to-noise ratio possible. (It is important to keep in mind that this applies to raw images but not to those captured as JPEGs because the main benefits occur in the process of the conversion. If you are shooting in JPEG, make the most accurate exposure you can, and make sure you're not clipping data on either end.)

Michael Reichmann does an excellent job of explaining this, so we asked him to share that explanation with you. The following section, "Expose Right," was written and contributed by him. For more information on Reichmann and his work, please visit his website, www.luminous-landscape.com.

"Expose Right" by Michael Reichmann

In the beginning there was the light meter. Photographers used them and saw that they were good. Then there was through-the-lens metering, and the people rejoiced. Automatic exposure followed, and photographers thought that the millennium had arrived. Eventually the millennium actually did arrive, and with it digital cameras with histogram displays; and the world changed again.

What hasn't changed over the years is the need for accurate exposure, which all of this technology is ultimately in aid of. But what constitutes proper exposure is quite different between film and digital. In this section, you'll see why and how to take best advantage of it.

Don't Blow It

Digital is very much like color slide film in that you want to avoid overexposure. Although it's often possible to recover some information from the shadows of an underexposed digital image, especially if a low ISO is being used, once overexposed beyond 255, there is no information to be retrieved. The individual photo sites or pixels have simply recorded 100 percent of the information that they can absorb, and this is a featureless white.

© Michael Reichmann

Note: We authors interrupt Michael here to say the exposure scale of a histogram goes from black at 0 to white at 255 in 8-bit capture; the same principle applies for 12-bit capture, where the maximum value is 4,095. For convenience sake, the convention is to describe histograms as extending from 0 to 255 whether for 8-bit, 12-bit, or 16-bit images.

This would lead most people to think that the best thing to do would therefore be to bias their exposure toward the left of the histogram—toward underexposure. This would avoid the risk of blown-out highlights, and since it's often possible to retrieve detail from underexposed shadow areas, what have you got to lose?

A lot actually, as you'll see.

Signals and Noise

Film has *grain*. These are particles of silver or organic dyes that, when exposed to light, turn dark to varying degrees. Fast films have more grain because they have more of these light-sensitive particles with which to absorb light.

Digital uses very tiny photo sites—sensor elements made of silicon that are sensitive to light. Essentially, if no light hits a sensor element, no voltage is generated, and a value of 0 or black is recorded. If the sensor element is flooded with light (overexposed), it records a maximum value of 255 (in an 8-bit image) and a corresponding voltage level is produced. Light levels in between are recorded as some value between 0 and 255.

Although silicon doesn't suffer directly from what we describe as grain, it does have a comparable issue. This is described as *noise*. Noise in this context is any form of non-image-forming energy (light is just one form of energy). Various things can cause noise to be recorded by the sensor. These include heat, cosmic rays, and several other exotic sources. All silicon chips have an inherent noise level. As a percentage of the total signal being recorded, it is usually quite small and unnoticeable. But it's always there, and depending on the exposure being recorded, it can become visible and annoying. This is somewhat akin to the noise that one sees on a TV screen when there's no channel broadcasting or antenna attached.

Note: We authors interrupt to add that usually the energy that causes noise is low enough in its intensity that it falls to the left (dark) side of the histogram.

This is where what we call the sensor's *signal-to-noise* (s/n) ratio comes in. If there's a lot of signal (data to the right side of the histogram), then the s/n ratio is high, the signal predominates, and the noise isn't visible. But if the signal is low (to the left of the histogram), then the s/n ratio is low, and one sees the noise because it represents a relatively high percentage of the total signal present.

So, the solution is clear. Take a photograph, check the instant review histogram, and make sure that the exposure is as far to the right of the histogram as possible without touching the right edge.

But wait. This has a problem. If you do this and you're shooting JPEGs, you'll see some fairly nasty-looking exposures—ones that appear very bright, inappropriately so. Of course, you can try to fix the shot in an image-editing program such as Photoshop. But because JPEGs are prebaked images (reduced to 8-bit mode and with predetermined exposure and color balance characteristics embedded in the file while in the camera), such adjustments can't really be performed while still retaining decent image quality. So, with JPEGs at least, the idea of biasing your exposures to the right of the histogram appears to be good in theory but not terribly practical.

Raw Mode

The answer is to shoot in raw mode. In raw mode the file contains the data that the sensor recorded. In addition, *tags* describe the camera's settings, such as white balance, sharpening, contrast saturation, and the like. But these tags are just that. The raw file itself is not changed in any way. It is also in 12-bit or 14-bit mode and in a 16-bit space (more on this in a moment). Finally, a raw file isn't compressed the way a JPEG file is. If it is compressed, which a few manufacturers do, it's done so losslessly.

Dynamic Range and Bit Mode

The concept of *bit mode* is important to properly understanding digital image quality.

Assume for the purposes of illustration that a digital SLR has a dynamic range of five stops. (It's usually closer to six stops, but let's not quibble.) When working in raw mode, most cameras record a 12-bit image. (Yes, we say it's in 16 bits, but the reality is that the camera is recording only 12 bits of information in a 16-bit space. This is better than 8 but not as good as a real 16 bits would be.)

A 12-bit image is capable of recording 2^{12} = 4,096 discrete tonal values in each component. One would think that therefore each f/stop of the five-stop range would be able to record some 4,096 divided by 5 = 850 of these steps. But, alas, this is not the case. The way it really works is that the first (brightest) stop worth of data contains 2,048 of these steps—fully half of those available.

Why? Because CCD and CMOS chips are linear devices. And, of course, each f/stop records half the light of the previous one and therefore half the remaining data space available. Table 1.2 tells the tale.

Table 1.2 Where Light Levels are Stored on Chips

F/Stop	Number of Levels
Within the first f/stop, which contains the brightest tones	2,048 levels available
Within the second f/stop, which contains bright tones	1,024 levels available
Within the third f/stop, which contains the midtones	512 levels available
Within the fourth f/stop, which contains dark tones	256 levels available
Within the fifth f/stop, which contains the darkest tones	128 levels available

This realization carries with it a number of important lessons, the most important of them being that if you do not use the right fifth of the histogram for recording some of your image, you are in fact wasting fully half of the available encoding levels of your camera.

But, we all know (or at least should by now) that the worst sin in digital imaging is to blow out the highlights—just as it was when shooting slide film. Once they're blown (past the right edge of the histogram), it's bye-bye data.

The Lesson

The simple lesson to be learned from this is to bias your exposures so that the histogram is snuggled up to the right of the histogram (as illustrated in Figure 1.17) but not to the point that the highlights are blown. This can usually be seen by the flashing alert on most camera LCD screens. Just back off so that the flashing stops.

Figure 1.17
A normal exposure shows a centered histogram (left). This histogram is shifted to the right for maximum signal/noise ratio (right).

Now when you look at the raw file in your favorite raw-processing software, such as Camera raw, the image will likely appear to be too light. That's OK. Just use the available sliders to change the brightness level and contrast so that the data is spread out appropriately and the image looks "right." This accomplishes a number of goals. First, it maximizes the s/n ratio. Second, it minimizes the posterization and noise that potentially occurs in the darker regions of the image.

Please be aware, though, that for proper results you need to make these corrections while working in 16-bit (12-bit) mode in a raw converter. Unlike what some people think, in RAW mode, the camera is not doing any nonlinear processing. All nonlinear processing takes place in the raw converter. This is why if you're going to try this trick, you must shoot in RAW and then manually readjust the image in the raw converter before exporting the file into Photoshop. By doing this you'll be maximizing the data bandwidth of your entire system.

Also be aware that by doing this, you are in fact effectively lowering the ISO used to capture the image, requiring slower shutter speeds and/or larger apertures. If you are holding the camera by hand or shooting moving objects, the trade-off may not be worth the reduced noise level.

But, if ultimate image quality is your goal and you have the ability to control all the variables, *exposing to the right* is a technique that will serve you well.

© 2004 Michael H. Reichmann, www.luminous-landscape.com

White Balance in Nature Photography

With film cameras, you used specific types of film according to the lighting conditions, and you used filters to further control the color casts. With digital, you have a somewhat equivalent, but more flexible, choice, which is white balance. As you know, the color (or temperature) of light varies throughout each day. It's a "warmer" color in the morning, and the world takes on a reddish/yellow glow. Your eyes adapt to that and compensate because you know that white is still white. (Think about when you put colored glasses on and a few minutes later the colors look "normal" again.) Later, when the bright sun is overhead, the color appears "cooler" or bluer. Your eyes continuously adapt so that you see neutral colors as neutral, and most people are rarely aware of color casts.

Your cameras are more literal—they record the colors exactly as they see them. With digital cameras you can use the white balance setting to render the neutral tones (any shade from white to black where the red, green, and blue values are all the same) as neutral, rather than rendering them with a color cast. For example, you need a different white balance in the cool bluish light of an overcast day than in the warm reddish light of a sunset. All digital cameras offer an automatic white balance setting in which the camera makes a best guess as to the correct lighting temperature. Surprisingly, most do quite a good job, as shown in Figure 1.18.

Figure 1.18
Auto white balance was used to capture this photo in the warm light of early morning. (Photo by Ellen Anon.)

However, some photographers think the best way to be certain of getting the correct white balance is to set it themselves. Most of these photographers are content to use one of the presets supplied with the camera such as Flash, Sunny, Cloudy, Shade, Fluorescent, and so on. With many cameras, using these settings ensures that the image you capture will appear as neutrally colored as possible, although other cameras tend to have a warm bias. If you don't use Auto White Balance, you must be vigilant about changing lighting conditions and changing your white balance accordingly. As you can see in Figure 1.19, if you use the wrong white balance setting, your picture may have a strong color cast. If you shot the image in RAW, you can easily correct this during the conversion process; but if you shot it in JPEG, a mistake like this could ruin the image.

Figure 1.19
The white balance here was accidentally set to Tungsten. A mistake like this can be deadly if the image is shot in JPEG.

But if you've ever gotten up before dawn to go out and photograph in the beautiful, warm, early morning light, you know that we nature photographers aren't always seeking to make neutrally colored images! Often, we want a color cast in our images, particularly a warm cast, as shown in Figure 1.20. This is one of the reasons we prefer to shoot in raw mode; we don't have to make a final decision about the white balance until we're converting the image, whereas with JPEG mode, the white balance is "baked" into the image. Our decision may be based more on the mood we want to portray than on what the actual lighting conditions were at the time.

Figure 1.20 This picture, taken at dawn, actually has a warmer color cast than what existed at the time, but the result is pleasing. Altering the white balance lets you effectively convey a mood. (Photo by Ellen Anon.)

If you are shooting in JPEG, you may want to try using the auto white balance feature, along with setting the white balance specifically. You may not only want to set the white balance for an accurate rendition of the scene, but you may also want to experiment a little. For example, if you use the Cloudy or Shade settings in fairly sunny conditions, it's similar to adding an 81A or 81B filter to your camera lens; these settings will add a warm cast to your picture. Product photographers must be concerned with absolute color accuracy in their photography. Nature photographers have the luxury of being able to be creative with the white balance and create, augment, or remove color casts as it suits their vision. You can use the white balance settings rather than filters to do this both with JPEG and with RAW.

When you capture your images as raw files, because the white balance you selected in the camera is not actually applied until you convert the image, you have the luxury of time to adjust the white balance as you want. Most raw converters provide a continuous temperature slider to set the white balance that best fits the mood of the image. You can tweak it in small increments to precisely obtain the effect you want. Because of this, many photographers elect to leave their cameras on auto white balance and then use the sliders in the converters to impart or remove color casts. Others still select what they believe is the best white balance setting while in the field so they can recall what the lighting was and how the image actually appeared. They prefer to have their images be as close to accurate, realistic color as possible. Who's right? Both are! It's a matter of your personal goals and preferences with your photography.

Photographing Elements to Composite Later

How many times have you looked up and commented on the great clouds or beautiful sunset but not taken the picture because foreground elements were missing? Or the opposite—you found a great subject, perhaps a bird posing wonderfully or a gorgeous scene, but the sky or background was completely blah? Or you could tell there was just too much contrast to be able to capture the picture? When you are in the field with your camera, it's important to remember that Photoshop enables you to combine images in a seemingly infinite variety of ways. You have to adjust your thinking to include seeing the potential for an image.

Skies, Clouds, and Moons

A number of situations lend themselves to photographing parts of a picture that you will later combine in Photoshop. You can create libraries of these image elements to use at some later time. Perhaps the most obvious elements to store are skies and clouds. Whenever you see a dramatic sky, photograph it! Place the images in a special folder labeled skies. You'll need more than one replacement sky, because one of the keys to creating believable composites is to match the direction and quality of the lighting. Sunsets are great to photograph, as are clouds—the blue sky with puffy white cloud types as well as impending storm clouds. When you start paying attention to clouds, you'll soon see that different types clouds tend to occur more in certain seasons. By having a collection of skies, when you find a great subject (perhaps that leopard in the tree while in Africa) or a beautiful scenic, you'll be able to remove the distracting white sky and make it appear that luck was with you in the field.

Figure 1.21 shows a picture that could have occurred but didn't. Capturing all these landing cranes in one shot was wonderful, but unfortunately the sky behind them was boring. A few minutes earlier, the sky in the very same spot had been dramatic, but there were no birds. This image is a combination of the birds with the sky that had been there a few minutes earlier.

Don't limit yourself to just skies and clouds, though. You can add all sorts of elements to pictures to add impact or create a sense of your own style. Ellen likes to keep a folder of moons to use as accent elements in pictures. She shoots full moons, crescent moons, moons against black skies, and moons in daylight skies. You'd be amazed at the variety of color casts in the moons. Then when she thinks a picture needs a little extra pop, she puts one in. (We'll explain how to do that in Chapter 8.) Sometimes she makes them a realistic size, and sometimes she enlarges them. Another person we know adds docks and has a collection of docks to add to scenic water pictures! You're the artist, and the choice is yours. Use your imagination, and keep your eyes open for other elements to collect to add to your images.

Figure 1.21 Sometimes nature doesn't cooperate and gives you a great subject but a boring sky, or vice versa. In Photoshop you can combine them to have the best of both worlds. (Photo by Ellen Anon.)

When photographing something that you're likely to want to later extract from the picture and use elsewhere, try to design your photograph to make it easier to remove the desired object. For example, it will often be easier to remove an item from a blurred background rather than a cluttered one, so consider using a wide aperture. You may need to take a step or two left or right or perhaps get down a little lower to help separate intricate background objects from your subject. A little care in the field can make your work in Photoshop much easier!

Be sure to store these photo elements in a consistent place that's easy for you to find. You don't want to have to look through all your pictures in order to find them. Of course, adding keywords to them can also make it easier to locate them when you need them.

Expanding Camera Capabilities

Sometimes you see a scene and know that you can't capture it in a single shot because of the technical limitations of your equipment. Photoshop provides ways to combine shots to create images not possible with a single exposure.

Your eyes can see a much greater range of tonalities than can your camera, where the dynamic range is limited to five to six stops of lights for digital captures and slide film. This means although your eyes may be able to see detail in both the highlights and the shadows in a scene, today's cameras may not be able to do so within a single exposure. The solution is to take a series of exposures, making sure you capture detail in all parts of the pictures. This could mean two or more exposures varying at least one stop each.

Some Helpful Definitions

Dynamic range

The range between the brightest and darkest points of an image.

High dynamic range (HDR) images

An HDR image contains a far wider dynamic range than can be displayed on a screen or printed on a printer. HDR images are often created from multiple exposures of one image and are stored in special file formats. They are of interest to photographers because you can convert them back to 8-bit or 16-bit images and compress the dynamic range, allowing you to get images with detail in both shadow and highlight areas of an image, more like what your eye saw when looking at the scene rather than what your camera captured.

If you're dealing with a static subject and shooting from a stable platform, you can take a series of exposures to later combine using Merge to HDR to create a 32-bit file. This file is called a high dynamic range (HDR) file, and we'll discuss it more in Chapter 8. In addition, there are several other ways to combine 16-bit exposures within Photoshop to extend the latitude. So even if your subject matter is not completely static, take at least two or three exposures: one or more that capture all the detail in the shadows and one or more that capture all the highlight detail. Make certain to keep your camera in precisely the same spot and not change the focus or aperture between the exposures; vary only the shutter speed. Chapter 8 will explain several techniques to put these pictures together to create a picture with as much or more detail than your eyes are accustomed to seeing.

Photographing Parts of the Scene Individually

Another limitation of your camera sometimes arises when you need more depth of field and shutter speed than what the amount of light will allow. This happened to Ellen in Bosque del Apache, New Mexico, when she saw the beautiful mountains and sunset in the distance with the cranes flying fairly close to her. Although she could see it, there was no way to capture the entire scene with adequate depth of field to have the cranes in focus as well as the mountains and have enough shutter speed to freeze the motion of the birds. Her solution was to photograph the birds in one frame and the background separately. Then she combined the two in Photoshop, as shown in Figure 1.22. In reality, the moon was behind her while taking those shots, but in the end, she decided to add it to the picture because she wasn't trying to create a documentary image but, rather, one that captured how it felt to be there. Photoshop made that possible.

Figure 1.22 There was no way to capture the birds and the mountains in a single shot because of the low light levels. Instead, individual shots were combined in Photoshop. (Photo by Ellen Anon.)

Ethical Considerations

Is the image manipulated? It sounds like such a straightforward question. But answering honestly may be more difficult than it appears, especially when responding to people not well versed in digital photography.

If you shoot in RAW, you essentially have a negative that needs to be processed during conversion. The settings you apply determine the appearance of the image, but these really aren't manipulating the image any more than chemicals do in a darkroom. Similar adjustments done in Photoshop, as opposed to in the raw converter, are considered by some to be manipulations. Many accept that it is necessary to clone out dust and to perform some sharpening since there is some slight softening of digital images by their very nature. A few people are bothered by basic exposure and color modifications, but most accept this as part of the processing, as long as the overall intent of the capture remains the same. Modifying the colors or tonalities within only a section of the image is more troublesome for some, and such changes are not allowed by several prestigious contests such as the Shell Wildlife Photographer of the Year or *Nature's Best* magazine. If you enter your image in a contest, be sure to follow their rules for what changes are and are not permitted.

Although cloning out dust is usually acceptable, there is debate about how much of an object one can clone out before the image is considered manipulated. Sometimes it's more environmentally responsible to clone out an object rather than remove it in reality. Sometimes it's impossible to remove it in reality. Unfortunately, for some this crosses the line into a manipulated image. Maybe it's an area that needs to be thought through more carefully.

Many gray areas exist. For example, it's common practice when photographing hummingbirds at feeders to put up a man-made background so that the birds are photographed against a pleasing, nondistracting background rather than clutter. This is acceptable. But if you took the image photographed with the cluttered background and, in Photoshop, replaced the background with a simpler one, many would insist the image is manipulated.

Ellen's feeling is that when she composites elements within an image, the image is manipulated, and she is careful to indicate this whenever reasonable. When asked, she responds honestly and labels images accurately. The bottom line for her is that photography is an art form, and her goal is to create images that express what she feels. For those of you who are more inclined toward scientific documentary types of nature photographs, the lines may be different. You have to decide what's right for you!

Removing Objects in the Field or Later in Photoshop

There's an old adage that reminds us to "Take only pictures and leave only footprints, and barely those if possible." But as nature photographers we know that sometimes there are distracting elements that are interfering with our picture. It may be an ill-placed stick, a wayward branch, or maybe a rock that's too light and bright. It seems harmless enough to move it and create a cleaner photo. Many times doing so may be fine. But have you considered that perhaps that rock or branch was serving a purpose to one of the many critters in our world? Perhaps the branch provided some protection against the wind or shielded visibility from a predator; maybe the rock provided a safe resting spot while looking for food. We know and see the world though our human perspective, and what seems inconsequential to us may actually have a significant impact on a variety of wildlife.

Does that mean you should never move anything in the environment? That would be an extreme and unrealistic position, but the reality is you may want to consider whether it would be smarter to remove the offending item later in Photoshop. Although it may create more work for you, you will be creating less stress on the nature around you. You are going to have to use common sense in making this choice. (We'll cover how to remove objects in Photoshop in Chapter 5.)

Software Choices: Aperture and Lightroom

A few years ago the software choices for digital photography were fairly limited. Photoshop has dominated the market for quite a while, and its sister products such as Photoshop Elements provided a reduced selection of tools offering some of the basic adjustments. Many photographers, amateur as well as professionals, have based their workflows entirely on using Photoshop for years. In fact, Photoshop offers a good workflow (which is what we're teaching you throughout this book), but it's not perfect. Photoshop was developed not only for photographers but also for graphic artists. The result is that it has numerous features that photographers don't need. And there are some features that photographers need but that Photoshop doesn't do quite as well as we wish. For example, Photoshop is not an image management device. Although you can add keywords in Photoshop, the process can be arduous, and Photoshop doesn't help you keep track of where you've stored the images. (Eventually, if you shoot enough, you can't keep all your images on your computer's internal hard drive—you must export them to external hard drives or gold DVDs, and so on.) Further, because Bridge is a separate program from Photoshop, you actually encounter three different user interfaces—Bridge, Camera Raw, and Photoshop. This can be confusing for some and is a little time-consuming as you go back and forth among them.

Apple introduced Aperture in late 2005, followed shortly by Adobe's announcement of a beta version of software called Lightroom. These new programs are designed from the ground up to meet the needs of photographers. In addition, they make working with raw files virtually indistinguishable from working with JPEGs or TIFFs. No separate converter software or interface is needed. Currently, they are intended to be used in conjunction with a program such as Photoshop, rather than as a replacement for Photoshop.

Aperture is designed to make your workflow easy and efficient from the moment you download images from your camera through locating your best images and showcasing them to others. When you connect your camera or card reader, an import window appears and nearly instantaneously so do low-res previews of your images. You choose where to store these images and how to name them. In addition, you can quickly add any metadata you choose, such as basic contact information and keywords. Aperture will import the images you select into a project. From there you can easily edit the images, using a magnifying loupe to check for sharpness and details—even within the thumbnails—to quickly identify the best images. You can compare similar images side by side.

With a single keystroke, a window appears containing most of the adjustments you're likely to need to make. You can save commonly made adjustments as presets, or you can adjust the sliders to tweak all aspects of the exposure and colors. These adjustments are stored as instructions while the master file remains untouched. The adjustments go beyond those typically available currently in most raw converters and include all the expected features as well as an outstanding Highlight/Shadow tool, individual color controls, Spot and Patch tools, red-eye reduction, cropping and straightening, toning, and more.

One of the major innovations of Aperture is the ability to generate versions of the image that are stored with the master file simply as instructions. That way you can create several variations of an image (see Figure 1.23)—perhaps a different crop, a black-and-white version and a sepia version, and so on—yet the demands for storage space on your hard drive are greatly reduced because the master file is not recopied each time. This makes your computer more efficient, and it makes it easy to find the different variations of your image. In Aperture you can add keywords at any time; search for images, including those you store offline; send emails; or create slide shows with a single click.

Figure 1.23 Experimenting with different variations of an image in Aperture is easy and requires only minimal additional storage space on your hard drive. (Photo by Ellen Anon.)

If you opt to use Aperture (or Lightroom), you're likely to find that you will not need to use Photoshop for all your images. You'll still need Photoshop when you want to make adjustments to just one particular area of your image, when you have more complicated cloning to do, or when you want to use any of the filters available in Photoshop. When using Aperture, if you want to open an image in Photoshop, it's just a keystroke away. The image will open in Photoshop, and you can make the desired changes. When you're done, you click Save, and Aperture will automatically update the image preview to reflect the changes you made in Photoshop. You can save all your layers when you work in Photoshop, and although the individual layers are not accessible from within Aperture, if you reopen that same file in Photoshop, all the layers will still be there.

Aperture provides equally efficient methods for creating slide shows, sending emails, creating books, creating websites, and making prints. Ellen has adopted Aperture as her primary workflow tool. For more about Aperture, see *Aperture Exposed: The Mac Photographer's Guide to Taming the Workflow* by Ellen Anon and Josh Anon (Sybex, 2006).

Lightroom provides similar functionality; however, it currently is not quite as full-featured as Aperture. It too provides a workflow enabling you to use raw images as easily as JPEGs or TIFFs. It has an intuitive interface that enables you to make many of the global color and tonal modifications that you may want to make and has a good keywording system to make it easy to find your images. Lightroom has the advantage that it will be available for both Microsoft Windows and Apple Mac OS, whereas Aperture is a Mac-only application. For more about Lightroom, see *Lightroom Workflow* by Tim Grey (Sybex, 2007).

If you opt to adopt Aperture or Lightroom as the basis of your workflow, you'll find that you make many or all the global exposure and color changes we discuss in this book in those programs. You'll still find it advantageous to work in Photoshop for some tasks. For example, we still use Photoshop for most of our cloning. We also use Photoshop anytime we want to make a change to part of the image and not have it affect the rest of the image—which means anytime we'd like to use a layer mask. As you'll discover later in this book, we use layer masks a lot! The ability to make a change and have it affect only the targeted area gives you more precise control over the final appearance of your images. We also use Photoshop when we want to use any of its filters as well as for all types of creative ventures including creating composites of all natures. Even if you use Aperture or Lightroom, it's worthwhile knowing what controls are available in Photoshop. That way if you encounter a difficult image, you'll have more tools available to you to work with it.

Storage Considerations

A comprehensive discussion of storage media is beyond the scope of this book. We'll cover only a few aspects here, which are especially pertinent for nature photographers.

Many nature photographers often do at least some of their photography away from home. We know one photographer who actually buys enough compact flash cards so that he can use a new one when needed rather than having to download and/or edit images while on the road. Although the cost of compact flash cards has come down considerably in the past few years, for most photographers this is not a practical solution. Even if you can justify it monetarily, it's impractical because it means you will have all your editing to do when you get home, and that can be overwhelming. In addition, it eliminates one of the major advantages of digital shooting—the ability to review the shots you took during the day and to learn from what went right and what went wrong so you can adjust your shooting the next day accordingly. Being able to view your images, preferably reasonably large, allows you to fine-tune your shooting skills and experiment with new techniques while still on location. That way you can return to a location if necessary or build upon a creative approach you tried.

A variety of independent handheld image storage and viewing devices have come on the market for the past few years. All of them have been promising, and most have had their issues. In addition, the screen sizes on most is too small to be as helpful as needed, although they're large enough to be tantalizing and tempting. At best these devices should be used as a secondary backup in our opinion. Canon recently announced a new storage device, similar to the Epson P that has been available for sometime, that holds some promise. (At the time we're writing this, we have not yet had a chance to test one.)

When we're on a photographic trip, we prefer to take a laptop along and make certain that it has plenty of space on its hard drive. That way we can download our images and view them at a reasonable size. (In addition, having the computer enables us to have email access while on the road.) Also, Ellen takes a small external portable hard drive. These drives are the size of a deck of cards. She backs up all the images she stores on her computer on this hard drive. That way if something happens to the computer, she still has a copy of all the files. If she is on a long trip that will involve a lot of shooting and not much time for editing, she'll bring along a second external portable hard drive for overflow images when her computer's hard drive becomes full. Ordinarily we recommend doing at least a first pass of editing each day to delete the images you are certain you don't want, but sometimes that's not possible. When we return home, we transfer the images to our main computer for further editing and archival storage.

After editing our images, we establish a Best Of folder for each shoot containing the images we want to keep. That folder gets backed up onto a RAID system. RAID stands for Redundant Array of Independent Devices. A RAID system consists of two or more hard drives that function together. There are several different types of RAID devices, but we use RAID-5. When you back up to a RAID hard drive, the data is automatically copied to all the drives. If one hard drive develops an error, it uses the information on one of the other drives to correct it. We think this provides the best storage system currently available.

Other photographers prefer to use DVDs or CDs. If you have a lot of images, the volume of DVDs and/or CDs can become unwieldy unless you have a clear-cut system for storing and identifying the discs. In addition, it's imperative to use gold discs, which are archival and are reported to last 100 years or so. Ellen uses the gold discs that are available from Delkin Devices. DVDs and CDs that are not gold may become unreadable in as little as one year! If you have been using regular DVDs or CDs to archive your images, we urge you to copy them to a gold disc.

Note: Whatever storage system you adopt, be consistent so that you protect your images and can easily locate them when you need them!

Bridge

After you're done photographing, you need an easy way to get your images from the memory cards onto your computer and to see how the pictures look. Although you may be anxious to start optimizing them right away, first you need to sort through them and decide which files to keep and which to delete. Adobe Bridge, a stand-alone application that comes with Adobe Photoshop, has a lot of features to help with this task. We'll show you how to take advantage of these features to make this part of your workflow as efficient as possible.

2

Chapter Contents
Customizing Bridge
Downloading Images
Bridge Views and Workspaces
Sorting and Editing
Additional Features

Customizing Bridge

Bridge is a program designed to be customized for each user's individual needs. It's a program that is used not only by photographers but also by graphic artists and others using any of the programs packaged in the Adobe Creative Suite series. Bridge's default views and behaviors may not match your workflow needs, so it's worth spending a little time learning to set it up in the most convenient way for you. We'll take you through the program step by step and make recommendations about what works best for us. That way you can customize your version according to your needs.

Note: Bridge is aptly named because it is the "connector" or "bridge" between the various applications that make up Creative Suite 3, such as Adobe InDesign, Illustrator, GoLive, Version Cue, Stock Photos, and so on, as well as Photoshop. It enables files created in one application to be viewed and opened in one or more of the other applications.

Setting Bridge Preferences

Bridge includes a Preferences dialog box where you can set a wide variety of options to adjust the behavior of Bridge to your liking. You access the dialog box by selecting Edit > Preferences (Bridge > Preferences on Macs) from the menu in Bridge. Because there are so many settings and most of them are simply a matter of personal preference, we'll simply highlight the major settings:

General   This section (see Figure 2.1) contains general settings related to the appearance and behavior of Bridge. Use the sliders in the Appearance section to control the background of the user interface as well as the backdrop for your images. The Accent Color drop-down menu enables you to choose a color and style for the highlight in the user interface. We find that the default settings work well, but this is largely a matter of personal preference.

Figure 2.1
The General section of the Bridge Preferences contains settings related to the display of images within Bridge.

Note: If you opt to experiment with the Appearance sliders, be aware that there is no way to automatically return to the default settings.

The Behavior section includes two options. The first automatically launches the Adobe Photo Downloader. Unless you are specifically using another program such as Aperture or Lightroom for your image importing (which we'll discuss later in this chapter), check the option to launch Adobe Photo Downloader when a camera is connected. This will launch the downloader when a memory card is connected and will save you time. We recommend checking the option to have Double-Click Edits Camera Raw Settings in Bridge. When this check box is cleared, raw files open into ACR hosted by Photoshop. When you check the box, the ACR dialog box opens without launching Photoshop. This may seem like a subtle distinction, but it may enable you to adjust settings more rapidly than you otherwise could; for example, you could be working in Photoshop while Bridge processes a large number of raw files in the background.

The Favorites Items section allows you to choose the image sources to be included on the Favorites tab. The Reset button at the bottom of this section allows you to reset the warning dialog boxes so that all are shown, even if you have previously checked the box to not show a particular message.

Thumbnails   The Thumbnails section includes options for the appearance of the thumbnails and associated metadata as well as for file handling.

The first check box enables JPEG and TIFF files to be edited using ACR. If you are shooting using one of these two file formats (which we don't recommend), check this option to take advantage of the tools and convenient ACR interface. However, if you shoot primarily in RAW and only occasionally want to use the ACR interface with JPEGs or TIFFs, consider leaving this option unchecked. The exact behavior of this preference changes depending on the preferences you have selected at the time the folder is cached.

- If "Double Click Edits Camera Raw Settings in Bridge" is checked, and "Prefer Adobe Camera Raw for JPEG and TIFF files" is unchecked, all unedited JPEGS will open directly in Photoshop.

- If "Double Click Edits Camera Raw Settings in Bridge" is checked, and "Prefer Adobe Camera Raw for JPEG and TIFF files" is checked, double clicking an unedited JPEG thumbnail will open the file in ACR.

- If "Double Click Edits Camera Raw Settings in Bridge" is unchecked, and "Prefer Adobe Camera Raw for JPEG and TIFF files" is unchecked, double clicking an unedited JPEG file in Bridge will open the file directly in Photoshop.

- If "Double Click Edits Camera Raw Settings in Bridge" is unchecked, and "Prefer Adobe Camera Raw for JPEG and TIFF files" is checked, to open a JPEG file from Bridge into ACR, press Ctrl +R/⌘ +R or choose File > Open in Camera Raw.

Note: Opening JPEGs and TIFFs in ACR is currently complicated as the Adobe engineers try to incorporate various contingencies into the behavior. Hopefully they will simplify it before too long. But for now you must consider which preferences you had selected at the time the folder was cached. If you change the preferences, you'll need to purge the cache (Tools > Cache > Purge Cache for Folder) in order to take advantage of the expected behaviors. Further, once a file has been edited, it will open that way. So if it previously was modified in ACR, it will initially open in ACR, and if it was previously modified in Photoshop it will open directly into Photoshop. Lastly, if you change the file handling preference for JPEGs or TIFFS within Photoshop itself, these behaviors will change to reflect that setting.

Next are options related to the quality of the thumbnails. Ideally you could have high-quality thumbnails appear at the speed of lightening, but realistically, higher-quality previews take longer to generate. Ellen finds the Convert To High Quality When Previewed option to be the best compromise for her. That way, image previews are generated quickly and then automatically changed to high quality when they are viewed.

The Do Not Process Files Larger Than option determines the size, in megabytes, above which Bridge will not generate a thumbnail for the image. It can be good to create such a limit (the default is 200MB), because building thumbnails for such large images can be time-consuming, resulting in reduced system performance. However, for photographers who frequently produce such large files, setting such a limit can be a source of frustration, because they aren't able to see thumbnails for many of their images. Consider this setting based on the relative advantages of placing a limit on the building of thumbnails for large files.

Three check boxes with drop-down menus allow you to specify additional information about the image to be displayed below the thumbnail. Again, it's a matter of personal preference and what information you want to have at your fingertips about each file. As shown in Figure 2.2, Ellen opts to show the date created, dimensions, and depth.

Figure 2.2

The Thumbnails section of Preferences contains important settings related to thumbnail quality and the behavior of TIFF and JPEG files.

The Show Tooltips check box determines whether information about the image is displayed as a pop-up tooltip when you hold the mouse over a thumbnail.

Metadata   This section (shown in Figure 2.3) allows you to specify which fields are displayed in the Metadata panel for each image. This extensive list includes a variety of metadata formats and fields that are not necessarily supported by all image formats. This section can be used both to include fields you're most interested in to maximize the amount of information displayed as well as to remove those items you're not interested in to keep the display more manageable. For example, most users don't need the GPS data (and only a few cameras such as some Nikons even support it), but it's a good idea to include the IPTC Core information that contains your contact and copyright information (if you added it during import or later) as well as some of the Camera Data (EXIF) and ACR information.

Figure 2.3

The Metadata section of Bridge Preferences allows you to specify which metadata fields should be displayed on the Metadata panel.

Labels   This section (see Figure 2.4) allows you to set preferences related to the labels you can use to rate and flag images. The check box at the top determines whether the Ctrl/⌘ key must be held to apply a rating or label to an image. We recommend you clear this check box so that you can simply press the appropriate number key rather than holding the Ctrl/⌘ key while pressing that key. The section below allows you to change the description of the colored labels. By default, the name is that of the color, but you can change this to reflect the categories you are using those colors for, if desired.

Figure 2.4
The Labels section of Bridge Preferences allows you to adjust the names of the colored labels and determine how keyboard shortcuts for rating and labels behave.

File Type Associations This section is another long list (see Figure 2.5)—the file types supported by Bridge. By default, most image formats are automatically opened by Photoshop. However, you can change the association so that files open in a different application. For example, you might choose to have Nikon NEF files open in Capture NX. Similarly, you can set different associations for specific file types within Bridge, if you prefer, using the drop-down menu to the right of a given file format to choose an application or to browse for the executable for the preferred application.

Figure 2.5
The File Type Associations section in Bridge Preferences allows you to specify which application should be used to open each supported file type.

Note: If you find you are unable to open a file in Photoshop, check the File Type Associations. Sometimes loading a new application or an upgrade will change the settings and cause files to open in another program.

Startup Scripts   This section enables you to select which scripts run automatically when you launch Bridge. We recommend turning off those you don't need since doing so may help Bridge run faster. As shown in Figure 2.6, check Adobe Bridge and Adobe Photoshop CS3, and consider checking Photoshop Services.

Figure 2.6

Select only those scripts that you need in order to improve Bridge's performance.

Advanced   This section (shown in Figure 2.7) contains several other settings. We recommend checking the option Enable Color Management in Bridge; however, for this to work correctly, you must have a correctly color-managed workflow including a calibrated monitor (see Chapter 4, "Foundations"). The option exists so you can see how images will look in applications such as browsers that are not color managed. In addition, if your monitor is not calibrated, you may get unpredictable results by having the option turned on.

Figure 2.7

The Advanced section of the Bridge Preferences contains a number of additional settings.

The second option is whether to Use Software Rendering. Software rendering can be helpful for those with older computers and/or lesser graphics cards whose hardware can't take advantage of some of the features in Bridge. For those with better graphics cards and newer computers, it's better to use the hardware acceleration. If you're not sure, you can easily try checking this option to see which way Bridge works better for you.

We recommend checking the option to Automatically Export Caches To Folders When Possible so that if you copy the folder to an external drive or a DVD, any changes you make in Bridge will be maintained. Otherwise, you may lose any ratings, labels, and metadata such as keywords that you have added.

Downloading Images

We're sure that you, like us, are anxious to get at your images immediately upon returning from a photo shoot. Of course, you need to download the images from your digital media cards before you can really get started. CS3 includes an excellent down-loader that makes this task easier than ever.

Start by inserting your digital media into the card reader (or connecting the external hard drive if you've used that for storage). In Bridge, choose File > Get Photos From Camera. A dialog box appears for the Photo Downloader. Click the button in the lower-left corner that says Advanced Dialog to access the interface shown in Figure 2.8.

Figure 2.8
The Photo Downloader is an extremely efficient way to download and rename your images. (Photos by Ellen Anon.)

Note: We recommend using an accessory card reader rather than connecting your camera directly to the computer. This is partly because we just find it more convenient to use a card reader, especially when we have a relatively large number of images to download. However, we also prefer keeping the camera safely in the camera bag rather than sitting on the desk with a cord attached, with the risk that cord might acciden-tally get pulled and the camera might crash to the floor.

Begin by choosing a location for your pictures. Click the Choose button to navigate to the desired location on your computer, and use it to create a new folder if necessary. Which folder you copy them to depends on your own organizational structure. Hopefully you've set up folders to organize your images based on your preference, such as the location, date, or other attributes of the images. If not, now is a good time to start. Ellen stores her images within Pictures. Then in the Create Subfolders drop-down menu, Ellen chooses Shot Date. That creates a folder within the location folder for each day so she can use the same location folder for multiple days of shooting while still keeping her images organized by date.

One of the handy features of the new downloader is the ability to rename the files while importing them. Ellen usually selects the Custom Name option and chooses a name that reflects the location, although some people prefer to use the species or subject name. It's a good idea to check the option to Preserve Current Filename in XMP so that if the file gets saved and renamed again later, you can easily find the original RAW file.

Although it may seem silly since Bridge is already open, we recommend checking the option to Open Adobe Bridge. Doing so opens a second Bridge window that automatically displays the images you are downloading. That saves having to navigate to them later.

We recommend you always store your files in at least two places since hard drives can fail. Photo Downloader enables you to simultaneously save copies of the images to a second location by checking the box by Save Copies To and then choosing the desired location. Obviously, if you want to use an external hard drive as your backup, it must be connected to the computer.

It's a good practice to create a metadata template containing your basic contact information such as your name, email, website, phone, or whatever information you want to include. Then you can select that template within Downloader, and it will apply the information to each file during the import. We'll explain how to do that shortly.

Lastly, if you want to import only some of the files from the card, click the Uncheck All button, and then manually check those you want to import.

When you're ready, click Get Photos. A new Bridge window will appear preset to the folder containing the newly imported pictures, which will already be renamed and have your contact metadata attached. That's pretty slick!

Once you've copied the images, the originals are still on your digital media card. Until you need to use that card, it serves as a backup copy just in case something goes wrong in the meantime (though you should still be backing up the images on your hard drive as well). When you're ready to use that digital media card again, reformat it in the camera to both erase the existing images and reinitialize it to give the file system on the card a clean start.

Creating a Metadata Template

In the days of slides, nature photographers used to label each slide with their name and contact information, helping to ensure that their slides were not lost. In today's digital world it's equally important to label your digital images with your contact information. The easiest way to do so is to create a template that can be applied to all your images as you import them.

To create a metadata template, go to the Metadata panel, click the small fly-out menu in the upper-right corner, and choose Create Template, as shown in Figure 2.9. In the new dialog box that appears, fill in the desired fields. Be sure to check each field that you want to include in the template. Even if text appears, if the field is not checked, it won't be included in the template. Name the template—Ellen uses Contact Info—and click Save. The template you just made will be available in the Downloader to apply to all images as you import then, as well as in the Metadata panel. You can apply the template from the Metadata panel by selecting the images and then going to the same fly-out menu and choosing Append Metadata. Select your template from the list that appears.

Figure 2.9
Create a metadata template to quickly add contact and copyright information to your files.

Note: To create a metadata template using earlier versions of Photoshop, choose File > File Info in the Bridge menu. In the dialog box that appears, complete the copyright information in the General section, then choose IPTC Contact, and finally fill in as much information as you want others to be able to access. When you're done, you must click the small right-facing triangle within the circle in the upper-right corner of the dialog box and choose Save. Do not simply click OK. Then give your template a name, and click OK.

Renaming Your Images After Import

Sometimes you may import images without renaming them and want to rename them later, or perhaps you want to change the name you initially used. Fortunately, it's quite easy to rename all or some of the images in a folder. To rename your images, take the following steps:

1. Either select the particular files you want to rename or select a folder in the Folders panel. In the latter case, the renaming will be applied to all the files in the folder.

2. Choose Tools > Batch Rename in the Bridge menu to open the Batch Rename dialog box (see Figure 2.10).

Figure 2.10

To rename images after you've imported them, use the Batch Rename dialog box.

3. Select whether you want your renamed files to be in the same folder, copied to another folder, or moved to another folder. If you copy or move them, specify where by clicking Browse.

4. For New Filename, we like to create a name that tells us essential identifying features about the images. This could be text that describes the place (such as Holland) or the subject (tulips), along with a date and/or the original preserved filename and an extension. The number of elements you use is your choice:

   - In the first drop-down box under New Filenames that says Current Filename by default, choose Text. The next box to the right will prompt you to type text. This is where you type the location, subject, name, and so on.

   - To the far right of this row are + and – radio buttons. Click the + button to get another drop-down box to add more parameters to your name. Ellen recommends using the Preserved Filename, although it's clearly a personal choice what you use.

   - If you do not use the Preserved Filename, then we suggest that you choose a sequence number (or letter) from the drop-down menu. Usually we specify a three-digit number, but if you don't use the date in your naming schema, you may prefer to use at least a four-digit number.

Note: Bridge will automatically preserve the file extension, so you don't have to use Extension as your final choice.

You'll see a preview of your new name at the lower right.

5. Under Options, if you did not already save the original filename to the XMP metadata, you can choose to keep the original filename in the metadata for the file. If you are renaming copies, this can be helpful in the event you ever want to refer back to the original files.

6. Under Compatibility, it's a good idea to select both Windows and Mac (your current operating system is selected by default).

Bridge Views and Workspaces

We know you're anxious to check out your images, but most nature photographers find that the default configuration (see Figure 2.11) of Bridge isn't a very efficient way to work. Fortunately, Bridge is very easy to customize, and making a few changes can make the difference between thinking that Bridge is awkward to use and thinking that it's wonderful. The Bridge interface is comprised of *pods* that can be moved and adjusted in size either manually or by using one of the presets, or a combination or both, to enable easier access to whatever features you're using. We'll show you several of the variations that we find most helpful.

Figure 2.11 By default Bridge opens with this view, giving you access to many of the features.

 Note: When using Bridge, maximize the interface window so that it uses your entire monitor. That way you'll be seeing as large an image preview as possible.

Filmstrip View

Most nature photographers use a "filmstrip" view to sort through their images. This view has a large Preview area with a much larger version of the selected thumbnail, along with a filmstrip view of all the thumbnails. The large preview makes it much easier to decide which images to keep and which to delete. In addition, the Favorites, Folders, and Filter tabs are on the left, making it easy to find the images you want to see. Click the number 2 icon in the bottom right of the Bridge interface **2** to switch to the horizontal filmstrip orientation, as shown in Figure 2.12.

Figure 2.12 The horizontal filmstrip view is a good starting place for viewing images. (Photo by Ellen Anon.)

Although the default horizontal filmstrip view is usable, Ellen modifies it. She prefers to have the filmstrip appear vertically on the right side, as shown in Figure 2.13, because vertical images appear considerably larger in the Preview pane that way. To change to a vertical filmstrip view, click and hold the lower-right corner of the number icons, and choose Vertical Filmstrip. Alternatively, choose Window >Workspace > Vertical Filmstrip.

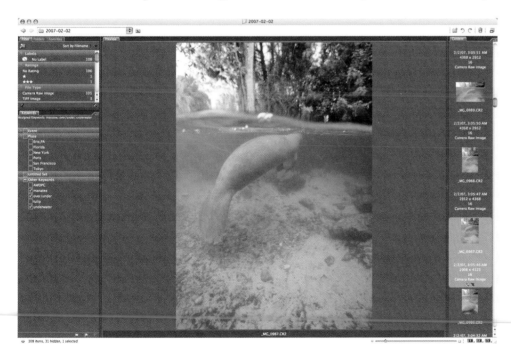

Figure 2.13 Using a vertical filmstrip affords more room for the vertical image previews. (Photo by Ellen Anon.)

Sizing Thumbnails

To adjust the size of the filmstrip, place the cursor over the vertical line separating the Preview pod from the Content pod. The cursor will change to a double-facing arrow, as shown in Figure 2.14. Click and drag to the right or left to increase or decrease the width of the Content pod. Just above the scroll bar is a tiny, somewhat difficult to see icon at the top right of the Content pod. Click it to reveal choices to display the thumbnails vertically, horizontally, or in the auto layout. For the vertical filmstrip view, Ellen prefers the vertical thumbnail display.

Figure 2.14

Adjust the size of the Content pod so that it's large enough to comfortably view the thumbnails but small enough so that you maximize the size of the image previews in the Preview pane.

To adjust the size of the thumbnails themselves, use the slider that's just to the left of the number icons. Simply click your mouse on the slider handle, and drag to the left or right to reduce or increase the size of the thumbnails. The thumbnail size and image layout adjust dynamically as you move the slider, making it easy to decide exactly what setting works best for you. It also makes it quick and easy to adjust the thumbnail size on the fly based on the particular task you're doing.

You'll want the thumbnails to be large enough that the metadata you've chosen in Preferences to appear with the thumbnails is visible. If the thumbnails are too small, the metadata won't appear. The idea is to make the thumbnails just large enough to reveal enough information to know which image is which but small enough that they don't unnecessarily take space away from the Preview pod. Click the small icon to the left of the slider to have Bridge automatically make the thumbnails as small as possible while still maintaining your configuration, and click the button to the right to make them as large as possible within the confines of the allotted space.

Customizing the Left Pod

On the left side of the interface is a pod containing the Favorites and Folders panels, and beneath it is one containing the Filter panel. You can adjust the width of these pods similarly to the way you adjusted the width of the Content pod. In addition, you can allocate more or less vertical space to each of these pods by clicking the horizontal line just above the Filter tab. Drag it up or down as you want. You can opt to have just a single pod on the left by clicking the Filter tab and dragging it on top of the Folders tab. In addition, you can view keyword or metadata information in these pods by choosing Window > Metadata Panel or Window > Keyword Panel. Then drag each panel to whichever pod is most convenient.

To reposition a panel, point your mouse at the title tab for that panel, and click and drag it to whatever pod is convenient for you. If several panels share a pod, simply click the tab of the panel you want to view to bring it to the forefront.

> **Note:** If you drag the Filter panel from its default location and place it by Folders and Favorites, the pod that originally contained the Filter panel will collapse unless you have placed another panel there.

> **Note:** Any panel in Bridge can be positioned in any pod by clicking the tab at the top of the panel and dragging it to the desired location. By doing this you could place the filmstrip on the left and the folders on the right or create any other configuration that suits your needs.

When initially viewing images, Ellen usually selects the Folders tab and navigates to the desired folder, so she can have the Folders panel fill the left pod. (If you have used Adobe Photo Downloader, it will automatically open a new Bridge window and navigate to the folder containing the newly imported images.) However, while she's sorting through her images, she likes to have the Filter and Keyword panels visible on the left. To quickly go between these two views, Ellen saved each view and then assigned them to the number icons at the bottom of the Bridge interface, as shown in Figure 2.15.

Figure 2.15 Creating a customized workspace and saving it to a numbered icon makes it easy to switch views. (Photo by Ellen Anon.)

To create and save a customized workspace, take these steps:

1. Choose the default workspace that initially is closest to what you want to use.

2. Adjust the size of the pods as described earlier.

3. Select which panels to have visible by choosing Window > Workspace and toggling the check marks on and off

4. Drag the panels to the desired pods.

Once you have configured the space the way you want it, save the workspace by Window > Workspace > Save Workspace or by clicking the lower right corner of the number icons and choosing Save Workspace. A new dialog will appear in which you name your workspace. In addition you can assign it a keyboard shortcut if you want. There are also options to save the current sort order and the physical location of the window. After you save your workspace, it's available from Window > Workspace or by clicking the lower right corner of the number icons as shown in Figure 2.16.

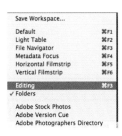

Figure 2.16
Choose a name for each workspace you save that clearly describes it, so you can quickly select the best workspace for any task.

Each numbered icon is "sticky" and will use the last saved workspace view you used after clicking it.

Light Table View

Sometimes it's helpful to be able to see more of the images at once without seeing a larger preview of a single image. The Light Table view (Window > Workspace > Light Table) shows only the Content panel (see Figure 2.17). This can be helpful when you want to get an overall look at the images. Tim often uses this view for a first pass at sorting through images.

This view is also excellent if Bridge didn't automatically rotate your verticals so they appear with the proper orientation (which requires that your digital camera support this feature). To rotate images, simply select them, and click the appropriate rotation button at the top of the Bridge window—these buttons have circular arrows indicating the direction of rotation. To select a group of images to be rotated, click the first one, then Shift+click the last one in the group, and finally click a rotation button. To rotate noncontiguous images, Ctrl+click/⌘+click the desired images, and then click a rotation button. When you rotate an image in Bridge, only the thumbnail preview is rotated. The actual image isn't rotated until you open it.

Resize the thumbnails using the same procedure as described earlier. Usually you'll want the thumbnails to be fairly small in this view since you're not checking the individual files for details but rather getting a sense of what images are in the folder.

Figure 2.17 Using the Light Table view allows you to see as many of your image thumbnails as possible for an initial sort.

Try It! To get more comfortable with the many options available in Bridge, point it to a folder containing some of your images, and adjust the various options we've discussed here for changing the interface including the view, pod size, and panel locations.

Stacking Images

As you go through your images, if you're like most nature photographers, you'll see that you have a series of very similar images. This is particularly true if you are a wildlife photographer seeking just the right head angle and subject position. Sometimes it helps to organize your images into *stacks*. That way you can rapidly glance through the stacked view to have a general idea of what you've captured and you can edit each stack individually.

To stack a group of images, first select them by Ctrl+clicking/⌘+clicking the images you want to group. If the images were shot in sequence and are all next to each other, click the first one and Shift+click the last one to select the entire series, press Ctrl+G/⌘+G to group them as a stack. Alternatively, you can stack them by choosing Stacks > Group as Stack. The stacked images will appear with an outline around them and a number on top indicating how many images are in the stack (see Figure 2.18).

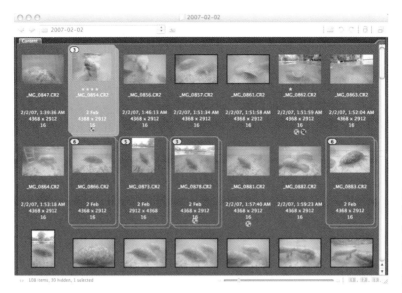

Figure 2.18
Stacking groups of similar images makes it easier to find specific sequences of images.

Ellen finds the following techniques helpful when working with stacks:

- To open an individual stack, click the number at the top of the stack. Click the number again to close that stack.

- To open all stacks, choose Stacks > Expand All Stacks, and to close all stacks, choose Stacks > Collapse All Stacks.

- To move an image in or out of an existing stack, click and drag it in or out of the stack.

The image on top of the stack will be the image that's the farthest to the left in the group when you open the stack. You can click any image in the stack and drag it to the right or left, thereby selecting which image will be on top of the stack. Usually you'll want to choose the best image from the group, as shown in Figure 2.19.

Figure 2.19
The image farthest to the left will appear on top of the stack.

To open just the top image in ACR, make sure that only the top image is selected. You can tell because the top image will have a gray background, and there will be a rim of black on the right and bottom before the outline of the stack, as shown in Figure 2.20.

Figure 2.20
When there is a black space to the right and bottom of the stack, only the top image is selected.

To open an entire stack in ACR, first click in the black space, which will then fill with gray. When the entire stack outline is filled with gray, the entire stack is selected, as shown in Figure 2.21. Double click in the main part of the thumbnail to open the images in ACR. To select just the top image, click in the space on the right and bottom so that it returns to black.

Figure 2.21
When there is no black space to the right and bottom of the stack, all images in the stack are selected.

Try It! Practice working with stacks on a folder of your own images. Create stacks, rearrange the files in them to change the one that appears on top, drag images in and out of the stack, and so on. We think you'll like this new feature once you get comfortable with it.

Sorting and Editing

Getting your digital images onto your computer and creating a good way to view them is certainly a start. But as you've probably noticed, images seem to accumulate quickly, and keeping them organized can be a bit of a chore, especially if you have a backlog of images stored in many folders. When you download your latest images, chances are you want to get started working with them right away. But the first step, of course, is to figure out what you have, which images are worth keeping, and which should be deleted. Then you can select the images you'd like to start optimizing,

A good approach is to plan to do at least two passes through your images. Ellen finds it helpful to reject the images that are obviously poor on the first pass and to mark those she's excited about with a star rating. She then takes a second look at the rejects before deleting them. That way no files are accidentally deleted. After that she may stack the images and go through them a second or third time, assigning more careful ratings as well as labels. We'll go into more detail about this process in this section.

If you haven't already navigated to the folder containing your images, do so using the Folders panel. It's a directory of everything on your computer. If you will be returning to this folder frequently, you may want to drag the folder to the Favorites panel. That way you can find it quickly without needing to look through the entire directory. To place it on the Favorites panel, right-click/Control+click the folder, and choose Add to Favorites. If both the Favorites panel and Folders panel are visible, you can simply drag the folder to the area under the words *Drag Favorites Here* on the Favorites panel. Then click the folder in Favorites to view the contents. Ellen uses the vertical filmstrip view customized to show Metadata and Filter or Keywords; you should select whatever view is easiest for you.

Instead of using your mouse to haphazardly click images that you want to view in more detail, we recommend taking a close look at all of the images in your collection.

Click the first image on the list (scroll to the top of the list if necessary), and then use the up and down arrow keys on your keyboard to navigate through the images. As you move up and down, the preview is updated based on the currently active image. This gives you a much better idea of the overall composition, exposure accuracy, and image quality so you can decide whether you should delete or keep the image. You can also start to get a better idea of which images deserve more attention as you sort through them.

Zooming and Comparing Images

As you go through your images, you need to know whether they are critically sharp. It's easy to tell when things are grossly out of focus, but judging critical sharpness can be challenging, especially on smaller laptop monitors. CS3 has added a Loupe tool to enable you to quickly check sharpness, as shown in Figure 2.22. To access it, simply click the image preview, and then drag it wherever you'd like. The pointed corner of the tool points at the area it will magnify. Alternatively, click anywhere on the image that you'd like to view at 100% magnification.

Figure 2.22 Using the magnifier makes it easy to check for critical sharpness. (Photo by Ellen Anon.)

By default the Loupe tool is set to 100%. To use greater magnification, up to 800%, Ctrl+click/⌘+click the tool. The magnification percentage is visible by the file-name at the center bottom of the Bridge interface. To decrease the magnification back to 100% click Ctrl+- (minus)/⌘+- (minus). To remove the loupe click the black rim of the magnifier.

Sometimes it's helpful to be able to look at two or more similar images simultaneously in order to decide which one is the best. To see more than one image in the Preview panel, Ctrl+click/⌘+click the images you want to see. The previews will automatically resize and move to accommodate as many images as you want to compare, as shown in Figure 2.23. To remove an image from the Preview panel, Ctrl+click/⌘+click it.

Figure 2.23 Being able to view multiple images simultaneously often makes it easier to decide which one is the best. (Photos by Ellen Anon.)

Rating Images

Bridge includes a rating capability that allows you to assign a value of one to five stars or "REJECT" to your images, much like you might rate a movie. In so doing, you can quickly go through your images and rate them so that when you're finished with the sorting and editing process, you'll know exactly which images are your favorites and which ones need to be deleted.

As you sort through your images, begin by rejecting those you definitely don't want to keep. To apply a REJECT rating, press Alt+Delete/Option+Delete. The image will remain in the folder but will be marked with REJECT in red. You could opt to delete each throwaway image instead, but then there is no safeguard if you accidentally reject/delete one that you later decide you should have kept. We strongly believe it's better to first mark the throwaways with a REJECT rating.

You'll also want to start thinking about which images are your favorites, since those are the ones you'll want to spend the most time optimizing. To assign a rank, simply press a number from 1 through 5 to assign a star rating.

> **Note:** You must change the Label preference in Bridge preferences to enable you to assign labels and ratings without pressing the Ctrl/⌘ key. Otherwise, the keyboard shortcut for applying ratings is Ctrl/⌘ plus a number key from 1 through 5. We have found no advantage to using the additional keystroke; it's much faster to do the rating by simply pressing a number key.

If you prefer to not use the keyboard shortcuts to apply ratings, select an image (or images), and move your mouse over the row of five dots below the thumbnail. The dots represent the possible star ratings, so click the first dot to rate it as one star, the second dot to rate it as two stars, and so on (these dots are visible only if the image is selected, but the star rating you've applied to an image will display regardless of whether it is selected). If you have multiple images selected when you click, the rating will be updated to the same value for all the selected images. You can also remove a rating by clicking to the left of the row of dots. The star rating display replaces the dots below the image, so you can see at a glance what you rated a given image (see Figure 2.24).

Figure 2.24
When you apply a rating to an image, that rating is reflected with stars displayed below the image thumbnail. (Photo by Ellen Anon.)

Labeling Images

The labeling feature in Bridge allows you to take the rating system a step further by assigning a color code to your images. You do this by applying a colored label to images in a way very similar to ratings. You can then filter the display to show only the images that are labeled or only those labeled with a specific color. The available colors for labels are red, yellow, green, blue, and purple.

To use these effectively, you'll first want to come up with a system that identifies what the colors mean. You might, for example, use the labels to identify categorizations of images. For example, you might use a yellow label to mark images to use for a contest or competition, a green label to mark images to illustrate an article, and a blue label to designate images for a slide show. It's a good idea to document your system so you won't get confused later as you are reviewing images that have been previously labeled or as you are trying to remember what color specific images should be labeled in a new group of images. Consistency is important to taking full advantage of this capability.

To label an image, you simply select it (or several images) and press the numbers 6 through 9; 6 for red, 7 for yellow, 8 for green, and 9 for blue (purple doesn't have a shortcut key). Alternatively, you can choose Label and then the desired color from the menu. You can turn off the label by hitting the number key a second time or by selecting Label > No Label.

When you label an image, a colored bar appears below the thumbnail (see Figure 2.25). This allows you to see at a glance which images were marked for a particular purpose, based on the system you're using for color-coding with labels.

Figure 2.25
When you apply a label to an image, a colored bar appears below the thumbnail in Bridge.

Of course, just seeing a colored bar or a star rating below the thumbnail image doesn't quite provide you with a powerful way to review your decisions about the images. By using the Filter panel, you can make even better use of the rating and labeling options.

Using the Filter Panel

When you have assigned a rank and/or label to all the images in your current project, you can sort the images by a particular parameter such as ratings or labels by choosing View > Sort > By Rating or View > Sort > By Labels from the drop-down menu on the right side of the Filter tab. In addition, Bridge shows how many images in the folder match each parameter. We prefer to use the Filter panel to allow Bridge to show only images meeting certain criteria. That makes it easier to select images for certain purposes.

The Filter panel enables you to choose which images to display at any one time according to a variety of parameters. You can select just one parameter such as stars, labels, or Reject, or multiple parameters. If the parameters are within the same category, such as Ratings, then selecting more than one parameter is the equivalent of saying, "Show all images with this rating *or* that rating." When you choose an additional parameter from a different category such as Labels, then you are instructing Bridge to show only those images that meet the conditions checked in both categories; for example, in Figure 2.26 they must have a rating of five stars and a yellow label. If you clear a label or rating for an image at this point, it will disappear from the current view if it no longer meets the display criteria. When you want to see all the images again, toggle off all the check marks in the Filter panel.

Figure 2.26 Use the Filter panel to selectively display images meeting specific criteria. (Photo by Ellen Anon.)

For example, you may choose to view images with three or more stars or those containing a label. You can then use the View > Sort options to reorder the images according to a variety of parameters including file type, bit depth, rating, labels, and so on.

In Ellen's workflow, after she has made the first pass through her images and rejected some of them, she filters the images to show only the rejects (see Figure 2.27). She then quickly looks through the images to make certain there are none she wants to keep. To delete the images, she will select them all (Ctrl+A/⌘+A) and then press Delete. A warning dialog box will appear asking whether to delete or reject the images. Choose Delete.

Figure 2.27 By selecting Filter > Rejects, you can glance through the images you rejected before actually deleting them. (Photo by Ellen Anon.)

Note: You may opt to check the box to cause the warning dialog box to not appear in the future since by rejecting the images first, you have introduced a safety step. It's a matter of personal preference to keep or eliminate this particular warning.

Using Keywords

Applying keywords to your images is essential if you want to be able to easily find particular images, or types of images, in the future. Although it may feel like a nuisance, it's important to apply keywords to your images early on in your workflow. It's all too easy to procrastinate and figure you'll do it later so that you can get on with the fun part of optimizing your images. But if you skip adding the keywords, you're likely to wind up with thousands of images stashed in various folders without an easy way to locate any particular image. By applying keywords, you can later search for an image using the Find command in Photoshop or using the search function on your computer.

Using Keywords to Locate Images

To find images using Bridge, choose Edit > Find. A new dialog box appears in which you specify the criteria for which to search. In the Criteria drop-down menu, choose Keywords. By using a series of keywords, you can do a more comprehensive search than just searching by filename. At the end of the line, click the + radio button to add additional keywords to use in the search. Under Results, choose If any Criteria are met or If all Criteria are met. Then proceed with your search.

Assign keywords every time you import images. In Bridge, you do so by highlighting one or more images, clicking the Keywords tab, and checking the keyword(s) to apply. It's really quite simple!

Keywords are organized into sets containing specific keywords in each set. By default Bridge has a few keywords and sets, but for most nature photographers these will not be of much use. You'll need to create your own. Fortunately, it's easy. First you need to think of what organizational scheme you want to use. Since Bridge does not use nested keywords, you'll need to create keyword sets according to how specific you want to be with the keywords. For example, in Figure 2.28, we have added a new keyword set for Birds. We can then add specific keywords such as Great Egret and Snowy Egret. In addition, we checked Florida for the location, but we could have opted to add a more specific location as a keyword.

Figure 2.28
Organize your keywords into sets so that you can quickly find the right keywords to apply.

Note: At the very least, you should have a keyword for the location of each shot and the subject matter. If you submit your images to stock agencies, you'll want to add keywords according to their recommendations.

To create new keyword sets, click the New Keyword Set icon , and then type the name for the set. To create new keywords, first select the set to contain the keyword, and then click the New Keyword icon. To delete a keyword or keyword set, select it, and right-click/Control+click, and choose Delete.

Although applying keywords in Bridge is not as flexible or robust as what is possible in other programs such as Aperture and Lightroom where you can use nested keywords, it's still worth doing.

Try It! Create a new keyword set and several new keywords, and apply them to various images. Although it may seem intimidating at first, once you do it, we're confident you'll see how easy it is to do.

Additional Features

Bridge contains a variety of additional features that we find useful. For example, we use Tools > Photoshop > Image Processor (see Chapter 11, "Time-Savers") to quickly batch convert images to other sizes and file formats, and we use Tools > Photoshop > Photomerge to stitch together a series of images into a panorama (see Chapter 8, "Composites"). We also use Tools > Photoshop > Merge to HDR to combine a series of shots in Bridge into a 32-bit file (see Chapter 8), and we use Tools > Photoshop > Contact Sheet to create contact sheets (see Chapter 10, "Output").

In addition, Bridge has a cool slide show feature that quickly generates a slide show of your images. That can be useful to show off some of your best images or to help you with your sorting and editing.

To create a slide show in Bridge, choose View > Slide Show from the Bridge menu, or press Ctrl+L/⌘+L. This will start a slide show of the selected images or all images in the current folder if none are selected. By default, the images will change every five seconds, but you can press the spacebar to play or pause the slide show. To move through the images manually, click the mouse, or use the arrow keys on the keyboard.

Choose View > Slideshow Options (Shift+Ctrl+L/Shift+⌘+L) to access a dialog box (see Figure 2.29) to specify options for the slide show. You can opt to have the slide show repeat, set the timing for the advances, whether the captions show, whether the images are scaled, as well as the transitions and transition speed. We think that the Dissolve feature is quite good and makes for a nice transition between images.

Figure 2.29
Add transitions and other controls to your slide show using the Slideshow Options dialog box.

While viewing a slide show, press the H key to access additional slide show commands, as shown in Figure 2.30. Notice that you can apply or change labels and ratings while viewing images in a slide show. Sometimes it's easier to decide which image you like the best by viewing the series of images in a slide show. Bridge makes it simple to remember which file you want by applying a label or rating. Press the 1–5 keys to add the appropriate number of stars and 6–9 to add a colored label.

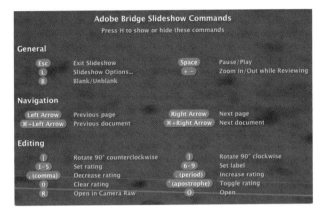

Figure 2.30
The slide show offers a number of useful features including the ability to easily add labels and ratings to images while viewing the slide show.

Try It! Open a folder in Bridge, and create a slide show. Try using the various commands and controls to customize the show. We think that once you try this feature, you'll like it a lot!

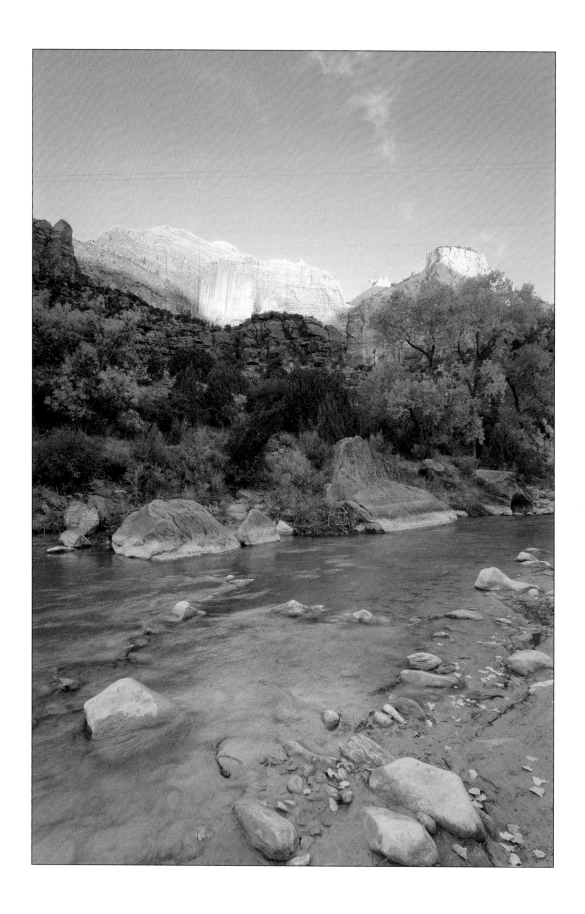

Adobe Camera Raw

Adobe Camera Raw (ACR) has been significantly improved in Photoshop CS3 and is the foundation of our workflow. Camera sensors capture information that needs to be converted to a form that we can see. Shooting in RAW gives us the chance to modify the algorithms used to convert the images. We can now do most global image adjustments within ACR, in a powerful and easy-to-use interface. What's more, we can even use ACR to adjust TIFF or JPEG files. We'll show you how to use ACR to adjust your images so that you're starting with the best possible files!

Chapter Contents
Using the ACR Interface
Using the Basic Tab
Setting the Other Tabs
Setting ACR Workflow Options and Saving Files
Batch Converting Multiple Images

Using the ACR Interface

The new ACR interface packs a lot of features and controls into its intuitive and easy-to-use interface. You can choose to make only basic corrections to your image or perform some quite sophisticated adjustments. We'll go through the interface step by step so you'll know precisely where to find each control.

Note: It's worth mentioning that ACR is different from the converter supplied by your camera manufacturer. The one that came with your camera may be able to take advantage of some proprietary information captured by your camera, and this can, in a small percentage of cases, result in better image quality in the conversion. However, there is a huge convenience factor in using the very user-friendly and generally faster converter included within Photoshop. You'll rarely, if ever, encounter a problem by using ACR.

Seeing Your Image Within ACR

By default when ACR opens, the image is set to Fit In View, so you see your entire image within the workspace. As shown in Figure 3.1, the small box in the lower left of the dialog box gives the current magnification of your image. To zoom in or out, click the – or + box there, or click the arrows next to the number to get a drop-down menu revealing a variety of common magnifications. To check for critical sharpness within your image, zoom to 100%. To return to the original view, select Fit In View from the drop-down menu, or use the keyboard shortcut of Ctrl+0/⌘+0.

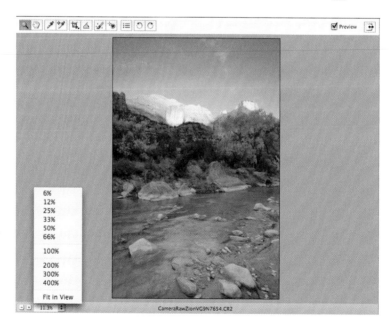

Figure 3.1
You have the option of seeing your entire image or zooming in to closely examine parts of the image. (Photo by Ellen Anon.)

Note: To change the default view, zoom, and other settings for *all* images you open, see the section "Controlling the Default Appearance of Your Image" later in this chapter.

When you are zoomed in beyond the Fit In View size, you can click the hand icon in the strip of icons at the top left of the ACR window, as shown in Figure 3.2, and then click within the preview and drag to inspect various parts of the image. Alternatively, you can simply hold down the spacebar while clicking and dragging within the preview. Note that you can also click the magnifying-glass icon in that same strip of icons to zoom into your image and hold down the Alt/Option key while clicking to zoom out.

Ⓐ Zoom tool
Ⓑ Hand tool (scroll-in preview)
Ⓒ White Balance tool
Ⓓ Color Sampler tool
Ⓔ Crop tool
Ⓕ Straighten tool
Ⓖ Retouch tool
Ⓗ Red-Eye Removal tool
Ⓘ Open Preferences dialog box
Ⓙ Rotate Image 90° Counterclockwise
Ⓚ Rotate Image 90° Clockwise

Figure 3.2 This strip of icons allows you easy, one-click access to a number of important features in ACR, including zooming, navigating, taking a reading of a point, selecting a point, cropping, straightening horizons, retouching, removing red-eye, setting preferences, and rotating the canvas.

If your image needs to be rotated, click one of the circle arrows ↻ ↺, or press the R key to rotate the image 90° to the right (clockwise) or the L key to rotate it 90° to the left (counterclockwise).

As you can see in Figure 3.3, you can select the Preview check box to toggle between a preview of the file with and without your changes. The preview is continuously updated.

Figure 3.3 Checking the Preview box and the clipping triangles in the histogram allows you to see whether there is any clipping in your image either from the way it was captured or because of the changes you make within ACR.

Next to that is the Full Screen icon . Clicking it toggles the ACR interface between full-screen and a smaller adjustable size. It's a matter of personal preference which you prefer.

In the upper-right corner of the interface is the histogram. It shows a graph for each color channel with the white luminosity histogram superimposed on top. In the upper corners of the histogram, as shown in Figure 3.3, you'll see two triangles. Clicking these triangles toggles the clipping previews on and off. When they are on, any highlights that are being clipped will appear solid bright red, and any shadows being clipped will appear solid vivid blue. This way you can readily see when you may have made an adjustment that would lead to accidentally throwing away detail in your highlights or shadows. With this obvious warning enabled, it's easy to modify your settings to retain as much detail as possible within your image. In addition, the triangles change colors to indicate which channels are being clipped. When there is no clipping, the triangles are black.

Note: *Clipping* means forcing pixels above or below a certain value to become pure black or pure white, thus losing detail in either your highlights or shadows.

As your cursor hovers over any point in your image preview, a readout of that point's RGB values appears beneath the histogram. In addition, some basic information about your lens, ISO, aperture, and shutter speed appears there.

Camera Raw Shortcuts

Windows	Mac	Action
Delete	Backspace	When Crop tool is active: Clear crop In Curve tab: Delete selected points on curve In Text field: Delete selected text In Filmstrip mode: Toggles "mark for delete"
Esc	Esc	Exit ACR (same as Cancel) When Crop tool is active: Clear crop
Alt+Cancel button	Opt+Cancel button	Reset
Tab	Tab	Move to next control
Shift+Tab	Shift+Tab	Move to previous control
Ctrl++	⌘++	Zoom in preview
Ctrl+-	⌘+-	Zoom out preview
Ctrl+Alt+0	⌘+Opt+0	Zoom to 100 %
Ctrl+0	⌘+0	Fit preview to window
Ctrl+Z	⌘+Z	Undo/redo last

Continues

Camera Raw Shortcuts *(Continued)*

Windows	Mac	Action
Ctrl+Alt+Z	⌘+Opt+Z	Undo multiple
Ctrl+Shift+Z	⌘+Shift+Z	Redo multiple
Ctrl+Shift+A or Ctrl+D	⌘+Shift+A or ⌘+D	Select primary image
Ctrl+O	⌘+O	Open
Ctrl+Alt+O or Alt+Open button	⌘+Opt+O or Alt+Open button	Open a copy
Ctrl+S	⌘+S	Save
Ctrl+Alt+S or Alt+Save button	⌘+Opt+S or Opt+Save button	Save with previous settings (no dialog box)
I	I	White Balance tool
Z	Z	Zoom tool
H	H	Hand tool
C	C	Crop tool
A	A	Straighten tool
S	S	Color Sampler tool
R or Ctrl+]	R or ⌘+]	Rotate right
L or Ctrl+[	L or ⌘+[	Rotate left
Arrow keys	Arrow keys	Adjust selected slider In Curve tab: Adjust selected curve point In Filmstrip mode: Select image
P	P	Toggle Preview check box
Alt+Shadows slider	Opt+Shadows slider	Show Shadows clipping in preview
Alt+Exposure slider	Opt+Exposure slider	Show Highlights clipping in preview
Ctrl+Tab	Control+Tab	Select next point in curve
Ctrl+Shift+Tab	Control+Shift+Tab	Select preview point in curve
D	D	Deselect point in curve
Ctrl+U	⌘+U	Toggle all Auto check boxes
Ctrl+K	⌘+K	Preferences
Ctrl+A	⌘+A	In text field: Select all text In Filmstrip mode: Select all images
Ctrl+Alt+A or Alt+Select All button	⌘+Alt+A or Opt+Select All button	In Filmstrip mode: Select all rated images
Alt+Synchronize button	Opt+Synchronize button	In Filmstrip mode: Synchronize selected with previous settings (no dialog box)

Cropping and Rotating Within ACR

Photoshop CS3 offers the ability to crop and rotate within ACR. Since you can embed your raw file in your image file as a Smart Object (see Chapter 5, "Workflows and First Steps," for more details), you can crop nondestructively using the cropping tool in ACR. By *nondestructively*, we mean that you can change your mind at some future time and change the crop without any loss of image quality. (Obviously when you crop, you're eliminating certain pixels from your final file.) Since cropping in Photoshop itself is nonreversible, it makes sense to crop in ACR whenever possible.

To use the Crop tool, simply click its icon ⌗ or press C on your keyboard, then click a beginning point in the image preview, and drag diagonally across the image. You can refine your selection by clicking any one of the small boxes appearing on the boundaries of the image and dragging them inward or outward as desired. You can move the crop around on the image by placing the cursor within the center of the area to be cropped and then clicking and dragging.

If you click and hold on the Crop tool, you'll see a drop-down menu listing various preset cropping options, so you can crop the image to a particular aspect ratio of your choosing (see Figure 3.4). You can even create custom settings for other aspect ratios that you frequently use such as 8×10. To do this, simply click the Custom option to reveal a Custom Crop dialog box. Fill in the boxes with the appropriate numbers, and click OK. To remove a crop, press Esc while the Crop tool is still selected, or choose Clear Crop from the Crop drop-down menu.

Figure 3.4

You can crop to a preset size or to a custom size within ACR. The Size menu will reflect the cropped file size. (Photo by Ellen Anon.)

As you set the crop to the desired size, notice that the Size menu on the bottom left has changed and now reads Crop Size, and the sizes reflect the number of pixels you have selected. This is quite helpful because if you realize you'll need a larger file size, you can select it and have the interpolation done within the converter.

ACR also enables you to easily straighten horizons. To do so, simply click the Straighten icon ▵, or press the letter A. Then click at the beginning of the *horizon*, or area that should be straight, and drag across to the opposite side. You are telling ACR what part of your image should be a straight horizontal or vertical line. When you release the cursor, you will see the preview rotated, and automatic crop lines will have been set, as illustrated in Figure 3.5. The Crop tool icon will automatically be highlighted or selected. To quickly reset your image to its original position, in the event that the straightening didn't work as planned, press Ctrl+Z/⌘+Z, or select Clear Crop from the Crop tool drop-down menu.

Figure 3.5 The Straighten tool automatically crops and straightens your image. (Photo by Ellen Anon.)

One potential drawback to cropping and rotating within the converter is that ACR limits your crop to the boundaries of the image, meaning you cannot rotate and crop in such a way that the boundaries extend beyond the pixel information at any point. If the placement of your subject matter dictates that you need to clone in additional background area after straightening the image, wait to crop and straighten the image within Photoshop.

> **Try It!** Open the raw image named ConvertRaw.dng on the accompanying CD or one of your own, and practice cropping and rotating it.

Using the Retouch Tool

One of the exciting new additions to ACR in CS3 is the Retouch tool , which is similar to the Clone and Healing Brush tools in Photoshop. If you are using a Smart Object–based flexible workflow (see Chapter 5), it's important to do as much as possible of your dust and scratch removal in ACR. That way, anytime you change the Smart

Object, your retouching will automatically change as well. If you use the flexible work-flow but do your cleanup in Photoshop, some changes you may make later to the Smart Object (your background layer with the raw file) may force you to have to redo the cleanup layer. For instance, if you make tonal or color corrections to the raw file, any cloning and healing that was based on the previous settings will no longer match.

The Retouch tool is particularly well suited to removing the dust that plagues most digital photographers. Unfortunately, since retouching in ACR is limited to circular spots, it is not well suited for object removal. That type of retouching is best done later in Photoshop.

To use the Retouch tool, follow these steps:

1. Zoom into your image to 100% magnification.

2. Set ACR to Full Screen mode.

3. Begin at one corner and systematically work your way through the image.

4. When you find a speck of dust, click the Retouch tool. As shown in Figure 3.6, several new options appear beneath the toolbar.

Figure 3.6 After clicking the Retouch tool, specify the Heal or Clone tool, as well as the radius and whether to show an overlay of the corrections.

5. Select either Heal or Clone in the Type drop-down menu. Clone will copy the pixels from another area that you choose to replace the dust, whereas Heal will copy the texture and blend the color just as the similar tools do in Photoshop. (For more in-depth coverage of cloning and healing, see Chapter 5.)

6. Check Show Overlay. That way a circle will remain showing areas that have been retouched, as well as the source for the retouching. That way, if you need to modify an area, you can redo it easily.

7. Click and drag over the dust to create a circle just slightly larger than the dust. A red circle appears to indicate this is the spot you are currently working on. As

you drag, the size of the circle changes. You can also modify the size of the circle, before or after you've created it, by adjusting the Radius slider.

8. Whether you are cloning or healing, a second circle will appear with broken lines. That indicates the source for the cloning or healing. To change the source, click within that circle, and drag it to the desired location.

9. Once you click the next spot, the previous red circle changes to a broken circle indicating the area that was retouched.

10. To modify a previously retouched area, click within the circle. If you place the cursor directly on the outline of the circle, you can drag to change its size. To change the source, click within the source circle, and drag.

11. To remove a single retouched spot, click within the circle, and press the Delete key on the keyboard. To remove all the retouching, click the Clear All button in ACR.

Note: The Red Eye Removal tool works similarly to the Red Eye Removal tool in Photoshop. Click and drag over the red pupils, and drag the Darken slider until the eye looks natural. Because red-eye removal is not a task faced by most nature photographers and the tool is straightforward to use, we won't go into more detail about using it.

Controlling the Default Appearance of Your Image

Bridge generates thumbnails and initial previews of your images to help you edit your images based on the ACR settings. These previews also serve as a starting place for your ACR adjustments. By default, they are set to use Auto settings and to apply some sharpening to generate these previews. You may decide that you would rather edit your images in Bridge, viewing the file previews with the settings you used to shoot them or some other combination of settings. ACR allows you to specify what settings it should use to generate the default thumbnails and previews. Click the Preferences icon in the toolbar ▤ to open the dialog box shown in Figure 3.7.

Figure 3.7

Click the Preferences icon to modify the default appearance of image previews in Bridge and ACR.

Specifying the General Settings

We recommend you use the default setting and save your image settings in sidecar .xmp files. These are the settings that contain the adjustments you make to the image, and it's useful to have them go with your image if you opt to open it in another application. More applications are able to read .xmp files and thus maintain consistency with the appearance of your image.

By default, ACR applies some sharpening to each image. This is to balance the slight bit of softening that is inherent within digital capture. Although using this sharpening may make your images look better initially, you have very little control over this sharpening. The sharpening tools in Photoshop offer far more control. We recommend that you change the Apply Sharpening To option to preview images only. This way you have the best of both: seeing your images with some sharpening within Bridge as well as ACR and also being able to use the more sophisticated sharpening available in Photoshop.

Specifying the Default Image Settings

ACR now includes several options for determining how you want to preview your images. There is an option to preview your images using auto-tone corrections for exposure, shadows, contrast, and brightness. For images from some cameras, these auto-corrections work fairly well and give you a good start on optimizing your images. With images from other cameras, the settings can be too extreme and result in clipped data or other less than ideal presentations. By default, CS3 ships with the Auto setting functionality turned on. This means that when you view your images in Bridge, you're seeing the raw files with the Auto settings applied. In reality, your raw file is still a raw data file; the settings are applied only to the previews, not to the raw files themselves. *When you open the image in ACR, you not only can but should modify any and all settings to customize the conversion as you desire.* The Auto settings are useful primarily as starting points.

We prefer to set ACR so that Auto is not applied to raw files. That way when you edit in Bridge, you'll be seeing your files as you shot them. Therefore, we recommend deselecting the Apply auto tone adjustments check box.

In the Default Image Settings section, we do enable Apply auto grayscale mix when converting to grayscale. In addition, if you use more than one camera body, Ellen recommends checking the option Make defaults specific to camera serial number. That way you can establish different settings for each camera. In particular, you may find that one camera requires a different amount of default color noise reduction or camera calibration settings.

Saving Settings

You may find with images shot under certain conditions that you frequently make similar adjustments. To save time, you can save these settings as a Preset. At other times you may want to return to the ACR default settings, or you may want to establish new

ACR default settings. To do any of these, click the small fly-out menu icon ≣◢ that's on the right side of the ACR interface about one third of the way down. It's actually on the far right edge of each adjustment tab. A new menu appears, as shown in Figure 3.8.

Figure 3.8

ACR enables you to save a group of settings as Preset or as the new default settings.

To save the settings for a particular image so that you can use them later for other images taken under similar conditions, choose Save Settings. A second dialog box, as shown in Figure 3.9, appears in which you select which parameters to save. Clicking Save will cause another dialog box to appear in which you give the setting a name. We suggest you give it a name that's specific enough that you will easily recognize its purpose. Unless you have a clear reason for changing it, store the settings in the default location.

Figure 3.9

When saving a group of settings, you can select as many or as few of the parameters as useful for any particular situation.

To use these settings, choose Apply Presets, or go to the last adjustment tab ▦, which contains a list of your presets.

To save your settings as the new default for ACR to use for all images (before they are individually adjusted), adjust the sliders and settings as desired, and then choose Save New Camera Raw Defaults. You will not see a dialog box asking which settings to save—it saves all of them. If you later change your mind, you can click Reset Camera Raw Defaults.

Using the Basic Tab

Whether or not you choose to use the Auto settings as your default, the chances are that you will often want to make some tonal and color adjustments to your image. The ability to easily make subtle tweaks, as well as major corrections, to your exposure is one of the many advantages of working with the ACR interface.

The Basic tab ◉ is visible by default when the ACR interface first opens and contains the white balance adjustments as well as some exposure and color adjustments.

Setting White Balance

One of the major advantages of using the ACR interface is the ability to fine-tune the white balance, or color cast. If you decide that you want to make your picture as neutral as possible, then including a card such as the WhiBal card (available at www .rawworkflow.com) within one frame of your pictures makes it easy to determine the correct white balance. Just use the White Balance tool 🖋, and click the gray tone in the card in your image. In fact, you can use this eyedropper to click any pixel within any image that you want to define as neutral, that is to say, any shade of gray from the lightest to the darkest gray, and the tonalities within the entire image are remapped accordingly.

However, for most nature photographers, pure neutral is not the goal for every image. We nature photographers tend to like the warm color casts of early morning and late day light. Sometimes we even like the cool colors of shadows and/or the harsh blue light on winter snow. And sometimes we like to pretend those color casts were present even when they weren't! In such cases, the white balance you ultimately select may be *correct*, but perhaps *not accurate*. Fortunately, there are no "white balance police" running around demanding that your choice of white balance must be true to life! However, if you're trying to depict your images more documentarily, then you'll want to make your white balance choices as accurate as possible.

 Note: There is a difference between accurate white balance and correct white balance. *Accurate* white balance portrays the lighting as it existed when you photographed the scene. *Correct* white balance is the ideal setting that gives the image the feeling you seek to express.

The Basic tab has two sliders that control the white balance or color cast of your image:

The **Temperature** slider refers to the temperature of the light (in degrees Kelvin). What you really need to know is that moving the slider to the left adds a blue cast to your image, similar to using an 80 A, B, or C filter. Moving the Temperature slider to the right adds a warm yellow cast, similar to using an 81 A, B, or C filter. In Photoshop CS3, Adobe has conveniently added a blue/yellow gradient to the Temperature slider, making it obvious which direction to move the slider.

The **Tint** slider controls the green/magenta color cast. Moving this slider to the left increases the greenish cast; moving it to the right increases the magenta cast. Again, in CS3, this slider is colorized to make it easy to know which direction to adjust the slider. We find that we tend to adjust the Tint slider less than the Temperature slider in general.

The major advantage this has over using a filter is that the adjustments are continual and gradual, so you can choose the exact amount of warming or cooling to make your image convey the mood you have in mind.

Unless you are color-blind (and we're being serious here, not sarcastic, having had several color-blind students), it's well worth getting into the habit of spending a little time adjusting the white balance because the changes you can make to the colors of your image here are subtly different from what you can do within Photoshop (see Figure 3.10). And if you are color-blind, you may want to get into the habit of setting the cursor on a specific point in the image and noting the RGB values that appear above the histogram. You can learn to interpret the values so you know when your image is slightly warm or cool.

Figure 3.10
Adjusting the temperature and tint sliders allows you to make finer adjustments to the color cast in your image than would be possible using traditional filters. (Photo by Ellen Anon.)

Adjusting Tonalities

The next group of sliders on the ACR Basic tab enables you to fine-tune the tonalities in your image, such as increasing or decreasing the exposure, contrast, and so on. We'll describe the sliders in the order that we usually set them.

Note: Although we usually follow a certain order adjusting these sliders, if one aspect of an image is significantly off, we'll adjust that first. Since you can readjust these sliders as much as necessary, you can set them in whatever order seems most logical to you.

Setting the Exposure and Blacks Sliders

The Exposure slider is similar to using Levels in Photoshop to set your white point. In plain English, this means you are selecting which tonal value (pure white, almost but not quite pure white, and so on) to make the lightest pixels within your image, and all pixels in the image are remapped accordingly. In many ways it's similar to modifying your in-camera exposure, but instead of being limited to a half or a third of a stop, or multiples thereof, you can choose from continuous values using tiny increments, up to four stops over or under the in-camera exposure. However, remember that if you overexposed your image in-camera to the point that no details were captured in the brightest highlights, using the Exposure slider does not restore the details. ACR cannot produce detail that was never captured in either highlight *or* shadow areas. However, it may make those blown-out areas a little less obvious by making them a very light shade of gray instead of bright white.

Note: To quickly reset any of the sliders in ACR to their default values, double-click the small triangle that specifies the value on the slider. It will automatically return to its default setting.

Use the Blacks slider to set the black point. You are telling ACR how close to pure black you want the darkest pixels within your image to be. Simply drag the slider to the desired value. Usually you won't have to drag the slider very far, because you're working on the linear-gamma data, that is, preconverted information.

To set your Exposure and Blacks sliders without accidentally clipping any pixels, do the following:

- Hold down the Alt/Option key, and drag the Exposure slider; the preview box turns completely black. Drag it to the right until you see colored pixels appearing. These are the first pixels that start to become pure white with no detail. Back off the slider slightly so there is no clipping, and release the mouse button.

- Hold down the Alt/Option key while sliding the Blacks slider to set the black point with no clipping. With the Blacks slider, the preview becomes totally white. When you see colored pixels begin to appear, back off slightly. By doing this, you have distributed the pixels in your image over the maximum tonal range using clipping previews.

Although you could just rely on the clipping warnings in the preview, holding down the Alt/Option key makes it easier to see clipping in small areas.

It's tempting for some photographers to assume that all pictures should have as wide a range of tonal values as possible. Indeed, many images look their best utilizing the full range of tonal values—which is what you're doing if you set the white and black points using the Exposure and Blacks sliders while utilizing the clipping previews. However, especially within nature photography, not all images are suited to using the full range of tonal values. For example, if you take a moody picture of a lovely foggy scene, as shown in Figure 3.11, you most assuredly don't want maximum contrast. You want a limited tonal range reflecting the limited tonalities visible through the fog. You need to look at each image and decide whether it should utilize the full range of tonalities.

Figure 3.11 Some pictures like this foggy scene must, by their nature, not use the full range of tonal values. Note that the histogram does not extend all the way to each end but rather is limited to more of the middle tonalities. (Photo by Ellen Anon.)

Using the Recovery and Fill Light Sliders

The Recovery and Fill Light sliders, which are similar to the Highlight/Shadow tool in Photoshop, are wonderful additions to ACR in CS3. These are valuable when, despite your best efforts, there is some clipping of the highlight and/or shadow values because of contrasty lighting. You can use the Recovery slider to recapture as much highlight detail as possible, while the Fill Light slider recovers shadow detail, as shown in Figure 3.12.

The best approach is to first set the Exposure slider so that the exposure is correct for most of the image. Then adjust the Recovery slider as necessary to regain as much highlight detail as possible.

Figure 3.12 The Recovery and Fill Light sliders can help expand the exposure latitude of an image so you can see detail in the highlights and shadows in contrasty scenes.

Note: If you overexposed or underexposed the image to the point that you didn't capture some of the highlight or shadow data, the Recovery and Fill Light sliders will not be able to recover it. It can't create information that you didn't capture. But if you were able to capture it on the sensor, then the Recovery slider will reveal it. Remember that the sensor contains more information than can be initially displayed—usually up to about a ½ stop more information in the highlights and up to 1½ stops more information in the shadows.

Set the Fill Light slider as necessary to recover detail in the darkest shadow areas. You may need to modify the Blacks slider setting as well. The trick is that you still want some true blacks in your image, but you want to see detail in the not quite black shadow areas.

Using the Brightness and Contrast Sliders

The Brightness slider shifts the majority of the pixels lighter or darker to make the overall image appear lighter or darker. Watch how the bulk of the histogram shifts as you move this slider each way. It's similar to moving the center slider within Levels in Photoshop. The more extreme the adjustments you make with the Exposure slider, the more likely it is you'll need to make adjustments using the Brightness slider. Don't forget to keep an eye out for any clipping you may introduce by increasing or decreasing the brightness.

The Contrast slider is similar to applying an S curve within Curves in Photoshop to increase or decrease the contrast within the bulk of the pixel values. If you watch the histogram as you adjust this slider, you'll see the bulk of the pixels being shifted away from the middle toward the extremes.

Contrast is primarily modified to those pixels in the middle tonalities with the lightest and darkest tonalities being less affected. Increasing the amount to greater than the default of +25 lightens values above the midtones and darkens values below the midtones. Similarly, reducing the value darkens values above the midtones and lightens values below the midtones to reduce the overall contrast. If you decide to adjust the contrast in ACR, be sure to check that you have not introduced any clipping to your highlights or shadows. You may have to readjust the other sliders.

> **Note:** Given the ability to make some fairly dramatic changes in exposure, it may seem like you don't have to worry about capturing the correct exposure in camera. In fact, as discussed in Chapter 1, "Thinking Digitally," the better your initial exposure, the better the final product will be. If the image is initially underexposed, you'll find that although you can correct the exposure, there is likely to be a lot of distracting noise in the final image. If you "expose to the right" (again, see Chapter 1), you will have the least amount of noise within your image, although you may have to adjust the Blacks slider, and possibly the Brightness slider as well. Exposing to the right with raw captures ultimately gives you the best possible result as long as you make certain you don't clip any highlights.

Modifying Saturation

ACR in CS3 added a check box to convert the image to grayscale, which immediately sets the Vibrance and Saturation sliders all the way to the left. You can further modify the appearance of a black-and-white image in ACR by using the HSL/Grayscale tab that we'll describe shortly.

ACR also added a Vibrance slider in addition to the Saturation slider. A good way to think about Vibrance is as a smart saturation slider. It affects colors differentially as it increases (or decreases) the saturation to reduce the chances of introducing clipping. Instead of applying increased saturation uniformly to all colors, it applies it heaviest to the less saturated colors and less to the more saturated colors. Often this creates a more pleasing result. Ellen finds that she can use higher amounts with the Vibrance slider and create images that pop but look natural.

At times you may want to use the Saturation slider in addition to or instead of the Vibrance slider. Be sure to check for unexpected clipping within the different color channels.

The Saturation and Vibrance sliders affect all the colors in your image. If you want to adjust specific color ranges, use the HSL/Grayscale tab that we'll cover shortly.

Note: Some images may benefit from reduced saturation or vibrance. Be sure to watch the histogram as you make any changes.

Setting the Other Tabs

There are a total of eight tabs, as shown in Figure 3.13, that have features to help you optimize your image. Many photographers are more than happy with the results they get simply by adjusting the sliders on the Basic tab. However, if you want to have even more control, you should venture into these other tabs after you've made your initial corrections on the Basic tab. We'll describe how to use the other tabs in the order they appear.

Figure 3.13 Click each of the tabs to reveal additional tools to fine-tune and adjust your image.

Setting the Tone Curves

The next tab is the Tone Curve tab ▨. By default this tab opens to the Parametric Curve, which is new to CS3. Ellen calls Parametric Curves "*Easy Curves*" because they're much easier and more intuitive for novices to use. But in addition to being easy, they're quite powerful and useful. Although she used to primarily use point curves, she routinely starts with the Parametric Curves in ACR.

As shown in Figure 3.14, there are four sliders beneath the typical Curves graph, with the histogram superimposed within it. Adjusting the Highlights slider primarily adjusts the brightest quarter of the tonalities. Adjusting the Lights slider primarily affects the midtones to light tones but may affect the lightest tonalities or the darks as well. The effect is most pronounced within the midtones to light tones. The Darks slider primarily affects the middle to darkest quarter of tonality, while the Shadows slider affects the darkest quarter of tonal values. As you adjust any of these sliders, the more dramatic the adjustment you make, the wider the range of tonal values that will be affected.

We suggest you spend a little time experimenting with these sliders and getting comfortable with them. They can be quite useful.

Note: Parametric Curves are also available in Lightroom.

The Tone Curve tab offers another tab to access the Point curve. This is the type curve that was in earlier versions of ACR and is found in Photoshop.

Note: A *tone curve* is an algorithm or set of instructions for how to process the raw linear data to make the image more visually accurate and/or pleasing. It's plotted in a gamma 2.2 space in order to make it easier to make the adjustments.

When you click the Point tab (illustrated in Figure 3.15), you'll see a drop-down menu for the Tone Curve, which by default is set to Medium Contrast. You'll also see a graph showing the actual tone curve superimposed over a graph showing the distribution of pixels. By clicking within the drop-down menu, you can choose the Linear curve option, which causes no additional contrast to be added to your image, or the Strong Contrast option to use a preset tone curve that adds more contrast to your image.

Figure 3.14
Creating customized curves to adjust midtone contrast is easy using the Parametric Curve slider controls.

Figure 3.15
By using the Point tab, you can access various tone curves, including the ability to make a custom curve to further refine your image.

However, the really useful part of the Point tab is that you can begin with any of the Tone Curve presets and modify the curve, using the preset points as well as any points you want to add, to create a custom curve for each image. The advantage of doing this here in ACR rather than later in Photoshop is that the curve is still operating on the linear data. As long as you have the clipping preview boxes checked in the histogram in ACR, you can see whether the changes you make are causing any clipping. If you're comfortable using curves, you may want to experiment with the Point Tone Curves within ACR. If curves are new to you, you may want to stick with Parametric curves until you are more familiar with using them.

Note: By holding the Ctrl/⌘ key and hovering the cursor over a pixel in the image preview, a circle will appear on the tone curve indicating where that point falls. To create a point on the curve at that location, click while holding the Ctrl/⌘ key.

Sharpening Preview and Reducing Noise: The Detail Tab

Three sliders are available on the Detail tab 🔺. The first, Sharpness, should be followed by (Preview Only) if you've set your preferences to have ACR apply the sharpening only to the previews, as discussed earlier in this chapter. You can drag the Sharpness slider to preview the effects of more sharpening, but the controls here are less sophisticated than what are available within Photoshop. We rarely use this slider at all.

The remaining two sliders help you control noise. Noise is a by-product of digital captures, more problematic when using higher ISOs and/or correcting underexposed images, and a bigger problem with some cameras than with others. Noise may be seen primarily in areas of darker tonalities, although it can extend into the midtones as well. As you can see in Figure 3.16, noise appears as variations in tones and colors in areas that should be smooth such as skies or skin tones.

Before

After

Figure 3.16

Noise appears as random variations in tones and colors in areas that should be smooth. Using the noise reduction sliders is an easy way to eliminate it. (Photo by Ellen Anon.)

ACR offers two sliders to deal with noise:

- The **Luminance Smoothing** slider deals with *grayscale noise*, the unexpected and unwanted variations in tonal values that appear. This type of noise is similar in appearance in many ways to film grain. By reducing these tonal variations, this type of smoothing may reduce the overall sharpness of your image, so keep these corrections to a minimum. It's a good idea to zoom into various critical areas of your image to 100% or even 200% to see how they're being affected as you make adjustments.

  Since luminance smoothing can reduce overall sharpness and blur fine detail, we prefer to do most luminance smoothing in Photoshop. That way we can use a mask to apply it only to problematic areas and retain full detail in our subject matter.

- The **Color Noise Reduction** slider reduces *color noise*, the unexpected color variations that often appear. Although this noise is most common in the darker tonalities, it can also sometimes be seen as green and magenta blobs in areas that should be neutral gray and as rainbow artifacts in the highlights. Again, zoom to a 100% or 200% view of the areas demonstrating problems with noise, and move the slider to reduce the color variations. Make the minimum amount of adjustment necessary to decrease the noise. We tend to use the Color Noise Reduction slider in ACR to remove as much color noise as possible when noise is an issue.

Note: Although the default value is set to 25, Ellen finds that with her camera a setting of 15 works well for most images. She saved this setting and created a new default as described earlier in this chapter. Occasionally she uses higher amounts with extremely noisy images.

Correcting Color: The HSL/Grayscale Tab

The HSL/Grayscale tab ▦ is new to ACR in CS3. HSL is short for *hue, saturation,* and *luminance* and is a very visual tool offering the ability to fine-tune each color range on a variety of parameters. For example, you can modify the yellows so that they are closer to orange or closer to green. You can also adjust the saturation of the yellows and then the *luminance*—or lightness/darkness—of them. This means you can make subtle—or not so subtle—adjustments to individual color ranges in your image without affecting other colors.

When you click the Hue, Saturation, or Luminance subtabs, the eight color range sliders change to gradients, as shown in Figure 3.17, indicating how moving the slider will change the appearance of the colors. You can set each color individually.

Figure 3.17 By using the HSL controls, Ellen fine-tuned the colors in this sunflower image. (Photo by Ellen Anon.)

Clicking the Saturation or Luminance tabs changes the eight color sliders so that they reflect increased and decreased saturation or modifications in luminance.

Spending the time to fine-tune the colors in your image may not be something you do to every image, but for some images, these tweaks can take an image from ordinary to extraordinary!

If you checked the Convert to Grayscale option on the Basics tab, then a Grayscale Mix tab will appear. Adjusting the sliders for each color lightens or darkens that color range. By using these sliders, you can alter the contrast within your image and create dramatic black-and-white versions of your images, as shown in Figure 3.18.

Figure 3.18 A straightforward grayscale conversion is often lackluster, but by using the grayscale controls you can create a more vibrant image. (Photo by Ellen Anon.)

Figure 3.18 *(Continued)*

Alternate Interpretations: The Split Toning Tab

The Split Toning tab ▤ is not one that we have found a lot of use for with nature photography. However, you may well find that a specific image lends itself to this creative interpretation based on a grayscale version of the file. The concept is that you assign one color for the highlights and a different color for the shadows so that you "split" the tones of the image.

Select the color by adjusting the Hue sliders, and set the intensity of the color-cast by adjusting the Saturation slider. Modifying the balance slider changes the proportion of highlight toning and shadow toning.

Fixing Aberration and Vignetting: The Lens Corrections Tab

The Lens Corrections tab ▥ offers solutions to some issues—specifically vignetting and fringing (chromatic aberrations)—that may result when using particular lenses with digital cameras. Some photographers never have and/or notice these problems, and that's fine. Others perceive them readily and are quite bothered by them.

Vignetting is darkening in the corners of your images. It typically occurs when a lens originally designed for 35mm film photography, and not optimized for digital cameras' sensors, is used with a digital camera that has a sensor that is smaller than the film area would have been. However, vignetting also sometimes results when using a lens hood with wide-angle lenses or even from using filters with wide-angle lenses. The Vignetting controls enable you to reduce or eliminate the darkening in the corners:

The **Amount** slider controls the amount of lightening or darkening that is applied to the corners.

The **Midpoint** slider controls where the adjustment gets applied. Larger values on the Midpoint slider increase the area that is affected, while smaller numbers reduce it.

Make adjustments in small increments while closely watching the effect on your image.

Note: Some photographers like to use the Vignetting controls to *add* darkening to the corners, similar to effects Ansel Adams created in the traditional darkroom to help draw the viewer's eye into the image.

Chromatic aberration, also known as *fringing*, occurs when the lens fails to focus the red, green, and blue wavelengths of light on exactly the same plane (the camera's image sensor); this causes color fringes along high-contrast edges. Chromatic aberration seems to be more of a problem with wider-angle shots, especially those made with lenses not optimized for digital cameras. It may be more noticeable toward the corners of the image, as shown in Figure 3.19.

Figure 3.19
Chromatic aberrations (fringing) is noticeable along the branch in this image, but you can easily remove it by adjusting the Chromatic Aberration sliders. (Photo by Ellen Anon.)

- The **Fix Red/Cyan Fringe** slider helps you to reduce or remove red/cyan fringing.
- The **Fix Blue/Yellow Fringe** slider addresses any blue/yellow fringing.

Before using these sliders it's a good idea to zoom in to 200% or more to easily see the fringing and the results of moving the sliders. Holding down Alt/Option while dragging these sliders limits which color channels are visible and makes it significantly easier to locate the best setting for each slider.

Accounting for Camera Variation: The Camera Calibration Tab

The Calibrate tab 📷 is one that most nature photographers never touch; those of you who do will need to use it only rarely. The purpose of the Calibrate tab is to tweak the performance of the built-in camera profiles to account for any variations between your camera and the one they actually used to build the profiles in ACR for that specific camera model.

If you notice that your images routinely have a slight color cast, rather than removing it in the Adjust tab, you can use the sliders here to set a correction. To do this accurately, you need to shoot a color checker chart, such as those available from GretagMacbeth (www.gretagmacbeth.com), and then compare it to a downloaded version with known values. You then move the sliders to match up the colors.

Using the Camera Calibration tab is considerably easier to do in ACR in CS3 than it was in CS2 because the controls have been reworked. Now they are intuitive. To modify the reds, use the controls in the Red Primary section; to adjust the greens, use the ones found in the Green Primary section; and similarly to adjust the blues, use the sliders found in the Blue Primary section. You can also adjust the tint of the shadows.

After creating settings for a particular camera, save them as the Camera Raw defaults by using the fly-out menu as described earlier in this chapter. Then go to the toolbar in ACR, and use the Preferences icon to access the Preferences dialog box. Check the option Make Defaults Specific To Camera Serial Number. That way if you have several cameras, ACR will use the correct camera calibrations for each one.

Setting ACR Workflow Options and Saving Files

At this point you're almost done with the ACR interface, but first you have to instruct ACR how you want the converted file saved.

Directly below the image preview in the ACR interface is a series of information that looks like a web link. Clicking it reveals the ACR Workflow Options dialog box, as shown in Figure 3.20.

Figure 3.20

Several important settings are found in the Workflow Options dialog box

Choosing the Space

The Space drop-down menu gives four options for the color working space:
- Adobe RGB (1998)
- ProPhoto RGB
- sRGB IEC61966-1
- ColorMatch RGB

Only the first three options are useful for nature photographers (we'll tell you why shortly).

Adobe RGB 1998 is the most frequently used color space for nature photographers seeking to make prints and archive their files because it is a reasonably wide color space and corresponds fairly well to the color spaces available in most inkjet printers. Many people prefer to use this space as their default color working space.

If you're planning to work with images in 16-bit color (and we recommend you do), you may consider using the ProPhoto RGB workspace. It's a wider space than the commonly used Adobe RGB 1998 and will allow you to use some colors that your camera may have captured but that are outside the gamut of Adobe RGB 1998. Some inkjet printers can print some of these colors. Further, if you have some clipping—that is, pixels that are at the extremes of the tonal values—in one or more channels, you may want to see whether changing to the ProPhoto RGB space allows you to capture more detail in those channels. The disadvantage is that if you are converting back to an 8-bit image, you may have more colors that need to be converted than if you had limited yourself to Adobe RGB 1998. This may lead to some posterization, or banding.

Occasionally, some people may want to use sRGB IEC61966-1. This is a narrower color space, but it's useful if your intended output is limited to projection, email, and/or web usage. If you think that there's any chance you may want to print the file, we recommend you use one of the other two spaces mentioned in this section (Adobe RGB or ProPhoto RGB) and convert to sRGB for the specific use. (See Chapter 4, "Foundations," for a more complete discussion of color spaces.)

ColorMatch RGB is a space that is wider than sRGB and narrower than Adobe RGB. This means it may have more colors than you can use for web use or projection but fewer than your inkjet printer is capable of printing. Therefore, one of the other spaces is usually a better choice.

Choosing the Depth

You have the choice of converting your image into a file with 256 possible tonal values (8 bits/channel) or a file with 32,768 possible values (16 bits/channel). The clear advantage to 16-bit is accurate and smooth reproduction of tonal variations. Prior to Photoshop CS, working in 16-bit was difficult, but if you have CS or later, the workflow is as easy for a 16-bit file as for an 8-bit file. The only slight disadvantages are that since the file is larger, your computer may process adjustments a little more slowly, you may need more RAM to process the files, and the files will take up more space in memory.

Note: Although it would seem logical that "16-bit" implies 2^{16}, or 65,536, tonal values, in fact Photoshop uses 2^{15}, or 32,768, when dealing with 16-bit files. Since most high-bit scans and digital captures currently range from 10-bit to 14-bit, this isn't an issue.

Choosing the File Size and Resolution

ACR provides a drop-down menu, found under the Size option, listing various file sizes specific to the camera used to take the image. Some of the sizes are marked with a plus sign (+) and some by a minus sign (–). One size has neither; it refers to the native resolution of the image with no interpolation. Most of the time this is the choice you'll want. If you are optimizing images for a slide show, you may prefer to use a smaller size.

Some people prefer to use a larger size if they know they will be creating huge files, believing that the interpolation done by ACR is better than the interpolation done later in Photoshop. We have not found any significant benefit to enlarging the file in ACR, and the drawback is that you are dealing with a larger file size that requires more memory space and longer processing times.

If you have cropped the image, the sizes available will reflect the crop. In that case, you may prefer to use one of the sizes with a + depending on the magnitude of the crop and the size of your intended output.

As we discuss in Chapter 4, the resolution, expressed in ppi (pixels per inch), merely refers to how tightly or loosely packed the pixels are; it doesn't change anything about the total number of pixels. The actual number of pixels is controlled by the file size that you choose. The resolution you set determines whether pixels are distributed 72 to an inch, 300 to an inch, and so on. Since one of the most common outputs is for print, we recommend setting your resolution to your print resolution setting (usually 300 ppi). This way, when your image opens in Photoshop, it is sized according to an output resolution of 300 ppi. We'll cover resizing images for print further in Chapter 10, "Output."

Opening an Image as a Smart Object

The check box to automatically have ACR open the file as a Smart Object is new to CS3. This is convenient, particularly if you opt to follow our flexible workflow (see Chapter 5). We recommend leaving this option checked. The Open Image button in the lower corner of the ACR interface will say Open Object if this option is checked or Open Image if it is not.

When you're done with the Workflow Options dialog box, click OK. Most of the time you'll leave the workflow options set without changing them. The settings are *sticky*, meaning that whatever choices you set there will appear when you open future images as well.

Finishing Up in ACR

After optimizing your image in ACR using as many of the features as necessary to make the file the best it can be, you have five choices:

Done   The Done button applies the changes but does not open the image. The image is still a raw file, and the changes are still tags. The thumbnail preview in Bridge will reflect the settings you chose in ACR, and those settings will reappear when you reopen the image in ACR.

> **Note:** If you are working with a JPEG or TIFF file in ACR, Done applies the changes, but you can see them only when you view the file in ACR. This is because the file itself remains untouched and the changes you made are stored as instructions to that file. To see the changes in Bridge you will need to use Save.

Open Image/Object

The Open button applies the changes to the selected image and opens it in Photoshop. The image is now converted, and the changes are a permanent part of the file. To toggle between Open Image and Open Object, hold down the shift key.

> **Note:** In JPEG and TIFF files the changes you made in ACR are applied to the image when you open it, but you will need to save the file in order to have the changes remain.

Open Copy   The Open Copy button is available if you hold down the Alt/Option key. This allows you to apply the current changes and open another copy of the same raw file within Photoshop using different settings. This is useful when you are trying some creative techniques such as a black-and-white version of your image or experimenting with different crops.

Save Image   The Save button converts the image and saves it; another dialog box appears, prompting you to choose a location, name, and format (such as DNG, JPEG, TIFF, or PSD) for your converted image. (If you don't want this dialog box to appear, hold down the Alt/Option key when you click Save.)

Cancel   The Cancel button closes ACR, and the settings you chose are not retained.

> **Note:** Digital negative (DNG) is a universal raw file format developed by Adobe to allow users to archive their raw images in a format that hopefully will continue to be accessible for years to come as converters become more sophisticated. DNG was developed as a response to the ever-increasing number of different raw formats and concerns that files archived in the camera manufacturer's proprietary raw format may one day be unable to be opened as camera manufacturers abandon older raw formats. The downside to the DNG format is that it's unable to store some information that exists within the original raw file but is proprietary to the camera manufacturer.

Try It!

Now that we've covered the basics of using ACR, it's time for you to try it. Open the raw file ConvertRaw.dng from the CD that accompanies this book, or open one of your own.

Take the following steps:

1. Begin by dragging the Exposure slider and then the other sliders. Don't forget to hold down the Alt/Option key while setting the Exposure and Blacks sliders to avoid clipping any pixels. Move the other sliders as needed. Experiment with each of them to get familiar with them.

2. Next, adjust the white balance. Try clicking the eyedropper in various areas to see how it affects the image. Fine-tune your results with the Temperature and Tint sliders.

3. Click the Detail tab, do any noise reduction that you need, and then experiment with the Lens Correction sliders.

4. Use the HSL/Grayscale tab, and create a black-and-white as well as a color version of the image.

Make certain to keep an eye on the histogram as you make your adjustments to ensure you don't accidentally clip any pixels!

Batch Converting Multiple Images

If you have a series of images that you want to convert, you can select them all in Bridge and then open them in ACR by either pressing Ctrl+R/⌘+R to open the Camera Raw dialog box while remaining in Bridge, pressing Ctrl+O/⌘+O to open the ACR dialog box hosted by Photoshop, or double-clicking one of the selected thumbnails. (You can set an option within Preferences in Bridge to indicate whether double-clicking opens the Camera Raw dialog box in Bridge or in Photoshop.)

> **Note:** Hosting ACR by Bridge can be a time-saver so that ACR can be converting images in the background while you continue to optimize other images in Photoshop.

When ACR opens, it opens in Filmstrip mode, as shown in Figure 3.21. The images to be converted appear in a vertical column on the left.

Figure 3.21 When selecting multiple images to convert, ACR opens in Filmstrip mode. (Photo by Ellen Anon.)

Selecting a number of images that you want to convert and having them open within a single Camera Raw dialog box can save time. You can choose settings for them individually or select a group to share some of the same settings. Although you are most likely to want to customize the ACR settings for each image, if you have a series of images, shot under similar conditions, that need some of the same settings, batch converting can be a huge time-saver. To batch convert a group of images in ACR, take these steps:

1. Click one of the images to select it, and then make all the adjustments you want to perform in ACR.

2. In the left pane, click the image(s) to which you want to apply these same settings. To assign the settings to more than one image at a time, Ctrl+click/ ⌘+click all the desired files.

3. Next, click the Synchronize button. A dialog box appears where you choose the parameters you want to copy from the file you just optimized to the other selected files (see Figure 3.22). Sometimes you may want to copy all the changes you made; other times you may want to select only a few, such as white balance or the dust removal. (Yes, you can even copy the retouching!)

Figure 3.22
You can choose which parameters to apply to all the highlighted images in ACR by checking them in the Synchronize dialog box.

4. Mark images to delete by pressing the Delete key. Those thumbnails now have a large red X on them.

5. When you are finished, click one of the buttons at the bottom right:

Save Images The Save button converts the images and saves them; another dialog box appears, prompting you to choose naming and a location for your images. (If you don't want this dialog box to appear, hold down the Alt/Option key when you click Save.)

Open Images/Objects The Open button applies the changes to the selected images and opens them as converted files in Photoshop.

Done The Done button applies the changes but does not open the images.

Foundations

We know that you want to continue working on your images as soon as possible, but there's some groundwork to be laid. Much of the work you'll do in Photoshop, and in fact most of the advanced work, involves using the various tools on the Tools panel. In this chapter, we'll introduce you to some of these tools to help you build a strong foundation for the adjustments we'll cover in later chapters. But before we do that, we'll help you set up Photoshop so that you can be as efficient as possible. In later chapters, you'll be putting these choices and tools to use, in some cases extensively.

4

Chapter Contents
Color Management
Setting Preferences
Views and Zooms
Selection Tools
The Brush Tool
The History Brush

Color Management

For any photographer, achieving accurate color is a key concern. You need to know that the way the image looks on your monitor is how it will look printed. Although you may take artistic license in how you optimize an image, you want to ensure that the print is an accurate reflection of your interpretation of the image. This means producing a print that matches the monitor display to the extent possible. This is the job of color management, and it can help you achieve greater consistency in your workflow.

Note: For more information on a complete color-managed workflow, see Tim's book *Color Confidence, Second Edition* (Sybex, 2006).

Monitor Calibration

The first step in a color-managed workflow is to calibrate and profile your monitor. We can't stress how important this is. If you don't have a calibrated display, the images you are evaluating and optimizing are likely to be at least slightly—and possibly significantly— inaccurate. They might look good to you on your monitor, but your prints are unlikely to match what you see. If you don't calibrate your monitor, you also have no valid reason to complain about prints that don't match your monitor. Calibrating your monitor is a critical first step to producing the results you are looking for with your images.

As far as we're concerned, calibrating your monitor is done properly only if you are using a package that uses a *colorimeter* (a type of sensor) to measure the color values of your monitor so that you can apply appropriate compensation (see Figure 4.1). There are several packages available that include a colorimeter. They are all good products and are available for both Microsoft Windows and Apple Mac platforms, although they vary considerably in price.

Figure 4.1
For monitor calibration, use a software package that includes a colorimeter sensor to measure the color behavior of your monitor and apply compensation to ensure an accurate display.

Some of the most popular monitor-calibrating packages are as follows:

Spyder2   The Spyder2 packages from ColorVision (www.colorvision.com) are some of the most user-friendly available, making them a good choice for those of you who are just getting started with a digital workflow and feeling a little intimidated, as well as more advanced users, without compromising on the quality of the results. They offer basic as well as more advanced packages with a variety of capabilities.

Eye-One Display   This is an advanced package from GretagMacbeth (www.gretagmacbeth .com) that produces exceptional results, including automatic compensation for ambient lighting in your working area. Eye-One Display is slightly complicated in operation, but it produces highly accurate results.

Huey   This is also from GretagMacbeth (www.gretagmacbeth.com), but it's an entry-level calibration device that takes the ambient room lighting into account.

MonacoOPTIX   X-Rite (www.xrite.com), the parent company of GretagMacbeth, also offers the MonacoOPTIX calibration system, which is another advanced solution and one of the most thorough in terms of the calibration process. It guides you through a large number of adjustments of your monitor settings to help ensure the widest dynamic range and best results possible.

Regardless of the solution you choose, the key is to calibrate and profile your monitor display and to do so on a regular basis. This is necessary because the monitor's display will shift over time. For CRT monitors, we recommend calibrating at least about every 30 days; for LCD monitors, about every 60–90 days should be adequate. Of course, you must calibrate your monitor under the same lighting conditions in which you'll be working.

Working Conditions

A calibrated monitor display ensures accurate color (to the extent possible) but doesn't ensure consistent color. That may sound a bit contradictory, but it emphasizes the importance of working under consistent conditions. As a nature photographer, you are well aware of the considerations of good lighting. You look for optimal conditions, with the sun at an optimal angle to produce a golden glow, for example. Just as varying lighting conditions can affect both the appearance of your subject and the ultimate quality of your photos, the conditions under which you work can affect the appearance of your monitor display. Different ambient lighting conditions will cause you to perceive the colors and tonalities differently on your monitor.

It is very important that you work under lighting conditions that are as consistent as possible and ideally somewhat dim. The monitor you are using as the basis of all your evaluations about an image emits light, and the light in the room can influence your perception of that light. If the room is too bright, you won't be able to see subtle details on the monitor. If the light isn't relatively neutral, it can affect the color appearance of the monitor display.

The ideal situation is to work in an environment that is consistently dark. That doesn't mean you need to work in absolute darkness. It just means that you want to minimize the lighting to the extent you are comfortable with and do everything you can to ensure the lighting is neutral and remains consistent from one session to the next. If you work on an image with early morning light filling the room and making the image on your monitor look warmer than it really is, you may overcompensate by adjusting the image to look too cool.

Minimizing the amount of artificial light in the room, perhaps by using a dimmer to keep the light at an appropriate level, is an excellent start. If you have windows in the room where you're working on your images, it is a good idea to close the blinds (or install blinds) so you can minimize the influence of outside light.

The bottom line is that you want to be working in an environment where the monitor is accurate, because it has been calibrated, and where it is consistent, because your working conditions are likewise consistent. This helps ensure that you are seeing accurate color on your monitor, which is the reference both for adjustments you're making to your images and for evaluating the accuracy of your prints.

Color Settings

Photoshop allows you to establish color management settings that determine its behavior related to the color in your images. Establishing appropriate settings is important to ensuring that your workflow results in accurate color and maximum image quality. You can adjust these settings by choosing Edit > Color Settings, which opens the Color Settings dialog box, as shown in Figure 4.2.

Figure 4.2

The Color Settings dialog box allows you to establish settings related to color management within Photoshop.

The Color Settings dialog box includes a More Options button that, when clicked, enlarges the dialog box to include additional controls. (It also enlarges the list of profiles on the Working Spaces drop-down menus to include all profiles available rather than only those designated as working space profiles.) Once you've clicked this button, it changes to Fewer Options, which returns you to the "basic" dialog box. Since we recommend leaving the advanced settings at their default values anyway, the main reason you might want to access the More Options version of the dialog box is if you want to use ProPhoto as your working space, which we'll discuss shortly.

A *working space* profile defines the range of colors (the color *gamut*) that will be available for your images. The Working Spaces section includes options for specifying which profile should be used as the working space for each of the color modes available (RGB, CMYK, Gray, and Spot). For most photographers, the only working space you need to be concerned with is RGB, which is the mode we recommend working with for all images until you have a reason to convert them to a different color space (for example, if a printing service insists that you perform the RGB-to-CMYK conversion). In most situations (including printing to most desktop printers), you will work on your images in RGB and keep them in RGB for the entire workflow.

For the RGB working space, we generally recommend using the one named Adobe RGB (1998). This is a good general working space with a relatively wide gamut, providing an appropriate space for a wide range of output options. This doesn't mean it's the best answer for everyone, but when it doubt, Adobe RGB (1998) is a good choice, and it is what we recommend unless you have a good reason to use something else. For example, some photographers may want to utilize the sRGB space as their working space, if their printer uses a workflow based on sRGB or if their images will be primarily displayed on the Web or via digital slide shows. Others may want to use the ProPhoto RGB space because it contains a few colors that most printers can print that are not contained in the Adobe RGB space. The downside of working in ProPhoto RGB is that it contains many colors that will be out of gamut when you go to print, so more colors will have to be converted.

Within the Color Settings dialog box, the Color Management Policies section provides settings that allow you to determine what Photoshop should do when you open an image that has a different embedded profile than the one you are using for your working space. As with the Working Spaces section, here you need to be concerned only with RGB. We recommend using the Convert to Working RGB setting here, with the assumption that if you've decided on a working space profile that's appropriate for your workflow, it makes sense to use that as the working space for all your images. Should you decide to use an image on a website, you can always convert to sRGB as part of the process of preparing the image.

Note: If you regularly work on images for other people, you may prefer to set this to Preserve Embedded Profiles so that you work with the image in the same space as the other person.

We generally prefer to have images converted to the working color space when they're opened. But in order to maintain maximum control over what is being done to our images, we also prefer to be given the option of what action should be taken for each image. Therefore, we usually select all three check boxes next to Profile Mismatches and Missing Profiles at the bottom of the Color Management Policies section. The effect is that the options selected from the drop-down menus will be the default (for instance, RGB images will be converted to the current working RGB space), but each time an image is opened that has a different profile embedded than your working space or no profile embedded at all, you'll be prompted so you can apply a different action on a case-by-case basis.

Note: If you select the check boxes in the Color Management Policies section but find you are always confirming the default action, clear the check boxes to prevent the extra step of dealing with the Missing Profile or Profile Mismatch dialog box.

Once you've established the preferred options in Color Management Settings, click OK to apply the settings. You don't need to restart Photoshop for the changes to take effect.

Setting Preferences

In addition to the color settings, there are a large number of preference settings you can establish within Photoshop. As the name implies, many of these are a matter of personal preference. However, we do have recommendations on some of the settings. Access the Preferences dialog box by choosing Edit > Preferences > General from the menu (Photoshop > Preferences > General on a Mac).

Note: Because there are so many settings within the Preferences dialog box, we won't cover all of them. Instead, we'll focus on those settings we think are most important.

General Settings

The General page includes a variety of settings that affect your overall experience in Photoshop, as you can see in Figure 4.3.

Figure 4.3

The General section of the Preferences dialog box includes settings that affect your overall experience in Photoshop.

Here are the settings you should be concerned with:

Color Picker: Adobe   Leave Color Picker set to the default of Adobe rather than using the color picker from the operating system.

Image Interpolation: Bicubic   This is the best general option for interpolation, with other settings being useful in specific situations. We'll address the details of interpolation in Chapter 10, "Output."

UI Font Size: Medium or Large   This is a welcome new setting in Photoshop CS2, providing relief for the tiny text size that results from running our monitors at extremely high resolutions. You'll find it very helpful from a readability standpoint to set this to Large. Note that this setting does not take effect until you restart Photoshop.

Options Check Boxes

The General page in the Preferences dialog box is dominated by a large number of check boxes that allow you to set a range of preferences. Here are some of the settings we find helpful in this section:

Automatically Launch Bridge: Personal preference   If you select this option, the Bridge image browser automatically launches whenever you start Photoshop. This can save time when you decide you want to launch Bridge, but it also slows down the Photoshop launch. If you use Bridge all the time, enable this setting. Otherwise, we recommend leaving it off.

Beep When Done: Personal preference   Tim turns this setting on because occasionally some tasks require a fair amount of time to process, and it isn't very productive to just sit there waiting for the Photoshop to finish. By turning on this setting, Photoshop beeps when a task is completed. That way, you can turn your attention to other matters while waiting for a major task to complete, knowing you'll be alerted when you're ready to continue. Ellen finds it annoying to have machines beep at her and prefers to check to see when a task is done. She finds that she rarely has to wait long enough for it to be an issue.

Dynamic Color Sliders: On   When selecting a color in the Color panel, it can be helpful for the sliders to change color as you adjust the color value so you can get a better sense of what color you'll achieve by moving a slider in a particular direction. We don't use the

Color panel very often, but we keep this setting enabled for those situations where we put the panel to use.

Export Clipboard: Off   This setting determines whether anything copied to the clipboard in Photoshop will be exported so other applications can use it. We recommend turning this feature off to reduce the amount of memory being used.

Use Shift Key For Tool Switch: On   Each tool in Photoshop has a shortcut key associated with it, allowing you to activate the tool quickly. Some tools actually have more than one tool associated with the same shortcut. By default, to switch among tools with the same shortcut key, you need to add the Shift key. We recommend leaving this option set because otherwise you can get some unexpected changes in tools when you press the shortcut key.

Zoom Resizes Windows: Personal preference   This determines whether a document window will automatically be resized as you zoom in or out. When this setting is turned on, as you zoom out on an image, the document window becomes smaller when the image no longer fills the screen; when you zoom in, the document window enlarges until the image exceeds the space available on the screen. This setting is a matter of personal preference, with some photographers (including Ellen) finding it helpful and others (including Tim) finding the automatic resizing annoying.

Zoom With Scroll Wheel: On   If you have a mouse with a scroll wheel, this setting can be helpful. It allows you to zoom in and out on your image by scrolling the wheel. We recommend turning this setting on.

Note: Use the Reset All Warning Dialogs button in this interface if you have opted to have Photoshop not show some of the warnings while working and then later discovered you'd prefer to have the safety cushion that some of these warnings provide.

History Log

The History Log section provides settings that can help you figure out how you performed a particular action on an image. When you enable this setting, you can have every step you perform on an image recorded in metadata so you can review the information later. *We generally prefer to leave this turned off* because there isn't an easy way to remove the information later. However, it can save the day if you apply a series of steps on your images and then want to know how to apply the same changes on another image. It is particularly helpful, for example, when applying a series of filters to an image or when experimenting with any creative technique.

When you select the History Log check box, additional settings become available. If you're going to use this option, we recommend setting the Save Log Items To option to Metadata so the information will always be saved with the image file. We also recommend you set the Edit Log Items option to Detailed so the information you collect is actually useful. The other options—Sessions Only and Concise—don't record the actual settings you used. Although they are helpful for other fields such as forensic work, they are not useful for most nature photographers.

Note: If you save the log information to a text file, the information for *all* images is saved in a single file, which isn't very efficient.

If you use the History Log option, you can review the saved information (which accumulates only after you enable the setting) by selecting File > File Info from the menu and clicking the History option in the left column (see Figure 4.4). Alternatively, you can view the information in Bridge > Metadata > Edit History.

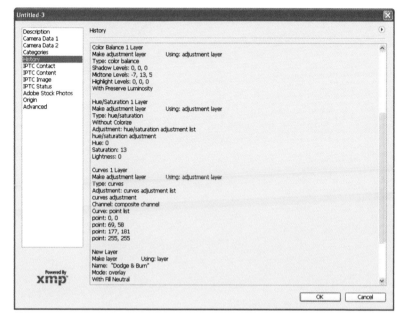

Figure 4.4
If you use the History Log feature, you can review everything that has been done to your image in the File Info > History dialog box.

Interface

The Interface section of Preferences is new in CS3. As shown in Figure 4.5, these options relate to the appearance of your workspace. We'll talk more about setting up your workspace later in this chapter; however, you establish some of your options here.

Figure 4.5
We recommend configuring these options as shown here.

Show Background Drop Shadow: Off   This option places a small drop shadow behind your canvas. Although this may look attractive, it can also be disconcerting if you are trying to create a drop shadow on your picture or when making other decisions about the edges of your image.

Note: You might want to turn this option on when showing your images to others to enhance your presentation.

Show Channels in Color: Off   We prefer to view the individual channels in grayscale so we can easily assess what detail information is contributed by each channel, so we leave this option off. Turning this on causes the channels viewed through the Channels panel to be displayed in their actual colors (red for the red channel, for example), rather than as grayscale images. Although this sounds like a good idea in terms of being able to interpret the color values for each channel, it actually becomes a challenge, because each of the component colors has a different perceived tonality, making comparison (and even viewing at times) difficult.

Show Menu Colors: Personal preference   This option is useful if you are new to Photoshop and use some of the preset workspaces that make certain menu items more obvious. We rarely take advantage of these features.

Show Tool Tips: On   We recommend turning this option on so that as you hover the cursor over an icon in the workspace, a brief explanation of the function associated with that icon appears.

Auto-Collapse Icon Panels: Off   Although it can be handy to save space on your monitor by collapsing the panels, when we expand a panel, such as the Layers panel, we prefer it to stay open.

Note: Only one panel at a time can be expanded when the panels are set to the collapsed mode.

Remember Panel Locations: Personal preference   This setting determines whether the panel arrangement you see when you start Photoshop will be the same arrangement you set when you last closed Photoshop. In general, if you moved panels within Photoshop, you probably did it for a reason, so this setting is probably a good thing. On the other hand, if you have saved a particular panel arrangement (as discussed later in this chapter), you may want to have Photoshop always return to the setting you've established, even if you've since shifted some panels. In that case, you'd want to disable this setting.

File Handling Settings

When you're finished with the General settings in the Preferences dialog box, click Next to continue to the File Handling section, illustrated in Figure 4.6. This section contains options related primarily to how files are saved.

Figure 4.6
The File Handling section of the Preferences dialog box contains settings that affect how files are opened and saved.

Two topics appear under the File Saving Options:

Image Previews: Always Save   The Image Previews setting determines whether a small preview thumbnail will be stored as part of the image file. We leave this setting on Always Save and check the option to save an icon for use in the Finder.

Append File Extension: Always   The File Extension drop-down list enables Photoshop to automatically append the filename with the correct extension. In addition, you can choose between uppercase and lowercase file extensions. This is really not a significant concern because either will work fine with current software.

Several options appear under File Compatibility including two that are new to CS3:

Prefer Adobe Camera Raw for JPEG Files   This option, new in CS3, enables you to use the controls in the Adobe Camera Raw (ACR) interface to make your initial adjustments to JPEG files as well. We recommend checking this option because ACR provides an interface where you can readily make most of the global tonal and color changes to your images.

Prefer Adobe Camera Raw for Supported Raw Files   This option is also new in CS3 and causes all supported raw files to be opened in the ACR interface. We recommend using this option because we think ACR does an excellent job with most raw files. However, if you are using other raw conversion software including Lightroom, your camera manufacturer's proprietary software, or other third-party software, you should leave this box unchecked.

Ignore EXIF Profile Tag: Off unless necessary   We recommend you leave this option off *unless* you're encountering problems with the color space embedded in your captures. This option in the File Compatibility section shouldn't be an issue for most photographers. If activated, it causes Photoshop to ignore the embedded color space in your digital captures. It's an issue only for images that have problems caused by their embedded profile, which is rare.

Ask Before Saving Layered TIFF Files: Personal preference   This controls the display of the TIFF Options dialog box. This setting is based on your particular workflow. Because Tim usually saves his TIFF files flattened (saving the master file with layers as a PSD), he leaves this option turned on so he's reminded if he's starting to save a TIFF file with layers. Ellen, on the other hand, tends to save her TIFF files with layers (or flatten them manually), so she turns this option off to avoid the extra click on the OK button in the dialog box.

Maximize PSD and PSB File Compatibility: Personal preference This option essentially controls whether a full-resolution composite image will be saved as part of the image file in Photoshop's native formats. The primary reason to enable this feature is to ensure that you're able to open the image as you intended it to appear with other versions of Photoshop—even if the algorithms determining how adjustments are applied get changed—or to enable applications that aren't able to build a thumbnail or preview from the layered file to utilize the full-resolution composite instead. It also provides a solution for situations where you have created a PSD file in a recent version of Photoshop and are sending that file to someone using an older version that doesn't support all the latest features. The disadvantage to using this setting is that file sizes are increased considerably (potentially doubled) when this option is used.

Note: The PSB file format can be opened only with Photoshop CS or later.

You'll see one check box under Version Cue:

Enable Version Cue Workgroup File Management: Off unless necessary Version Cue is a separate Creative Suite application (not included with the stand-alone version of Photoshop) that allows multiple people to work from one set of files without conflict or allows one person to work on a file with multiple versions.

The final option in the File Handling settings concerns the recent file list:

Recent File List Contains: 10 Files This option allows you to specify how many files should be listed on the Open Recent list found on the File menu. We find the default of 10 is usually adequate.

Performance

The Performance section of Preferences controls some of the behind-the-scenes issues that help Photoshop run smoothly and quickly. There are four sections in this part of Preferences: Memory Usage, History & Cache, Scratch Disks, and GPU Settings, as shown in Figure 4.7.

Figure 4.7

The new Performance dialog box enables you to control computer memory–related options.

Memory Usage   The Memory Usage setting is quite important for overall system performance. As you have no doubt figured out, Photoshop wants to have access to as much memory as possible. The Memory Usage setting determines how much memory Photoshop reserves for its use. Although you would generally expect to benefit from setting this to the maximum value, that can actually lead to problems. Very high settings can lead to stability issues, and on many computers, setting the value to 100% can even prevent Photoshop from loading.

Photoshop assesses the amount of RAM that's available on your computer after the operating system and other programs stake out their portion, and then it suggests an ideal range for how much to allocate to it. We recommend setting the value at the high end of the recommended range to provide as much memory to Photoshop as possible without running the risk of system stability problems.

Note: For best performance, your computer should have a minimum of 2GB of RAM and ideally more. Although Photoshop can run with less, you'll find yourself spending time waiting for things to process.

Scratch Disks   In the Scratch Disks section of the Preferences dialog box, it's important to establish appropriate settings to ensure optimal performance for Photoshop. Whenever Photoshop doesn't have adequate memory to perform a task, it depends upon hard drive space to simulate additional memory; the hard drive space used is referred to as a *scratch disk*. (Think of it as providing a scratch sheet of paper for Photoshop to use for figuring out complicated problems.)

When Photoshop must resort to scratch disk space, you want to make sure it's working optimally. If you have more than one internal hard drive, you can specify which drive Photoshop should use for start-up and which for memory-intensive processing tasks. To maximize performance in this situation, use the arrow keys in the dialog box to point Photoshop toward a secondary internal hard drive that isn't being used by the operating system. If you have more than two drives installed, you can also establish settings for Third and Fourth, keeping in mind that you want to set these in order of optimal performance, with the fastest drive first and the drive used by the operating system listed last. Most external drives offer much slower performance than internal drives, so they either should not be used for this purpose or should be last in the order.

If you have a drive separated into multiple partitions, you won't achieve a benefit by making these changes. You achieve the benefit by using a separate physical drive for the scratch disk usage.

History States: 40 to 60   This determines how many steps you'll be able to undo on the History panel. In other words, if you've made a mistake, how many individual steps can you undo in order to get back to the point where you actually made the mistake? The default setting of 20 is relatively low, especially for certain tasks such as image cleanup with the Clone Stamp tool. However, setting the value too high consumes a relatively large amount of memory when you are doing a lot of work on your images. Therefore, we recommend that you strike a compromise, using a value of 40 to 60. This is usually adequate for being able to go back and correct a mistake, even if it takes some time to realize what you've done, while not consuming a huge amount of memory.

Cache Levels: 6   The Cache Levels setting determines how many zoom settings are stored in memory for your image so the image and histogram can be drawn more quickly when zooming in and out on your image or performing adjustments. The performance difference here is minimal, so we generally leave the setting at the default value, which is 6. We leave the GPU Settings options in their default checked positions.

Cursors

In the Painting Cursors area of the Cursors section, you can adjust the cursors used for your mouse pointer when working with brush tools within Photoshop. *We recommend Normal Brush Tip and Precise.* Setting Preferences for accurate cursor displays (see Figure 4.8) is essential. Otherwise, although you may be using an icon that shows you what tool you're using, you won't know precisely where you are creating the effect on the image.

Figure 4.8
The Cursors section of Preferences is used to control the appearance of the pointer so that it is as useful as possible.

Standard   The Standard option causes the mouse pointer to display a small icon of the tool you're using. Although this helps remind you of which tool is in use, it doesn't help much in evaluating the size of the brush being used or the specific area to be affected.

Precise   The Precise option uses a "target" display that makes it easy to see exactly where you'll paint on the image with a given tool, but it doesn't give you any size information.

Normal Brush Tip   The Normal Brush Tip option uses a mouse pointer that matches the shape and size of the brush you're using, with softness accounted for by showing the perimeter of the brush as the point where the opacity of the brush edge is 50%. (See the left image in Figure 4.9.) That means the soft edge of the brush actually extends beyond the shape shown for the brush, but the shape represents the primary area being affected.

Full Size Brush Tip   The Full Size Brush Tip setting uses a full display of the actual brush size, with a fuzzy edge to the mouse pointer representing a soft brush. (See the right image in Figure 4.9.) However, this brush size represents the full extent of the brush, which can be a bit misleading for soft-edged brushes since they generally have no effect all the way out to the edge of the full brush size.

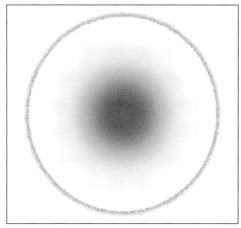

Figure 4.9 The Normal Brush Tip setting (left) causes the brush edge to be defined at the point where the opacity of the brush is at 50% for soft-edged brushes. The Full Size Brush Tip setting (right) causes the full extent of the brush to be shown (including a representation of a soft edge) even though there may not be any effect out to that distance when painting.

There is one additional option under Painting Cursors:

Show Crosshair In Brush Tip   The Show Crosshair In Brush Tip check box allows you to specify whether you want to see a crosshair in the center of the brush, so it's easier to see exactly where the center of the brush is. This can be helpful in a variety of situations, and we don't find it to be a distraction, so *we recommend leaving it turned on*.

Note: The Caps Lock key toggles the display of brush cursors between the Precise and brush options, so if you're not getting the display you expect based on Preferences, check the status of your Caps Lock key.

For Other Cursors, use the Precise option so you can see exactly where in the image you're clicking when using one of the nonbrush tools. In most cases, this option displays a crosshair or "target" for the nonbrush tools.]

Plug-Ins

If you use a number of plug-ins, you can opt to store them in a separate folder and have Photoshop automatically access the folder. Since we tend not to use many plug-ins, we leave this option unchecked. To use it, click the check box, navigate to the appropriate folder in the dialog box that appears, and click Choose. If you have an older Photoshop serial number associated with these plug-ins, you can add that to the Legacy Photoshop Serial Number box.

Note: For the Transparency & Gamut; Units & Rulers; and Guides, Grids, Slices, & Count; and Type settings, we recommend the default settings. The settings themselves aren't of significant consequence for optimizing photographic images, so we won't cover those sections here.

Views and Zoom

With Photoshop set up just the way you like it, you're ready to start actually looking at your images. Photoshop provides a variety of ways to do just that. This includes ways to display the image with Photoshop and ways to navigate around within your images with various tools.

Windows and Workspaces

The first thing we recommend doing when you open an image is to size the document window appropriately. In general, this means maximizing the document window so you can see as much of the image as possible (as illustrated in Figure 4.10). To do this, press Ctrl/Command+0. We're always a bit surprised at the number of people in our workshops who are working with their images sized so small that the majority of their monitor is filled with blank gray space. You can work far more accurately when you can see the image in more detail.

Figure 4.10 It's generally best to maximize your document window so you can see as much of the image as possible while working in Photoshop. (Photo by Ellen Anon.)

Screen Modes

Photoshop CS3 offers four screen modes: Standard Screen, Maximized Screen, Full Screen with Menu Bar, and Full Screen. These screen modes change the background surrounding your image as well as how you view your image. To toggle through the screen modes, press the F key; each time you press it, the mode will change to the next one in the series. You can also access the screen modes from the Change Screen mode icon in the Tools panel (see Figure 4.11) or from View > Screen Mode.

Figure 4.11

You can access the four screen modes via the Change Screen Mode icon at the bottom of the Tools panel.

In Standard Screen mode, your image has its own window, and on a Mac, your desktop will be visible. In earlier versions of Photoshop, this mode was popular because it allowed for scroll bars when the image was viewed at magnifications greater than the space available on the monitor. The presence of the scroll bars made it easy to navigate through the image.

Photoshop CS3 introduced Maximized Screen mode, which is an improved version of Standard Screen mode. Your image appears within a gray background that is linked to the panels on each side of the monitor. Just as in Standard Screen mode, when the image is zoomed larger than the working space, scroll bars appear to help you navigate smoothly and reliably. This has become Ellen's preferred working space, as shown in Figure 4.12.

Figure 4.12 The Maximized workspace has the best features of both Standard Screen and Full Screen modes. (Photo by Ellen Anon.)

The Full Screen modes are similar to maximized except that the area potentially utilized by your image extends underneath the panels. When you zoom in on your image, part of it may be hidden, and no scroll bars appear. You can move the image by holding down the spacebar, clicking on the image, and dragging it.

It's a matter of personal preference which mode you prefer to do most of your work in, but it's generally agreed that Full Screen mode is best when presenting your images to others.

If you're working with only one monitor and therefore have Photoshop's panels on your primary display, you can press the Tab key to toggle these panels on and off.

Configuring Panels

You can also adjust the arrangement of the various panels within Photoshop to suit your own preferences. The default arrangement places the History panel to the left of the image and the Histogram, Color Swatches, and Layers panels to the right, as shown earlier in Figure 4.12. We don't find this to be the best use of space for our needs. Most nature photographers have little use for the Color Swatches panel, so we suggest removing it by clicking the small X in the upper-right corner of that panel. You can remove panels by clicking the small X in the upper right corner or you can rearrange panels by clicking the tabs and dragging them where you want. By doing this, you can rearrange what panels are clustered where. We often use the setup shown in Figure 4.13. You'll notice that many of the panels are collapsed in our working space.

Figure 4.13 Configuring the panels the way you feel most comfortable will help you work more efficiently in Photoshop. (Photo by Ellen Anon.)

The Tools panel changed in CS3 to a single column as the default configuration. We prefer this view, but if you're more comfortable with the double column setup that earlier versions of Photoshop used, click the gray area by the two triangles at the top of the Tools panel, just above the PS icon, as shown in Figure 4.14.

The panels on the right side of the monitor have traditionally used a significant amount of monitor real estate. If you were working with a dual-monitor setup, it wasn't as much of an issue, but with a single monitor, it was frustrating to have so much space devoted to the panels rather than your image. In CS3, the panels are not only completely flexible as to their arrangement, but they are also collapsible, as shown in Figure 4.15. In their collapsed states, they're readily accessible; you can expand an individual panel by clicking it, as shown in the figure. We find this is a workspace arrangement that we use frequently.

Figure 4.14

In CS3 the Tools panel can appear as either a single column or a double column.

Figure 4.15

Collapsing the panels you are not using saves space on your monitor and is less distracting.

Note: Press the Tab key to hide the panels on the right. When you want to access them, hover the cursor over the dark translucent stipe at the right edge of your monitor and they'll magically appear. When you move your cursor away from that area, they'll disappear again.

Throughout this book you'll become familiar with many of the panels you can use, and you'll start to develop a preference for which panels you want to have visible and how you want them arranged. You may even find that you prefer to establish different configurations for different tasks or for different types of images. Fortunately, it's easy to switch between various panel arrangements. To start, set the panels where you want them.

Note: Prior to CS3, panels were called palettes.

Once you establish a workspace that's convenient for you, save it so that you can return to it easily if you move panels around while working. To save the workspace, select Window > Workspace > Save Workspace from the menu, enter a name for the arrangement you have established, and click Save (as shown in Figure 4.16). Then, any time you want to access or refresh this workspace, select the name of your saved settings from the Window > Workspace menu, and the configuration will be loaded immediately. You can save a variety of different workspace configurations if you find that you prefer certain arrangements for different tasks or types of images.

Figure 4.16

The Save Workspace dialog box allows you to provide a name for the panel configuration you have established so you can easily load it in the future.

Zoom Tool

The Zoom tool is the most basic of navigation tools, but it does include some hidden features that can be helpful. To select the Zoom tool, click its icon on the Tools panel 🔍, or press Z on your keyboard.

 Note: If you're using any other tool, you can switch to the Zoom tool by pressing Ctrl/Command+ spacebar. When you release the spacebar, your tool switches back.

In the most basic use, after selecting the Zoom tool, click anywhere in your image to zoom in by one preset percentage level. When you do so, not only is the image enlarged on the screen, but also the point you clicked becomes the center of the new display. To zoom out, select the minus (–) option on the Options bar, or simply hold down the Alt/Option key while you click. When zooming out, the same basic behavior occurs in reverse. The image zooms out by one level, and the point you clicked becomes the center of the new display.

 Note: You can also zoom in or out (without changing the center of the view) by pressing Ctrl/Command and the plus (+) or minus (–) key. Also, if your mouse has a scroll wheel, you can use that for zooming in and out.

The Zoom tool also offers one special capability that makes it incredibly powerful. If you click and drag with the Zoom tool, you create a *marquee* (dashed box) on your image. When you release the mouse, the area you dragged the box around is zoomed as much as necessary to fill the document window. This is an excellent way to zoom in on a particular area of your image to give it a closer look.

Another handy hidden feature of the Zoom tool is the ability to quickly go to a 100% view of your image, which is an excellent way to evaluate sharpness and look for small problems such as dust spots within the image. To quickly return the zoom percentage to 100%, simply double-click the Zoom tool's icon on the Tools panel *or* press Ctrl+Alt+0/⌘+Option+0. You can also access some of these commands when the Zoom tool is active by right-clicking the image and choosing the desired option from the context menu.

Note: At irregular magnifications, artifacts may appear, causing distortions, or the selection marching ants may not be visible. One place this commonly occurs is with photos showing the texture in cloth. At some magnifications it may look as though the cloth is a fancy silk moiré rather than ordinary fabric. The most accurate magnification is 100% , but you can eliminate most magnification artifacts by using a magnification of 50% as well. If something looks odd in your image, check the magnification to see whether it's a problem with the image itself or an artifact.

Evaluating Sharpness: The Proper Magnification and Practice

Determining whether an image is critically sharp is a major aspect of the image review process that leads up to the actual optimization workflow. Many photographers have a difficult time evaluating the sharpness of a digital image displayed on their monitor, especially those who have spent many years evaluating the sharpness of images on film by utilizing a high-powered loupe.

The first step to evaluating sharpness for a given image is to view it at 100% magnification (or Actual Pixels). To do this, you can use the Zoom tool or the keyboard shortcut Ctrl+Alt+0/⌘+Option+0. At this magnification, one image pixel is represented by one monitor pixel. As a result, you're seeing all the actual pixels within the image for the area that can be seen on the monitor. If you don't have the display set to 100% magnification, the monitor is either using more than one pixel to represent each pixel in the image (if the zoom percentage is greater than 100%) or is not showing all pixels for a given area within the image (if the zoom percentage is less than 100%).

After you're viewing the image at 100% magnification, look to see whether the edges within the subject matter of the image have good contrast. This is the key attribute of an image with crisp focus. Learning to see what a sharp image looks like on a monitor display takes some practice, and the only way to accumulate that practice is to evaluate a large number of images.

Besides simply reviewing the images on your monitor, it can be helpful to first make prints of some of your images and then compare the printed image (where you'll have an easier time evaluating sharpness) to the image on the monitor at 100% magnification. Comparing these images gives you a better idea of how the monitor display translates into actual image sharpness.

Hand Tool

The Hand tool provides a way to navigate around your image when the magnification is higher than 100% and it therefore spills over the document window. You can think of this tool as behaving the way your own hand would if you were evaluating a large print on a table. Instead of moving your head around to look at different areas of the image, you can simply move the "print" with your hand. You can activate the Hand tool by clicking its icon in the Tools panel 🖐 or by pressing H on your keyboard.

With the Hand tool active, drag around on the image. The image moves in the direction you drag, with the display being updated in real time so you can watch the image slide around as you move the mouse.

Note: The Hand tool can't move your image around if the image is zoomed out to the extent that you can see the entire image at once.

Another handy trick is to use the Hand tool to quickly display your image at a magnification that allows it to fit within the space available without being obstructed by the panels (if they are docked to the side of the screen) or to fill the screen display area (if they are not), resizing the image window if necessary. To do so, double-click the Hand tool in the Tools panel. This is a great way to quickly get an overview of the image for evaluating overall composition, tonality, and color.

Note: If you're using any other tool, you can switch to the Hand tool by pressing the spacebar. When you release it, your tool switches back.

Navigator Panel

The Navigator panel consolidates many of the features of the Zoom and Hand tools into a single package and provides an efficient method for moving around your image to evaluate various portions of it (see Figure 4.17). If the Navigator panel isn't visible, choose Window > Navigator from the menu to make it active.

Figure 4.17
The Navigator panel provides a convenient way to navigate around your image. (Photo by Tim Grey.)

The Navigator panel provides a thumbnail preview of the currently active image. A red box indicates which portion of the image is being viewed in the document window, so you always have a sense of what portion of the image you are seeing. The bottom-left corner of the panel includes a zoom percentage indicator for reference.

The zooming features of the Navigator panel are utilized primarily with the slider in the bottom-right corner of the panel window. The "little mountains" button to the left of the slider allows you to zoom out by one preset percentage level each time you click it, similar to Alt+clicking/Option+clicking your image with the Zoom tool. The "big mountains" button to the right of the slider allows you to zoom in by one preset percentage level. You can exercise greater control over the zooming process by adjusting the slider left (to zoom out) or right (to zoom in).

Within the thumbnail display for your image, the red box serves not only as an indicator of which area of the image is currently being viewed but also as a way to change the view of the image to look at a different area. If you drag the boxed area around within the thumbnail display, the document display changes in real time to reflect the area defined by the box. This is similar to the use of the Hand tool for navigating around your image.

> **Note:** You can't move the outline in the Navigator panel if the entire image is currently visible.

You can click a particular point in the thumbnail to center the outline on that spot. This is a great method to use when you want to spot-check various portions of the image. For example, if you're trying to evaluate critical sharpness, check various areas of the subject and even areas at various distances from the camera to see the effect of depth of field. By simply clicking those points in the thumbnail of the Navigator panel, you can check multiple areas of the image quickly and easily.

One last trick in the Navigator panel allows you to reproduce the effect of drawing a marquee on your image with the Zoom tool so you can quickly fill the screen with a particular portion of your image. To do so, hold the Ctrl/⌘ key, and click and drag within the thumbnail display of the Navigator panel to draw a box over the area you want to view. When you release the mouse button, the image is automatically zoomed and repositioned so that the area you drew the box around fills the available space.

Navigating by Keyboard Shortcuts

If you love using keyboard shortcuts to speed up your workflow, there are a variety of options for navigating around your images during the evaluation process (as well as during your actual optimization workflow). If you tend to keep one hand on the keyboard as you work, this may be your preferred way to navigate. Even if you prefer to use the mouse as much as possible, remembering a few of these keyboard shortcuts can help improve your workflow by adding to your arsenal of tricks for working with your images. Table 2.1 recaps the most common navigational shortcuts.

Table 2.1 Keyboard Shortcuts for Image Navigation

Windows Shortcut	Mac Shortcut	Action
H	H	Activates the Hand tool.
Z	Z	Activates the Zoom tool
Ctrl++	⌘++	Zooms in
Ctrl+-	⌘+-	Zooms out
Ctrl+Alt+0	⌘+Option+0	Zooms to 100% magnification (Actual Pixels)
Ctrl+0	⌘+0	Zooms document window to fit on the screen
Spacebar	Spacebar	Temporarily activates the Hand tool regardless of currently active tool
Ctrl+spacebar	⌘+spacebar	Temporarily activates the Zoom tool regardless of currently active tool
Ctrl+Alt+spacebar	⌘+Option+spacebar	Temporarily activates the Zoom tool in zoom-out mode regardless of the currently active tool

Note: In Windows, if you have a check box or other control active in a dialog box while trying to hold the spacebar to access the Hand tool, you may not get the behavior you are expecting. This is because you can use the spacebar to toggle such controls. To avoid this, click an empty area of the dialog box so that no control has the focus before using the spacebar as a shortcut key.

As you've seen in this section, there are many options in Photoshop for navigating around your images during the evaluation and optimization processes. Instead of trying to decide which particular methods work best for your needs, make an effort to become familiar with all of them. Doing so will ensure that you have the maximum number of techniques available for any given situation. What you'll likely find is that although you have your favorite methods for navigating around your images, in certain situations other methods are more convenient. By being comfortable with all the available methods, you'll have maximum flexibility and control when working on your images.

Try It! To gain familiarity with the Navigator panel, open the image NavPanel from the accompanying CD and zoom in to various areas of the image, deciding on a specific area to view and then navigating to that area so it fills the monitor display. Then save a workspace with the panel arrangement you prefer to use when working on your images

Selection Tools

We're including the selection tools in this chapter on foundations because making a selection is required for many of the more advanced topics we'll cover in later chapters. You can make a selection in a variety of ways, and which approach is best depends upon the characteristics of the specific image as well as your own preferences. Focusing on the selection tools now introduces and reinforces the general techniques you employ when working with most of the tools in Photoshop. We recommend you experiment with and learn the different tools that perform similar basic tasks to help you get more comfortable using Photoshop and the various tools it offers. That way you'll be able to use the best one in any given situation.

You can use selections for making targeted adjustments and for other tasks, as we'll discuss in later chapters. For example, you can select the sky to apply adjustments that affect only the sky, or you can select a foreground subject to enhance it so it stands out from the landscape better. In the following sections, we'll look at some of the selection tools most commonly employed by nature photographers, as well as some behaviors common to all the selection tools.

The Lasso Tool

The Lasso tool provides maximum flexibility and is very intuitive because it allows you to literally draw a custom shape around the pixels you want to select. This is very helpful for situations where the more automated selection tools don't provide the accuracy you need, requiring you to trace by hand. For example, if you are trying to select a dark bird against a dark background, other tools may not be able to tell the difference between the two. The Lasso tool allows you to define the specific shape and location of the selection edge. Activate the Lasso by choosing it from the Tools panel �e or by pressing L on your keyboard.

The Options bar for the Lasso tool (shown in Figure 4.18) contains some settings that allow you to adjust the behavior of the Lasso tool. These include four modifier options, which we'll discuss in the next section. Also on the Options bar for the Lasso tool are the Feather and Anti-Aliased controls. We recommend leaving Feather set to 0 px (we'll explain what feathering is and how to feather a selection later) and Anti-Aliased selected (to help smooth portions of the selection lines that are not perfectly horizontal or vertical).

Ⓐ New Selection
Ⓑ Add to Selection
Ⓒ Subtract from Selection
Ⓓ Intersect with Selection

Figure 4.18 The Options bar for the Lasso tool lets you decide how to use the tool.

Zoom in on the area you want to select. Creating an accurate selection is easiest to do when you magnify the image to clearly see the edge you're trying to select. Carefully position your cursor along that edge; then click and hold the mouse button. Drag the cursor along the edge so you're effectively tracing that edge to define your selection, as illustrated in Figure 4.19. Take the time to be as precise as you can so the selection you create is as accurate as possible.

119
■
SELECTION TOOLS

Note: For tools like the Lasso that require you to draw on your image, using a tablet such as the Wacom Intuos3 (www.wacom.com) can be a tremendous help, providing you with greater control and precision. In addition, using a pen and tablet feels more natural to many people.

Figure 4.19
When working with the Lasso tool, you can trace along any shape within your image to define your selection. (Photo by Tim Grey.)

When working on a zoomed portion of your image, the area you're trying to select might extend outside the document window. In that case, as you near the edge of the document window, press and hold the spacebar. This temporarily accesses the Hand tool, so you can click and drag the image to change the area you're currently viewing. When you're finished moving the image, release the spacebar, and continue dragging the cursor to extend the selection you're in the process of creating.

When selecting an area of the image, be sure to define all of it, dragging the cursor all the way back to your original starting point and releasing the mouse button to finish the selection, as shown in Figure 4.20. If you don't finish at the same point you started, Photoshop automatically completes your selection by extending a straight line from the point where you release the mouse button to your original starting point, which is obviously less than ideal in most situations.

Figure 4.20
When you finish tracing the object you want to select, returning to your starting point, the selection will be completed. (Photo by Tim Grey.)

Working with the Lasso tool can require a steady hand and a bit of practice. It isn't always the fastest or easiest way to create a selection, but it does offer exceptional flexibility.

Selection Modes

Sometimes when you are making a difficult selection, you may want to make part of your selection first and then add or remove sections. With the Lasso selection tool under control, you can make more complicated selections by adding pixels to or subtracting pixels from a selection. Start by using the Lasso tool to create a basic selection. To the right of the Tool Preset drop-down list on the Options bar is a set of four buttons (these are labeled back in Figure 4.18) that allow you to modify the behavior of these (and other) selection tools.

The first button, New Selection, causes the current selection tool to behave in the "normal" manner, creating a new selection whenever you use the tool. With this option active, when you click and drag to create a selection, it replaces any existing selections. Each time you click and drag with the first button selected, you are starting to make the selection from scratch.

The second button is the Add To Selection option. With this option chosen, whenever you use a selection tool to surround pixels, the new selection is added to the existing selection. For example, if you use the Lasso tool to create a selection around a flower but then realize you left a part of the flower out of the selection, choose the Add To Selection option, and then select the area you missed. It is then added to the overall selection (see Figure 4.21). You can also hold the Shift key to access the Add To Selection option regardless of the current state of the tool.

Figure 4.21
The Add To Selection option for
the Lasso tool allows you to add
a new area to your selection,
creating a larger final selection.
(Photo by Tim Grey.)

The third button in the set is the Subtract From Selection option, which allows you to subtract pixels from an existing selection. When this button is selected, drawing a selection causes the surrounded pixels to be omitted from the existing selection, as shown in Figure 4.22. You access this option by holding the Alt/Option key when using any selection tool. You must still draw a closed shape to define the area of the selection you want to subtract.

Figure 4.22
The Subtract From Selection option for the Lasso tool allows you to remove an area from your selection, creating a smaller final selection. (Photo by Tim Grey.)

The Add and Subtract options are extremely helpful, and you'll use them extensively as you build complicated selections that require a fair amount of fine-tuning. The last button of the four, the Intersect With Selection button, is one that is not too useful for most nature photography. When you choose this option, creating a new selection when you have an existing selection results in a selection of only the pixels in the areas where the two selections overlap.

The Magnetic Lasso

The Magnetic Lasso is very helpful for selecting objects within your images where reasonably good contrast exists along the edges defining that object. Instead of selecting precisely where you drag, the Magnetic Lasso defines a selection by periodically placing anchor points as you drag the cursor around an object, automatically identifying the locations of highest contrast as you move the cursor around the edge. In other words, this tool often simplifies the process of identifying exactly the area that you want, reducing the need to work extremely slowly and carefully, as you must with the Lasso tool. It makes the selection jump to the edges of the area that you're trying to select.

You'll find the Magnetic Lasso 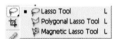 under the regular Lasso on the Tools panel. Click and hold the cursor (or right-click) on the Lasso tool to open the fly-out menu, and choose Magnetic Lasso (see Figure 4.23). You can also press L on your keyboard to activate the current Lasso tool, and then press Shift+L to toggle through the selection tools until you access the Magnetic Lasso.

Figure 4.23
You can find the Magnetic Lasso tool under the Lasso tool on the Tools panel.

Besides the standard controls found on the Options bar for the other selection tools (and discussed in the prior section on the Lasso tool), the Options bar contains some special controls for the Magnetic Lasso tool. (Figure 4.24 shows the Options bar.) The first is the Width control; as you "paint" with the Magnetic Lasso, the Width control determines the size of the area in which you'd like Photoshop to search for contrast. You could enter a value in pixels to determine the size of the edge width for the Magnetic Lasso, but obviously this is a rather arbitrary decision. Instead, simply place your cursor along the edge where you'll start making the selection, and use the left or right square bracket key ([and]) to reduce or enlarge the size of the edge width, respectively. You want the width to be small enough that the strongest area of contrast within the sample area is the edge you're trying to select but large enough that you don't have to be overly precise in dragging the mouse pointer along that edge.

Figure 4.24 The Options bar for the Magnetic Lasso tool includes some specialized settings in addition to those found with the regular Lasso tool.

The Edge Contrast setting determines how much contrast the Magnetic Lasso should seek. For high-contrast edges, if you use a higher setting, you won't need to be as precise as you move the mouse along that contrast edge. For low-contrast edges, use a lower setting, but be more precise in dragging the mouse along the edge you're trying to select. Frankly, the change in behavior achieved with different settings is very slight, so we recommend setting Edge Contrast to the default value of 10% .

The Frequency setting determines how often anchor points are placed as you drag the mouse pointer over the edge. A higher Frequency value causes anchor points to be placed quickly in close proximity to each other; a lower value causes them to be placed farther apart. (Figure 4.25 illustrates both of these situations.) Lower settings are best for well-defined edges, whereas higher settings tend to work well for more nebulous edges. A Frequency value of 60 is a good general starting point, and you can then revise that number based on whether the anchor points are being placed at an appropriate rate (the allowed range is 0 to 100). It's generally better to have a higher frequency with more anchor points rather than a lower frequency so the shape of the selection better matches the edge of the object you're trying to select.

 Note: The faster you move the cursor with the Magnetic Lasso tool, the farther apart the anchor points are spread as compared to when you drag it slowly.

Figure 4.25
A low Frequency setting for the Magnetic Lasso causes anchor points to be spaced out relatively far apart, while a high setting causes them to be placed closer together. (Photo by Tim Grey.)

The final setting on the Options bar is a Pen Pressure check box. This setting applies only if you are using a tablet. With this check box selected, varying the pressure you apply to the stylus (pen) affects the edge width. Pressing harder causes the width to decrease as though the pressure is focusing the edge width onto a smaller area. Less pressure causes the edge width to enlarge, so the Magnetic Lasso looks for contrast across a broader area.

With the Options bar settings established, you're ready to start creating a selection with the Magnetic Lasso tool. Position the cursor over the contrast edge you want to select, and click the mouse button once to place the initial anchor point. Then drag the cursor along the edge of the object you are trying to select. Photoshop automatically places anchor points at the area of highest contrast within the target area (Width), with spacing based on the Frequency setting. If you get to an area of the image where contrast isn't adequate for the Magnetic Lasso to accurately place an anchor point, click the mouse to manually place an anchor point. For example, if you have a well-defined subject such as a flower against the sky, the Magnetic Lasso will likely do a good job. But where the flower overlaps foliage or other flowers below it, the Magnetic Lasso may not be able to identify the edge, requiring you to place anchor points manually by clicking. We often find it helpful to manually place an anchor point where the selection needs to abruptly change directions.

At times you'll find the Magnetic Lasso doesn't do a very good job of placing anchor points where you want them, placing them in inappropriate places. When that happens, you need to delete anchor points before trying again in the problem area of the image. First, move the cursor back to the last place where you want an anchor point. Then, press the Backspace/Delete key once for each anchor you want to remove. They are removed starting with the most recently created point. You can then adjust the width with the square bracket keys, or change other settings on the Options bar, and drag again along the edge. If you can't find settings that work well for a particular area, place the anchor points manually by clicking the mouse.

> **Note:** Sometimes the Magnetic Lasso tool seems to have a mind of its own and runs amok. When that happens, place the cursor over the last good anchor point before it ran off, and repeatedly hit the Backspace/Delete key. Doing so will remove all the extra anchor points and put you back in control of the tool.

To access the regular Lasso tool while working with the Magnetic Lasso, press and hold the Alt/Option key as you click, and drag the cursor along the edge you want to define by drawing freehand. Click again without the Alt/Option key to return to the Magnetic Lasso. (Note that if you inadvertently release the Alt/Option key while dragging, you will be using the Polygonal Lasso tool rather than the Freehand Lasso tool.)

If you decide you want to cancel the selection in progress, simply press the Esc key; all anchor points are removed, and there is no active selection (unless there was a selection active before you started using the Magnetic Lasso).

> **Try It!** To get more comfortable working with this tool, open the image MagneticLasso on the accompanying CD, zoom in on the eye of the owl, and use the Magnetic Lasso to create a selection of the eye.

The Magnetic Lasso tool is powerful, but it isn't perfect. Although it does a good job of selecting based on contrast in the area you drag the cursor over, in most cases it won't create a perfect selection, as you can see in Figure 4.26. However, it usually creates a good basic selection, making it an effective tool that can sometimes save you time in creating selections. Think of it as a tool for creating a rough selection, knowing you'll have to modify that selection after creating it. Tim frequently uses the Magnetic Lasso and finds it saves him considerable time in the overall process of creating the perfect selection, whereas Ellen prefers to use other tools such as the Quick Selection tool that we'll cover later in this chapter. By learning the nuances of each tool, you too will develop your own favorites that work best for you.

Figure 4.26
The Magnetic Lasso tool doesn't generally create perfect selections, as you can see here when we zoom in, but it does provide you with a good basic selection with minimal effort. (Photo by Tim Grey.)

Note: The third Lasso selection tool is the Polygonal Lasso tool. However, for nature photography, this tool tends to be less useful than the tools described in this section because it is designed for creating selections comprised of straight lines.

The Magic Wand

When the Magic Wand tool creates a selection with a single click of the mouse, it seems truly magical. When too many clicks are required, it can be a bit frustrating. The trick is knowing what type of image is best suited for this tool and how to configure the settings for the best result.

The Magic Wand lives underneath the Quick Selection tool. To access it, click the Quick Selection tool in the toolbar, and select the Magic Wand from the fly-out menu. The Magic Wand functions by sampling the pixel that you click and then comparing other pixels to see whether they are a close-enough match. If they are, they are included in the selection.

Before setting the options for the Magic Wand tool, it's important to check a setting on the Options bar for the Eyedropper tool. Although these tools don't seem related, the Magic Wand tool uses the Sample Size setting from the Eyedropper tool to determine the actual value to use in evaluating pixels for inclusion in the selection. Choose the Eyedropper tool from the Tools panel, and choose an option from the Sample Size drop-down menu on the Options bar, as shown in Figure 4.27.

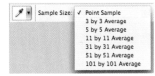

Figure 4.27

The first step in using the Magic Wand tool is to set an appropriate option from the Sample Size drop-down menu on the Options bar for the Eyedropper tool.

The most useful options available for your purposes when you select the Eyedropper tool are 3 By 3 Average and 5 By 5 Average. As their names indicate, they sample a grid of pixels (a total of 9 or 25 pixels, respectively) surrounding the one you click and average their values. This average value is then used as the basis of the Magic Wand tool selection. Averaging helps to compensate for any local variation among pixels and is more reliable than sampling a single point. We recommend using the 3 By 3 Average setting, because it provides a good balance for most images. The 5 By 5 Average setting has a higher risk of averaging the pixel values to the point that the result isn't as accurate based on the pixel area you clicked.

Note: The Point Sample option causes only a single pixel to be used as the basis for pixel comparison by the Magic Wand tool. This can certainly increase precision, but it also introduces potential errors. For example, you could click a dust spot or a pixel with variation caused by grain or noise, and the resulting selection wouldn't match what you were intending to create. For this reason, we don't recommend using the Point Sample option.

After you've established an appropriate Sample Size setting on the Options bar for the Eyedropper tool, choose the Magic Wand tool so you can adjust the settings and create your selection.

The key to using the Magic Wand tool effectively is the Tolerance setting on the Options bar (see Figure 4.28). This setting determines how different the pixel values can be and still be considered a match. With a low setting, pixels must be very similar to the value of the pixel you clicked to be included in the selection. With a high setting, even pixels with very different values can be included in the selection. The tolerance ranges from 0, which would mean a pixel must be identical to the sampled pixel in order to be selected, to 255, which would result in the entire image being selected.

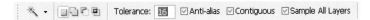

Figure 4.28 The Tolerance setting on the Options bar for the Magic Wand tool is key to getting the best results.

The Magic Wand tool is obviously best suited for images with broad areas of similar tone and color that you want to select. An example is an area of open sky with no clouds (see Figure 4.29). Because the pixels already have similar values, a relatively low Tolerance setting should be appropriate. Tim typically starts with a Tolerance value of 16, whereas Ellen often starts with a value of 30 and works from there.

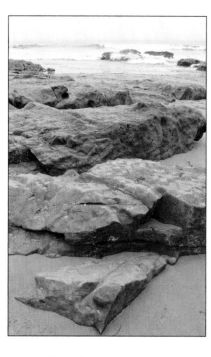

Figure 4.29
The Magic Wand tool is best
suited to images with broad
areas of similar tone and
color, such as the sky in this
image. (Photo by Tim Grey.)

Click the area of the image you want to select and adjust the Tolerance setting based on the result. If too many pixels from areas you don't want to select are selected, Tolerance is too high; cancel the selection (choose Select > Deselect from the menu), and reduce the Tolerance value.

Of course, you could spend a lot of time chasing the right Tolerance value. We recommend taking a tempered approach, trying to find a *good* value without spending too much time finding the *perfect* value. Opt for a Tolerance setting that is a bit lower than needed. Then use the Add To Selection option and Refine Edge feature (that we'll describe later in this chapter) to build up the final selection.

Note: It's usually better to start with a Tolerance value for the Magic Wand that results in a selection that encompasses less than the area you are trying to select and then build up the selection with the Add To Selection option.

It's important to keep in mind that when you add pixels to or subtract pixels from a selection by using the appropriate options with the Magic Wand tool, the selection is modified based on the pixel you click after making your initial selection. Also, keep in mind that you can adjust the Tolerance setting between mouse clicks when using the Add and Subtract options, giving you even greater control. Each time you click with the Magic Wand tool, pixels throughout the image are evaluated based on the Tolerance setting, regardless of whether the pixels are already selected.

Although the Tolerance setting is the pivotal setting for the Magic Wand tool, the Contiguous option is also important. The Contiguous option affects which pixels are evaluated. When you click a pixel with the Magic Wand, Photoshop looks outward from that pixel to find matching pixels. If it encounters a pixel that doesn't match closely enough based on the Tolerance setting, that pixel creates a border so that pixels outside the areas defined by that border aren't considered. In other words, all pixels in the final selection are contiguous, or touching each other.

Using the Contiguous option is helpful when a tonality appears not only in the area you want to select but also in areas you don't want to select. By clicking Contiguous, the Magic Wand will not include those pixels that are in other areas of the image. For example, if you wanted to select the two swans shown in Figure 4.30, by selecting Contiguous you help the Magic Wand limit the selection to the swans rather than including the snow in the mountains.

Figure 4.30
Using the Contiguous Option enables you to select a subject when similar tones are present elsewhere in the image. (Photo by Ellen Anon.)

At other times, you need to select similar areas that are noncontiguous. For example, you may need to select a sky in an image where the sky shows between the leaves and branches of a tree. Turning off the Contiguous option causes Photoshop to evaluate every pixel based on the pixel you click with the Magic Wand tool, as shown in Figure 4.31.

Figure 4.31
Turning off the Contiguous option for the Magic Wand tool allows you to select multiple noncontiguous areas in a single step.(Photo by Tim Grey.)

The Sample All Layers check box allows you to determine whether Photoshop evaluates pixel values based on all layers in the image or on only the currently active layer. Because you're viewing the image based on all visible layers, it usually makes sense to keep this option turned on. In fact, you can use this setting to make the Magic Wand tool more effective by creating a temporary adjustment layer that accentuates the difference between areas you do want to select and those you don't.

The Anti-Aliased check box serves the same purpose as it does with the other selection tools discussed earlier in this chapter, and we recommend leaving it selected.

Try It! Open the image MagicWand on the accompanying CD, and practice by creating a selection of the sky that doesn't encroach on the clouds.

The Magic Wand tool is best for selecting areas of an image that have similar tone and color. If the area you're trying to select contains too much variation, evaluate the image to see whether you can easily select the opposite of what you really want. For example, if you want to select everything in an image except the sky, it might be easier to select the sky and then invert the selection (Select > Inverse).

When using the Magic Wand tool, it's important to check your selection at 100% magnification. At other magnifications there may be small "blinkies" that you can't see. These "blinkies" are actually pixels that may be erroneously selected or not selected. Rather than have to click over and over with the Magic Wand and use Add To Selection/ Subtract From Selection, it's often much easier to refine the selection with the Freehand Lasso set to Add To Selection/Subtract From Selection. We'll talk more about this in the next section of this chapter.

The Magic Wand is a favorite selection tool for many nature photographers, and it's one that Ellen used frequently in earlier versions of Photoshop.

The Quick Selection Tool

The Quick Selection tool ⬚ is new to CS3 and has quickly become one of our favorite selection tools. It's easy to use, and it actually gets "smarter" as you work with the Add To and Subtract From Selection options. Rather than having to trace along the edges to make a selection, you click and drag the cursor over the areas you want to select. The selection grows as you drag the cursor.

The Quick Selection tool is actually a brush tool. To determine the size of the tool, set the brush size in the Options bar, or use the bracket keys to increase and decrease the size. We find that using a fairly small brush gives the best results; the larger the brush, the less precise the area that is selected. By using a small brush in detailed areas, we can make reasonably accurate selections in many cases, as shown in Figure 4.32.

If the selection is not updating fast enough, you may need to drag a little more slowly and continue to hold down the mouse.

If you stop dragging and then click elsewhere, the tool will automatically change to Add To Selection. The selection will grow to incorporate the new area but not necessarily areas in between the original selection and the new area.

To remove an area from the selection, choose the Subtract from option in the Options bar and then drag over the area to be removed. You may need to reduce the size of the tool.

In areas of lower contrast, you may need to alternate between adding to and subtracting from the selection. Holding down the Alt/Option key will enable you to rapidly toggle between the two modes. As you do so, Photoshop is actually refining the algorithm to make the selection more accurately and quickly.

To further adjust the edges of the selection, click the Refine Edges button, discussed in the next section.

Figure 4.32

It was easy to make a good
selection of the horse and
cowboy by using the Quick
Selection tool. (Photo by
Ellen Anon.)

Using the Refine Edges Controls

When using the selection tools, there is a Refine Edge button on the toolbar [Refine Edge...]
that is particularly helpful with the Quick Selection tool. In addition, it has become our
method of choice for controlling the appearance of the edges of a selection no matter
how we made the initial selection. It's taken the place of the simple Feather command
in our workflow as well as the elaborate method we used to use in which we created a
layer mask for a selection and blurred the edges of the layer mask.

You can use these same controls with selections made using any of the tools, and
you can also access them by choosing Select > Refine Edge. The Refine Edges dialog box
appears, as shown in Figure 4.33. This is a major new addition to CS3. Its purpose is to
enable you to modify the edges of a selection so that it blends or separates from the background as needed. In earlier versions of Photoshop, these same issues were addressed by a
series of steps that included blurring the layer mask and then using Levels to adjust the
edge of the layer mask. The Refine Edge dialog box is easier to use and more precise.

Figure 4.33

The Refine Edge dialog box
provides tools to perfect the
edges of the selection.

Within the Refine Edge dialog box, you'll see a series of sliders and boxes. The five boxes near the bottom enable you to preview the selection in different ways, as shown in Figure 4.34.

Standard shows the selection as the traditional series of marching ants around the edge of the selection. The presence of the marching ants can make it difficult to determine the precise location of the edges.

Quick Mask hides the background under a transparent veil of red while the selected area remains in clear view.

On Black shows the selection floating on a pure black background. In many cases, this makes it easy to see the edges. This is our default setting.

On White is similar to On Black, but the selection sits on a white background. This too can be helpful when trying to determine edge detail. Whether black or white is preferable depends on the colors in the selection.

Mask changes the preview to a traditional black-and-white mask view.

To toggle among the views, click the different boxes. Whichever view you last used is "sticky" and what will be used initially the next time you open the dialog box.

In addition to the boxes, you'll see five sliders. Increase the Radius slider to improve the edge selection in areas with low contrast and/or fine detail. The larger the radius, the more gradual the edge, while the smaller the radius, the more discrete the edge. Larger radius settings preserve more details along the edges but may include some artifacts. You can remove such artifacts by increasing the Contrast slider.

Moving the Contrast slider to the right can remove artifacts along the edges. In addition, increasing the contrast retains gradual transitions in larger areas but makes slightly soft edges crisper.

Adjust the Smooth slider to reduce any jagged edges along the edge of the selection. At times this may cause some fine detail to be lost. In such cases, adjust the Radius slider to recover the detail.

The Feather slider is the familiar Feather command Photoshop users have been using in earlier versions of Photoshop. It produces a uniform, gradual blur along the selection edge. The Radius slider is a more sophisticated version of feathering. We recommend using the Radius slider rather than Feather.

Nudge contracts the selection edge when moved to the left and expands the selection when it's moved to the right.

By using the Refine Selection Edge controls, you can control the appearance of the edges of your selections more precisely to make transitions more accurate than what was readily possible to do using earlier versions of Photoshop. We recommend using these controls with most of your selections.

Standard

On Black

On White

Quick Mask

Mask

Figure 4.34
Depending on the image, different previews make it easier to see the edge detail of the selection.

Feathering Selections in Versions of Photoshop Prior to CS3

When using earlier versions of Photoshop to create selections, we recommended keeping the Feather option set to zero pixels with those tools that have a feather option. This means that pixels inside the selection are completely selected, and pixels outside the selection are completely unselected, with no transition in the degree of selection along that edge. However, when the selection is actually put to use, as the basis of hiding or revealing pixels in a composite image, for example, or as the basis of a targeted adjustment that applies only to the selected area, a nonfeathered selection is generally a bad thing. We recommend beginning with no feathering because it's nearly impossible to determine ahead of time how much feathering you'll need.

Feathering a selection results in a gradual transition along the edge of the selection. For example, if you feathered a selection by 10 pixels, there would be a transition from pixels that are 100% selected to pixels that are 90% selected, and so on, until reaching the point where the pixels aren't selected at all. (Yes, that's right—a single pixel can be partially selected.) This creates a soft edge along the selection boundary and results in an equivalent smooth transition along the edge of the adjustment you apply in a targeted fashion using a selection.

You can feather a selection edge as soon as it is created by choosing Select > Feather from the menu. The Feather Selection dialog box appears, where you can enter a value for the number of pixels by which you'd like to feather. Of course, as you can imagine, it can be difficult to judge how many pixels you want the selection edge to transition across. For this reason, we generally recommend that you save your feathering for later. In most cases, a selection is used as the basis of a mask for an image or adjustment layer, defining where that particular layer should be visible. You can apply a blur to this mask to produce the same effect as you would achieve by feathering a selection, but with more control and precision. We'll cover these topics further in later chapters.

Combining Tools

We've covered a few of the key selection tools here, primarily to help build a foundation for the use of tools within Photoshop, as well as get you started on creating selections you'll use to apply targeted adjustments to your images. There are some other, more advanced ways of making selections that we'll cover when we talk about creating composites in Chapter 8. *However, we want to stress here that you can mix and match any of the selection tools or methods in Photoshop to create the perfect selection.* It's fine, and often helpful, to begin a selection with one tool and use another tool to refine it.

In the workshops we teach, we often see participants getting stuck on a single selection tool for a given task. For example, if they're trying to create a selection of the sky, they naturally start with the Magic Wand tool. If that tool isn't providing a very good solution in a particular portion of the sky, we often see the person struggling to find just the right Tolerance setting and just the right pixel to click in order to get the selection perfect. The result is a lot of frustration as the photographer has to repeatedly undo a step in their selection process and then redo that step with different settings.

You can avoid (or at least minimize) this sort of frustration by combining various selection tools to create a selection. For example, when selecting a sky, you might start with the Magic Wand tool to create a basic selection and then employ the Lasso tool to clean up that selection and the areas the Magic Wand tool wasn't able to select effectively. Always keep in mind that every tool or method for creating a selection in Photoshop can be utilized in building a selection, adding to or subtracting from the selection as appropriate, using the means most appropriate for each given area of a selection as you work to create the final result.

Note: Of course, selections by themselves don't do anything for your images. But in later chapters we'll show you exactly how to put selections to use for creating targeted adjustments.

Combining selection tools can be a tremendous help when trying to build a specific selection that can't be created all by itself. For example, if you have a group of flowers set against the sky and you want to select only the primary grouping, the steps might go like this:

1. Use the Magic Wand tool with an appropriate Tolerance setting to select the sky. After the initial mouse click on the sky, hold the Shift key and click in additional areas to build up a selection of the entire sky. Be sure to uncheck the Contiguous option on the Options bar if there are areas of sky isolated by other elements in the image.

2. Inverse the selection so that everything except the sky (the flowers in our example) is selected, choosing Select > Inverse from the menu.

3. Choose the Lasso tool. Hold the Alt/Option key for the Subtract From Selection option, and draw a loop around the area you want to exclude from the selection (in this example, flowers other than the principal ones you're concerned with).

4. Zoom in on the edge of the selection, and use the Add To Selection (hold the Shift key) and Subtract From Selection (hold the Alt/Option key) options to clean up the edge of the selection so that it matches the edge of the object you're trying to select.

Try It! To gain a better understanding of how you can combine various selection tools on an image, open the image CombineSelection on the accompanying CD, and perform the steps described in this section.

Saving and Loading Selections

After you've created a selection, particularly if it was time-consuming and/or challenging, you probably want to save it for future use, just in case. Once you save a selection and then save the image file in an appropriate format (such as Photoshop PSD or TIFF), the selection is then saved as part of the image file, so you can always reload the selection in the future if needed.

Note: Selections are saved as alpha channels. As you may know, RGB images are comprised of individual channels that describe the amount of red, green, and blue light that should be combined to produce the color value for each pixel. An *alpha channel* is a special channel in addition to these RGB channels, and it is generally used to store selections for an image.

To save a selection, choose Select > Save Selection from the menu, which opens the dialog shown in Figure 4.35.

Figure 4.35
The Save Selection dialog box allows you to specify a name (as well as other settings) for the selection you are saving.

Although you can save selections in different documents with the same dimensions, it's generally best to save your selections within the image for which you've created the selection. Therefore, leave the Document setting to the default value, which is the name of the current document.

The Channel drop-down list should be set to New so the selection is saved as it is. If an existing selection has been saved, you can also choose that selection from the Channel drop-down list and merge the current selection with the previously saved selection. We don't recommend this option, because it merges two separate selections together so they can't be used separately in the future.

The Name is the key setting (and generally the only one you need to change) in the Save Selection dialog box. Be sure to save the selection with a descriptive name that will make sense to you in the future when you need to load a selection, since you may be choosing a selection from a list of names when you load it.

If you're using the New option from the Channel drop-down list, the Operation section of the dialog box has only a single option to create a new channel. Otherwise, you'll have the same options as you have for each selection tool to create a new saved selection: Add To Channel, Subtract From Channel, or Intersect With Channel. When you click OK, the selection is saved as an alpha channel, which you can view on the Channels panel.

Note: Saved selections aren't truly saved until you save the image in which you stored them. If you save a selection but then close the image without saving it, the selection isn't saved.

In the future, you can "load" the selection—that is, select the same pixels once again—by choosing Select > Load Selection from the menu and choosing the name from the Channel drop-down list, as shown in Figure 4.36.

Figure 4.36
The Load Selection dialog box
allows you to recall previously
saved selections.

Note: Not all image file formats allow you to save selections, because they don't all allow you to save alpha channels, which is how a selection actually gets stored. If you're going to save a selection, it should be part of your master image file saved as a Photoshop PSD or TIFF image file.

The Brush Tool

As a nature photographer using a camera to produce artistic images, you may not think you'd need to utilize the Brush tool in Photoshop. After all, if you capture an image with a camera, you certainly don't need to draw an image from scratch. However, there are actually many situations where you'll use the Brush tool while optimizing your photos. For example, we use the Brush tool extensively with Safe Dodging and Burning layers and for painting on masks to identify areas where we want targeted adjustments to apply. (We'll cover both of these topics in later chapters.)

Note: The Quick Selection tool we just covered is actually a form of a brush tool, and the Clone Stamp and Healing Brush tools are advanced types of brush tools that allow you to clean up your images; we'll cover those in Chapter 5, "Workflows and First Steps."

The Brush tool allows you to paint pixels with great flexibility. This comes in handy for a number of different adjustments you can make by painting on a layer with special properties or for painting on a mask (which you'll learn about in later chapters) to change where adjustments will apply to your image, for example. By learning how to work with the Brush tool, you open up many opportunities for making more advanced adjustments and taking full control of your images.

To get started, create an empty document by choosing File ➢ New from the menu. The New dialog box appears. Choose 5×7 from the Preset drop-down list, make sure Color Mode is set to RGB, and click OK. Then select the Brush tool either by clicking the paintbrush icon on the Tools panel or by pressing the B key.

Figure 4.37
To practice with the Brush tool,
create a new document to serve
as your blank canvas.

Next, look at the color swatches on the Tools panel (see Figure 4.38). The large squares indicate the current foreground and background colors (represented by their relative positions). For painting, think of the foreground color as the color you'll actually be painting with and the background color as an alternative color you have quick access to when you need it. If you want to change either of the colors, simply click the corresponding box to open the Color Picker dialog box (shown in Figure 4.39). Click (or click and drag) the vertical color bar to define the basic color you want, click the large area to select a specific color to paint with, and then click OK.

Figure 4.38
The color picker area on the Tools panel shows you the current status of your foreground and background colors.

Figure 4.39
The Color Picker dialog box allows you to select a specific color value to use.

To set the colors back to the default values of black and white, just click the smaller thumbnail at the bottom-left corner of the color swatches on the Tools panel. You can also set these defaults by pressing D on your keyboard.

Since the foreground and background color options are mostly a way to have two colors readily available when working with the Brush tool, you often want to be able to switch back and forth between them. At the bottom-right corner of the color swatches is a double-headed curved arrow icon. Click this icon to switch the foreground and background colors, or perform the same action by pressing X.

The Options bar contains several settings that allow you to modify the behavior of the Brush tool (see Figure 4.40). Near the far left is a Brush drop-down list where you can select the type of brush you'd like to use. Click the drop-down list to see the available options, shown in Figure 4.41. The Master Diameter setting controls the size of the brush you're using in pixels. It's much more effective to adjust the size of the brush based on its relative size in your image, so we'll set the size in a moment. The Hardness setting determines whether your brush will have a hard edge or a soft and "fuzzy" edge, or somewhere in between. We'll discuss specific settings for various situations in later chapters, but for now, experiment with different settings to get a sense of how this setting affects the brush.

Figure 4.40 The Options bar for the Brush tool contains several settings that allow you to adjust the behavior of this tool.

Figure 4.41
The Brush drop-down list
contains several settings for
adjusting the type of brush
you'll use to paint.

At the bottom of the Brush drop-down list is a scrollable list containing a variety of brush shapes. The first group contains hard-edged brushes of various sizes, and the second group contains soft-edged brushes of various sizes. Below that are a variety of brushes with more artistic shapes, which you can use in a variety of applications.

Note: You can also access the options from the Brush drop-down list by right-clicking/Ctrl+clicking the image when the Brush tool is active or by clicking the Brushes panel icon in the Dock .

Once you've set the basic properties of the brush, adjust the remaining settings on the Options bar. The Mode drop-down list allows you to adjust the blending mode for the brush, which affects how the "paint" you are drawing with interacts with the underlying image. We recommend leaving this set to Normal. We'll tell you under what circumstances you might need to change blending modes in later chapters.

The Opacity setting controls how opaque or transparent the paint you're drawing with appears. At full opacity, the paint completely covers the underlying pixels, effectively replacing them. At a reduced opacity, the underlying pixels show through. (Figure 4.42 illustrates both of these situations.) We'll use the Opacity setting to vary the strength of the painting in several adjustments we'll discuss in later chapters, but for now, play with various settings to get a sense of how they affect the behavior of the Brush tool.

Figure 4.42 The Opacity setting allows you to determine whether your paint strokes completely cover up the pixels below them or allow them to partially show through.

The Flow setting and Airbrush option control the variability of the Brush tool, causing it to behave like an airbrush or can of spray paint, where the longer you hover over an area, the more the paint spreads out. Because this creates a somewhat unpredictable response from the Brush tool, we recommend leaving the Airbrush option off, which means the Flow setting is ignored.

You're just about ready to take the Brush tool for a test-drive, but you still want to adjust the size of the brush. So, place the cursor on the new document you created, and evaluate the size of the brush. Then, press the left and right square bracket keys ([and]) to reduce or enlarge the size of the brush, respectively.

 Note: To draw a horizontal or perpendicular straight line, hold down the Shift key, and then click and drag the cursor.

 Note: The Caps Lock key toggles the mouse pointer display between Precise and the brush size settings. If you're not able to see the circle that defines the shape of your brush, check the status of Caps Lock.

Brush Panel

The Brush panel is located on the right side of the monitor in the Dock. Clicking the icon opens the Brush Panel dialog box. You can select preset brushes and set the same parameters you set in the Brush Preset Picker on the Options bar, but in addition you can modify brush tip options. Most of these options are more useful to graphic artists than to nature photographers, but if you use a graphics tablet such as a Wacom, you'll need to use this dialog box to set the brush so that the opacity of your stroke varies with pen pressure. This will be useful when painting on layer masks. (We'll be doing that extensively in later chapters.)

To vary the opacity of your brush stroke according to the pressure applied with your stylus, follow these steps:

1. Attach the graphics tablet, and install any necessary software.

2. Select the Brush tool.

3. Click the Brushes panel, or go to Window > Brushes

4. Select Other Dynamics. Then choose Pen Pressure from the Controls menu under the OpacityJitter slider control, as shown in Figure 4.43.

 Try It! Now comes the fun part. You have an empty canvas before you, and you know how to adjust the behavior of the Brush tool. So, start painting away! Get comfortable working with the Brush tool, using the mouse (or a stylus) to paint strokes on the canvas. Be sure to adjust all the various settings for the Brush tool, including the color, Hardness, Opacity, and the size of the brush, so you get comfortable adjusting those various parameters. You can then use the Brush tool with confidence in the wide variety of situations we'll describe in later chapters.

Figure 4.43
Setting Pen Pressure to control opacity is extremely useful when painting on a layer mask using a graphics tablet.

The Color Replacement Tool

The Color Replacement tool is a specialized Brush tool, with properties that allow you to alter the color of specific areas within your image. It actually produces similar behavior in most cases to what you could achieve with the Brush tool in conjunction with specific settings, but it provides extended capability above and beyond what the Brush is capable of doing. The Color Replacement tool is useful for fixing small areas of color problems within an image, where you need to change the color without changing the tonality or texture of the area.

For this type of use, we typically work with the Color Replacement tool with the following options set:

Mode set to Color, so we're changing the color in the image.

Sampling set to Continuous (the first of the three option buttons), which causes the tool to change color anywhere we paint, not just based on an initial sampling point, for example. Occasionally we use the second button, Sampling, once to replace just a certain color.

Limits set to Contiguous, to adjust only those colors that are contiguous to those we paint over.

Tolerance at 100%, so all areas we paint on are adjusted.

When you paint with the Color Replacement tool with the settings recommended here, it changes the color of the pixels under the brush, preserving tonality and texture. For example, if you have some color contamination on a flower because a flower of a different color was very close to the lens and resulted in a wash of color that is completely out of focus, you could use this tool to paint an appropriate color to fix the flower.

Painting with a neutral color (such as black) changes the color to a shade of gray.

If you want to paint a color correction, you naturally need to find an appropriate color to paint with using the Color Replacement tool. To do so, simply hold the Alt/Option key, and click an appropriate color within the image to make that color the foreground color. You can then paint with that color in appropriate areas of the image using the Color Replacement tool to change the color as needed.

Try It! To practice using the Color Brush tool, open the image ColorReplacement on the accompanying CD, select the Color Replacement tool, set the foreground color to a muted orange, and paint on the red flower on the left to change its color. Be careful to paint only the red flower, zooming in and using a small brush as needed when painting near the foreground flower.

The History Brush

The History Brush tool is unique—it allows you to selectively paint certain areas of your image to take them "back in time," reflecting what they looked like before certain tasks were performed. This allows you to perform actions on the entire image and then undo those actions in specific areas as desired.

Note: Neither of us uses the History Brush often, preferring to use various layers and masks to produce the same results. However, some users favor the History Brush, so we present it here as an option. Ellen finds the History Brush helpful when using the Extract filter.

As its name implies, the History Brush is a brush tool, allowing you to paint on the image. The difference is that instead of painting pixels, you're painting an area to change it back to the way it looked at an earlier time. Let's take a look at an example to help you understand this concept.

Start by opening an image and applying an artistic filter to that image. For example, you might select Filter > Distort > Glass, adjust the settings for this filter, and click OK. Then select the History Brush from the Tools panel ⟨⟨⟨ icon ⟩⟩⟩. (You can also access it by pressing Y on your keyboard.)

By default, when you paint with the History Brush, it changes the areas you paint on to what they looked like when you first opened the image. However, you can change the *source* for the History Brush to any history state on the History panel. To do so, click the box to the left of the name of the history state (which defines the action performed at that step) on the History panel. This places a small History Brush icon in that box, as shown in Figure 4.44, so you know it is the source for this tool.

Figure 4.44
On the History panel, click the box to the left of the state you want to paint back to, defining the source for the History Brush tool.

For example, in your new, blank practice document, you've only opened an image and applied the Glass filter to it, so you don't have too many options. However, you can set the source to the Open step (the last step done before the application of the Glass filter) to specifically select that history state as the definition of how you want to change the pixels or what steps you want undone for them as you paint.

With the source set, you're ready to paint. Note that you have the same options on the Options bar for the History Brush as you do for the regular Brush tool. In most cases, you want to use a soft-edged brush of an appropriate size, the Normal blend mode, and a 100% opacity. Wherever you paint, the effect of the Glass filter in this example is removed, returning those areas of the image to their original appearance, as shown in Figure 4.45. However, at times you might want to paint at a reduced Opacity setting, for example when you want to "tone down" an adjustment in certain areas of the image rather than eliminating the effect altogether.

Figure 4.45
With the History Brush, you can selectively paint areas back to the way they looked before making a particular adjustment. (Photo by Tim Grey.)

Think of the History Brush tool as a "selective undo" tool. Anytime you've changed pixel values in an image and want to tone down or eliminate the effect in certain areas, this tool allows you to do exactly that with very good control. However, if you have made certain types of changes to your image such as cropping it or changing the bit depth, you'll need to change the source to a state that reflects the same conditions, rather than the initial image. Otherwise, the tool refuses to work.

Building Tool Knowledge

In this chapter, we explained how to use a handful of the tools you're most likely to use in Photoshop, providing you with an introduction to the use of these tools. Because so many of the tools in Photoshop behave similarly in a general sense, you can apply your knowledge of one tool to using another. Of course, in later chapters we'll describe additional tools and techniques for optimizing your images.

Workflows and First Steps

5

Now that you have Adobe Photoshop set up the way you want it and you've used Adobe Camera Raw (ACR) to make the most of your global tonal and color changes, usually you have at least a little more work to do. If you get in the habit of following a routine approach when optimizing your images, you'll find you're working more efficiently. We'll suggest two versions of an overall workflow that you can modify to suit your particular needs. One version is more flexible and takes advantage of Smart Objects and Smart Filters, while the other is more traditional.

Chapter Contents
Flexible and Traditional Workflows
Initial Cropping and Straightening in Photoshop
Understanding Layers
Doing Cleanup in Photoshop

Flexible and Traditional Workflows

Digital workflows are works in progress that evolve as technology and software change. With each new version of Photoshop, new features affect our workflow. For example, our workflow habits changed when adjustment layers became part of Photoshop (yes, there was a time when Photoshop had no adjustment layers), they changed when it became easy to use adjustment layers on 16-bit files, and they changed yet again when converting raw files became easy, just to mention a few of the features that caused us to modify our workflow.

With the arrival of CS3, our workflow has evolved again; this time we have established a *flexible workflow* as our recommended workflow when optimizing an image for future use, particularly printing. The flexible workflow takes advantage of Smart Objects and Smart Filters to maintain the most editability while simultaneously maintaining the most nondestructive workflow possible. Ultimately this leads to the highest quality files possible.

However, there are times you may have a specific output in mind and/or need to make fewer changes and prefer to follow a more traditional workflow. We'll describe both our flexible and traditional workflows in detail so you can choose what's right for you. You'll see that both these workflows are actually quite similar. But first we'll explain Smart Objects and Smart Filters so you can better understand their roles in changing our workflows.

 Note: If you are using an earlier version of Photoshop, then you'll need to follow our traditional workflow.

Smart Objects

Smart Objects were introduced in CS2, but they were of limited use for nature photographers, so we didn't readily incorporate them into our workflow. With the addition of Smart Filters and a vastly more robust ACR in CS3, it's time to make use of Smart Objects.

Smart Objects are actually containers that you create within a file that can store (among other things) your original image file, including a raw file. By using a Smart Object, you embed your original raw file inside the master file you create while doing your image optimization.

The Smart Object raw file will then retain all its original characteristics and be fully editable. In other words, you can modify the settings used in ACR for your image at any time, even while in the midst of working on the file in Photoshop, and those changes will appear in the current file.

If you don't use a Smart Object, then once you choose your settings in ACR, those settings are fixed into place when you open the file in Photoshop. If you later decide that you wished you had used different settings in the conversion, you would have to start all over again in ACR and then in Photoshop. But if you had begun with the raw file opened as a Smart Object, double-clicking the background layer of your file would open the ACR dialog box so that you could modify the settings.

Note: A Smart Object can contain either raster or vector data from other Photoshop files or even files from other programs such as Adobe Illustrator. You can also create a Smart Object from one or more layers of an image by selecting those layers and choosing Layer > Convert to Smart Object. You won't be able to access ACR by double-clicking those layers because in this case the Smart Object is referencing whatever was on those layers of your file rather than the raw file itself.

You can edit a Smart Object over and over again with no loss of image quality because the Smart Object always refers back to the original image data. This means that in addition to being able to repeatedly modify color and exposure settings in ACR, Smart Objects enable you to crop nondestructively! If you set a crop in ACR and later decide it was too severe, it's no problem at all if you're using a Smart Object. You simply double-click it, access ACR, and modify the crop.

Smart Objects also make it possible to repeatedly resize the image within Photoshop, making it larger or smaller *with no loss of quality.* Clearly opening your raw file as a Smart Object lends a tremendous amount of flexibility to your image optimization workflow.

To open a raw file (or any other file format) as a Smart Object from ACR, check the Open in Photoshop as Smart Objects option in Workflow Options, and then choose Open Object (or in Photoshop choose File > Open as Smart Object). See Chapter 3, "Adobe Camera Raw." When the file opens, you'll see that the background layer is marked as a Smart Object, as shown in Figure 5.1.

Figure 5.1
Smart Object layers are marked as such in the Layers panel.

Smart Filters

Smart Filters are a long awaited and frequently requested feature that is new in CS3. Smart Filters are *editable* filters.

In the past you applied a filter to a pixel layer, and once you clicked OK in the filter dialog box, you had no way to modify the settings. The only exception was the Edit > Fade command, available only immediately after applying the filter, that could reduce the strength of the effect or apply it using a different blending mode. You had no way to access the filter dialog box and modify your settings. Smart Filters change that—with them your filter settings are forever editable similar to adjustment layers.

The only "catch" to using Smart Filters is that they can be used only on a Smart Object layer. However, it's easy to change any pixel layer into a Smart Object by choosing Filter > Convert for Smart Filters. Photoshop will automatically change the layer so that it can receive a Smart Filter.

Any filter that can be applied as a regular filter can be applied as a Smart Filter, and a bonus is that the Shadow/Highlight adjustment can also be applied as a Smart Filter. Once you change the active layer to a Smart Object, when you select a filter, it will automatically be applied as a Smart Filter. (Pretty smart, yes?)

Note: Photographers have wanted to be able to apply a Shadow/Highlight adjustment as an adjustment layer rather than directly on a pixel layer since the arrival of the Shadow/Highlight adjustment feature. Because of behind-the-scenes technical issues, it could not readily be made available as an adjustment layer. Instead, the Adobe engineers made it possible to apply the Shadow/Highlight adjustment as a Smart Filter.

An Example of Smart Filters in Action

Let's take a look at Smart Filters in action. You can follow along with the image Smart-Filter on the accompanying CD.

1. Begin by opening the image SmartFilter. We'll pretend that for whatever reason we did not initially open the file as a Smart Object. (If you did open the image as a Smart Object, skip step 2.)

2. Choose Filter > Convert to Smart Filters. A warning dialog will appear (Figure 5.2). We recommend checking the option to not have this warning reappear.

Figure 5.2
The Smart Filter warning

3. Choose Image > Adjustments > Shadow/ Highlight, and adjust the settings as desired. Click OK.

Note: For more details about using the Shadow/Highlight feature, see Chapter 6, "Exposure Adjustments."

4. Notice that the adjustment appears as a Smart Filter on the background layer (Figure 5.3).

Figure 5.3
A Smart Filter in the Layers panel

- There's a layer mask you can use to control which parts of the image are affected by the filters. We'll cover using layer masks in detail in Chapter 6 and Chapter 7.

- The Smart Filter icon leads to a new dialog box, as shown in Figure 5.4, in which you can specify the opacity of the effect as well as a different blending mode. We'll talk more about these features in Chapter 9.

Figure 5.4

The Smart Filter Options dialog box lets you choose different blending modes and opacities for each filter.

- To modify the settings you used in the Shadow/Highlight dialog box, double-click directly on the words Shadow/Highlight in the Smart Filter layer, and make the desired changes.

5. If you want to add an additional filter, open the Filters menu, and choose the desired filter. It will appear beneath the other Smart Filters in the Layers panel, as shown in Figure 5.5.

Figure 5.5

You can add additional-filters, and they appear on the same layer.

6. Unfortunately, all Smart Filters are governed by the same layer mask in CS3, so if you need to apply two or more filters to different areas—for example, if you wanted to apply noise reduction to part of the image—you are forced to use a workaround.

- Begin the workaround by copying the initial Smart Object layer. To do so, drag the original Smart Object layer to the Create New Layer icon in the Layers panel ![]. A copy of the layer is created complete with any Smart Filters you used.
- Choose Layer > Smart Objects > Rasterize to change the copy layer into a regular layer containing the effects of the previous Smart Object layer.
- Choose Layer > New Smart Object to turn this composite layer into a Smart Object so that you can apply an additional Smart Filter, and use the associated layer mask to apply the effect to a different part of the image.

As you can see, using Smart Objects and Smart Filters creates the potential for unparalleled flexibility in your workflow with editability combined with no loss of image quality. Therefore, we recommend the following to you as the backbone of your flexible workflow. Ultimately, you should modify our workflow to suit your specific needs.

The Flexible Workflow

Your image optimization workflow actually begins when you initially choose an image in Bridge for further work. We find that by following a similar series of steps, we work more efficiently. The order of the steps remains the same, although depending on the needs of each individual image, we may omit one or more step. The flexible workflow is of particular benefit when working with raw files, although it can be used with JPEGs or TIFFs as well. Figure 5.6 lays out this particular plan of work.

Figure 5.6
Following the flexible workflow, and customizing it according to the needs of individual pictures, will enable you to use a single file as both the master file and the output file.

Note: To take advantage of the flexible workflow, we open raw files as well as JPEGs and TIFFs in the ACR converter, as explained in Chapter 3, "Adobe Camera Raw." If you're using a version of Photoshop prior to CS3, then you can open only raw files in ACR; JPEGs and TIFFs will open directly in Photoshop. In that case, you'll need to follow our traditional workflow and make all your modifications in Photoshop.

To begin, double-click the image, and take a good hard look at it in ACR. Think about what you like about the image and those aspects you want to emphasize, and decide what elements you need to modify. It's important to have an overall game plan in your head when optimizing images to keep you on track. Otherwise, it's easy not to know what to do next and even not to know when you're done! It sounds silly until it happens to you—suddenly you realize you've been working on an image for a long time and can't decide whether you're done. Having a game plan in mind makes it easier to know where you're going and when you've arrived! So, the first step is to look at the image and the histogram and decide what you want to do.

The next step is to use ACR to make most of the global tonal and color adjustments, in addition to cropping, straightening, and cleaning up as much dust as possible. (See Chapter 3 for details.) It's important to do as much work as possible in the raw converter so that you're starting with the best image possible. Remember that with raw files almost all the settings we specify in ACR are actually changes to the algorithms used to convert the information captured by the photo sites on the sensors into a visible image, rather than changes to the pixels. Although we work as non-destructively as possible in Photoshop, ultimately all the changes we make in Photoshop modify the pixels. The greater the changes we make there, the greater the potential for some image degradation. Changes made in the raw converter do not generally result in image degradation—except when clipping is introduced or areas are cropped out. However, the changes made in ACR to JPEGs and TIFFs are changes to the actual pixels—which is why we recommend shooting in RAW for most nature photographers.

When you finish in ACR, open the image as a Smart Object. At this point, your image may be done except for sizing, sharpening, and/or noise reduction, or you may need to work on it further. We consider making the following adjustments in this order. Keep in mind that on most of your images you won't need to do all these steps.

1. If you think your image could benefit from a Shadow/Highlight adjustment because it allows finer control than the similar Fill and Recovery tools in ACR, or because you want to apply it to only a certain part of your image, begin by making a Shadow/Highlight Smart Filter. (We'll go into detail about this in Chapter 6.) Most images will not need this step.

2. If you need to straighten and crop your image in a way that will result in needing to clone in some additional background, do that next. (Otherwise, crop in ACR.) We'll talk more about this later in this chapter. Note that the cropping that you do here is not reversible, unlike the cropping done in ACR, and some people prefer to do this as a last step in their workflow.

3. If you need to do any further cloning/healing, it should be the next step. That way changes to additional adjustment layers will change the work you do on this layer as well.

4. If you want to make tonal adjustments to a particular part of your image, follow the procedures described in Chapter 6 for making targeted tonal adjustments using layer masks.

5. If you want to make further color adjustments such as a Selective color adjustment or a Color Balance adjustment taking advantage of the controls in Photoshop, or to adjust the color in a particular part of your image, follow the procedures described in Chapter 7.

6. If you want to apply some creative filters, do that next.

7. Finally, follow the recommendations for output workflow that we cover in Chapter 10, "Output," for resizing and sharpening your images.

Note that by using a Smart Object as your background layer you can do your resizing and sharpening on your master image. However, many people will feel more comfortable saving their master images without resizing and sharpening and instead creating a duplicate copy, the way we recommend in our traditional workflow. The choice is yours.

No matter what workflow you follow, make it a habit to save and save often! When you first open your image after using ACR, you will need to save your image. You can opt to use PSD or TIFF formats. PSDs tend to be slightly larger, but both formats can retain the integrity of your layers. As a matter of habit, we tend to use the PSD format for layered files and TIFFs for flattened files, but you could just as easily do the opposite. By using one format for layered files and one for flattened files, it's easy to recognize which file is which. The important point is to save the image after every step that has been at all time-consuming. You never know when a computer is going to decide to crash...and in our experience, it's usually when you have been struggling and working for a long period of time and haven't saved what you're working on!

The Traditional Workflow

There are times when even those who use the flexible workflow will choose to use the traditional workflow. If you have images that you converted using another program, you may want to use the traditional workflow—illustrated in Figure 5.7—particularly if you have only a few adjustments to make.

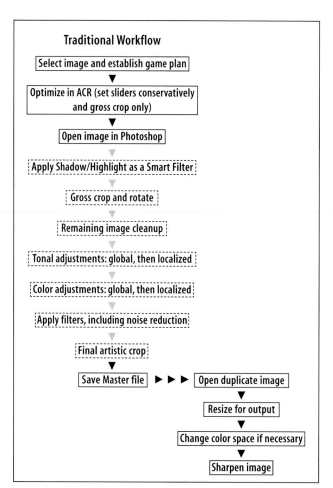

Traditional Workflow

Select image and establish game plan
▼
Optimize in ACR (set sliders conservatively and gross crop only)
▼
Open image in Photoshop
▼
Apply Shadow/Highlight as a Smart Filter
▼
Gross crop and rotate
▼
Remaining image cleanup
▼
Tonal adjustments: global, then localized
▼
Color adjustments: global, then localized
▼
Apply filters, including noise reduction
▼
Final artistic crop
▼
Save Master file ► ► ► Open duplicate image
▼
Resize for output
▼
Change color space if necessary
▼
Sharpen image

Figure 5.7

Following the traditional workflow, and customizing it according to the needs of individual pictures, will enable you to efficiently optimize your images..

In addition, anytime you begin by creating a composite—whether it's a panorama, creative, or to extend exposure latitude, and so on—you will not have a raw file as the basis of your master file. Technically you could opt to create the composite, save it, and then open it in ACR and use the flexible workflow. The advantage would be using the ACR interface; however, many people will find it just as easy to use the traditional workflow.

Numerous combinations of these two workflows are possible, and ultimately you should follow a predictable pattern, either by following our steps exactly or by borrowing from each of the workflows to create a workflow that works for you.

Just as with the flexible workflow, the workflow begins by looking at the image carefully and developing a strategy. Focus on how you'll maximize the strengths of the image and remove or minimize any of its shortcomings—that's what optimizing is all about! We'll assume that this file is not a raw file and that you have opted not to use ACR to make the global adjustments, but instead have just opened it in Photoshop.

Once you have in mind the changes you want to make, we approach the adjustments in the following order:

1. If you are using a file that does not have a raw file original associated with it—for instance, if you captured in JPEG or if you created a composite file such as a panorama—begin by creating a duplicate of the image file. To do so, choose Image > Duplicate. That way you will optimize the copy and preserve the integrity of the original file just in case you need to refer to it in the future.

2. Begin with any initial cropping and straightening that may be needed. Because cropping in Photoshop is not reversible, this is not a final artistic tight crop but rather a rough, loose crop to eliminate areas that there's absolutely no chance of wanting in the final image. At the same time it's a good idea to straighten the image if the horizon is crooked. We'll describe how to do this using the Crop tool or the Measure tool later in this chapter. There's no sense in taking the time to correct pixels that you aren't going to be used.

3. The next step is to remove any dust spots by using the cloning and healing tools. We'll talk more about how to do this later in this chapter. This is also a good time to remove any objects you don't want from the picture.

4. At this point you have the basic image but need to make whatever adjustments are necessary to the exposure. This may involve using the Shadow/Highlight tool if there are blocked-up shadows or extremely light (but not completely blown-out) areas or using Levels and possibly Curves adjustment layers to bring out the details in our image. We'll explain how to do this in detail in Chapter 6.

5. After we're satisfied with the exposure, it's time to work on the color within the picture. Most images benefit from a slight boost in the saturation of the color, and sometimes we need to modify the hue or color casts within the image. We'll be using adjustment layers for this, of course, and we'll talk about how to do it in detail in Chapter 7. (Using adjustment layers will become second nature to you, and we'll talk more about them and why they're so important later in this chapter.)

6. If you want to apply any creative filters, do so at this point.

7. With most images in the traditional workflow, you've now created the master file—the optimized version that you save without resizing it and without sharpening it.

Note: Save the master file as a TIFF or a PSD file, since both allow you to save the file with the layers intact. It's not uncommon to return to an image that was previously optimized and realize that perhaps you prefer the color to be slightly different or you want more or less contrast in a particular part of the image, and so on. If the adjustment layers are there, these minor modifications are quick and easy. If you have to make them on a flattened file, then you're risking some slight image degradation by changing and therefore damaging the pixels again. In reality, such damage is likely to be slight, but since you're after the best finished product you can make, you want to save with your layers intact.

The reason to save your file without sharpening it in the traditional workflow is because sharpening must be done according to the final output size. When you resize the image—interpolating to either increase or decrease its size—you need different sharpening values. You want your master file to be at the native resolution without any interpolation since interpolation also inherently slightly degrades the image quality. We'll talk more about resizing and sharpening in Chapter 10.

Following this same basic series of steps with each image allows you to work efficiently and without needless repetitive steps that might in reality conflict with one another. Of course, there are times some of the steps in the traditional workflow aren't necessary, and those steps are omitted. You'll have to decide what your image needs are and how much you want to fine-tune the exposure and color within your image.

Initial Cropping and Straightening in Photoshop

The goal of all the adjustments in ACR is to create the best possible file from the data collected on the camera sensor when you took the picture. Although by now the image may look pretty good, there are some things you can't do within ACR such as applying filters, creating composites, resizing specific items, and sharpening. And it's possible you'll want to tweak some of the exposure or color settings in parts of the image. We perform these tasks in a routine order to continue optimizing the file to make the best final image possible. We'll go through how to do the various modifications in Photoshop in detail beginning here and continuing on through the next few chapters.

Let's begin by assuming you're using the traditional workflow and that you have opted not to use ACR with a JPEG, a slide from a scan, or a composite. We're going to go through our routine traditional workflow in detail. Of course, if you've used the flexible workflow, you could opt to use any of these steps as well.

Initial Cropping

If there is some portion of your image that you're absolutely positive you would never want to be included in your final image, it's a good idea to crop it out at the beginning of your workflow. This includes cropping those black edges that often appear when scanning slides. Those black edges can throw off the histograms as well as the Levels and Curves adjustments you'll be making. We recommend that you don't do a final tight artistic crop at this point because it's quite possible that by the time you're done optimizing the image, you may change your mind and want a tad bit less cropped out. If you did a tight crop at the beginning, this means you would have to start all over again.

To crop an image, take the following steps:

1. Select the Crop tool ⊞ by clicking it.

2. To crop your image to a particular aspect ratio—for example, 8×10—you can set these values in the Options bar at the top of your screen, as shown in Figure 5.8, and then click and drag within the image. To clear these settings, click the Clear button.

Figure 5.8 You can enter specific dimensions to crop your image to any desired size.

Note: To mark out a crop manually—without constraints on height, width, or resolution—place your cursor in any corner of the image approximately where you want to begin the crop, click, and drag diagonally, releasing the cursor after you are close to where you want the crop to end. The area to be cropped out darkens so you can preview how the image will look.

The Options bar changes, adding a Shield check box, which controls how, and whether, the area to be cropped away is darkened. Select the color and opacity of the shield by clicking the color swatch. We recommend leaving the Shield box checked and the color set to black at 75% opacity. This way you get an effective preview of your crop for most images. If the outer edges of your image are quite dark, you may want to use a different color for the Shield. We leave the Delete box checked rather than Hide.

Note: Although it's not often needed in nature photography, if you check the Perspective box, you can transform the crop by pulling out the corners as desired. You can use this feature to straighten buildings that appear to be tipping away.

3. Fine-tune the crop boundary. You can change the size and proportion of the crop (if you're using a freehand crop rather than a specific aspect ratio) by dragging the handles at the sides and corners of the boundary. To reposition the crop within your image, place your cursor within the remaining image area, click, and drag. If you entered both Height and Width values before you started, you can change the size of the crop area but not its proportion.

4. Once the crop boundary is where you want it to be, to make Photoshop perform the crop do one of the following: press Enter/Return, double-click within the image area, or click the check mark on the Options bar.

Note: To crop an image to match the dimensions of another image, open both images. Click the one that has the correct dimensions, click Front Image, and then click the other image. Notice that the dimensions of the first image are specified in the Height, Width, and Resolution boxes. You can now readily crop your second image to match the size of the first.

Straightening Horizons

This is an easy way to straighten a horizon while using the Crop tool:

1. Begin by using the tool to draw a crop on the image. Don't worry about placing it precisely yet.

2. Click the small square box in the middle of the horizontal line closest to the horizon, and drag it so that it is just on top of the horizon.

3. Now place your cursor outside the crop area. Notice it changes from an arrow-head to a double-arrowed icon. Click and drag it up or down to rotate the crop, and make the horizontal line follow your horizon, as shown in Figure 5.9. When you are satisfied that the crop line parallels the horizon line, release the cursor..

Figure 5.9
Drag one edge of the crop close to the horizon, and then rotate it until it parallels the horizon line. (Photo by Ellen Anon.)

4. Now click the center box on that crop line to drag it back to an appropriate place in your image. The rotation of the crop should remain as you reset all the outside edges, as you can see in Figure 5.10.

Figure 5.10
Carefully drag the edges of the crop where you want them while leaving the rotation alone. (Photo by Ellen Anon.)

5. Be careful not to drag the corners of the crop beyond your image, or you'll have empty areas in the cropped version that you'll need to create background for or recrop. However, in some instances, it might actually be better to go too far than not far enough.

Now when you click Enter/Return or double-click the image to perform the crop, it rotates the image as well as straightens it in one step, as illustrated in Figure 5.11. That's pretty cool and very convenient!

Figure 5.11 Cropping and rotating the image in one step is easy and saves time. (Photo by Ellen Anon.)

Note: An alternative method for straightening an image, one that is particularly effective with reflections, is to use the Measure tool, located with the eyedropper tools. Click the subject's eyes or other identifiable point and then drag to the same point in the reflection. Choose Image > Rotate Canvas > Arbitrary. A dialog box will appear that has the precise angle and direction needed to rotate the canvas. Click OK, and the image will be straightened. You'll need to crop the image after straightening it.

Try It! Open the image called Straighten on the accompanying CD, or one of your own, and use the Crop tool to straighten the horizon.

Understanding Layers

Before proceeding any further with the workflow, you have to understand layers—what they are, why they're so important, and how to make them. Most Photoshop novices are initially intimidated by the concept of layers. But in reality, they're quite simple and easy to understand.

Let's begin by thinking of a couple of prints that are the same size. If you took one print and placed it on top of the other print, you would no longer be able to see the print that's on the bottom. You know it's there, and you know if you remove the top print or make a hole in the top print that you would see the print that's underneath. But when one print is simply on top of the other, you see only the top print. Those prints are actually two layers. Agreed? In Photoshop each of these prints is called a *pixel layer*.

Pixel layers contain pixels, which are the building blocks of your image. Pixel layers work much the same way as stacking prints on top of one another. Whatever pixel layer is on top is what you see.

Note: Right now we are discussing how pixel layers behave in the Normal blending mode. Later in this book we'll discuss some more advanced behaviors of layers using different blending modes. For now, we'll keep it simple.

But wait, there are actually two types of layers: layers that have pixels and adjustment layers, which don't have any pixels at all! *Adjustment layers are simply instructions for changing the appearance of the pixel layers.* For example, they may contain instructions to make the pixels lighter or darker; more or less contrasty; more or less saturated; or bluer, redder, and so on. In other words, adjustment layers modify the appearance of your image but not the content. It would be similar to putting a filter over your top print in our analogy and viewing the print through the filter. Your print would look warmer if it was a slightly yellow filter, bluer if it was a blue filter, and so on. The filter would change the appearance of your print but not the content.

Note: Adjustment layers modify the appearance of every pixel layer below them.

You could perform all the modifications you make in adjustment layers directly on your pixels by choosing Image > Adjustments and selecting the type of adjustment you want to make. *But that's exactly what we want you to avoid doing!* Every time you work directly on a pixel, you damage it and you risk losing some quality in your final output. By using *adjustment layers*, you can see the changes you have made, but they are not applied to the pixels until you either print the file or flatten it. This way you can make multiple changes and affect the pixels only once.

Even better is the flexibility that working in layers gives you. You can return to your image at any time in the future, even after closing it, as long as you have saved the image file with the layers intact, and you'll be able to modify the adjustments you made. You can increase them, decrease them, eliminate them, and so on—all without damaging your pixels.

And the best part is that it's so easy to actually select the adjustment layers. You simply click the New Adjustment Layer icon ⊘ at the bottom of the Layers panel, as shown in Figure 5.12, and choose from the menu. Almost all the adjustments that are available from the Images > Adjustments in the menu bar are available from this list. By selecting them here, the adjustment is automatically performed as an adjustment layer.

We have a couple more thoughts for you about layers. If you place a pixel layer on top of one or more adjustment layers, the adjustment layers don't have any effect on that pixel layer because the adjustment layers are below it rather than above it. It's like taking another print and putting it on top of the stack—you're going to see what's on top, and what's underneath is not going to affect it.

Figure 5.12

To make an adjustment layer, click this icon, and choose the type of adjustment you want.

Now imagine you have a print with a great sunset, and you have another print with a silhouette of a group of birds flying by. If you took the print with the silhouette of the birds flying and placed it on top of the sunset picture, you'd see only the silhouette picture. But you could cut the birds out of that print and lay them on top of the print below. Now you'd see the sunset with the silhouetted birds flying through it. In Photoshop this is akin to having a pixel layer that is partially transparent (the part that you removed from the print is the transparent part) and partially filled with pixels (the silhouetted birds) resting on top of the original pixel layer—the sunset. The sunset is the background layer, and the layer with the birds is only partially filled with pixels. In other words, pixel layers can be partially transparent and partially filled with pixels.

This is enough theory for now about layers, but we'll be talking more about them later in this book. Take the time to reread this section again slowly if you're feeling a little shaky about layers.

Doing Cleanup in Photoshop

Digital cameras seem to include a dust magnet on the sensors (not really, but it seems so!). Therefore, you have to carefully go through your images and remove these blobs. Scanned images also often have dust and/or scratches on them that you need to remove. First you'll learn about the three tools in Photoshop that you can use, and then you'll go through the actual steps to use on an image.

> **Note:** Even if you used ACR, you may prefer to do your cleanup in Photoshop if there are complicated areas that need cleaning up.

The Photoshop Cleanup Tools

The Clone Stamp tool, the Healing Brush tool, the Spot Healing Brush tool, and the Patch tool are all useful in removing dust spots, removing unwanted objects from your image, and even filling in areas when you need to enlarge your canvas. They're very similar tools, but they're also different in some important ways.

When using any of these tools, we always begin by creating a new layer for the cleanup. To do so, click the Create New Layer icon ▣ at the bottom of the Layers panel next to the trash can. This creates an empty pixel layer on which you will place new pixels to hide the imperfections in your image. By doing the cleanup on a separate layer, you don't have to worry about permanently changing any pixels in the file. In addition, you can't use these tools on a Smart Object layer.

The Clone Stamp tool 🔖 may be the easiest to understand. It simply copies the pixels that you specify from one place to another place using the following steps:

1. Place the cursor over the area from which you want to sample.

2. Hold down the Alt/Option key, and click.

3. Then release the Alt/Option key, and position the cursor over the area that you want to replace and click. It's that simple!

If you just keep clicking to sample an area and then clicking to put it somewhere else, you're likely to end up with a series of circular replacements that are easy to spot. On the other hand, if you click and drag for long distances, you're likely to get repeated patterns that are also a telltale sign of a poorly optimized image. The trick is to just drag a little around the replacement area and make certain not to have an identifiable repeated pattern.

Most of the time you should make sure to use a soft brush and adjust the size of the brush, using the bracket shortcut keys as explained in Chapter 4 so that the brush is just slightly larger than the smaller dimension of the dust you're trying to remove. If you are cloning out a large area, then you'll have to use a small enough brush to be able to convincingly re-create the background. You'll become an artist at borrowing pixels to re-create that area of the picture.

It's important to remember to have Sample All layers checked in the Options bar at the top of your screen. If it seems like nothing is happening, it's probably because this isn't checked. Also make sure the Adjustment Layers Icon ▨ in the Options bar is turned on so that adjustment layers are ignored when cloning. That way if you return to the cleanup layer after you've made some further adjustments, you won't have to manually turn off the adjustment layers as you did with versions of Photoshop prior to CS3. (Otherwise, if you clone on a lower layer after you've added adjustment layers, the adjustments are applied twice to the cloned pixels, which means they don't match the image.)

Most of the time you also want Aligned checked. This means that the source you are sampling from moves in keeping with the movement of the cursor at the destination. Otherwise, every time you unclick and then click to continue cloning, the source resets to where you initially began sampling. Therefore, you'll be creating repeated patterns.

CS3 added a Clone panel (Figure 5.13) in which you can specify several different sources for your cloning. The sources can be located in the same image or in different images. To create a source preset, click one of the Clone Source icons, then hold the Alt/Option key, and click the desired point in the image; a target with a number will mark that spot. This is helpful so you can easily identify which clone source to use. Although we don't often find this too useful with nature photography images, it's possible that you may encounter certain situations where using multiple source presets would be very helpful. For example, if you removed an object or added canvas and need to create a new area of background, it might be helpful to have several different source points preselected.

Figure 5.13
The Clone panel adds features to the Clone Stamp tool including presets and the Show Overlay option.

However, we do find that the Show Overlay option can be helpful. By checking this option, an overlay of the source you're using appears superimposed on your image. That makes it easier to know how far to drag when cloning. Ellen finds this particularly helpful to reposition an object within an image, as shown in Figure 5.14. However, sometimes seeing the overlay follow your cursor is annoying. This is an option to use when it's helpful and turn off at other times; it's not one that we always or never use.

Figure 5.14
Using the overlay made it easy to move the swans. (Photo by Ellen Anon.)

The Healing Brush tool operates very similarly to the Clone Stamp tool. Press Alt/Option+click to define the source area, and then release the Alt/Option key and click the area you want to change (the destination). However, the Healing Brush copies the *texture* of the source area and blends the colors so that a natural-looking correction results in which texture has been added and color has been blended from the source and destination. This can be quite useful to create natural-looking corrections, especially in areas of sky and clouds. Its behavior initially seems less predictable when used near edges with strongly contrasting tonalities. In the Options bar, make sure that Source: Sampled is checked and that Pattern is unchecked. As with the Clone Stamp tool, you usually want Aligned and Sample All Layers checked as well. Adjust the brush size and hardness as with the Clone Tool.

The Spot Healing Brush operates like a "smart" Healing Brush. You don't have to define a source; instead, you simply click the tool and then click and drag your cursor over the area that needs fixing. This can work extremely quickly and efficiently in areas of low detail such as sky and clouds, but at other times you may prefer the additional control of being able to specify the precise source that the Healing Brush uses.

Make certain Proximity Match is selected in the Options bar. Usually the Spot Healing Brush works best if it's a little larger than the narrowest dimension of the area to replace, but just one click of the bracket keys larger than what you would use with the regular Healing Brush. We've found that the Spot Healing Brush can be a huge time-saver.

Note: If initially the Spot Healing Brush gives you an unacceptable result, adjust the size with the bracket key to slightly larger or smaller, and try again. Often a slight adjustment to the brush size or the direction that you drag enables Spot Healing to work effectively.

Using these tools well takes some practice. Be careful not to create repeated patterns that make it obvious you "fixed" something. Taking the time to do a careful job in removing unwanted areas and re-creating background areas is well worth it if you want the image to look natural.

Try It! To get familiar with the behavior of these three tools, open the image called Cloning on the accompanying CD, and play with each tool, noting what happens when you sample in one colored or textured area and then try to heal or clone to the same or a different area. See how each tool behaves in each situation and near edges.

Darrell Gulin offers the following cleanup suggestion based on his workflow creating dramatic images of butterflies and moths.

Repairing Wings Using the Patch Tool

by Darrell Gulin

© Darrell Gulin

When I am working with raising and photographing moths and butterflies, they can damage their wings and scales so easily. The Patch tool has been a lifesaver for me to fix minor—and sometimes not so minor—damage to their wings.

The Patch tool, located under the Healing Brush in the Tools panel, is on my toolbar at all times. I use the Patch tool with Source Mode selected on the Options bar. This means I select the area to be cloned out and move the selected area to an adjacent area that looks good, or what I want in the image. The sample of the Io Moth's wing tips was almost 95% corrected with the Patch tool.

Zooming, Navigating, and Layering for Cleanup

To remove those dust or scratches, you first need to zoom into the picture to a 100% view by double-clicking the Zoom tool. You need to check your image in a systematic way to ensure you don't miss any areas. We recommend beginning in the upper-right corner. Make sure the blue scroll bars are as far to the right as they go and at the top, as shown in Figure 5.15. To navigate through the image, you can drag one of the scroll bars. When you reach the other side, take the cursor, place it in the white area next to the other scroll bar, and click. This advances that scroll bar to the next unit so you don't miss anything. Continue this process throughout the image.

Note: Since most people read left to right, top to bottom, it may seem that starting in the upper-left corner is more logical. However, Ellen finds that by going against the common direction, it tends to force people to slow down and proceed carefully, thereby helping them find each little dust spot, rather than casually skimming through the image and missing some. Of course, ultimately you should establish a procedure that works for you.

Figure 5.15 Begin navigating through your image in a systematic way by placing the blue scroll bars at the top of the vertical axis and to the right on the horizontal axis. (Photo by Ellen Anon.)

Next, put some of your knowledge about layers to work. Rather than doing any cleanup directly on the background layer, you're going to make a new pixel layer to do your cloning and healing. To make a new pixel layer that initially has no pixels in it, click the Create New Layer icon next to the trash can icon at the bottom of the Layers panel. Notice in the panel that a new layer has appeared. To name this layer—so you know what you were doing in it if you return to the file later— double-click the words *Layer One*, and then type the new name. You want a short but clearly identifiable name, such as Cleanup or Dust and Scratches, as shown in Figure 5.16.

Figure 5.16
Make a new layer to do your cleaning up on, and be sure to label the layer.

Note: Naming your layers is a good habit to develop. Initially while you're working, it may seem unnecessary, but the more layers you create, the more likely it is that you'll forget exactly what you were doing in any one layer.

Once you're familiar with the tools, you've examined your photo, and you have a layer available, you're ready to clean up your image.

Removing Dust

In most cases, removing the spots created by dust and dirt on your camera's imaging sensor is a relatively easy job. Create a new layer as described in the previous section, zoom in, and begin carefully navigating throughout your image checking for dust (see Figure 5.17). Our first-choice tools for removing these spots, particularly in sky areas, are the Spot Healing Brush and the Healing Brush. Often they blend the corrections seamlessly into the image with little effort. However, sometimes you'll find that the Clone Stamp tool is a better choice, particular when working in areas of high detail. You'll know quickly whether one of the Healing brushes is going to work.

Figure 5.17
Carefully navigate through your picture at 100% magnification to find the dark blobs resulting from dust on your camera's sensor. (Photo by Ellen Anon.)

Whether you're using the Clone tool or one of the Healing brushes to remove dust spots, select a brush size just barely larger than the smallest dimension of the offending spot. For example, if it's a hair, the brush should be just wider than the width of the hair. Click and drag the tool along the length of the hair to remove it. The brush doesn't need to be large enough to cover the whole thing in one click. In fact, more often than not, you'll run into trouble if you try to do that. Sometimes you need to zoom in even further and use a very tiny brush.

The single most important trick to remember to successfully use these tools is to click and then drag the cursor just a smidge. This avoids the appearance of "correction circles."

Try It! Open the image named Dust from the accompanying CD or one of your own, and practice removing the dust spots.

Removing an Undesirable Object

Eliminating an object—whether it be a branch, a bird, an animal part, or whatever has crept uninvited into your image—is very similar to removing dust. But doing a good job requires finesse, patience, and practice. In fact, careful cloning is actually an advanced technique!

Note: Sloppy cloning is one of the telltale signs of a poorly optimized image. If you've done your job well, no one should have a clue that anything was removed from the image.

When you decide to remove an object from your image, you need to think even more like an artist. Imagine what the background would look like if you could see through the offending object, and then work to create that background by using the existing pixels in the rest of the picture or by borrowing pixels from another picture.

Often you'll need to begin by using the Clone Stamp tool. Zoom in to focus on that portion of your image so you can work precisely. Click and drag the cursor a small distance to "paint" over the offending object, and then sample another spot and continue working. Balance dragging the cursor with resampling.

After you have hidden an object, you need to look at the area even more carefully. If you are creating something with distinct patterns or textures, such as grasses or ocean waves, you should probably work with the Healing Brush on top of the cloned area. Sample from a variety of different areas where the lighting, size, and direction of the textures match what you need to fill the spot. You can also vary the opacity of the Clone Stamp tool or the Healing Brush, along with their sizes, by changing the Opacity setting in the Options bar. By combining these different approaches and tools, you can create a very natural-looking replacement area.

Cloning from a Separate Image

You can use an entirely different image as the source for your cloning! Open both images, making certain they are the same size, resolution, and color space. Place your cursor on the image you want to copy from, and click while holding the Alt/Option key; then release the Alt/Option key, place the cursor on the other image where you'd like to replace the pixels, and click and drag.

Here's a trick to make it easy to remove an object that comes right up to your subject, for example, a stick that comes right up to a bird's body. Before you do any cloning or healing, use the Lasso tool to carefully outline the part of the subject that you need to protect and then make a loose selection into the area where you'll be working, as shown in Figure 5.18. When you do your cloning and healing, Photoshop does not allow the effects to extend beyond the boundaries of the selection you just made. That way you don't have to worry about accidentally affecting your subject.

Figure 5.18 By making a selection before you do your cloning or healing, you can protect your subject matter so you don't accidentally damage it while fixing another part of your image. (Photo by Ellen Anon.)

Try It! Open the image named Extra Pelicans from the accompanying CD, and remove the background pelicans while creating natural-looking water. Don't worry if it takes you more than one try. It takes many people more practice than they think at first, but once you get the hang of it, it'll be an invaluable skill to have.

Creating New Background on Empty Canvas

Sometimes you may find that your subject is too tight in the frame, whether because you framed it poorly, the subject moved, you cropped the image, or you had too long a lens for the subject. No matter what the cause, you can add canvas to remedy the situation by following a similar procedure as described previously after expanding the canvas size.

To increase the canvas size to allow more space around your subject, choose Image > Canvas Size. The dialog box tells you the current size of your image. In that dialog box, take the following actions:

1. Check the Relative box. This tells Photoshop that the number you put in the box is the number of inches or pixels (depending on the unit you choose) to *add* to your image.

2. Fill in the desired increase in pixels or inches.

3. To specify where to add the additional canvas (top, bottom, right, or left), click in the Anchor area to anchor the image on one or two sides. In this way you can choose to add canvas to one, two, three, or four sides of your image, depending where you anchor it.

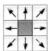

4. You can also specify what color to make this new canvas:

   a. To get a jump-start on creating a new background, choose Other from the drop-down menu. This opens the Color Picker dialog box.

   b. The cursor turns into an eyedropper icon; click a similar background color in the image.

   c. Click OK in the Color Picker dialog box.

5. Now click OK in the Canvas Size dialog box. Your newly added canvas starts out in a similar color to what will be needed.

At this point you can use the Healing Brush along with the Clone Stamp tool to create the patterns and tonalities that you would naturally expect to see there. Don't forget to alternate between the tools as necessary. Again, you're going to have to use some artistic imagination to visualize how this additional background might have looked and then create it from pixels in other places in this image or by sampling pixels from similar images.

Note: An alternate quick way to expand your canvas is to use the Crop tool to draw around your image. Increase the size of the window around your image by dragging the bottom-right corner of the image window if you are not in Full Screen mode. Drag one or more of the side boundaries of the crop out beyond the image. Click OK, and your image will be cropped (which means expanded in this case) using the background color in your Tools panel.

Try It! Open the image named Add Canvas from the accompanying CD, and try adding canvas while making the background appear natural.

We've covered a lot of territory in this chapter beginning with deciding upon a workflow, followed by the initial steps we routinely take in optimizing our images. Each step is a building block to make your final image the best it can be. In the next chapter, we'll cover ways to improve the exposure to maximize the detail and impact of your image.

Exposure Adjustments

Nature photography—and all photography for that matter—is about light and creating a proper exposure that records that light. Once you've captured the optimal exposure, you can use Photoshop to make the most of the information you've captured. As you've already seen, we make most of our global exposure adjustments in ACR. In this chapter, we'll guide you through methods to fine-tune the exposure for your images in Photoshop, many of which are quite similar to those found in ACR, and then discuss how to limit those tonal corrections to specific parts of your image.

EXPOSURE ADJUSTMENTS

Chapter Contents
Shooting for Optimal Exposure
Tonal Adjustments with Levels
Targeting Adjustments with a Layer Mask
Safe Dodge and Burn Layers
Curves
The Shadow/Highlight Adjustment

Shooting for Optimal Exposure

The ability to perform exposure adjustments in imaging software leads some photographers to feel they can be a little less careful during the original capture. We strongly advise you against believing that. Creating the very best images in a digital workflow requires that you start with the very best quality. Therefore, focus on creating the best exposures in the field, and select only your very best exposures to work on in Photoshop (see Figure 6.1). By ensuring you have achieved an appropriate exposure in the original capture, you'll achieve maximum detail in the image. Your adjustments can then focus on revealing the maximum amount of detail possible and emphasizing particular areas of your image, as we'll discuss in this chapter.

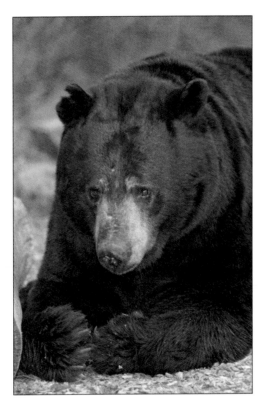

Figure 6.1
Achieving optimal exposure is an important first step for any photograph. It is especially important when you need to preserve detail in shadow areas, such as in the fur of this bear. (Photo by Ellen Anon.)

As we discussed in Chapter 3, "Adobe Camera Raw," in Photoshop CS3 you can make most, if not all, your global adjustments in ACR not only for raw files, but for JPEGS and TIFFS as well. However, there are times you'll choose to use the original tools within Photoshop as well. For example, you may want to tweak the settings you used for your conversion—particularly if you opted to use a converter other than ACR—or you may want to create an adjustment to apply to one part of your image. In addition, the exposure tools in ACR and Photoshop are very similar, but sometimes they differ in significant ways that will make you favor one over the other.

When considering the best exposure, keep in mind Michael Reichmann's advice back in Chapter 1, "Thinking Digitally," to "expose to the right" in the camera.

Tonal Adjustments with Levels

The Levels adjustment provides good basic control over tonal adjustments for your images, with the capability to adjust contrast by independently controlling shadows and highlights within your image, as well as to adjust the overall brightness. In ACR you can make similar adjustments by setting the Exposure, Blacks, and Brightness sliders. However, there are still times you may choose to use Levels within Photoshop, particularly if you want to make changes to only one area of your image. We'll talk about making localized adjustments later in the chapter, but first we'll cover how to use Levels to make a global adjustment.

We recommend using Levels to adjust contrast and brightness rather than the adjustment called "Brightness and Contrast" because the Levels adjustment offers far more accurate control of your settings. In addition, you may opt to increase contrast using Curves to increase the contrast in a particular range of tonalities rather than throughout the entire tonal range. We'll talk about Curves later in this chapter.

The primary component of the Levels dialog box is a histogram display (shown in Figure 6.2) that charts the distribution of tonal values within your image. Those values are represented from black at the extreme left to white at the extreme right. This gradation of tonal values appears as a gradient bar along the bottom of the histogram chart. The shape of the histogram chart tells you about the distribution of tonal values within the image. For example, histogram data that is shifted toward the left indicates that the image is generally dark. However, that doesn't necessarily tell you anything about the quality of the image; it may simply be a dark scene. Similarly, a brighter image has a histogram shifted toward the right.

Figure 6.2

The Levels adjustment revolves around a histogram display that charts the distribution of pixels among the available tonal values within your image.

The key things to watch out for on the Levels histogram are clipping and gapping. *Clipping* is an indication that information has been lost in the highlights or shadows of your image. *Gapping* is represented by gaps in the histogram and indicates tonal values that are not represented in your image.

Clipping is indicated on the histogram display by data running off the end of the chart. Clipping may be displayed in two ways. One is as a thin spike at one end of the chart. This is most commonly seen at the highlight end and is often caused by specular highlights within your image such as reflections from water, glass, or metal. In other words, it isn't necessarily a major problem within the image because you don't expect to see detail in such highlights.

Note: As we mentioned in Chapter 1, "Thinking Digitally," clipping seen in a luminosity histogram always indicates that some pixels in your image are pure black or pure white, but clipping in an RGB histogram can occur when one or more channels has a value of 0 or 255. In such cases, there may or may not be black or white pixels in your image. For example, pure red would have RGB values of 255,0,0 and would indicate potential clipping at both ends of the histogram even though the pixels are pure red, not black or white. The histogram in Levels shows RGB information or individual histograms for each of the channels. To check, click the Histogram options fly-out menu 📄≣| in the Histogram panel, and choose the Expanded View. Then in the Channel drop-down menu, choose Luminosity or RGB.

The other type of clipping is more likely to represent a problem within your image, especially if it occurs in the highlights where it is usually important to retain detail. In this type of clipping, the data of the histogram gets cut off abruptly at the end of the chart (see Figure 6.3), rather than ending gracefully before the chart ends. If you think of the histogram as representing a mountain range, ideally the mountains should gradually drop down to the flatland before the chart ends. If instead the mountains end suddenly in a steep cliff, detail is lost in the area that would have gradually lowered to the base of the chart. All pixels within the "missing" tonal values have been clipped to the minimum (pure black without detail) or maximum (pure white without detail) value at that end of the histogram chart.

Note: Remember, the correct shape histogram will vary according to the distribution of tonalities in your image. Not all subjects will have "mountains" as the correct shape of their histogram; some may have an even distribution of pixels throughout the tonal range, others may have several "mountains," and so on. Refer to Chapter 1 for more information about histograms.

Figure 6.3

Clipping of data in your image is exhibited by a histogram chart that appears "cut off" at one end, as with the highlights in this histogram.

Ideally, your image shouldn't exhibit any clipping when you get started with your adjustments. If it does, it is often preferable that the clipping occur in the shadows rather than in the highlights, because your eyes are usually more forgiving of lost shadow detail in a photographic image than blown highlights. However, be careful not to *produce* excessive clipping because of creating excessive contrast as a result of your adjustments in Levels.

Note: There are times that you may deliberately create clipping in the highlights. For example, if you are shooting a scenic and the sky is a very light and boring gray, you may choose to overexpose the scene to make it easier to replace the sky. If you do, make certain you're not also blowing out highlights in the rest of your subject matter. Additionally, if a scene is overly contrasty and you are shooting several versions of it to make an exposure latitude composite, some versions will have clipping in the shadows and others in the highlights.

Another potential problem to be aware of is gapping in the histogram. Think of the histogram chart as a bar chart consisting of many narrow bars so that the final result typically looks like a curving data display rather than one composed of individual bars. However, when gapping occurs, you start to see the individual bars that create the data display, as shown in Figure 6.4. Gapping indicates that certain tonal values are not represented by any pixels in the image (or are represented, but only by very few pixels).

Figure 6.4

Gaps in the histogram indicate tonal values that are not represented within the image.

Note: Gaps in the histogram rarely occur for 16-bit files because many more values are available than the 256 represented by the histogram display. Sixteen-bit files have 65,536 tonal values per color channel available, compared to 256 values per channel for an 8-bit file. As a result, 16-bit files can lose a significant number of tonal values without obvious gapping or the posterization.

Gaps in the tonal values indicate that smooth and subtle transitions between tones and colors within the image may be compromised. Instead of making a gradual change from one value to another with 10 values in between, for example, the transition may be from one value to another without any transition values between them. This lack of smooth gradations is referred to as *posterization* (see Figure 6.5). This sort of flaw isn't often seen out of the camera, only by making strong adjustments in Photoshop, particularly in 8-bit images.

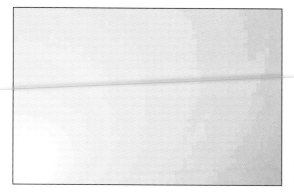

Figure 6.5

Posterization is represented by a lack of smooth gradations within an image.

However, gaps in a histogram are not an immediate indication of a serious problem with your image. Minor gaps of only a few pixels wide, representing just a few tonal values, aren't likely to be visible with the human eye. In fact, it isn't until the gaps become relatively extreme (at least 10 tonal values) that they are likely to be potentially visible in the final output. Although gaps certainly indicate a potential problem, they don't define image quality by themselves. If you have significant gapping in an image, use caution not to make extreme adjustments that may worsen the situation, and closely evaluate the final image to ensure there isn't visible posterization.

Note: Ultimately your goal is to provide the best looking image, not the best looking histogram! So if a histogram exhibits gapping, consider it a caution to carefully check the appearance of your image, but don't consider gapping a problem if the image looks good.

Revealing Detail

Nature photographers are often focused on the detail within the image, so tonal adjustments often revolve around revealing and enhancing detail and texture in the photo. The Levels adjustment allows you to do exactly that by enhancing contrast and adjusting brightness to reveal the desired level of detail while maintaining an appropriate tonality within the image. In CS3, chances are you'll have made these global adjustments in ACR, but we'll describe making global Levels adjustments first and then explain how to limit them to certain parts of the image.

Let's make a Levels adjustment so you can see this in action. Begin by creating a new adjustment layer for Levels by clicking the Create New Fill Or Adjustment Layer button on the Layers panel ⬤ˌ. This adds a new Levels adjustment layer on the Layers panel, and the Levels dialog box appears.

Note: We make all our adjustments as adjustment layers rather than applying them directly to the background image. This decreases the potential image degradation that occurs as changes are made to the image, as well as making it easy to modify the adjustments. To avoid any confusion when creating an adjustment, we recommend accessing the adjustment layers from the bottom of the Layers panel rather than from the main menu.

For most adjustments with Levels, you need to adjust only three controls; you'll find all three directly below the histogram display in the Levels dialog box:

- The black point slider (for shadows) is at the far left.
- The white point slider (for highlights) is at the far right.
- The midtones slider is in between the two.

Together, these controls allow you to adjust the overall contrast (by shifting the black point and white point sliders) and brightness (with the midtones slider) of your image with excellent control.

We recommend establishing overall contrast before fine-tuning brightness. Therefore, start with the black point and white point sliders. These provide contrast adjustment by allowing you to vary the amount of adjustment being applied to the shadow and highlight areas of your image. As a result, you can, for example, sacrifice more detail in the shadows to improve overall contrast without losing significant highlight detail.

As a general rule, most nature images benefit from having the brightest pixel value set to white and the darkest pixel value set to black, to maximize contrast and tonal range within the image and to ensure that as much detail as possible is visible. In other words, after making adjustments, your histogram should stretch (in most cases) nearly the full width of the chart, with few gaps in that range. Obviously there are plenty of exceptions to this, but it is a good basic rule. Because you know that the last data point at either end of the histogram chart represents the darkest and brightest pixels, you could make a very basic adjustment by dragging the black point and white point sliders inward to the point where the data begins at each end of the histogram (see the example in Figure 6.6).

Figure 6.6
A basic start with Levels involves bringing the black and white point sliders in to where the data begins on the histogram.

Of course, this is a somewhat arbitrary way to approach an image. Although it indeed produces good results for most images, it isn't an ideal solution for everyone. We recommend using clipping previews to help you set the black and white points.

The Clipping Preview

Although a basic visual evaluation of your image while making adjustments with Levels is certainly effective, it can be even more helpful to use the clipping preview display available in Levels. This display allows you to see exactly where you are losing detail within your image as you adjust the black point and white point sliders. As a result, you can make a much more informed decision about the settings you'd like to use for these sliders.

When you start with an image that lacks strong contrast and want to maximize the contrast without sacrificing detail in highlights or shadows, the clipping preview display allows you to see exactly where you'll begin to lose detail based on your specific adjustment of the black point and white point sliders.

We recommend adjusting the white point first, simply because highlight detail tends to be the more critical adjustment. To enable the clipping preview display, hold the Alt/Option key while you adjust the highlight slider/white point. Your image display initially changes to a completely (or almost completely) black display. This indicates that no pixel values (or very few) are clipped to white before you make any adjustment. As you continue to hold the Alt/Option key, slide the white point slider to the left. You'll see more pixels showing up as you move the slider, as shown in Figure 6.7. As a general rule, we recommend adjusting the white point until pixels just start showing up in the clipping preview and then back off just a hair. This is the point where you've maximized contrast and tonal range within the image, while sacrificing minimal highlight detail. Of course, the benefit of the clipping preview display is that you're able to make an informed decision about the amount of detail you're sacrificing to achieve the level of contrast you'd like to see and about that detail's location.

Figure 6.7 Holding the Alt/Option key gives you a clipping preview as you adjust the white point slider in Levels, so you can see where you start losing highlight detail and in which areas of the image.

Note: The colors of the pixels that show up in the clipping preview display indicate the color channels that are losing detail within the image. The pixels won't appear as pure white or black in the image until the clipping preview shows those values. However, even if they aren't pure white or black, they are probably very close if any channels are clipping, so you can generally treat such values as though they were indeed white or black.

The process for setting the black point is nearly identical: hold the Alt/Option key while adjusting the black point slider, and a similar clipping preview appears, except that now it starts completely (or almost completely) white, with pixels showing up to indicate where you're losing shadow detail (see Figure 6.8). As discussed previously, we are generally willing to sacrifice more shadow detail as opposed to highlight detail to maximize contrast. The clipping preview allows you to make an informed decision about how much detail you're giving up with a particular adjustment and the location of that detail, so you can better determine the extent to which you can push the black point to produce the desired contrast level.

Note: As you make changes to your image, the histogram in the Histogram panel will dynamically update to reflect those changes.

Figure 6.8 The clipping preview while adjusting the black point slider shows you where you're losing shadow detail in the image.

After you've adjusted the black and white points by using the clipping preview, you're ready to adjust the midtone slider for overall brightness. Because this doesn't affect the extreme tonal values within the image, there isn't a clipping preview for the midtone slider. You need to rely on a visual evaluation of the image for this adjustment. Think of this slider as a brightness control. Moving the slider changes which pixel value within the image should be mapped to a middle-gray tonal value, but the result is a brightness shift. This adjustment doesn't have any rule of thumb you can follow in terms of positioning the slider at a particular point along the histogram chart, so you need to make a decision based on a visual review of the image.

Try It! To practice utilizing the clipping preview in Levels, open the image Levels on the accompanying CD. Use the clipping preview to adjust the white point and the black point, and adjust the midtone slider visually.

Photography is very much a visual pursuit, so it makes sense to perform a visual review of the image and decide whether you're happy with the results of the adjustment you've made. You may want to back off the adjustments slightly in some situations to minimize the risk of introducing excessive contrast or in other situations, you may want to bring the sliders in just a bit farther to produce stronger contrast. It's up to you to determine the best adjustment for a particular image.

Note: If you're having trouble making appropriate adjustments, hold the Alt/Option key to change the Cancel button to a Reset button in most dialog boxes in Photoshop. If you then click the Reset button, all settings in the dialog box return to their default values.

When you've adjusted all three sliders, you've finished the basic tonal adjustment with Levels. Click OK, and the Levels dialog box closes. As with any other adjustment layer, if you change your mind about the adjustment at a later time, you can simply double-click the thumbnail icon for the Levels adjustment layer on the Layers panel, and the dialog box appears, with the sliders positioned exactly as you left them the last time you clicked OK.

Note: The Levels dialog box also includes eyedroppers that allow you to click areas of your image to automatically set the black, white, and neutral values. We'll talk more about those in Chapter 7, "Color Adjustments," when we talk about color casts.

Targeting Adjustments Using a Layer Mask

Making overall adjustments to bring out the maximum amount of detail in your images is a common goal, but one of the reasons for using the tonal adjustments within Photoshop, in addition to those you already made in ACR, is so that you can apply the changes to only certain areas of the image. You may want to do this to help emphasize your subject or to reveal detail in areas of your picture that have different lighting. Doing so requires the use of a layer mask to target the adjustment to a particular area of the image.

Every adjustment layer comes with a layer mask. It's the white box that appears in the adjustment layer next to the icon for the type of adjustment. The shape of the mask matches the shape of your image, as shown in Figure 6.9.

Figure 6.9
Every adjustment layer automatically comes with a layer mask.

Think of a layer mask as a visibility control for the changes you make on that layer. Initially by default, the mask is white. Wherever a layer mask is white corresponds to areas of your image where the changes made on that layer will be visible. Wherever a layer mask is black corresponds to areas of your image where the change will not be visible. Imagine superimposing the layer mask over your image—the areas underneath white parts of the mask will show the changes you make on that layer, and the areas of the image underneath black parts of the mask will show no effects of that layer.

There are several ways to make parts of the layer mask black. There are two ways that are particularly useful for nature photographers. The first is by creating a selection before you make the adjustment layer, and the second is by painting parts of the layer mask black. We'll talk about both these approaches in more detail.

Note: A *layer mask* identifies which areas of a particular layer will be visible. In this case, we're talking about layer masks on adjustment layers, so the mask determines where the adjustment applies and where it doesn't. White on the layer mask indicates areas where the adjustment layer affects the image, and black indicates areas where it does not affect the image.

Masking a Selection

When you create a selection first and then create an adjustment layer, we refer to it as *masking a selection*. Creating an adjustment layer that is masked based on a selection is easy, especially since you've already seen some of the methods you can use to create selections in Chapter 4, "Foundations." This is the method Tim commonly uses.

To mask an adjustment layer based on a selection, start by creating a selection that defines the subject you'd like to modify, as shown in Figure 6.10.

Figure 6.10
The first step in emphasizing a particular area of your image with a targeted tonal adjustment is to create a selection defining that area.
(Photo by Tim Grey.)

Then create a new adjustment layer of the desired type (in this case using Levels). Because a selection is active when the adjustment layer is created, Photoshop assumes you want to mask the adjustment layer based on the selection. Therefore, the adjustment layer applies only to the areas that were selected when you created the adjustment layer.

Notice that when the adjustment layer appears in the Layers panel, the layer mask is partially white and partially black. The white areas match the shape of the selection you originally created (see Figure 6.11). When you make adjustments to the Levels dialog box, as in this example, the adjustment affects only the area that was selected when the adjustment layer was created.

Figure 6.11
When you create an adjustment layer with an active selection, the mask for that adjustment layer reflects the shape of the selection, so the adjustment applies only to that area of the image.

Note: On a layer mask, black blocks and white reveals the layer's effect.

Using this concept, it's very easy to see how you could create a selection to define the area you want to emphasize and then create a Levels adjustment (or a different type of adjustment as appropriate) to adjust that area and draw more attention to it. Remember that our eyes tend to go to areas that are brighter and more contrasty, so if you want to help make your subject stand out from the background, you could make two Levels adjustments. In the first you may adjust the background to be a little darker and less contrasty, and in the second you may adjust the subject to be a little bit brighter and perhaps more contrasty as well. (See Figure 6.12.)

Figure 6.12 By making adjustments using layer masks, you can help emphasize your subject by applying one type of adjustment to the subject and a different one to the background. (Photo by Ellen Anon.)

Painting on a Mask

In some situations you don't want to create the adjustment layer mask based on a selection. For example, when you're going to adjust an image area that is defined by relatively nebulous edges, creating a selection to start from can be a challenge. When the edge of the area you want to adjust isn't well-defined, it's often easier and more efficient to paint directly on the mask to control where the effect is visible. The concept is that you paint with white or black on the mask to control the visibility of the effects of that layer. This is actually Ellen's preferred method, whenever possible, so she can skip the sometimes laborious process of creating a selection before making a targeted adjustment based on that selection.

Almost all of us have been using a paintbrush since we were preschoolers, so creating a mask by painting is usually a very natural and intuitive approach. To use this approach, take the following steps:

1. Create an adjustment layer, in this case a Levels adjustment layer, by clicking the Create New Fill or Adjustment Layer button at the bottom of the Layers panel.

2. Make an adjustment so you can see an effect in the image. Concentrate on making the particular section of your image look the way you want, and don't worry that the rest of the image may be "ruined." We'll use the layer mask to restore those areas to their "before" states.

Note: We recommend making an exaggerated adjustment when you're first learning to use an adjustment layer so it's easier to see exactly where in the image the adjustment layer applies.

3. To modify the mask for an adjustment layer, select the Brush tool. We usually use a soft brush (0% hardness), but in some instances you will want to use a harder brush or even a totally hard brush to make a discrete edge.

4. Press D to set the colors to their defaults of black and white, and then press X as needed to switch foreground and background colors.

5. Zoom in so you can easily see the area you want to change.

6. Place your cursor on the image, and begin painting with black as your foreground color to remove the effects of your adjustment from that area.

7. If you make a mistake, reverse your brush colors by pressing X so that white is your foreground color. Then paint over the area to correct the mistake. Layer masks are very forgiving!

To help you see exactly where you have masked the image and where the effect will appear, press the \ key. This will create a type of quick mask over your image. A transparent red layer will appear over the masked areas, as shown in Figure 6.13. As you paint with black, the red area will increase; to remove it from an area, paint with white. OK, we know it's a little confusing to paint with black and have it appear red, but remember you're not really painting on the image. You're painting on the layer mask, and the red is there as a superimposed version of the mask that's easier to see. To remove the quick mask, press the \ key again. This is one of Ellen's favorite tricks!

183

TARGETING ADJUSTMENTS USING A LAYER MASK

Figure 6.13
By pressing the backslash (\)
key, a red mask will appear
over the parts of your image
that are masked, helping you
to see whether you need to
refine the mask.

Note: Another way to view the mask is to Alt/Option+click the adjustment layer mask. That way the mask appears in place of your image preview, making it easy to clean up small areas that may have been missed in painting.

One of the benefits of using layer masks is that if you later decide you need to further revise the layer mask, simply click the adjustment layer to make it active and paint as needed to change the areas where the adjustment is blocked or revealed.

At times, you'll want the adjustment layer to apply to a very small area of your image, but that area won't be conducive to making a selection. In such situations, it may seem that the only solution is to paint with black throughout most of the image. An easier way is to begin with a layer mask that is already filled with black and then paint the areas where you want the effect to show with white. To do this, take these steps:

1.   After creating the new adjustment layer, choose Edit > Fill from the menu.

2.   Select Black from the Use drop-down list, and click OK (see Figure 6.14). This fills the layer mask with black, blocking the effect of the adjustment from the entire image.

Figure 6.14

You can use the Fill command to fill a layer mask with black and then paint with white to apply the adjustment to specific areas of the image.

3.   Use the Brush tool with the foreground color set to white to paint the adjustment in the areas where you'd like it to be applied.

Note: You can also use Alt/Option+Delete to fill a layer mask with the foreground color and use Ctrl+Delete/⌘+Delete to fill a layer mask with the background color.

So far you've seen how you can paint with black or white on an adjustment layer mask to target specific areas where the adjustment should be blocked or revealed. If you'd like to only partially block or reveal the effects of an adjustment layer, then the layer mask will need to be a shade of gray. The darker the gray, the more the effect will be blocked, and the lighter the gray, the more it will be revealed, as shown in Figure 6.15. Rather than using the Color Picker to select a shade of gray, because it's easy to accidentally select a non-neutral gray, which can lead to unexpected results, we recommend continuing to use the default colors of black and white but reducing the opacity of the brush. To reduce the opacity of the brush, use the Opacity box in the toolbar Options bar. And, as mentioned previously, paint with a soft-edged brush if necessary to produce a gradual transition between the areas that are and are not affected by the adjustment layer.

Figure 6.15
You can use shades of gray on an adjustment layer mask to have the effect partially revealed within the image.

Of course, you can also combine the two approaches to creating a mask. You could start by creating a selection that defines the area you want to adjust and then paint on the layer mask to fine-tune the area you want to have affected by the adjustment. This allows you to utilize the best of both techniques to achieve the best results possible in your images.

Blurring the Layer Mask

If you used a selection that wasn't feathered to create your mask (as we generally do since you'd then be guessing at how much feathering you want) or if you used a hard-edged brush to adjust the layer mask for an adjustment layer, the transition between the areas you adjusted and those you didn't will be relatively harsh, as you can see in Figure 6.16. Sometimes this works well, but other times you may want a more natural transition.

Figure 6.16
When you use a nonfeathered selection or a hard-edged brush with a layer mask, the transition between adjusted and nonadjusted areas will be relatively harsh.

To create a more natural effect, apply a blur to the layer mask when you've finished defining its shape to create a smooth transition between adjusted and nonadjusted areas. By using this method, you can see the actual effect in the image rather than guessing by how many pixels you should feather a selection. Most of the time you may not need to do this, but sometimes it can improve your final results, particularly if you are planning to make a large print.

Make sure the appropriate layer mask is selected first and then select Filter > Blur > Gaussian Blur from the menu to open the Gaussian Blur dialog box (shown in Figure 6.17). With the Preview check box selected, start with a value of 1 pixel, and adjust the slider up or down to achieve the desired effect in the image. You want to produce a gradual transition between the areas you're adjusting versus not adjusting (see Figure 6.18), but not softening the effect so much that the adjustment blends across too large a distance. When you've found the appropriate value, click OK to apply the blur to the mask.

Figure 6.17
Applying the Gaussian Blur filter on the mask for your adjustment layer allows you to soften the edge of the mask.

Figure 6.18
After blurring the adjustment layer mask, the result is a more gradual transition between adjusted and nonadjusted areas of the image.

Note: We used this technique more often in earlier versions of Photoshop before the Refine Edge options were available. However, even now, the technique can come in handy and is worth knowing.

Try It! Open the image BlurMask on the accompanying CD, select the layer mask for the Levels adjustment layer, and apply a Gaussian blur to the mask to soften the vignette effect in the image and help you gain a better understanding of the process for blurring a layer mask.

Creating a Virtual Split Neutral-Density Filter

One particularly helpful example of another tool that you can use to place pixels onto an adjustment layer mask is the Gradient tool. This allows you to place a gradient on a layer mask, resulting in an adjustment that affects one side of the image completely but gradually tapers off in a given direction until it has no effect at the other side of the image. The most common example of using such a gradient is in a composition where you would otherwise shoot with a graduated split neutral-density filter, such as when you need to darken the sky without darkening the foreground of an image. But the advantage of doing it in Photoshop is that you can customize the filter to the exact size you need.

To create a virtual split neutral-density filter, follow these steps:

1. Start by creating a new adjustment layer that produces the desired effect in the area of the image to which you want it to apply. For example, you may create a Levels adjustment layer that darkens the sky in an image by moving the midtone slider to the right. After you've made the adjustment, click OK in the dialog box for the adjustment to apply the settings on the layer.

2. Select the Gradient tool from the Tools panel (the shortcut key is G). On the Options bar, click the drop-down list for the gradient editor, and choose the first gradient thumbnail on the list, which is the Foreground To Background gradient. Next, select the Linear option for the Gradient tool on the Options bar (shown in Figure 6.19), which is the first in the set of five buttons allowing you to choose a style for your gradient.

Figure 6.19 To use a gradient on a layer mask, select the Foreground To Background gradient with the Linear option from the Options bar.

3. Press D to set the colors to the defaults of black and white, and set white to the foreground color (pressing X to switch foreground and background colors if necessary). You're now ready to create a gradient that transitions from white to black.

4. You want to create the gradient on the layer mask for the adjustment layer you just created, so make sure that is the active layer on the Layers panel. Then click and drag the image to create a gradient: the foreground color starts where you first click, with a smooth gradation to the background color where you release the mouse, as shown in Figure 6.20. The length of the line you drag determines the distance over which the gradient transitions, and the direction determines the angle of that gradient. To lock the gradient to 45-degree increments, simply hold the Shift key as you drag.

Figure 6.20
Draw the gradient on the layer mask so the adjustment tapers from adjusted to nonadjusted areas.

5. In the example of darkening the sky, click the area of sky that represents the lowest area you still want the adjustment to affect completely, and drag downward to the point where you don't want any effect at all. If you're not happy with the initial gradient you created, simply click and drag again to replace the gradient with a new one. The result is an adjustment that blends smoothly, from applying completely in one area of the image to having no effect on another area (see Figure 6.21).

If your image requires an odd shape to the split neutral-density filter, you can modify the layer mask by painting on it to add or remove the effects where necessary. This can be useful when shooting in the mountains where the sky may be very light, but the mountains dark, and the sky area may be V-shaped.

Figure 6.21
By applying a gradient mask to the adjustment, you're able to produce an adjustment that gradually blends, as with the sky darkened in this example. (Photo by Tim Grey.)

Safe Dodge and Burn Layers

Dodging and burning are techniques borrowed from the wet darkroom, where you can use your hands or various instruments to block light from specific areas of an image. The longer the light from the enlarger strikes any given area, the darker that area will be. Blocking light to small areas during exposure is referred to as *dodging* and results in the blocked areas being lighter in a print than they otherwise would have been. *Burning* is the opposite: blocking light from *most* of the image so you can concentrate light for a portion of the exposure on one particular area, darkening that area of the print.

In Photoshop you can produce similar effects. In fact, Photoshop includes Dodge and Burn tools on the Tools panel, but we don't recommend using them because you must apply them directly to an image layer, and they don't offer quite the flexibility of the method we'll present here.

Setting Up

The method we recommend for dodging and burning uses one layer for dodging and another for burning and takes advantage of layer masks and layer blending modes. Blending modes are different ways of combining layers. So far all the layers we've worked with in the examples have been in Normal mode, but Photoshop contains numerous algorithms for different ways to combine two layers. You can combine layers so that the tonal values are added together or multiplied, or the darker value used, or the lighter values, and so on. You don't have to become an expert on each of the algorithms; we'll use just two of them here: Screen and Multiply. We'll talk more about blending modes in Chapter 9, "Creative Effects."

Note: We prefer this method to the older Overlay method because it's more forgiving and easier to use.

Although setting up the dodging and burning requires a lot of steps, the procedure is easy and can be automated by creating an action (see Chapter 11, "Time-Savers").

To set up layers to use for dodging and burning, do the following:

1. Create a new Levels adjustment layer, but do *not* make any changes; just click OK. This creates an adjustment layer in the Layers panel even though you aren't making any changes with it yet.

2. Double-click directly on the name of the layer (Levels1), and change it to Dodge.

3. In the Blending Modes drop-down menu on the Layers panel, choose Screen, as shown in Figure 6.22. The entire image will become one full stop lighter, which in most images means that it will instantly be overexposed. Don't worry—we're not going to leave it that way for long!

Figure 6.22
Take advantage of blending modes to create dodge and burn layers that can be easily modified.

4. In the menu bar, choose Edit > Fill > Use Black, and click OK. The layer mask should now be black, and your image should look the way it did before we began setting up for dodging and burning.

5. Create another Levels adjustment just as you did in Step 1, and name it Burn.

6. Change the blending mode of this layer to Multiply.

7. In the menu bar, choose Edit > Fill > Use Black, and click OK.

8. Select the Brush tool by selecting it on the Tools panel or by pressing B on your keyboard. Make sure to use a soft-edged brush, as shown in Figure 6.23.

Figure 6.23
Use a soft-edged brush when dodging and burn-ing your image with this method.

9. Set the opacity of the brush to 15% although you may well want to adjust this as you proceed since it controls the strength of the dodging and burning.

> **Note:** It's important to set the brush to the Normal blending mode in the tool Options bar, while the layer itself is set to Multiply or Screen.

> **Note:** If you're using a tablet, you can also use pen pressure of the stylus to determine the Opacity set-ting when dodging and burning with this method.

10. Press D to set the colors on the color boxes in the Tools panel to their default values of black foreground and white background. Note that you can switch the foreground and background colors by pressing X as you're working, allowing you to easily switch between black and white.

Now you're ready to apply selective lightening and darkening to the image.

Painting with Light

With your new layers and the Brush tool properly configured, you're ready to start painting with light. Paint with black to darken portions of your image, and paint with white to lighten your image. Because you're painting at a reduced opacity, the result is relatively modest. If necessary, you can paint over areas multiple times to build up an effect. The best effect is usually subtle. When someone looks at the final image, they shouldn't get the impression that you were using dodging and burning techniques. How-ever, when you toggle the visibility of the dodge and burn layer off and on, you'll see a difference between the images.

It's important to understand the behavior of the Brush tool when working at a reduced opacity for this technique. As long as you hold down the mouse button, the effect does not accumulate no matter how many times the mouse passes over a particu-lar area. However, if you release the mouse and start painting again, the effect is uneven if you partially overlap areas you've previously painted. Therefore, it's important that you click and hold the mouse button while painting until you've covered the entire area you want to adjust. Then, release the mouse, and start painting again in additional areas you'd like to change.

> **Try It!** To practice dodging and burning, open the image DodgeBurn from the accompanying CD, and use the method presented here to add drama to the rock formation, enhancing texture and contrast.

Dodging and burning are two of our favorite techniques in Photoshop. We think this has a lot to do with the capability to paint with light, bringing out details in various areas of the image or simply emphasizing particular features (see Figure 6.24). So much of the image optimization process seems very mathematical, adjusting sliders and other controls to apply formulas to an image. The processes of dodging and burning are different, allowing you to work directly on the image. As a result, they feel more artistic than other methods and enable you to take great control over tonal adjustments.

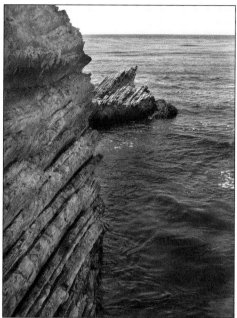

Figure 6.24 Dodging and burning allow you to enhance detail or add drama to various areas of your image with tremendous flexibility, producing an image that has been adjusted in a subtle way but with a big difference in the final result. (Photo by Tim Grey.)

Correcting Mistakes

Of course, now and then you may be less than satisfied with an adjustment you've made when using this technique. Fortunately, because you apply it using a layer mask, it's easy to fix mistakes even if it's too late to simply undo a step on the History panel.

There are two basic ways to correct your mistakes. If you were painting with white as your foreground color, make black the foreground color, and set the opacity to 100%. Paint over the problematic area, and begin again.

Alternatively, if you are dissatisfied with all the dodging or burning you did, return to Edit > Fill > Use Black, and reset the layer mask to black. Then you can start over.

Curves

The Curves adjustment in Photoshop has a reputation as being one of the most difficult controls to master. Although becoming comfortable with it can take some time and practice, it provides an incredible level of control over your images. It enables you to change the brightness values and contrast within your image, and it allows you to accomplish this by applying varying degrees of adjustments to pixels of different tonal values. Simply put, you can concentrate contrast or brightness modifications in certain tonal ranges. As with Levels, you can accomplish the same effects within ACR, but the Curves tool in Photoshop has some features that make it more convenient.

Nonetheless, we recommend that while you are first getting accustomed to using Curves that you begin with the Parametric curves that are available only in ACR. Unfortunately, they are not part of Photoshop itself. We find that they provide an easy way to get comfortable with working with Curves. Refer to Chapter 3 for more about using Parametric curves.

As with all controls that are available as an adjustment layer, the first step in utilizing Curves is to create a new adjustment layer from the Create New Fill or Adjustment button at the bottom of the Layers panel.

The key to understanding the Curves adjustment is the concept of "before" and "after" values. All adjustments in Curves are based on shifting the value of all pixels at (or near) a particular tonal value. Therefore, think in terms of brightening the midtones or darkening the highlights, for example, when working with Curves.

The Curves dialog box shows a "curve" overlaid on a grid (see Figure 6.25), all of which is superimposed over the histogram. Of course, at first the curve isn't a curve at all, but a straight line at a 45° angle. As you learn to "read" the curve, you'll see that this 45° line represents no change in the image. The gradient along the bottom of the grid represents the "before" tonal values, and the gradient at the left shows the "after" values. If you follow a vertical line up from a specific tonal value on the gradient below the grid to the point that intersects the curve line and then follow in a straight line to the left until reaching the after gradient, at this point the "before" and "after" values are exactly the same. Changing the shape of the curve alters the relationship between the "before" and "after" values, resulting in a change in the appearance in your image.

Figure 6.25

The Curves dialog box shows a "curve" that by default is actually a straight line at a 45° *angle*.

The grid behind the curve line is provided simply for reference, and you can set it to either a 16-square grid or a 100-square grid. In general, the 16-square grid is preferred by those working in prepress, because they tend to think about quarter tones, midtones, and three-quarter tones. However, most photographers prefer the 100-square grid, and that is the setting we recommend. To toggle between the two settings, hold the Alt/Option key, and click the cursor anywhere within the grid. Keep in mind that changing the increments has absolutely no effect on the actual adjustment being applied.

In the bottom-left corner of the Curves dialog box is a button that allows you to access options for the Curve display, as shown in Figure 6.26.

Figure 6.26

Photoshop CS3 has new options for controlling the Curves display.

We recommend leaving the Show Amount of option set to Light; Pigment/Ink % is more often used with prepress. Switching to Pigment/Ink % toggles the gradient at the bottom of the grid. Having black in the top and right of the gradients appeals to those in prepress because they think of an increased value as more ink on paper, which produces a darker result. However, for photographers we recommend configuring the gradients with white at the top and right so that an increase represents more light and a brighter image. Changing the gradient configuration doesn't have any impact on the image, and any adjustments you've made with Curves are automatically mapped accordingly, as shown in Figure 6.27.

Figure 6.27 Changing the gradient configuration by changing the Show Amount of option changes the location of the white point or black point in the dialog box, but the curve shape is automatically adjusted, so the adjustment doesn't change.

We keep all four boxes in the Show section checked:

Channel Overlays enables the individual curve for each channel to appear superimposed on the master curve if you have made any changes to the individual channels. If there are no changes to the individual channels, then the other curves don't appear.

Histogram enables the original histogram to be displayed under the curve.

Baseline retains the original curve (line) as well as a curve to indicate your changes.

Intersection Line adds a vertical and horizontal line as you click a point and move it. This makes it easier to visualize the changes you're making.

Clipping Preview

The Show Clipping check box enables you to look for clipping in your image at any time while the Curves dialog box is open. When you check the Show Clipping box, the image turns either nearly or all white, or nearly or all black. A white background is used to check for clipping in the shadows, and a black background is used to check for clipping in the highlights. Any areas where there is clipping will appear in color to indicate the particular channel that's being clipped, and if all three channels are clipped, then the area will appear black or white—whichever is the opposite of the background color. This makes it easy to see where there's any clipping and to decide whether you need to modify your adjustments to try to eliminate it. Sometimes the clipping will be in dark shadows that should be black or in specular highlights that should be pure white. At other times the clipping preview may show you that you've unintentionally lost detail in your subject.

You can use the clipping preview to accurately set the white and black points in your image. In versions of Photoshop before CS3, we recommended setting the white and black points in Levels because Curves didn't have a clipping preview, but this has changed in CS3. To set the white and black points in Curves, do the following:

1. Open a new Curves adjustment layer from the Create New Fill or Adjustment Layer button at the bottom of the Layers panel.

2. Check the Show Clipping option. The image will turn white.

3. Click the small white triangle on the bottom right of the histogram. The image will turn black.

4. Drag the triangle to the left until colored pixels begin to appear in the preview, as shown in Figure 6.28.

Figure 6.28 Use the clipping preview in Curves to establish the white and black points.

5. Back the slider off until there is no clipping, if possible. That sets the white point.

6. Click the small black triangle on the bottom left of the histogram. The preview turns white.

7. Drag it to the right until colored pixels appear, and then back off until there is no clipping, if possible. That sets the black point.

8. Uncheck Show Clipping to return to your image preview.

Dragging the triangles toward each other will increase the contrast in the image and eventually introduce clipping. For the maximum amount of contrast in your image, drag these sliders toward the center until colored pixels appear, and then back off slightly. Then, to change the overall brightness of the image or to refine the contrast within a certain range of tonalities, apply anchor points to the curve.

Anchor Points

You generally want to use anchor points for changing relationships between the "before" and "after" values in your image, which in turn creates the actual tonal adjustment. Anchor points allow you to place a handle on a particular point on the curve and adjust its position. When you do so, Photoshop automatically smoothes out the curve to connect all the anchor points, providing a seamless transition in your adjustments.

The curve always starts off with anchor points at the extreme ends. You can adjust the position of these points by setting the black point and white points within your image as we just described in the "Clipping Preview" section.

To see the basic functionality of anchor points, position your mouse at about the middle of the curve, and click. This places an anchor point at that position, which you can move around to change the shape of the curve, as you can see in Figure 6.29. Move the anchor point upward to lighten the image and downward to darken the image. The result is similar to adjusting the midtone slider in Levels. It differs in that the tones closest to the point you moved on the curve are altered more than tones farther away from that point. In fact, the effect tapers off toward the ends of the curve.

Of course, this hints at the incredible power of Curves. You can place up to 14 anchor points on the curve to perform adjustments on pixels at various tonal values within the image—but you'll usually need only a handful (typically one to three) to accomplish your goals with the image. By carefully positioning and adjusting these anchor points, you can exercise tremendous control over the tonal adjustments applied to the image.

Clicking the curve to place anchor points is sort of like working blind because you don't get any feedback about which area of the image you're going to adjust. Also, you're usually thinking in terms of a specific area within the image, and you want to find the position on the curve that represents the tonal value for that area. Fortunately, there's a way to make an informed decision about where to place anchor points.

Figure 6.29

To get a sense of the basic control in Curves, click at about the middle of the curve line to create an anchor point, and then drag it around to see the effect in your image. (Photo by Tim Grey.)

First of all, if you point the mouse at your image and click, a small circle appears on the curve showing you where the tonal value for the pixel under the mouse falls (see Figure 6.30). If you drag the mouse around on the image, the circle bounces around as it updates its position based on the tonal value under the mouse. This display allows you to see exactly where particular areas of your image fall on the curve.

Figure 6.30 If you click your image, a small circle appears on the curve line representing where the tonal value you're pointing at with your mouse falls on the curve. (Photo by Ellen Anon.)

Even better, if you hold the Ctrl/⌘ key when you click the image, an anchor point is created on the curve for the tonal value of the pixel under your mouse. You can even drag around the image to review the range on the curve before releasing the mouse to place the anchor point. This allows you to place anchor points very precisely based on the area of the image you'd like to focus your adjustments on.

Note: The Curves dialog box includes eyedroppers with which you can set black, midtone, and white points in the image. We'll talk about using these in Chapter 7.

Adjusting Anchor Points

After you've created one or more anchor points, you can adjust them to change the relationship between the "before" and "after" values on the curve. You lighten or darken specific values by raising or lowering an anchor point, respectively.

You can move the anchor points by dragging them with the mouse, but you can apply a more precise adjustment by clicking an anchor point to select it and then using the arrow keys to adjust its position. You are typically thinking in terms of lightening or darkening and therefore would adjust the anchor points up or down to change the after value, but you can also move the anchor point left or right. Although this is actually changing which "before" value you are adjusting, we prefer to think of this as simply fine-tuning the relationship between the "before" and "after" values by taking greater control over the specific shape of the curve.

Note: At this point, you're performing only tonal adjustments with Curves. In the next chapter, you'll learn how to adjust the curves for individual color channels to apply color adjustments to your images.

As you're adjusting the anchor points, you'll begin to see the relationship between the shape of the curve and the effect on the image:

- Raising or lowering the curve in a particular area affects the brightness of the pixels within the tonal range represented by that portion of the curve.
- Making a portion of the curve steeper than the original 45° line represents an increase in contrast.
- Areas that you change to be shallower than the original 45° line represent reduced contrast.

As you understand these relationships, you'll be better able to read the curve as well as apply the desired adjustments with minimal effort.

Creating the S Curve

One of the most common adjustments recommended for Curves is the S curve. This curve shape applies an increase in contrast to the midtones of your image while preserving detail in highlight and shadow areas. Because we tend to respond better to photographs with higher contrast in the midtones, you can apply this adjustment to many photographic images and have good results.

Note: Moody, foggy images do not need S curves, nor do images that are already contrasty.

To create an S curve, we recommend placing anchor points about 20% in from the black and white endpoints on the curve (see Figure 6.31). Then move the upper of these anchor points to the left slightly and the lower anchor point to the right (see Figure 6.32). You don't need to move them much to produce a nice boost of contrast in your image; often moving the anchor points by one or two clicks with the arrow keys is sufficient.

Figure 5.31 To create an S curve, start by placing anchor points about 20% in from the white and black endpoints of the curve. (Photo by Tim Grey.)

Figure 6.32 To complete the S curve, move the anchor points inward to achieve the desired increase in midtone contrast.

Another great feature of using Curves for such an adjustment is that you can focus your S curve on either the highlights or the shadows within your image. If you want to boost the brighter tones more than the darker ones, move the anchor point that's closer to the white endpoint farther inward than the anchor point you added near the black point.

If you're also applying more sophisticated adjustments with Curves, you may want to make one Curves adjustment layer specifically for the S curve and another for adjustments that apply to various tonal values within the image. Renaming each of these adjustment layers helps you stay organized as you move through your workflow and when you return to the image later.

Locking Down the Curve to Limit Changes

When you move anchor points on the curve, Photoshop automatically adjusts the shape of the curve to provide a smooth transition between all anchor points. Although this is a good thing, sometimes it causes adjustments in areas where you don't want any applied. When this happens, you must prevent changes—"normalize" the shape of the curve—in the areas you don't want altered.

Note: If your Curves adjustment is causing undesirable color shifts in your image, change the blending mode for the Curves adjustment layer to Luminosity (using the drop-down list at the top of the Layers panel) after closing the Curves dialog box. This ensures that the Curves adjustment layer affects only tonal values, not color values, within the image.

For example, if you're trying to focus some adjustments to the brighter areas of your image, you'll find that adjusting the anchor points causes a bend in the curve that also affects the darker areas (see Figure 6.33). To lock the curve, place a new anchor point near the existing anchor point on the side representing the tonal values to which you want to limit changes. Then place two more points on the curve close to that point. The three points together "lock" the section of the curve so that changes on one side of those three points essentially don't affect the curve on the other side (see Figure 6.34).

Figure 6.33 At times you will adjust a portion of the curve that you want to affect only to find that the entire image is being adjusted because of the shape the curve takes on. (Photo by Tim Grey.)

Figure 6.34 Using an additional anchor point, you can lock down the area of the curve you don't want to have affected, bringing it back near the original starting point.

You can also place anchor points outside those you placed for adjustment, producing something of a barrier outside the range you're adjusting. This won't always prevent adjustments from applying to the rest of the curve, but it helps when the adjustments you're making are relatively minor.

The bottom line is that you can use anchor points not just for producing desired changes within the image but also to adjust the shape of the curve to compensate for unintended consequences of your adjustments. Think of these anchor points as handles that allow you to control the shape of the curve and use them to produce exactly the result you have in mind.

> **Note:** The best advice we can offer for working with Curves is to use very small adjustments. It doesn't take much to cause a significant change in the image, and frustration with Curves is most often caused by adjustments that are simply too strong.

Curves Presets

Another helpful addition to Curves in CS3 is the Preset drop-down menu. Adobe has created a series of frequently used curves that you can apply with a single click (see Figure 6.35). That way you can quickly add a small amount of contrast or other common curves without having to re-create the curve yourself. You can also choose one of the preset curves and then modify it to suit your needs by clicking the anchor points and moving them and/or adding anchor points.

Figure 6.35
Using the new Curves presets can be a time-saver.

In addition, you can create your own presets that will appear in the drop-down menu. To create your own presets, take these steps:

1. Open an image, and create a curve. For example, perhaps you frequently add contrast just to the middle tones, and you prefer a little more contrast than what the Linear Contrast (RGB) preset applies. You could start with the preset and modify it, or you could create a completely new curve.

2. When you have the curve the way you want, click the Preset Options box ▤, and choose Save Preset.

3. In the next dialog box (Figure 6.36), give your curve a name, and make sure it's specific enough that you'll know immediately which curve is which. Leave Where set at the default folder Curves. That way your new preset will appear in the drop-down menu.

Figure 6.36
Name your curves so you can tell them apart.

4. Click Save, and your new preset appears in the Preset drop-down menu, as shown in Figure 6.37.

Figure 6.37
Once you create and save your custom preset, it appears in the Preset drop-down menu.

Note: The Curves Pencil tool isn't a feature we use often, but occasionally it comes in handy. You use it to hand draw all or part of the curve. This is particularly helpful when you add a series of anchor points that are close together and make significant adjustments to them because the curve sometimes becomes quite bumpy. By using the Pencil tool to draw a smoother curve in that area, you avoid the problem of abrupt changes within the image and bring the adjustment under control. You can smooth your hand-drawn curve by clicking Smooth. After refining the shape of the curve, click the Anchor Points button to the left of the Pencil button to return to a curve with defined anchor points. The position and quantity of the anchor points are updated based on the new shape of the curve.

Try It! To start getting more comfortable with Curves, open the image Curves on the accompanying CD, and make some adjustments, starting with a simple S curve adjustment and then working to fine-tune the overall tonality to your liking.

The Shadow/Highlight Adjustment

The Shadow/Highlight adjustment is an excellent way to reveal subtle detail in the shadow and/or highlight areas of your images. Although you could theoretically produce very similar results with sophisticated use of Curves, the Shadow/Highlight adjustment is far easier to use when you need to recover detail that has been lost in shadow or highlight areas because of excessive contrast. It's similar to the Fill Light and Recovery sliders in ACR, which we covered in Chapter 3, but it has additional controls so you can fine-tune the results.

Note: Some photographers are tempted to try to use Shadow/Highlight to fix all their exposure problems. We don't recommend that because the Shadow/Highlight adjustment works by reducing contrast. That's fine for small tonal ranges, but it's not usually a good idea to do throughout the entire image. We find it's far more effective to limit the Shadow/Highlight tool to recovering detail in the deep shadows and recovering highlights in very light areas.

Although you can't apply the Shadow/Highlight adjustment as an adjustment layer, in CS3 you can use it as a Smart Filter. As we discussed in Chapter 5, "Workflows and First Steps," a filter that's applied as a Smart Filter behaves similarly to an adjustment layer. The advantage of using it as a Smart Filter is that you can tweak the settings as needed, and you can add a layer mask to it to target the effects to certain areas of your image. For example, perhaps you have a portrait of a dark animal against a dark background. You may want to reveal details in the shadows of the animal, but not in the background.

Note: In Photoshop CS2 you have to apply Shadow/Highlight directly to a pixel layer. If you are using CS2, you'll need to duplicate the background layer and then apply the Shadow/Highlight adjustment directly on the copy layer. To do so, click the thumbnail for the background layer, and drag it to the New Layer button at the bottom of the Layers panel.

We recommend using the Shadow/Highlight adjustment early in your workflow, as the first step after you open the raw file as a Smart Object. To do so, take these steps:

1. If your background layer is not already a Smart Object, you'll need to convert it to one by choosing Layer > Smart Objects > Convert to Smart Object. That way you can use Shadow/Highlight as a Smart Filter.

2. Choose Image > Adjustments > Shadow/Highlight. Shadow/Highlight will automatically be opened as a Smart Filter, as shown in Figure 6.38.

Figure 6.38
Photoshop CS3 enables you to use the Shadow/Highlight adjustment as a Smart Filter.

The default dialog box for Shadow/Highlight in Photoshop includes only the Amount sliders for Shadows and Highlights (see Figure 6.39), and you should rarely use it in this abbreviated form. (We'll talk about Show More Options in just a second.)

In effect, think of the Amount slider for Shadows as allowing you to decide how much to lighten the darkest areas of your image, and the Amount slider for Highlights provides a similar ability to darken the brightest areas. Your first reaction may be that doing so simply reduces contrast and produces a muddy image. However, keep in mind that this adjustment is designed for situations where contrast is too high or when you want to extract more detail from the darkest and brightest areas of your image. When used with modest settings, the result is an effective increase in detail without a problematic loss of contrast.

Figure 6.39
The default Shadow/Highlight dialog box includes only basic controls for adjusting your image.

Using the basic Shadow/Highlight control is a simple matter of adjusting the sliders to extract the desired level of detail in the image. As you make these adjustments, use care not to overcorrect, which can create an image that is excessively flat or that has an artificial appearance.

The real power of the Shadow/Highlight control is enabled when you select the Show More Options check box. This enlarges the dialog box to include many additional controls for fine-tuning the adjustment (see Figure 6.40). The controls are divided into three sections. The Shadows and Highlights sections provide similar controls for adjusting areas of your image based on tonal value; the Adjustments section provides additional controls for improving specific aspects of the image.

Figure 6.40
When you select the Show More Options check box, the Shadow/Highlight dialog box expands to include more controls.

The controls in both the Shadows and Highlights sections are the same, although they obviously target different areas of the image based on tonal value:

Amount   The Amount slider affects the strength of the adjustment you're making to the area.

Tonal Width   To adjust the range of tonal values that will be affected by this adjustment, use the Tonal Width slider. A low value causes only a limited range of tonal values within the image to be affected, whereas a high value allows the adjustment to apply to a wider range. In other words, you expand or contract the area to be adjusted by defining a tonal range. Try to limit the tonal width to as narrow a range as possible to give you the desired results.

Radius   The Radius slider determines how far outward from pixels that fit within the defined tonal range the adjustment will spread. This provides the ability to blend the adjustment to produce a more realistic effect.

> **N o t e :** You'll find the best settings with experimentation. Usually you'll want the Tonal Width setting to be as limited as possible and still affect the desired tonal range. Often we find effective radius settings around the 25–40 range and again at the very high range of the scale. Don't hesitate to drag the sliders and experiment.

After you've adjusted the controls in the Shadows and Highlights sections, use the Adjustments section to fine-tune the final result. The Color Correction slider is really a saturation adjustment that affects the darkest areas of your image. This control allows you to compensate for shadow areas that often have reduced saturation compared to other areas of the image because there isn't adequate light to enhance the colors. After you've brightened up shadow areas, you'll likely want to increase the saturation slightly so those areas match the rest of the image.

Similarly, brightening shadows and darkening highlights helps extract more detail but results in an overall reduction in contrast. The Midtone Contrast slider allows you to apply some compensation by adjusting contrast for just the midtone values within the image, leaving the shadow and highlight areas you've already adjusted relatively unchanged.

The Black Clip and White Clip settings allow you to specify how much detail can be sacrificed in the image when making adjustments by using Shadow/Highlight. We recommend leaving these values to their default of 0.01% to minimize the loss of detail.

> **N o t e :** Don't let the Save As Defaults button lull you into thinking you can establish one set of adjustments for Shadow/Highlight that will be appropriate for all images. Each image deserves its own custom settings.

Once you've established the optimal settings in the Shadow/Highlight dialog box, click OK to apply the adjustment to your image, as you can see in the examples in Figure 6.41.

Figure 6.41
The Shadow/Highlight adjustment allows you to extract detail in your image with relative ease. (Photo by Tim Grey.)

Try It! Open the image ShadowHighlight on the accompanying CD, and work with the Shadow/Highlight adjustment to extract as much detail as possible while maintaining appropriate overall contrast.

Greg Downing has been an avid birder and nature lover for more than 30 years. His connection with nature and interest in avian subjects evolved naturally into a career of photographing birds, selling prints, and teaching photography. He gives some tips on using the Shadow/Highlight tool.

Shadow/Highlight Tips

by Greg Downing

Although there are other methods for targeted tonal adjustments, particularly with newer versions of Photoshop, the Shadow/Highlight (S/H) tool is still very popular with some nature photographers because it is relatively easy to use. The tool permits independent tonal adjustments over the darks and lights, allowing photographers to make precise corrections to high-contrast images or images captured in difficult lighting conditions. The Shadow/Highlight tool can even revive an image and often save the day when used correctly.

Following are some tips for making the most of this tool.

Make Shadow/Highlight Adjustments in a Layer

As with all tonal adjustments, I recommend using adjustment layers in order to allow additional refinements either later in your workflow or even at a later date if the image is saved with the layers intact. Unfortunately, the Shadow/Highlight tool does not work as an adjustment layer, but here's an easy tip to overcome this limitation:

Create a duplicate background layer and run a fairly strong Shadow/Highlight correction on this new layer; then fine-tune the effect by adjusting the overall opacity for the layer.

As I mentioned, unlike actual adjustment layers, you cannot change the amount of Shadow/Highlight adjustment should you later desire to do so. However, you can always go back and adjust the opacity of the layer, apply or adjust a layer mask, or trash the layer altogether or start over should you change your mind.

(We authors interrupt to mention that in CS3 you can apply the Shadow/Highlight adjustment as a Smart Filter which enables you to readjust the settings at any point in the future.)

Add a Layer Mask

The S/H tool is a global tool, meaning it affects the whole image based on the settings used. This is not always desirable, and more often, smaller local adjustments are preferred. For these precise local adjustments, you can apply the S/H adjustment to a duplicate layer as described in this section, focusing only on the areas of importance. Next, apply a layer mask set to Hide All (Layer > Add Layer Mask > Hide All) and brush the adjustment into only those areas needing correction. Again, you can make the initial S/H adjustments fairly strong and then fine-tune them by adjusting the opacity, size, and softness of the brush you use for the mask, as well as the opacity of the entire duplicate layer.

This also lets you to make stronger adjustments in one area of the image and more mild adjustments in another area, allowing ultimate control.

Continues

Shadow/Highlight Tips *(Continued)*

Use Separate Layers for Each Type of Adjustment

If you find the need to make adjustments to both the shadows and the highlights, in the same image, try using a separate layer for each for ultimate control. This way you can apply your mask and adjust your overall layer opacity for both shadows and highlights independently.

As with most tonal and color adjustments in Photoshop the tendency to go too far should be avoided. Often times subtle adjustments are all that you need to make a noticeable improvement in your images. The use of layers gives the photographer the ability to toggle the adjustment on and off (by clicking the layer visibility on and off) in order to better evaluate the final results.

Shown here are before and after examples of an image that was corrected using these tips. Notice the additional subtle detail extracted from the light and dark areas of the image using these methods.

Before

After

Becoming adept with the Shadow/Highlight tool and using it in combination with a duplicate background layer and a layer mask opens your images to new possibilities, perhaps even bringing some old photos back to life.

© Greg Downing, www.gdphotography.com

Emphasizing Your Subject

Exposure is everything in photography, and for nature photographers it can be even more critical. Being able to reveal detail hidden within your images, and to emphasize key areas of those images, can be a tremendous advantage for the final result. By practicing the adjustments covered in this chapter, you'll be able to exercise tremendous control over your images, taking them far beyond what you'd be able to achieve if you used only the camera to control your exposure.

Learn to emphasize your subject by making it subtly lighter, brighter, and/or more contrasty than the background, by using layer masks. By taking advantage of the different exposure tools in conjunction with layer masks, you can tweak the tonalities in different areas of your image, creating a final print (or other output) that would have taken incredible skill and long hours in a traditional darkroom.

Color Adjustments

Expressive images with the most impact use color wisely to direct our attention and elicit reactions. Color often creates strong emotional reactions, drawing you into a photo or making you pass it by. Nature photographers have more choices to make about the colors in their images than do most photographers. Other types of photographers must maintain neutral colors, but we nature photographers are often looking for color casts, such as the warm glow of early morning light. Although we're often trying to create as natural-looking an image as possible, we also have a great deal of latitude to modify colors to make our images more expressive.

7

—

211

COLOR ADJUSTMENTS

Chapter Contents
Recognizing Color Casts
Removing Color Casts
Adding Color Casts
Modifying Colors to Match Nature or Add Impact
Layer Masks and Color Adjustments

Recognizing Color Casts

Sometimes you may look at your image and decide that the colors just aren't quite right, but you may or may not be able to identify which color is the culprit. At other times you may not even be aware there is a color cast until you do some checking. There are several ways to detect a color cast.

Using Hue/Saturation to Reveal a Color Cast

An easy way to identify a color cast is to open a temporary Hue/Saturation adjustment layer—click the adjustment layer icon at the bottom of the Layers panel, choose Hue/Saturation, and drag the Saturation slider all the way to +100. Although your picture will look weird, this will show you where there are colors that don't belong. Think for a minute about what colors you'd expect to see versus what you do see, since the colors are supersaturated. Pay attention to the hues to determine whether there are unexpected colors appearing.

Note: Although it's possible to create any adjustment layer from the main menu bar—by choosing Layer > New Adjustment Layer—we recommend opening all adjustment layers from the icon at the bottom of the Layers panel. By using the icon, you won't accidentally find yourself choosing Image > Adjustments on the main menu and working directly on your pixels.

As an example, Figure 7.1 shows a picture of a snowy egret with no obvious color cast and the same image with the Hue/Saturation slider pulled all the way to +100. Although you expect the water to turn blue or blue/cyan and the sand to turn yellowish, you do not expect the egret to be magenta. Clearly there is at least a partial magenta cast to this image.

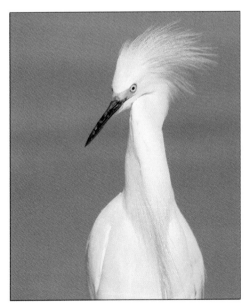

Figure 7.1 At first glance, there is not an obvious color cast in this picture (left). Boosting the saturation to +100 reveals an unexpected magenta cast in the snowy egret (right). (Photo by Ellen Anon.)

It may be difficult to determine whether the cast is a single color such as cyan or a combination such as blue and cyan (Figure 7.2 shows an example of this). Note that early morning outdoor pictures on what will be a sunny day often have a cyan cast to them. Pictures taken in shade often have bluish casts. Magenta casts are also common, particularly with landscape pictures or images that include a partly cloudy sky.

Figure 7.2

Initially you may not be certain whether there is a color cast in the lava (top). Increasing the saturation to +100 reveals a definite cyan cast (bottom). (Photo by Ellen Anon.)

If pulling the Hue/Saturation slider has revealed an obviously problematic color cast, it can be tempting to just go to the channel containing that color and reduce the saturation. Occasionally that approach will work, but the problem is that it reduces the saturation of that color throughout the entire image, even in areas that should be that color. There are several more useful approaches to removing the color cast that we will describe shortly.

After using the Hue/Saturation adjustment dialog box to identify a color cast, click the Cancel button to remove this layer. You only need it temporarily to give you an idea of whether you need to consider doing something to remove a color cast.

Using the Info Panel to Reveal a Color Cast

When we talk about "neutral" in a digital picture, we're referring to the relationship of the red, green, and blue values for any tone, from pure white (where the RGB values are 255,255,255) to pure black (RGB values 0,0,0), as well as all tonalities of gray in between in which the red, green, and blue values are all nearly identical. Neutral also means that pixels that should be pure red will have an RGB reading of 255,0,0; pure green will be 0,255,0; and pure blue will be 0,0,255. The farther away from these readings any pixel is that should be neutral gray or pure red, green, or blue, the more of a color cast there is. We nature photographers rarely, if ever, need to be concerned with *total* neutrality. In fact, outdoor lighting almost always imparts a color cast—sometimes warm, sometimes cool. Nonetheless, it's important to understand what neutral would be.

Understanding the values that neutral pixels should have enables you to check for a color cast by using the Info panel. If there are any areas of the picture that you know should be neutral (pure white, gray, or black), zoom in, and place your cursor over that area. Take a look at the Info panel to see the red, green, and blue values of that point.

If the pixel is neutral, the values should be all the same (or very close). If one value is higher than the others, then there will be a cast in that direction. For example, if an area that should be neutral has roughly equal blue and green values but a higher red value, there is a reddish cast to the picture. Conversely, if the number for one channel reads lower than the other two channels, then the cast is toward the opposite color of that channel. Table 7.1 lists all the ways that one RGB channel might differ from the other two, creating a color cast.

Table 7.1 Identifying a Color Cast via the Info Panel

If This Value Is Off	This Cast Will Be Seen
Red high	Red
Red low	Cyan
Green high	Green
Green low	Magenta
Blue high	Blue
Blue low	Yellow

In Figure 7.3, a reading taken from the wing of the white pelican should be close to neutral. Instead, it shows markedly lower red values, reflecting a cyan cast throughout the image.

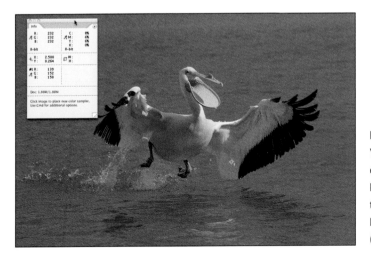

Figure 7.3
You know this image has a cyan color cast because the RGB values of a sample from the white wing (point #1 in the Info panel) are 139,152,150. (Photo by Ellen Anon.)

> **Note:** Remembering the basic RGB colors (red, green, and blue) and their opposites (cyan, magenta, and yellow) will make your color adjustments much easier and predictable. Red and cyan are opposites, and green and magenta are opposites, as are blue and yellow. Once you appreciate this fact, you'll know to add cyan to reduce a red cast, add green to reduce a magenta cast, add blue to reduce a yellow cast, and so on.

If you have determined that there is a color cast in your image, you'll have to decide whether to eliminate it. Not all color casts are bad! Remember that part of the reason many nature photographers prefer early morning and late afternoon light is for the lovely warm (yellow/red) quality it imparts to their subjects as opposed to the more neutral or cooler light that may occur in the middle of the day.

Removing Color Casts

There are a number of different approaches to removing color casts, and depending upon the individual circumstances, one approach is likely to be superior in one situation, whereas another approach may be more effective in another. For that reason, we'll present several ways to deal with color casts, some of which are objective and some subjective.

Subjective Methods for Removing a Color Cast

First we'll look at the subjective ways to remove a color cast from your image. Some of these approaches allow Adobe Photoshop to do most of the work for you, while others offer considerable individual control over the process and invite a great deal of personal preference.

Using the Gray Eyedropper

If there's an area that you know should be neutral—it can be any tonality from almost white to almost black and any shade of gray in between—there is a very simple way to eliminate the color cast in your picture.

1. Create a new Levels adjustment layer by clicking the Create New Adjustment Or Fill Layer icon at the bottom of the Layers panel and selecting Levels.

2. Make sure to take the time to double-click the word *Levels* and rename the layer; we use the name "color cast." That way, if you return to this file later, assuming you save it with your layers intact, you'll know exactly what you did in each layer.

3. Click the gray (middle) eyedropper to select it, and then click the area of your image that should be neutral. Photoshop will automatically define the point you click as "neutral" (that is, having equal red, green, and blue values) and will remap the rest of the image accordingly.

You can also do the same thing using the gray (middle) eyedropper in the Curves Adjustment Layer box; the results will be just slightly different, since Levels uses a linear algorithm to do the remapping whereas Curves naturally uses a tone curve. Practically speaking, the results will be very similar in most cases. The results are also very similar to using the White Balance eyedropper in ACR.

Try It! Open Colorcast1 from the accompanying CD or an image of your own that you suspect has a color cast but includes an area you think should be neutral. First, determine whether there is in fact a color cast (either use the Hue/Saturation slider method or check the Info panel). Next, create a Levels adjustment layer, and click the middle eyedropper on a neutral pixel to remove the cast. Turn off the visibility of the Levels layer (by clicking the eyeball next to it in the Layers panel). Add a Curves adjustment layer, and click the same point with the Curves middle eyedropper. Then, alternate viewing the Curves and Levels layers' visibility to compare the results.

Using Individual Channels within Levels

When you made a Levels adjustment layer in Chapter 6, "Exposure Adjustments," to make tonal adjustments, you used the composite RGB channel (named Master in the Levels dialog box). This means that the adjustments you made affected all the channels. Now, instead of working in the composite channel, you'll modify one channel at a time. This is another subjective way to achieve the desired color balance within an image. You will need to use the Channel drop-down menu, as shown in Figure 7.4.

Figure 7.4
To adjust a color cast within Levels, use the individual color channels.

To modify the color cast one channel at a time, take the following steps:

1. Create a new Levels adjustment layer, and rename it "color cast."

2. Select the Red channel, and adjust the midpoint slider to achieve the desired balance between red and cyan. Don't move the endpoint sliders in the individual channels because this will increase the contrast within that channel and could lead to lost data.

3. Open the Green channel, and move the midpoint slider to modify the balance between green and magenta.

4. Finally, repeat the process with the Blue channel until you're satisfied with the balance between the blue and yellow.

In the image shown in Figure 7.5, we've removed the warm yellow cast and made the picture closer to neutral by moving the midpoint slider in the blue channel.

Figure 7.5
By adjusting the midpoint sliders within the individual color channels in Levels, you can remove or introduce a color cast as desired. (Photo by Ellen Anon.)

Using Individual Channels within Curves

You can also remove a color cast within a Curves adjustment layer by using the individual RGB channels one at a time. You need to set a point usually that's close to the middle and gently raise the curve upward or downward. If, however, you want to affect the colors primarily in the highlights or shadows, then set a point closer to the ends of the curve—perhaps one-quarter to one-third of the way up or down the curve, as shown in Figure 7.6.

> **Note:** When making a Curves adjustment layer to adjust tonalities and exposure, you may want to set the blending mode of the layer to Luminosity to avoid unwanted color shifts. However, when using a Curves layer to adjust color, you need to leave it in Normal mode.

Just as when you used Curves in Chapter 6 to adjust tonalities, you could choose to affect only a segment of the tonal range—such as the highlights or shadows—by placing three points on the curve to "lock it down" and prevent the remaining tonalities from being affected. It's important to realize that only slight adjustments are necessary. You'll be surprised how a seemingly tiny adjustment can have a huge impact on your image.

Figure 7.6

Slight changes in the individual color channels of Curves can have a dramatic impact on the color within your image. (Photo by Ellen Anon.)

Try It! Open Colorcast2 from the accompanying CD (or one of your own images), and try adjusting the color balance within the image, first using the individual color channels within a Levels adjustment layer. Hide the visibility of the Levels layer, and create a Curves adjustment layer. Adjust the curve individually within each color channel, and compare the results of the two techniques. See which you prefer; initially, it's likely that Levels will seem easier, although Curves allows for finer control.

Using a Color Balance Adjustment Layer

A Color Balance adjustment layer may be the most generally useful approach to correcting color casts. In essence, it presents the sliders from each of the individual color channels within Levels in one interface, along with the ability to set the sliders to affect primarily the midtones, shadows, and/or highlights. As you pull the sliders, you are shifting the color values in your image toward the basic colors (red, green, and blue) or toward their opposites (cyan, magenta, and yellow), as shown in Figure 7.7.

Figure 7.7
Color Balance provides an easy interface to adjust the balance within each color channel as well as to make those changes to the midtones, highlights, and/or shadows.

The Tone Balance section is set by default to affect the midtones when you first open a Color Balance adjustment layer. When Midtones is checked, the changes you make on the sliders affect the majority of the pixels and tones in your image, excluding only the brightest and darkest values. Selecting the Highlights or Shadows option instead allows you to primarily adjust the most extreme tonalities in your image. You may want to adjust each of them slightly differently.

This can be quite useful in some situations common to nature photography. For example, if you have a white bird photographed in early morning light on water, you may want to emphasize the warm light on the bird but not make the water appear too discolored. To do this, click Highlights, and adjust the sliders to allow for more yellow and red and possibly magenta than in the midtones and shadows, where you might be attempting to limit the color cast, as shown in Figure 7.8.

Figure 7.8 Adjusting the Color Balance sliders differently for the highlights than for the midtones enables you to leave more of a color cast on the white bird, while limiting the color cast on the water. (Photo by Ellen Anon.)

Setting the best position for the sliders can be challenging and is a subjective decision. If there is a strong color cast in your image, it's often easiest to begin by working with the corresponding slider in the midtones. For example, if there is a strong cyan cast in your image, start by adjusting the Cyan/Red slider for Midtones. Then, if necessary, adjust the other sliders for midtone values; after that, click Highlights and adjust, and then click Shadows to set those sliders. You may be happy with the color balance after adjusting only the midtone sliders since they affect the majority of the pixels within most pictures.

On the other hand, you may find it necessary to adjust each slider several times, and you may even discover that you can't decide which setting you like best. At that point, we offer two suggestions:

- Pull the slider that's creating a problem for you to an extreme position, and start again. You might even pull it all the way to the right, then reset it and note the setting, and then pull it all the way to the left and readjust it to where it looks best. Hopefully you'll be able to find a position that looks good to you.

- If you're still not sure, it's time to get up and walk away from your computer for a couple of minutes. When you come back, note your gut-level reaction to the picture. Are the colors good, or are they too much toward a specific color cast? Trust your immediate reaction, don't overthink it, and then make any necessary changes.

Objective Method for Removing a Color Cast

At times, even nature photographers prefer to make their images as neutral as possible, and in such cases an objective approach may be best. We've also encountered some photographers who are color-blind and who don't have the luxury of having someone close by to comment on the colors within their images. Sometimes they feel safest using an objective method to correct color casts.

To objectively remove a color cast, you use all three eyedroppers in a Levels adjustment layer. Initially you'll identify and set the white and black points, and then you'll have Photoshop define them as neutral.

As you already know, you can hold down the Alt/Option key while pulling the endpoint sliders within Levels to identify the lightest and darkest pixels within your image. However, you don't want to have to rely on your memories as to exactly where they're located. Instead, we'll show you how to mark them to be sure you're accurately targeting the darkest and lightest pixels within your image.

To objectively remove a color cast, take the following steps:

1. Begin by choosing the Color Sampler tool. It's located on the Tool panel with the Eyedropper tool (see Figure 7.9). Make certain to set the Sample Size option on the Options bar to 3×3 Average rather than to its default value, which is a one-point sample. The 3×3 Average option causes Photoshop to read an average of nine pixels, which prevents you from accidentally selecting a pixel that is different from its neighboring pixels.

Figure 7.9 The Color Sampler tool allows you to mark particular pixels within the image (left). It's best to set the Color Sampler tool to use a 3×3 sample to avoid accidentally sampling an aberrant pixel.

2. Create a Threshold adjustment layer via the same icon and drop-down menu that you've been using to access the other adjustment layers, as shown in Figure 7.10.

Figure 7.10
Open a Threshold adjustment layer to identify the darkest and lightest pixels within the image.

3. You see a histogram with only one slider, and your image is in black and white, with no tones in between (see Figure 7.11). Move the slider all the way to the right until the image preview becomes totally black.

Figure 7.11
Your image will appear in black and white, with no in-between tonalities.

4. Slowly move the slider to the left, and stop when you see the first pixels begin to turn white. These are the lightest pixels in your image.
5. Zoom in by pressing Ctrl++/⌘++ to clearly identify the lightest pixels. Accuracy is vital here. Click OK.
6. Now, with the Color Sampler tool still selected, place your cursor over the lightest pixels in your image, and click. The tool leaves a small circle with the number 1 on your image. (Alternatively, you can hold down the Shift key and use the Eyedropper tool.)

7. Zoom out to see your entire image by pressing Ctrl+0/⌘+0.

8. Double-click the Threshold layer icon to reopen it. This time move the slider all the way to the left so that the preview becomes entirely white. Gradually move it to the right, and note where the first black pixels appear. These are the darkest pixels in the image.

9. Again, zoom in as necessary to clearly see these pixels, and then click OK.

10. Place your cursor over one of the darkest pixels, and click. This time, the Color Sampler tool leaves a small circle with the number 2.

11. Zoom out again by pressing Ctrl+0/⌘+0 to see your whole image.

12. Since you no longer need the Threshold adjustment layer, drag it to the trash can to remove it. The selected pixels remain marked, and you have an objective indicator of the darkest and lightest pixels within your image, as shown in Figure 7.12.

Figure 7.12
The darkest pixel (bottom edge) and lightest pixel (corner of the mouth) in your image are marked with a numbered target so you can easily identify them. (Note the red circles are here for illustrative purposes only; you won't see them on your image.) (Photo by Ellen Anon.)

13. Now create a Levels adjustment layer as usual. Be sure to rename it to indicate you're using this one to remove a color cast.

14. Next, you're going to set the values for the black and white points that you want Photoshop to use. If you have previously saved default values for black and white, you can skip this step:

    a. Double-click the black eyedropper to open the Color Picker dialog box. Type values of R = **10**, G = **10**, and B = **10** for the black point, and click OK. (If you have established a different set of black values for your printer, use them here.)

    b. Double-click the white eyedropper, and the Color Picker dialog box reappears. Type values of R = **244**, G = **244**, B = **244**, as shown in Figure 7.13, for the white point, and click OK.

    c. Click OK in the main Levels dialog box. Because you've changed one or more eyedropper values, Photoshop asks whether you want to set these as your default values. Click OK.

Figure 7.13

By typing values into the Color Picker, you can set the black and white values within your image and then save them as the default values for Photoshop to use in the future.

Note: Because most of our printers can't print in ways that allow us to differentiate shades of black all the way to 0,0,0 or whites all the way to 255,255,255, we have to use slightly different values. Once those are set, we can save them as default values. The actual ideal values for your printer may vary and can be determined by printing out test strips of blacks and whites at various values—(8,8,8), (12,12,12), (15,15,15), and so on—to determine where you can begin to see differences in the dark tones. You can do a similar test strip for the whites. The values suggested in step 14 work for many people.

15. Now click the white eyedropper, and then move your cursor onto your image. Carefully and accurately align the cursor with the point the Color Sampler tool marked with the number 1. When you have precisely aligned the cursor and the sampled point, click OK. This remaps that point to an RGB value of 244,244,244, or neutral white. Verify this by looking at the Info panel, which shows you the "before" and "after" values of the targeted points.

16. Repeat the same process with the black eyedropper. In most cases, the color cast within the image is neutralized (see Figure 7.14). In some images, however, you also need to use the gray (middle) eyedropper and click somewhere in the image that should be neutral.

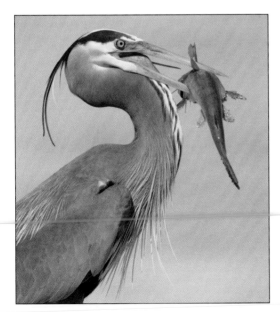

Figure 7.14

Compare this neutral version of the heron with the original in Figure 7.12. (Photo by Ellen Anon.)

17. To remove the little circles with the numbers by them, reselect the Color Sampler tool, and hold down the Alt/Option key. As you approach a circle, your cursor changes to a scissors. When you click, the circle is removed. Alternately, simply hide them by choosing View > Extras from the menu. This toggles the visibility of the color samples. Simply hiding them can be a time-saver if there is any possibility that you might want to modify your color-cast adjustments.

Try It! Open the image on the CD named Colorcast3 or one of your own images, and try removing the color cast using the objective method. You can compare the results with what you obtain using your favorite subjective method.

This approach may seem quite long, but actually it's pretty straightforward and a good way to set your black and white points as well as to remove a color cast objectively. You could also use the eyedroppers in a Curves adjustment layer to achieve similar results. You would follow the exact same procedure described in this section from within the Curves dialog box.

Award-winning nature photographer John Shaw agreed to share his version of the color-cast correction process with us.

Neutralizing a Color Cast
by John Shaw

Let's open a scan of a film image taken during a Colorado blizzard. There is a definite blue bias to the image, and while snow in overcast conditions often really does show a blue component, this is rather extreme.

© John Shaw

Let's use a Levels adjustment layer (adjustment layers are always the best way to do non-destructive editing) and Threshold to find the lightest and darkest areas of the image. To do this, choose Layer > New Adjustment Layer (actually I always use the shortcut icon at the bottom of the Layers panel, as shortcuts are a great help in Photoshop), and click Threshold for the type of layer you want to create. Your image turns into black and white, and a dialog appears with one slider.

Neutralizing a Color Cast *(Continued)*

As you mouse over your image, notice that you get an eyedropper tool. Right-click or Ctrl+click to get a context menu, and set the eyedropper to a 3×3 sample. Move the slider to the left and watch your image for the last place there is a solid black. When you find this location, position the eyedropper over it, and Shift+click to set a color sampler point. Now pull the slider to the right, watch for the last solid white area of the image, and Shift+click again with the eyedropper to set another color sampler point. You might have to enlarge your screen image while setting these points.

Click Cancel in the Threshold dialog box; you used it only to set those two color sampler locations, nothing else.

Make sure your Info panel is visible, and open a Levels adjustment layer. You'll see three eyedroppers in the dialog box. Click the white eyedropper (the right one), and then click the white color sampler point you set in the image. Look at the Info panel for this point, and you'll see two sets of RGB values displayed for that point. The first set is the original "before" values; the second ones are "after" you clicked the sampler point. Note the highest numerical "before" value. Now in Levels, open each channel, and move the white input slider until the "after" numbers in the Info panel all match that highest "before" value.

Repeat this process for the black color sampler point you set. Select the black Levels eyedropper, click the black point, and move the Levels black output slider until all those numbers match in numerical value also.

You have now neutralized any color cast. Of course, if you don't want a perfectly neutral result, you can change the numbers just partially, leaving one channel more prominent.

© John Shaw, www.johnshawphoto.com

© John Shaw

Adding a Color Cast

The reality is that nature photographers get up ridiculously early in the morning and stay out photographing until the sunset is completely over because we *like* our pictures to have the warm special light of early and late day. We tend to prefer the color casts imparted by this light because our photos have a different feeling in them and often create more impact on the viewer than more neutral versions of the same subject. It's possible to create color casts to simulate that light using the same subjective techniques we used before to remove color casts.

For example, if you're using the middle (gray) eyedropper from within Levels or Curves and you click an area that should not be neutral, Photoshop will still be obliging and redefine the values of that point to be neutral anyway, and the rest of the image then has a color cast. This can be a good thing! You can introduce a slight warmth to your images this way by clicking a point that actually should be slightly bluish or cyanish, as shown in Figure 7.15. Conversely, you can make them appear cooler by clicking a pixel that should actually be slightly yellowish or reddish. Remember that Ctrl+Z/ ⌘+Z undoes your last step, so you can use a trial-and-error approach in finding the right spot to use. Obviously, this is a subjective way to determine the color balance within your picture that relies on Photoshop to do most of the work for you.

Figure 7.15
By clicking the middle eyedropper on a point that should be slightly bluish, you can impart a warmer color cast to an image. (Photo by Ellen Anon.)

If you prefer to use a Color Balance adjustment layer, simply adjust the sliders to achieve the desired effect. No one but you has to know that the picture wasn't taken in the earliest morning light!

Photoshop also offers a Photofilter adjustment layer option. Choosing this adjustment layer allows you to select from a drop-down menu containing a variety of color tints, including some with familiar names like 81A (see Figure 7.16). You can adjust a Density slider to control the strength of the effect. Although this is a quick and easy way to add a color cast to your image, the disadvantage is having to settle for tints predetermined by the folks at Adobe who wrote Photoshop rather than choosing the exact color cast that suits your image.

Figure 7.16
The Photofilter adjustment layer contains a number of familiar-sounding filters.

Modifying Colors to Match Nature or Add Impact

After you've adjusted the overall color cast of your image—whether to neutralize it or to add a color cast—you often want to work with the colors a little more to help convey the mood and impact you have in mind. Colors elicit emotional reactions from those who view your pictures. For example, pastels can be calming, while bold primary colors can be energizing, as shown in Figure 7.17. A blue cast in a snow scene can add to the sense of coldness and perhaps isolation. Warm yellow light rays drifting through trees or lighting flowers may give a sense of peacefulness and well being or spirituality.

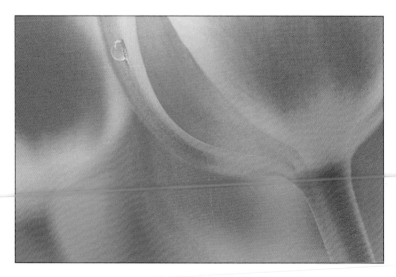

Figure 7.17
Colors elicit emotional reactions from the viewer, so it makes sense to adjust the colors accordingly. (Photo by Ellen Anon.)

It's well worth the effort to spend the time to make certain the colors in your pictures elicit the reactions you have in mind. The two primary tools you'll use for this are Hue/Saturation adjustment layers and Selective Color adjustment layers.

Adjusting Hue and Saturation

In CS3 you may opt to make most of your hue and saturation adjustments in the raw converter. However, there will be times when you want to use the Hue/Saturation adjustment within Photoshop.

Most photographers who use Photoshop are comfortable opening the Hue/Saturation dialog box (which of course we recommend you do as an adjustment layer) and adjusting the saturation of their image. This is one of the more intuitive adjustments within Photoshop, and it can make your images come to life. However, be careful not to go to excess with saturation, not only because the colors will look fake but also because you risk losing detail as you increase the saturation. This is the result of more and more pixels being shifted toward the purest colors, resulting in a loss of detail in those areas. With most images, you'll find a saturation increase in the composite channel of 6 to 12 is usually effective. Of course, this varies among files from different cameras as well as individual preferences.

Although you can modify the saturation of all the colors within your image by using the composite or "Master" channel, which is the default when you open the Hue/Saturation adjustment layer, one extremely useful feature is the ability to target a particular color range from the drop-down menu (see Figure 7.18). This way you can modify colors individually by selecting the desired color and changing the saturation—or hue—of a single color within your image.

Figure 7.18
The Hue/Saturation dialog box enables you to target not only the composite channel but individual colors as well.

In addition to choosing a particular color, you can target a specific range of colors to modify within the Hue/Saturation dialog box. However, you can't do this from the composite channel; you have to begin within a specific color channel from the drop-down menu. Select the range of colors to modify by first clicking the eyedropper in the Hue/Saturation dialog box and then clicking the color you want to adjust.

Don't worry if you're not sure which color to choose from the drop-down menu. It doesn't matter which one you begin with, because once you click with the first eye-dropper, Photoshop automatically changes to the correct color channel. You can increase the range of colors to be modified by clicking with the plus eyedropper or decrease it by clicking with the minus eyedropper.

Alternately, you can refine the range of colors to modify by adjusting the Color Range bars that appear between the two color gradients when you have specified a particular color channel (see Figure 7.19). This process is a bit more advanced than the other adjustments you've been making.

Figure 7.19

You can set the range of colors to be adjusted by moving the Color Range bars that appear between the two color gradients at the bottom of the Hue/Saturation dialog box.

To refine the range of colors to modify, follow these steps:

1. We recommend initially dragging the Saturation slider all the way to the left so that the selected range of colors is shifted to gray, as shown in Figure 7.20. This helps you to see what areas of the image you're modifying.

Figure 7.20

By moving the saturation slider to the left, the range of colors you will be modifying appears in gray on the color gradient.

2. Click the bars, and drag them to increase or decrease the targeted range of colors. This limits or expands the colors that will be affected by the adjustments you make to the sliders.

3. Click the two triangles outside the bars to define the extent of feathering of the color adjustments. These triangles control how gradual the transition is between the modified and original colors so that the adjustment is less obvious.

4. Having selected the target range of colors, move the Hue, Saturation, and Lightness sliders to achieve the desired effect.

Try It! Open the file HueSat from the accompanying CD or one of your own images, and select a single color and then a range of colors to adjust. Try changing not only the saturation but the hue as well.

Colorizing an Image

There are times when your original image may contain very little color information and instead contain a lot of neutral values. This happens sometimes in pictures of foggy or cold misty situations around trees. In such cases you may find that simply adjusting the Hue and Saturation sliders is not enough to add the color that you want. An answer is to use the Colorize option in the Hue/Saturation dialog box. Colorize changes the image into a duotone, and you use the Hue slider to select the desired color. The Saturation slider then adjusts the intensity of the color.

The Colorize option was helpful when one of our students had a lovely image of a gray covered bridge set amidst trees. He wanted to make the bridge red, but just changing the hue and saturation alone didn't work, so he used the following procedure.

To add color to neutral areas such as the gray bridge, follow these steps:

1. Select the area to be colorized using any of the selection tools discussed in Chapter 4.

2. Open a Hue/Saturation adjustment layer and check the Colorize box.

3. Notice that the Hue and Saturation sliders have moved substantially. Adjust all the sliders to colorize the targeted portion of your image as desired.

Another use of the Colorize option is to create a tint such as a sepia tint with a black-and-white image. We'll cover how to do this, as well as how to convert images to black and white, in Chapter 9, "Creative Effects."

Fine-Tuning with Selective Color

Sometimes a color may still not look right despite your best efforts at adjusting the color cast and making Hue/Saturation adjustments. The Selective Color adjustment layer, accessible from the same place as the other adjustment layers, enables you to modify the hue of specific colors, as well as whites, neutrals, and blacks (see Figure 7.21). This tool enables far greater control over the exact hue of any specific color than is possible within Hue/Saturation, as well as the ability to adjust color casts in whites, neutrals, and blacks.

Figure 7.21

The Selective Color Options dialog box allows you to modify the color components of specific colors as well as the whites, midtones, and blacks within your image.

Note: Similar adjustments that can be made with Selective Color can be made in the Hue/Saturation/Luminance tab of ACR. However, ACR does not have the option to adjust the whites, neutrals, and blacks within the same dialog box.

First, select the color you want to modify by clicking the appropriate color. For example, if you've adjusted an image but the blue of the sky seems off, you can alter the shade of blue, as shown in Figure 7.22. Notice that the sliders are labeled Cyan, Magenta, Yellow, and Black this time, because Selective Color was originally designed for use with CMYK output. But it works equally well with RGB! If you increase cyan, you are decreasing red, and if you decrease cyan, then obviously red increases. Similarly, increasing or decreasing magenta alters the percentage of green used in the color, and changing the amount of yellow will alter the amount of blue. By changing the percentage of each component of a color, you have fine control over the specific hues.

Figure 7.22

Selective Color was used to improve the shade of blue in the sky by making it slightly warmer. (Photo by Ellen Anon.)

So in the case of your blue sky, you might want to increase the cyan and blue components to make a better shade of sky blue (which is composed of both blue and cyan tones). If you increase the black within the Blues menu, the blue will get darker. In a sky, it's likely you'll need to work with the drop-down menus for Blue and Cyan and adjust the components within them.

Extremely precise adjustments are possible within each of the colors in the Selective Color Options dialog box. Those photographers who are latent artists may particularly enjoy this ability to fine-tune colors.

You will find that as you make a color more pure, there may be less need to increase overall saturation as much. This can lead to a more natural and pleasing final result in your image.

To add a little extra "pop" to your pictures, select Black as your target color, and then increase the percentage of Black by a small amount such as 2. The actual amount varies by image. This gives many images the illusion of being slightly sharper.

You can use Selective Color to remove some stubborn color casts by choosing Neutrals in the Colors list and adjusting the sliders as needed. One of our students came to a workshop with a shot, taken under unusual lighting in a mausoleum, that had a strong cyan cast. The only method that was successful in removing the color cast was to virtually eliminate cyan from the Neutrals and Whites within Selective Color.

Note: For more in-depth coverage of controlling color within your image, see *Color Confidence, Second Edition* (Sybex, 2006).

Layer Masks and Color Adjustments

So far we've described a variety of approaches for modifying the color within your entire image, all of which use adjustment layers and all of which adjust the color across the entire area of your photo. But there will be times when you want to target a specific part of your image to change, a part that will be determined by the subject matter rather than by a particular color range. For example, you may want to increase the saturation of your subject more than the background to help draw attention to your subject. Of course you'll be using layer masks to do that. Given the importance of gaining a solid understanding of layer masks, rather than force you to flip back to Chapter 6 to refresh your memory, we'll review the process here.

Creating Layer Masks via Selections

One way to affect only a portion of your image is to select that area, using any of the selection methods covered in Chapter 4 before you make the adjustment layer. This technique works well if you have a well-defined area you want to adjust, and it's Tim's preferred method. By making a selection prior to opening an adjustment layer, whatever adjustment you choose will impact only the selected area. If you then look at the layer mask that Photoshop automatically includes with every adjustment layer, you'll see that the area you selected appears white and the rest of the mask is black. As discussed in Chapter 6, any place in your image that corresponds to where the layer mask is white is affected by the adjustment in that layer, while any part of your image corresponding to where the layer mask is black is not affected. White shows the changes, black hides the changes.

You might want to draw attention to your subject's eyes, for example in the portrait of a crane in Figure 7.23.

Figure 7.23

If you have selected only the eyes of your subject, most of the layer mask will be black while the area representing the eyes will be white. (Photo by Ellen Anon.)

To draw attention to the eyes, take these steps:

1. To begin, select the eyes using the Elliptical Marquis, Quick Select tool, or Magnetic Lasso tool.

2. Create a Hue/Saturation adjustment layer (using the icon at the bottom of the Layers panel). Notice that the layer mask is almost entirely black. The only parts that will be white are two small shapes that correspond to the eyes you selected, as shown in Figure 7.23.

3. Increase the saturation of the eyes as desired to make them more prominent and also slightly increase the lightness by a value of 1 or 2. This subtly draws attention to the creature's eyes.

Just as when making tonal adjustments using selections, we don't recommend that you feather the original selection, because there's no way to tell how many pixels you should use. You could use a trial-and-error approach, but what we prefer is to apply a Gaussian blur to the adjustment layer after you've made your adjustment. The blur actually affects the layer mask and enables you to create a feather or blending between the areas that were changed and those that were not. The benefit to this method is that you can control exactly how much feathering is needed.

Continuing on with our example…

4. Choose Filter > Blur > Gaussian Blur from the menu.

5. Make certain the Preview box is checked, and then move the Radius slider to change the blur on the transition edges (see Figure 7.24). The result is a feathering amount specific to the needs of the individual image and a pleasing transition between the areas that were and were not modified. Usually you will need a very small radius, often less than 1.0, but of course this varies by image.

Figure 7.24
Using a Gaussian blur on your layer mask feathers the transition between the areas that were changed and those that weren't.

Try It! Open the image called Eyes from the accompanying CD, and try not only increasing the saturation of just the eyes but also changing the hue using a Hue/Saturation adjustment layer. Using the same selection, try also adjusting the hue using a Selective Color adjustment layer.

Creating Layer Masks Without Prior Selections

Many people (including Ellen) prefer not to have to make selections whenever possible. They find that it's often easier to simply paint on the layer mask to define the areas they want to be affected, as outlined in the following steps:

1. First, use an adjustment layer to make the desired changes. Train yourself to focus only on the parts of the image you want to change and ignore what happens to the other parts since they will masked out later.

Note: If you don't get the adjustment exactly as it needs to be, you can modify it later after you create the mask by double-clicking the thumbnail on the layer.

2. Make certain your colors are set to foreground black and background white. To do this, press D, or click the small black and white boxes at the bottom-left of the color swatches in the Tool panel ◼ .

3. Now, making certain that the adjustment layer is still selected in the Layers panel, select a moderately soft-edged paintbrush, place your cursor on your image, and begin to paint over the areas you do not want to be affected. Zoom in as needed so you can paint accurately.

4. Continue editing your mask, as described in Chapter 6:

   • To undo your painting (for example, if you accidentally paint over some areas you do want to be affected), toggle your foreground color to white and paint over those areas.

   • To have an adjustment only partially affect an area of your image, reduce the opacity of your brush on the toolbar.

   • Press the \ key to create a red overlay showing the masked areas superimposed on the image.

   • To see a preview of the mask, Alt/Option+click the layer mask icon. You can paint directly on the mask preview if desired.

   • When you've finished, if necessary, Alt/Option+click the layer mask icon again to return to your image preview.

Note: Although learning to use a pen tablet, such as the Wacom Intuos3, takes time, using the tablet can ultimately help you easily make far more effective layer masks.

Using a Mask for Color Adjustment without a Selection

Let's apply the no-selection mask technique to an image of a burrowing owl with a green background. (This image is called BurrowingOwl on the accompanying CD.) To increase the saturation of the colors within the owl but not affect the background in order to help draw attention to the bird, take these steps:

1. Create a Hue/Saturation adjustment layer by clicking the Create A New Adjustment Layer icon at the bottom of the Layers panel.

2. Increase the saturation to make the owl look good. Ignore what's happening to the background.

3. You could continue to follow the steps exactly as outlined previously, but in this case, it would be easier to have the mask be entirely black—hiding the effect of the layer—and then paint with white over the bird to reveal the effect on the bird. To quickly fill the layer mask with black, choose Edit > Fill from the menu, and choose Black for Contents.

Note: A shortcut for filling a layer mask with black is Ctrl+Backspace/⌘+Delete.

4. Now use your Brush tool to paint on your image preview using white as your foreground color. As long as your adjustment layer is still selected, you are actually painting on the layer mask and not the image itself. Paint with white over the bird to reveal the increased saturation only on the bird, as shown in Figure 7.25.

Figure 7.25
Filling with black allows you to quickly create a black layer mask, upon which you'll paint with white to reveal the changes you made in that layer. (Photo by Ellen Anon.)

5. Next, modify the hue of the background using Selective Color. Create a new Selective Color adjustment layer (via the icon in the Layers panel), and label it Background Hue.

6. Modify the colors until they are pleasing, and click OK.

7. To save the time of re-creating a mask to affect only the background, click the Hue/Saturation adjustment layer to make it active.

8. Hold down the Alt/Option key, click directly on the layer mask icon, and then drag it on top of the Selective Color adjustment layer. A dialog box appears asking whether you want to replace the mask. Click Yes.

9. Unfortunately, this mask is the opposite of what you need, because you want to change the background on this layer. To invert the mask, choose Image > Adjustments > Invert from the main menu. The inverted mask enables you to modify the background without affecting the bird. Copying layer masks from layer to layer and inverting them as needed can be a time-saver.

Note: If you've created a layer mask on one layer and want to further modify the same areas using another adjustment layer, Ctrl+click/⌘+click the layer mask icon in the first adjustment layer *before* creating the new adjustment layer. Photoshop creates an active selection based on that mask. Then when you open a new adjustment layer, the same mask appears.

Note: To copy a layer mask from one layer to another hold down the Alt/Option key, click the layer mask you want to copy and drag it to the one you want to replace.

Using layer masks is easy and gives you incredible ability to fine-tune the color (and tonal values) within specific areas of your image. Regardless of which approach you prefer for creating your layer masks, being able to enhance parts of your image—such as the eyes of your subject—is invaluable. In fact, Arthur Morris, one of the world's foremost bird photographers, contributed the following sidebar describing several tricks he uses to enhance the eyes of the birds in some of his outstanding photos.

Digital Eye Doctor

by Arthur Morris

In *The Art of Bird Photography*, I wrote, "When viewing wildlife, or wildlife art, we tend to make immediate eye contact. Consequently, if a bird's eye is in sharp focus, it gives the photograph an impression of overall sharpness." While optimizing my bird photographs in Photoshop, I often have the chance to improve the look of a bird's eyes, and I have developed a useful bag of tricks for doing just that. Doing so can add greatly to the drama and impact of an image.

In many cases, simply sharpening the eyes can substantially improve an image. To do so, first zoom in so the eye fills the window. Next, select the eye using either the Lasso or Magnetic Lasso tool. (Sometimes I will select both the eye and a patch of sharply defined feathers surrounding the eye.) Feather the selection one pixel before sharpening to avoid the cookie-cutter look. Then choose Filter > Sharpen > Unsharp Mask. I generally sharpen (to taste) with an Amount from 300% to 500%, a Radius from 0.2 to (rarely) as much as 0.5 pixels, and the Threshold at 0. On average, I work with these settings: 375, 0.25, and 0.

The same technique can be used to lighten or darken the eye and possibly the feathers of the face that surround the eye or eyes. Many birds have dark or black eye masks, and some have black hoods. With these, it is often necessary to lighten the eye so that it becomes visible. At times you may want to lighten the eye and the surrounding feathers. When optimizing images of birds with light or pastel *lores* (the area between the eye and the base of the bill) or patches of light-colored feathers around the eye, it is often helpful to darken these areas to intensify the color. To lighten or darken an area, simply use the Lasso tool to select the area and then feather the selection; I use one pixel of feathering for an eye, two pixels when working with tracts of feathers. Then create a Levels adjustment layer (Layer > New Adjustment Layer > Levels) and lighten or darken the selection by moving the middle slider.

When using flash to photograph birds, the eyes are often rendered quite funky. Red-eye and steel-eye (an odd-looking silvery crescent on the eye) were common when using flash with film, but with digital (which is more sensitive to flash than film), the effects are both wider ranging and even more detrimental to the image. When examining a flashed bird's eye at high magnification, unnatural highlights and lightened and artificially colored pupils are often revealed. Most folks simply ignore these problems, but the fix takes only minutes. I always examine the eye closely by magnifying it greatly, using a box drawn around the eye with the Zoom tool to do so.

I often use the Clone Stamp tool to repair red-eye, purple-eye, steel-eye, and other unnatural highlights that may affect small or significant areas of the pupil. After making such repairs, however, the pupil, which should be black, often appears far too light. Simply select the pupil with the Lasso tool, feather the selection one pixel, create a Hue/Saturation adjustment layer (Layer > New Adjustment Layer > Hue/Saturation), and then reduce the Saturation as much as 100%. Next, choose Select > Reselect (Shift+Ctrl+D/Shift+⌘+D) and feather the selection again. Then create a Selective Color layer (Layer > New Adjustment Layer > Selective Color), and add blacks to either the neutrals or the blacks until the pupil is rendered a pleasing black. It often helps to compare the eye of a flashed bird with the unflashed eye of the same bird or species.

After my recent trip to Homer, Alaska, to photograph eagles in the dead of winter (−5 degrees Fahrenheit!), I found often that I needed to either lighten or darken the yellow iris and to intensify the yellow

Continues

Digital Eye Doctor *(Continued)*

as well. To select the iris only, first circle it with the Lasso tool. In the Options bar, click the Subtract From Selection button, and then use the Lasso tool to circle the pupil. This *removes* the pupil from your previous selection, which included the iris *and* the pupil. The end result is that you now have only the iris selected. After feathering the selection one pixel, lighten or darken the iris as needed. If you want to boost the color, reselect and refeather and then either work the Yellow channel only in Hue/Saturation or add Yellow (and possibly a point or two of black) to the yellows in Selective Color. (Similarly, click the Add To Selection button when you want to work on both pupils or on both eyes.)

Original

Before correction

After correction

After correction

After correction

By carefully examining the eye or eyes of their subjects, repairing and improving the damaged areas, and then lightening or darkening them as needed, nature photographers can quickly and easily improve the impact and the quality of their images. With wildlife, the "eyes" have it!

If you've followed our workflow so far, you've cropped and rotated your image if necessary, removed any dust or scratches, made any necessary exposure adjustments, and modified the colors so that your image has the desired impact. Be sure to save your image at this point with your layers intact as your master file. The chapters following provide additional ideas of ways to create and present your images.

Composites

Many nature photographers are initially loath to consider making composites, believing that this is somehow "cheating" or "dishonest." There is a clear need for photographers using Adobe Photoshop to be ethical and reveal when they have made changes so that their images no longer reflect the reality of what they saw and what existed. However, sometimes combining elements from several pictures can create more impact and be more representative of an experience. Ironically, compositing techniques can actually enable photographers to more accurately and realistically depict what they saw in certain circumstances such as with a panorama, an exposure composite, or a focus composite.

Chapter Contents
Creating Panoramas
Expanding Dynamic Range
Extending the Depth of Field
Combining Elements from Multiple Pictures

Creating Panoramas

The advent of the digital darkroom freed photographers from being tied to the constraints of any one particular camera format, whether it is 35mm, 2×2, or some other format. By using Photoshop, you can stitch together a series of images to create a photograph of a particular shape that better suits the subject. An added benefit of stitching together several frames is that the larger file you create enables you to make prints that are substantially larger than you could if you simply used a wider lens and cropped a single frame.

In-Camera Considerations

When photographing images to be combined into panoramas, following certain techniques while shooting enables you to stitch the images together with a minimum of headaches. If you choose to ignore some of the following procedures (and we admit that at times we do), you may still be able to stitch the segments together, but it's likely it will take longer and the results may not be quite what you had hoped:

- Use a tripod.
- Not only do you need to use a tripod, but you also need to level it! If your tripod does not have a level built into it, place a small bubble level on a top-flat surface to help get it level. This is important because you want the camera to rotate on a level axis. If you enjoy shooting panoramas, consider buying a tripod leveler such as the panning clamp with level from Really Right Stuff (www.reallyrightstuff.com).
- Level your camera as well by adding a double bubble level to the flash shoe of your camera (see Figure 8.1). Taking the time to level both the tripod and the camera means there will be a minimum of "stair-stepping" as you combine the images. Otherwise, you'll lose part of the image because you'll have to crop to get rid of the stair-stepping.

Figure 8.1
Using a bubble level on top of your camera as well as leveling your tripod will make your panoramas stitch together much more easily. (Photo by Ellen Anon.)

- You can shoot a panorama without a tripod, but you will lose part of the image near the top and bottom with a horizontal panorama and near the sides with a vertical panorama. When the segments are combined, you're likely to discover that you accidentally changed the relative height and angle of the camera slightly between shots. If you must shoot without a tripod, allow extra room in your framing.

- Plan your shots, allowing for an overlap of about 20–30 percent in most cases, as shown in Figure 8.2. It's helpful to identify key objects/points within each frame that you will use as anchors to help line up each segment. In the first image, this should be within the right 20–30 percent of the frame for a horizontal panorama; for a vertical panorama it would be in the bottom 20–30 percent. As you rotate the camera to take the next shot, place that same anchor point in the left (or top for a vertical panorama) 20–30 percent of the frame, and identify a new object on the right (or bottom). Repeat this process for as many frames as necessary.

Figure 8.2 Plan your shots ahead of time, allowing for an overlap of 20–30 percent between frames and an identifiable anchor point. (Photo by Ellen Anon.)

- Although it may seem counterintuitive, it can be quite helpful to shoot a horizontal panorama using the camera in vertical format since it reduces distortion.
- Meter the scene, and *manually set your exposure* to a compromise between the readings for the various segments. While some exposures for some of the frames that you shoot will be slightly off this way, you avoid having huge exposure variations that may result if you use one of the autoexposure techniques such as aperture priority. The autoexposure modes may set an entirely different exposure for each frame, making the final panoramic image a series of mismatched exposures.
- If you are using a digital camera, *set your white balance manually*. Auto white balance can lead to a slightly different temperature being used in each frame.
- Avoid using a polarizer because the intensity of the polarizing effect varies as your shots vary their angle in relation to the sun, causing parts of the sky to be darker in some frames than in others.
- To minimize having to correct for distortion, use a focal length longer than approximately 35mm.
- Always start by taking the farthest left (or top) image first. This helps avoid confusion later when you combine the sections.

- When shooting a panoramic series digitally, it's beneficial to shoot a frame at the beginning and at the end of the sequence that will clue you in when you're editing that these images are part of a panoramic series. Otherwise, it's all too easy to delete images, wondering why you composed them so poorly. One trick we use is to take a shot of our hand at the beginning and end of each series.

- Compositionally, you need a logical beginning and end to the panorama, just as you would have if you were shooting a single-frame image.

Note: Photographers who shoot panoramas frequently are aware of the benefits of eliminating, as much as possible, the distortion effects of parallax. This is achieved by pivoting the lens around what is commonly termed the *nodal point*. Technically, this requires moving the camera and lens back slightly from the tripod pivoting point. Companies such as Really Right Stuff (www.reallyrightstuff.com) produce accessories, including the Omni-Pivot Package, to help with this.

Photomerge

Photomerge has been dramatically improved in CS3 so that, at long last, it's easy to stitch even 16-bit panoramas together. Photomerge automatically arranges and blends multiple images to create a panorama with just a few instructions from you. This is a tremendous time-saver, rather than tediously manually stitching the images together as we did in earlier versions of Photoshop. Since Photomerge can save the file in layers, we still have the option to tweak the image alignment when necessary, but Ellen has found that Photomerge often does a surprisingly accurate job.

Note: For those with earlier versions of Photoshop, instructions for manually stitching a panorama together are available as a free download from Ellen's website at www.sunbearphoto.com.

1. There are two ways to get started with Photomerge:
   - The easiest way to begin is to highlight the images you wish to use in Bridge—by holding the Ctrl/⌘ key and clicking the images—and then choose Tools > Photoshop > Photomerge from Bridge's menu. If these images are raw files, Photoshop automatically converts them using whatever default you have set within ACR. If you have not made any changes to the default, Photoshop uses the Auto Adjust settings.
   - If you prefer, select the images to use within Photoshop by going to File > Automate > Photomerge.

2. You need to set the source to use either images you have previously opened, files you specify, or a folder. Check the box to have Photomerge automatically blend the files as well as to specify the type layout you want it to use (see Figure 8.3). Photomerge then creates a layered file containing all the images, properly placed with layer masks applied.

Figure 8.3

Instruct Photoshop which images to select to merge by specifying open files or folders, and check the box to have Photoshop automatically arrange the images.

You have the following options:

- Use Auto to have Photomerge determine the best approach for the layout. Usually it will choose Cylindrical.

- Choose Perspective to have Photomerge apply corrective perspective distortion. This can be useful with some HDR alignments and other layouts with smaller angle compositions, that is, those shot with longer lenses.

- Cylindrical is often the best choice for wide-angle compositions, and with 360° compositions you must use it. Photoshop first projects the images onto a cylinder and then unwarps them.

- Choose Reposition to have Photomerge create a canvas and align the images with no distortion applied. If you have shot the panorama carefully, this is the choice you will use most of the time, unless there is a specific reason to use one of the other layouts.

- The Interactive layout invokes a dialog box similar to that used in Photomerge in CS2. You can manually rotate each file as desired and specify the vanishing point if you choose to apply perspective distortion. When you click OK, a layered panorama is created using only the distortions and changes you specify.

Note: The Set Vanishing Point tool in the Interactive layout works only when you have checked the Perspective Correction tool in that dialog box.

The panorama results will vary depending on the layout you choose, as shown in Figure 8.4. If you have Photomerge apply a distortion in the layout, the processing time increases, and this can be quite slow if you're creating a panorama from numerous large 16-bit files. However while you're waiting for your computer to generate the panorama, remind yourself it's a lot faster than doing it manually!

Reposition only

Using Auto

Figure 8.4 Using some of the layouts applies distortion, particularly at the edges of the panorama. Notice the difference between an image that was repositioned only and one where Auto was used.

Note: If you are dealing with a difficult group of files to align and blend because an object, person, or animal significantly changed position between frames, it's best to open the files in Photoshop, apply a layer mask to block out the object wherever necessary, and then invoke Photomerge. Photomerge will respect the layer mask and know which frame should contain the moving thing. Otherwise, Photomerge may or may not do a good job with the alignment and blending.

Advanced Image Stitching

In CS3 there is another way to stitch images together that can be useful with some tricky images, including HDR panoramas. To begin in Photoshop, choose File > Scripts > Load Files into Stack. A dialog box appears in which you specify which images to stack. Photoshop will create a new file containing each image as a layer. Locking a layer will set it as the center for any distortions. Select all the layers, and then choose Edit > Auto Align Layers. A dialog box appears in which you choose the Layout, similar to the one in the Photomerge dialog box discussed earlier. This places each file into the correct alignment on a correctly sized new canvas. You can apply any type distortion or transformation necessary to each layer, as well as apply layer masks to instruct Photoshop to remove part of a layer from the final composite. The last step is to choose Edit > Auto-Blend layers to seamlessly blend the colors and exposures. Photoshop adds layer masks in this step that you can tweak, although the specific adjustments used in the blending are not available.

Ellen has found that this method is particularly helpful with group shots of people. Even nature photographers sometimes have to take group shots of people, and when they do so, they often are reminded why they prefer nature photography! Seriously, in group shots, often one person is blinking in a shot, looking away, or otherwise not appearing their best, while in another shot that person is OK, but another person has problems. Using the script to load the images as a stack and then Auto-Align, makes it simple to use the layer masks to select the best shot of each person for the final composite.

Usually Photomerge does a good job, but very occasionally it fails. It's a good idea to zoom in to ensure that Photomerge has done a good job of aligning each segment. Use the Move tool if necessary to nudge a layer into place. Of course, moving one layer will make it likely that you'll need to move the other layers as well.

Try It! Open the series of images: Pano 1a, Pano 1b, and Pano 1c images on the accompanying CD, and practice stitching them together. If you prefer, use a series of your own images. We recommend starting with a panorama of no more than three or four sections.

Matching the Exposures of Each Segment of the Panorama

With earlier versions of Photoshop, we often had to manually create and blend our panoramas. This is rarely necessary now that the Auto-Align and Auto-Blend algorithms are so good in CS3, but it's conceivable you might shoot a series of images that Photoshop can't perfectly blend. Ellen has seen this primarily in panoramas including the sun at sunrise or sunset with auto white balance, as shown in Figure 8.5, or if a cloud suddenly obscured the sun in the midst of a series of manual exposures for a panorama that were calculated when the sun was shining.

Figure 8.5 Unless you manually set the white balance and exposure for your panoramas, you're likely to get some variation in colors and tonalities between the files.

If you discover that the exposures of the various segments of the panorama do not match, follow these steps:

1. Click the layer containing the second segment of the panorama to make it active.
2. Zoom in to magnify the area where the first segment and the second segment overlap and where the differences in exposure are evident.
3. Click the Channels panel.
4. Select the Red channel by clicking the word *Red*. When viewed in grayscale, the differences between the two layers are usually easy to see, as shown in Figure 8.6.

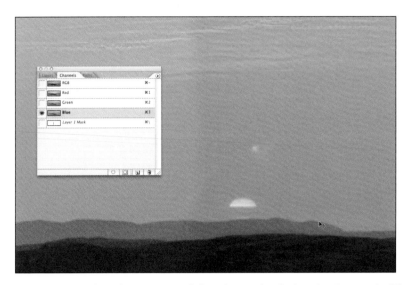

Figure 8.6 Viewing the overlapping area in each channel separately makes it much easier to see the differences.

5. Choose Image > Adjustments > Levels on the menu bar. Note that this is one of the few times we'll have you working directly on the pixels. Unfortunately, when you're working within channels, you can't readily use adjustment layers.

6. Click the Midpoint slider, and drag it to match up the gray tones in layer 2 with those in layer 1. When they appear the same, as in Figure 8.7, click OK.

Figure 8.7 Adjusting the Midpoint slider in Levels within each channel enables you to easily match exposures.

7. Repeat the same process for the Green and Blue channels, one at a time.

8. Repeat these steps for each frame you need to match to another until your final image matches in color and tonalities (see Figure 8.8).

Figure 8.8 The final image has consistent color across the various segments.

Occasionally, a simple linear correction (which Levels applies) can't resolve the changes in exposure between the segments, in which case you need to use Curves rather than Levels in each channel to accurately match up the different segments. This happens more often when the quality or quantity of the lighting is changing dramatically. Follow the same procedure as described in this section, but use Curves instead of Levels.

Try It! Open PanoMatch1 on the accompanying CD, and practice adjusting the exposures to get them to match. If you're looking for a challenge, open PanoMatch2, and match those exposures! (Hint: You'll need to use Curves rather than Levels to get them to match.)

Composites
by Joe McDonald

Shooting digitally, my photography now has far fewer limitations. Think about it. The basic laws of optics normally restrict our vision, but for virtually my entire career I've been further limited not by what I could see but what my camera could capture. Limitations imposed by the depth of field or the angle of view or the exposure latitude all conspired to force me to make images not as I saw them but as I knew my medium could render them. We all lived with this and probably didn't even think about it, for it was the reality of photography at the time.

Continues

Composites *(Continued)*

Digital has changed all of that for me: I now make images with the "reality" of the scene in mind. This can take any number of forms. Sometimes I simply have too much lens, but by shooting a panorama, I still get the image size and detail I wanted while encompassing more of the habitat as well. On other occasions I'll shoot focus composites, focusing on the foreground if it bears interest and on the main subject so that the finished image lacks the unnatural dimension typical of long lens shots. If necessary, I'll add some Gaussian blur to a background to draw more attention to the subject.

Restrictions created by a broad exposure latitude have been significantly reduced. Often I'll "shoot for the middle," knowing that I can convert a raw image twice, once biasing for the underexposure and once for the over. Usually I'll cover myself for those shots by shooting two exposures, metering for each value. That way, if the exposure latitude was indeed too broad for a single image, I'll have a good chance of recording the scene if I use two separate images.

This has simply made my photography more fun because I'm not frustrated or stymied by past limitations. I'm free to try things, probably way more than I'll ever have time to work with in the digital darkroom, but that's secondary. The fun part is the shooting, and with digital, I feel I have the potential of capturing what I truly see.

© Joe McDonald, www.hoothollow.com

Expanding Dynamic Range

Until recently, the dynamic range or exposure latitude that we could capture in a single image was limited by camera and film technology. Often, especially during the midday hours, there was too much contrast to be able to capture in a single shot. We had to choose to give up detail in the highlights, the shadows, or both. Photoshop enables us to combine several images of the same subject, taken using different exposures, to retain detail in the highlights and shadows while simultaneously having the midtones properly exposed. It's almost magical how we can create an image that reflects what we actually saw, no longer limited by the latitude of film.

There are three techniques we'll describe to extend the exposure latitude in an image:

- Manually
- The "cookbook" approach, where Photoshop does most of the work for you
- Merge to HDR

Expanding Latitude Manually

When you encounter a situation in which there is too much contrast to capture detail in the entire scene in a single shot, take several shots at different exposure levels, and combine them using these steps:

1. Use a tripod, and take your first shot, exposing for the shadow areas. Check your in-camera histogram to ensure that the shadow areas do *not* spike against the left side of the histogram. If they do, take another shot, adding more light to the exposure.

2. Without moving the camera, take another shot, this time exposing for the highlights. This time when you check the histogram, make certain that there are no spikes against the right side of the histogram. If there are, reduce the amount of light in the exposure (see Figure 8.9).

Figure 8.9 Check the histograms to make certain that the dark exposure has captured detail in the highlight areas and similarly that the light exposure has captured all the shadow detail. (Photo by Ellen Anon.)

3. In some cases, you may want a third shot exposing for the midtones.

Note: It's not enough to simply expose for the midtones and bracket the shot by half a stop in both directions. Bracketing that way is usually insufficient to allow ample differences in the exposures to re-create as much detail as your eyes saw. Instead, make sure to check the histogram with each shot to ensure that the portion of the image you are exposing for falls within the bounds of the histogram, as discussed in Chapter 1, "Thinking Digitally."

4. Open each image in Photoshop.

5. Choose the Move tool, and while holding the Shift key, click one image and drag it on top of another. By holding the Shift key, they should line up in perfect registry.

6. To check to see whether they are lined up perfectly, reduce the opacity of the top layer to 50 percent. If perchance they are not perfectly aligned, use the arrow keys to nudge the top layer until it does line up. (If you are using files from a film scan, you'll almost certainly need to fine-tune their alignment.)

7. Return the opacity of that layer to 100 percent.

8. Click the Add Layer Mask icon to create a layer mask on the top layer.

9. Choose a brush tool that is soft to medium hardness, and set the brush opacity to 100 percent initially.

10. Make sure the foreground color is set to black and the background color is set to white by hitting the D key.

11. Paint with black in the layer mask to reveal parts of the underlying image layer, leaving the well-exposed parts from each layer visible, as shown in Figure 8.10.

Figure 8.10
Create a layer mask on the top layer to reveal parts of the image below that are better exposed.

12. Zoom in, and work carefully.

13. If you make a mistake, simply switch to white (by pressing X), and paint with white in the layer mask.

14. You may want to reduce the brush opacity to partially reveal the underlying layer in areas.

15. If you have a third exposure, follow the same procedure, and drag it on top of the other two while holding down the Shift key.

16. Add a layer mask to this layer, and paint with black to reveal the underlying layers in the appropriate places.

17. You can proceed with the rest of your workflow in one of two ways:

   • Flatten the image when the desired tonal range is achieved and proceed to modify it using your normal workflow as you would a single image.

   • Make a Stamp Visible layer (see Figure 8.11)—a single layer containing your desired final exposure. To do this, click the top layer in the Layers panel.

Then, while holding down the Alt/Option key, click the Layers panel menu at the top of the Layers panel. Continue holding the Alt/Option key, and click Merge Visible. Do not release the Alt/Option key until you see a new thumbnail icon appear in the layer you created.

Figure 8.11
A Stamp Visible layer contains all the information of the layers beneath it in a single layer that serves as the initial layer in your normal workflow.

The "Cookbook" Approach to Expanding Latitude

Sometimes combining two exposures is fairly straightforward, as it was in the example we used for the manual method of combining exposures. But sometimes the highlight and shadow areas are scattered throughout the image, making the manual method quite time-consuming. Fortunately, there's an easy way to have Photoshop do most of the tedious work for you in combining two images (see Figure 8.12).

Figure 8.12 You can have Photoshop use the lighter image to create a mask to use while combining two different exposures. (Images courtesy of Rick Holt.)

Take these steps to combine the two images:

1. Drag the *dark* image on top of the light image by using the Move tool while holding the Shift key. It's important that the darker image goes on top.

Note: For this approach to be successful, the images must align perfectly. After dragging the darker image on top of the lighter one, reduce the opacity of the dark one, and nudge it into place using the Move tool and the arrow keys on the keyboard, as you did when arranging the sections of a panorama.

2. Add a layer mask to the dark image layer.

3. Make the background image active by clicking the background image layer, and press Ctrl+A/⌘+A to select the entire background image.

4. Press Ctrl+C/⌘+C to copy the image to the clipboard.

5. Highlight the dark image layer; hold down the Alt/Option key, and click the Layer Mask icon to make the mask appear where you usually see your image. It will be completely white at first.

6. Press Ctrl+V/⌘+V to paste the contents of the clipboard onto the white mask. Your layer mask should now appear to be a black-and-white version of the Background layer, as shown in Figure 8.13.

Figure 8.13
Hold down the Alt/Option key, click the Layer Mask icon, and then press Ctrl+V/⌘+V to make the mask appear in place of the image preview.

7. Apply a Gaussian blur (Filter > Blur > Gaussian Blur) with a radius between 0.5 and 40. Modifying the Gaussian blur is important to make the final result appear natural. The exact amount of blur needed can vary significantly according to the image.

8. Click the image icon on the darker layer, and press Ctrl+D/⌘+D to deselect. Your image should now reflect the best of both exposures (see Figure 8.14).

9. You may want to fine-tune the tonality of the image using a Curves adjustment layer if necessary or by further modifying the layer mask.

10. Create a Stamp Visible layer, as you did in the final step of the completely manual method, and continue with the regular workflow.

Note: Open the images on the accompanying CD called CanyonDark and CanyonLight, and try combining them using the "cookbook" approach.

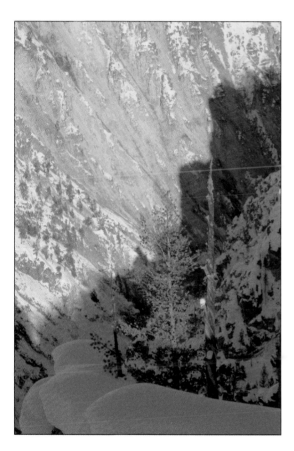

Figure 8.14
By using the lighter image to create a mask for the darker image, Photoshop does most of the work to create a composite using the best of both exposures.

Expanding Latitude via Merge to HDR

Photoshop CS2 introduced Merge to HDR and the feature has been improved in CS3. Merge to HDR is a tool to combine multiple exposures (ideally three to seven exposures of the identical subject) into one 32-bit image.

Using 32-bit enables the image to have a greatly expanded dynamic range so that the final image can contain detail in shadow areas and in highlights that normally cannot be present in a single image. In fact, 32-bit offers more latitude than what you can even see on your monitor. However, the 32-bit image can then be converted back to 16-bit or 8-bit. Merge to HDR creates an image containing the maximum amount of detail and color information possible, with very little work on your part. It ensures that the transitions among the exposures are gradual, with no harsh obvious edges. It sounds too good to be true, doesn't it?

In the earlier version, nature photographers were likely to experience several difficulties using this tool. If anything changed between exposures—a tree branch blowing slightly in the wind, a leaf, anything moving—Merge to HDR often failed to give a good final image. Similarly, if there was any camera movement, it also didn't work. In CS3 the Auto-Align algorithms have been tremendously improved. In addition, you can add a layer mask to an image to hide part of an image to help with objects that move. Although there is still no option in this version of the tool to allow you to manually align the images, it works far better than the initial version.

 Note: It might seem the answer would be to take a single raw file and convert it at numerous settings; however, this won't work, because the algorithms used in Merge To HDR require different *linear* data.

Situations with high contrast and static subjects are best for creating Merge to HDR composites. For example, the sun rising or setting behind a mountain offers an ideal opportunity. Normally, some of the detail in the mountain would be lost while trying to capture the colors of the sunset.

If a scene lends itself to using Merge to HDR, take the following steps in the field:

1. It's essential to use a tripod and not move your camera between exposures. Use a cable release if possible.

2. Take a series of shots, varying the exposure by changing the shutter speed, not the aperture (which would change the depth of field). If you use aperture priority, then you simply need to dial in different exposure compensation amounts for each shot.

3. Vary the exposures by one to two f/stops each. Don't try to bracket by small increments such as 1/3 to 1/2 stops, as you might if you were trying to capture a single well-exposed frame.

4. Check the histogram to make sure that your darkest picture includes detail in the brightest part of the image, that is, there are no spikes on the right of the histogram and no flashing highlight warnings. Similarly, check to make sure that your lightest image (which has flashing highlights) has no spikes on the left side of the histogram. You want to make certain to capture detail in all the shadows.

5. Don't vary the lighting by using flash in one picture and not the next.

After you have downloaded your images to your computer, access Merge to HDR through Bridge directly or through Photoshop using these steps:

1. To select the files to use in Photoshop, choose File > Automate > Merge to HDR. The Merge to HDR dialog box (see Figure 8.15) appears. Click Browse to select the desired images, and then click Open, or if you have already opened the images, simply select Use Open Files.

Figure 8.15

Select your desired images in the Merge to HDR dialog box.
(Images courtesy of Josh Anon.)

2. Check the Attempt To Automatically Align Source Images box.

3. To select the images to use directly from Bridge, simply highlight the desired images, and choose Tools > Photoshop > Merge to HDR.

4. Click OK.

5. This leads to a Merge to HDR dialog box, shown in Figure 8.16. You can zoom in to see the results more closely, if desired, or uncheck one of the source images displayed along the left side to exclude it from being part of the final image. The image preview automatically updates to reflect this change.

Figure 8.16
The Merge to HDR dialog box allows you to preview the results of the merge as well as specify the white point and bit depth for the composite.

6. Choose a bit depth for the merged image from the Bit Depth menu. To store the entire dynamic range, you must choose 32-bit.

7. Move the slider below the histogram to set the white point for previewing the merged image. We usually recommend moving this slider all the way to the right to retain your highlight detail. This affects the preview only in a 32-bit image, since there is more information than what can be displayed on a monitor (or print). You are not discarding any information yet. If you choose to save the merged image as an 8- or 16-bit-per-channel file at this point, then moving this slider is applying exposure edits to your final image, and you are discarding some information. The same conversion dialog box as shown in Figure 8.17 will appear. There you can specify the exact conversion settings.

Figure 8.17
You can choose from several different approaches to convert your image back to 16-bit (or 8-bit).

8. Click OK, and Photoshop creates the merged image.

9. Currently, there are only a few tools and adjustments that can be used with 32-bit images, but Ellen has found it helpful to use the Exposure adjustment, which was specifically designed for 32-bit images. Adjusting each of the sliders adjusts the brightness of the image slightly differently:

   - The Exposure slider is calibrated in stops and increases (or decreases) brightness throughout the image, but it affects the highlights more than the shadows.

   - The Offset slider increases or decreases the brightness of the shadows far more than the highlights.

   - The Gamma slider adjusts the brightness in a similar way to the Brightness slider in ACR. Although all tones are affected, the middle tonalities are affected the most.

10. Although you can make a few other adjustments in 32-bit mode including Levels, Hue/Saturation, and the Channel Mixer, you will have to convert your image back to a 16-bit-per-channel file for most adjustments and output. To do so, choose Image > Mode > 16 Bits/Channel.

11. In the HDR Conversion dialog box (shown earlier in Figure 8.17), choose from among several options in the Method drop-down list:

    - Choose Exposure and Gamma to manually adjust the brightness and contrast.

    - Choose Highlight Compression to compresses the dynamic values in the HDR image to fall within the bounds of a 16-bit image. Photoshop automatically converts the image for you.

    - Choose Equalize Compression to compress the dynamic range of the image while trying to preserve some contrast. This is also an automatic method.

    - Choose Local Adaptation (see Figure 8.18) to adjust the tonality by calculating the amount of correction necessary for specific brightness regions throughout the image. If you choose this option, you can adjust the tone curve in a manner similar to adjusting curves, as discussed in Chapter 6, "Exposure Adjustments." This is often the most useful choice.

Figure 8.18

Using Local Adaptation and modifying the tone curve and then making further adjustments including Shadow/Highlight, Curves, and Hue/Saturation, allowed us to convert this HDR image to 16-bit, while retaining a great deal more info in the shadows and highlights.

12. Initially your image may appear rather flat. Using adjustments such as Shadow/Highlight, Curves, and Hue/Saturation you can increase the visible details, as well as the midtone contrast, and make the image come alive.

Try It! Open the images from the accompanying CD called HDR 1, HDR 2, and HDR 3 and experiment with creating a 32-bit file and then converting it back to a 16-bit file.

Extending the Depth of Field

Nature photographers sometimes encounter situations where we want to maximize our *depth of field* (the range of apparently sharp focus within an image) but we encounter technical limitations. Perhaps the range we want to be in focus is too great for the lens, or the wind is blowing so we have to use a relatively fast shutter speed to freeze the motion. Using the faster shutter speed may mean we can't use as small an aperture as we'd like for a correct exposure without resorting to higher ISOs, which can lead to problems with noise.

Using a compositing technique similar to that for manually increasing the exposure latitude, you can combine two or more photographs in which you varied your focus to increase the depth of field. This can be a huge advantage at times, since you can shoot at whatever shutter speed you need to freeze the action. It can also allow you greater depth of field than would be possible in certain situations, such as macro photography.

Note: When using zoom lenses, changing the focus changes the focal length slightly, so this technique tends to work best with fixed focal length lenses.

Here are the steps you can take to extend the depth of field by combining two or more images:

1. Take two or more shots, varying the focus for each. For example, focus on the foreground in one shot and on the midground for the next shot while the camera is on a tripod, as shown in Figure 8.19.

Figure 8.19
Take two or more shots, varying the focal point. (Photo by Ellen Anon.)

2. Do not change the exposure, only change the focus.

3. Use your depth-of-field preview button to see what areas will be in focus and allow for overlap between the shots.

4. Open all the shots in Photoshop. If they are raw files, synchronize the settings for all the files, as discussed in Chapter 4, "Foundations."

5. Drag one image on top of another with the Move tool while holding down the Shift key to align the images in perfect registry.

6. Check to see that they are aligned perfectly by reducing the opacity of the top layer. Use the arrow keys if necessary to slightly move the top image and then return the layer to 100 percent opacity.

Note: Sometimes you may not be able to perfectly align the images, in which case later you'll have to zoom in and carefully create the layer mask.

7. With the top layer highlighted, click the Add A Layer Mask icon at the bottom of the Layers panel.

8. Press D to make sure the foreground and background colors are set to black and white. Press X to toggle between white and black as the foreground color.

9. Choose a medium hard brush of the appropriate size with 100 percent opacity. You need to zoom in and work carefully, adjusting the size and hardness of your brush as necessary.

10. Paint with black on the layer mask to reveal parts of the underlying image (see Figure 8.20).

Figure 8.20 Use the layer mask to reveal the sharp areas of both images, which creates the appearance of increased depth of field.

11. Repeat this process if you have more than two shots you are combining.

12. Make a Stamp Visible layer that will be a single layer containing a flattened version of your composite image. To do this, first create a new layer on top of the others by clicking the Create A New Layer icon at the bottom of the Layers panel. (It's not necessary to create the new layer first if you are using CS2 or CS3.) Then, while holding down the Alt/Option key, click the small 3 line icon at the top right of the Layers panel. Continue holding the Alt/Option key, and click Merge Visible. Do not release the Alt/Option key until you see a new thumbnail icon appear in the layer you created.

13. Continue with your normal workflow.

Try It! Open the images called DOF1 and DOF2 on the accompanying CD, and practice combining them.

Helicon Focus

by Joe McDonald

Digital photography's ability to capture what we truly see goes even further with the Helicon Focus filter, available from Helicon Products at www.heliconfocus.com. This filter maximizes depths of field via software, thus overcoming the limits of a len's optics. Using this filter, one can combine a series of images shot at various points of focus into a finished product that stitches the focused areas into one. It does this quickly and simply, provided you follow the proper photography techniques when making the initial image capture. Here's how.

Make sure you use a tripod and that your subject is immobile. If your camera or your subject moves, you won't get a proper registry with the stitch. Focus on the closest point in your image, and take a shot. Roll the focus slightly so that the focus moves a bit further back, and take the next shot. Continue this process until everything you want in focus in your finished image has been shot.

Don't be conservative with your shots, because the filter works best when there is a thorough series of images with just slight variations in focus. You may have to work relatively quickly, too, when dealing with animate subjects that might move or be blown by the wind.

After downloading the images to your computer, simply open up the Helicon Focus software, choose File > Open New Images, and navigate to the series of images to composite. Select them, click Open, and a list of the images will appear in the source menu. Click Run; the filter begins its work, and you'll see the results as the image begins to take form, literally increasing the focus depth as you watch in the large preview window.

Continues

Helicon Focus *(Continued)*

When the image is done, choose File > Save As, and save the image in the appropriate file. On occasion, minor artifacts may appear in out-of-focus areas, but these are easy to deal with by using the Clone Stamp in Photoshop.

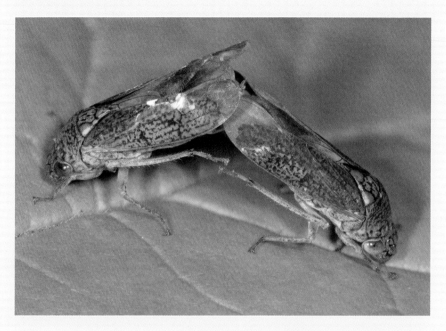

With the Helicon Focus filter you will obtain images with incredible depths of field, virtually impossible to obtain via conventional photography. If you're shooting close-ups, macro, or even scenes where the range of focus is just too great, you'll simply love it.

© Joe McDonald, www.hoothollow.com

Combining Elements from Multiple Pictures

When you start combining elements from various pictures, you begin to be more creative with your images. Ethically, it's important to acknowledge that what you're presenting is not a documentary photograph but rather a photo illustration or photo art. That doesn't make it inherently more or less valuable than a straight photograph—just different. Often, a photo illustration can convey the essence or spirit of a place better than a single straight photograph. But creating something that didn't exist and claiming it is not a manipulated photograph creates trouble for all photographers. The image in Figure 8.21 has impact, but it's a composite and needs to be presented as such.

Figure 8.21 Images like this can often be confused with "lucky" shots and ethically must be presented as composites. (Photo by Ellen Anon.)

Advanced Selection Methods

Chapter 4 covered some of the basic selection tools, but when you make composites, sometimes you need more sophisticated means of making selections. Different techniques work most effectively with different images, so it pays to understand several different approaches.

If you know ahead of time that you're likely to want to use one part of a picture as a composite, it's a good idea to try to photograph it so that it contrasts as much as possible from the background. That makes it easier to select, no matter which technique you choose.

Color Range

The Color Range tool is similar to the Magic Wand tool, but it's more powerful. It's particularly useful in selecting skies when there are trees in the foreground. To access it, choose Select > Color Range. This tool allows you to select multiple areas of different colors at one time. You can even specifically select the highlights, midtones, or shadows with this tool. In addition, you can preview the effects of some of your settings.

Let's use Color Range to select the sky in an image by taking the following steps:

1. Make certain the Select box is set to Sampled Colors, and use the left eyedropper to click an area in your image to specify as the target color. (You can also use the pull-down menu from the Select box, and choose a specific color, such as red, or highlights, midtones, or shadows.)

2. Your selection is white in the preview box. (Selected areas are white, unselected areas are black, and gray areas are blurred selection edges.)

3. Drag the Fuzziness slider to adjust the tolerance. Higher tolerances select more colors; lower values select fewer colors. The preview box shows how the Fuzziness value is affecting the selection (see Figure 8.22).

Figure 8.22 With just a couple clicks of the eyedroppers and adjusting the Fuzziness slider, you can easily select a sky from this image. (Photo by Ellen Anon.)

4. It's likely you'll need to use the Add To eyedropper (the one with the + by it) and click additional areas of the background until you have successfully identified the entire sky area. Similarly, you may need to use the Subtract From eyedropper to remove areas from the selection. As you do so, you'll need to readjust the Fuzziness slider.

5. Click OK, and Photoshop turns the white area into a selection.

6. If Color Range has identified other areas that you do not want to be selected and you cannot eliminate them using the Subtract From eyedropper and the Fuzziness slider, use any of the other selection tools (such as the Lasso or Magic Wand tool) to remove them from the selection, as discussed in Chapter 4, "Foundations."

 Note: You can use more than one color as the basis for your selection by selecting the middle eyedropper tool and clicking an additional color in your image. Similarly, you can use the farthest-right eyedropper to click a color range to remove from your selection.

The Color Range tool tends to create selections with blurry edges, whereas the Magic Wand creates more definite selections with anti-aliased edges. Color Range is often an extremely effective way to select a sky. Later in this chapter we'll explain how to actually replace a sky that you select this way.

Creating a Selection from Within a Channel

This sounds a lot more difficult than it is, but don't let the sound of it intimidate you. Recall that your images have pixel information in three channels: a red channel, a blue channel, and a green channel. You access these channels by clicking the Channels panel, as shown in Figure 8.23. By default, Channels shares a panel window with Layers.

Figure 8.23
To access the individual channels, click the Channels panel.

Sometimes it's easier to make a selection using one of the three color channels rather than the RGB image itself. This is the case when there is good contrast within a particular channel. For example, making a selection of a sky based on a channel is quite useful when the sky meets trees and vegetation with many fine branches.

Use this approach to select the sky in the poppy image you just used with the Color Range tool:

1. Choose Channels, and then click each of the three channels, one at a time, to determine which has the best contrast in the area of interest. With the poppy picture, clearly the blue channel offers the best contrast to separate the sky and the flower, as you can see in Figure 8.24.

Figure 8.24
Looking at the red, green, and blue channels, it's clear that the blue channel offers the most contrast between the sky and the flower.

2. Make a copy of the channel offering the most contrast—in this case, the blue channel—by dragging that channel layer to the New Channel icon at the bottom of the Channels panel.

3. Maximize the contrast between the area you want to select and the rest of the image by choosing Image > Adjustments > Levels. This is one of the few times

you make changes directly on the pixels because there is no way to create an adjustment layer for a channel. Drag in the black point and white point sliders to turn the preview nearly black and white, as illustrated in Figure 8.25. A small transition area of gray is actually beneficial.

Figure 8.25 Use the sliders in the Levels dialog box to turn this channel into black and white.

4. To fine-tune the selection, you'll most likely need to use the Brush tool and paint some areas with black and some areas with white.

5. Once you have a black-and-white preview created (which is actually a mask), click the Load Channel As Selection icon ⬭ at the bottom of the Channels panel. This creates a selection based on the mask you just created. The white areas are selected.

6. You can invert the selection (by choosing Select > Inverse on the main menu) if you find that you have selected the opposite part of the image.

7. After going through all this to make a selection, it's a good idea to save the selection by choosing Select > Save and naming it (see Figure 8.26). That way, you can refer to it in the future.

Figure 8.26
After making a time-consuming selection, it's a good idea to save the selection.

Extracting an Object from Its Background

Photoshop provides the Extract dialog box to select an object and remove the background. You might want to do this if you have a subject that you're preparing to import into another image. For example, if you have been on an African safari and have a great picture of a lion you'd like to put in another setting, use the Extract tool to select the lion.

Most people find it takes some practice to use this tool successfully. The trick is to use it carefully to retain edge detail in the portion you're preserving. Fuzzy-edged objects, such as furry or feathered critters, are often challenging. Nonetheless, this tool can work well at times and is worth a try if other selection methods don't seem to work easily.

Note: The Extraction filter works only on 8-bit files.

Take the following steps to extract an object from its background using the Extract tool:

1. Open an image with an object you want to separate from the rest of the image.
2. Choose Filter > Extract.
3. In the Extract dialog box, choose the Edge Highlighter tool , and use it to trace along the edges of the object you want to preserve.
4. Try to have about two-thirds of the border outside the object and one-third inside it. You can change the brush size as you work. Use a smaller brush when outlining well-defined areas and a large brush for less well-defined areas such as fur or feathers (see Figure 8.27).

Figure 8.27
Outline the object to be extracted, trying to keep two-thirds of the border outside the object. Use a larger brush on less-well-defined areas such as feathers. (Photo by Ellen Anon.)

5. Make sure your outline completely surrounds the object to be extracted. You can use the edge of the image as part of the outline.

6. Click the Fill tool , and click once inside the outlined object. This fills the inside of your highlighted outline with a colored tint and tells Photoshop that this is the part you want to keep (see Figure 8.28).

7. Click the Preview button to see how your extraction will look, as in Figure 8.29.

Figure 8.28 Filling an area tells Photoshop that this is the area you want to keep.

Figure 8.29 Click the Preview button to see the extraction results.

8. You may have to go back and work on your highlighting along some of the edges if the extraction isn't as accurate as you hoped; zooming in may be helpful. Use the Eraser and Edge cleanup tools while in the preview to perfect the edges.

9. Click OK to perform the extraction.

10. After performing the extraction, use the History Brush (as described in Chapter 4) to help perfect the extraction if areas were removed by mistake. To do this:

   a. Choose the History Brush .

   b. Click the original image in the History panel to set it as the source, and then paint back in any missing areas in your selection. If the original image was 16-bit, you'll need to place the History Brush by a preextraction layer in which the image is 8-bit.

   c. Use the Eraser tool to remove any pixels that should not be there.

Note: For more information on making selections, see *Photoshop Masking and Compositing* by Katrin Eismann (New Riders, 2004).

Combining Elements from Various Images

Perhaps you have several images, each containing elements that you would like to combine into a single image. Often, the relative sizes of the various elements need to be modified—you can take care of that during the process of compositing the elements. In the next example, we'll create a composite of some birds, a background, and a moon:

1. Open your destination photo (the photo that you are going to use as the main photo), set its resolution to 300 ppi by choosing Image > Image Size, and *uncheck* the Resample Image option. You don't want to interpolate the file now; just set it to the same resolution. See Figure 8.30 for our destination photo.

Figure 8.30 This is the destination photo that we'll use as the foundation for our composite. (Photo by Ellen Anon.)

2. Open a file containing an element you're going to use, and also set it to a resolution of 300 ppi. In our example, we'll use an image with a group of cranes flying (see Figure 8.31).

Figure 8.31
We're going to select these flying cranes to use in our composite. (Photo by Ellen Anon.)

3. Use your preferred selection tool to isolate the element. In this case, it's easy to use the Color Range tool to select the cranes. Don't forget to use Refine Edges to soften the edges so that they look natural, not cut out and pasted.

4. Choose Select > Save Selection, and type a name for the selection. This enables you to return to this selection at any time by choosing Select > Load Selection.

5. Use the Move tool, and drag the selection you just made to the destination image.

6. Use the Edit > Free Transform tools to size, rotate, and place these elements (see Figure 8.32).

Figure 8.32
Size, rotate, and place the new elements using the Free Transform tool.

7. Note that the elements you just dragged in are on their own layers. It's quite possible they may need some tonal or color adjustments to match the destination image. To make an adjustment layer that affects only a specific layer, hold down the Alt/Option key while clicking the icon to make a new adjustment layer. Check the box that says Use Previous Layer To Create Clipping Mask, as shown in Figure 8.33.

Figure 8.33
By holding down the Alt/Option key while creating a new adjustment layer, you can check the option to have only the previous layer affected by the adjustments you make.

8. Repeat this process if there are other elements from other pictures you want to include. In this case, add a moon as well (see Figure 8.34).

Figure 8.34 The final image also contains a moon that was added.

9. You may want to save the composite with the layers intact as a master file so you can further modify it in the future. It's quite possible that you may want to slightly adjust the position of one of the composited items or its size.

10. Proceed with your normal workflow.

Lighting Angles Matter

It's important to pay attention to lighting angles. Many Photoshop novices create composites that would require the earth to have several suns. This detracts from the impact of the final image. Paying attention to subtle details can make the difference between an impressive image and one that evokes comments of "Oh, that was Photoshopped." Although you will be ethical and indicate when an image is a composite, you still want to elicit reactions of "Wow!"

Replacing a Sky or Other Background

Now that you've learned a variety of methods for selecting a sky, you're going to put them to use. Nature photographers often find they have a great subject with a boring sky (or other background). It's wonderful when things naturally come together and the subject, lighting, and background are all perfect. But realistically, all too often the sky or background may be great when there are no subjects, and the subjects may be great when the sky is not. This happens on African safaris, it happens while photographing birds anywhere…you name the situation, and you can bet there will be times when the sky/background just doesn't cooperate. Photoshop makes it easy to replace the dull background with one that enhances your subject matter.

To replace a sky (you can follow along using the images ReplaceSky1 and ReplaceSky2 on the accompanying CD), follow these steps:

1. Open an image that needs a new sky (destination image), and set it to a resolution of 300 ppi.

2. Open an image of a preferred sky (or other background), and set it to a resolution of 300 ppi as well. Make sure that your new sky is at least as large as the destination image; making it slightly larger can be helpful too so that you can move the new sky to position the clouds or lighting precisely where you want them. As you can see in Figure 8.35, the sky image should be a picture of just a sky, not including other subject elements.

Note: Sometimes the better sky may simply be a more dramatic cloudy sky. You don't want to combine a bright blue sky with billowy clouds and a foreground taken on a very cloudy day unless you're prepared to make some sophisticated color changes to your foreground. Paying attention to the subtleties of color will make your composites more believable.

FFigure 8.35 Open an image with a sky that needs to be replaced, and open an image with a better sky. (Photos by Ellen Anon.)

3. Click the destination image, and make a selection of the dull sky using your preferred selection method. The Color Range tool is often the most efficient choice for selecting the sky.

4. Access the Refine Edge tool by clicking any of the selection tools in the Tools panel such as the Lasso tool. Use Refine Edges to soften the edges of your selection

5. Choose Select > Modify > Expand, and enter **1** pixel. Click OK. This expands the entire selection by 1 pixel to help ensure that there are no sky pixels left.

6. Click your good sky image, and use the Move tool to drag the new sky image on top of the destination image.

7. Rename the sky image layer New Sky.

8. Create a layer mask on the New Sky layer by clicking the Add Layer Mask icon at the bottom of the Layers panel. Magic! Your new sky replaces the old one, since the layer mask reflects the selection you just made, as shown in Figure 8.36.

Figure 8.36 When you create a layer mask on the New Sky layer, it reflects the selection of the old sky you already made, and magically the new sky appears.

9. If you didn't use Refine Edges, you'll need to soften the edge of the selection to make the transition to the new sky more natural. Click the layer mask to select it, and make certain the layer mask is highlighted, not the image thumbnail. Choose Filter > Blur > Gaussian Blur, and enter a value from 0.5 to 1.5 pixels. You can see the results on your image and gauge how much blur to add by what looks good. Click OK.

10. With the layer mask still active, you can further control exactly where the mask begins by choosing Image > Adjustments > Levels and moving the sliders. You are modifying the tonalities in the mask, which in turn modify the edges of each image layer.

11. You can choose the area of the new sky (the background) you want to show by *unlinking* the layer mask on the New Sky layer. To do this, click the link icon between the New Sky image thumbnail and the New Sky layer mask, as shown in Figure 8.37. Now click the image thumbnail, and choose the Move tool. You can move the new sky without affecting the mask, so you get to choose which part of the sky to show. Very cool!

Figure 8.37 By unlinking the image thumbnail and the layer mask, you can move the new sky to reveal whatever part of it best complements your picture.

Once you grasp the basics of compositing, you're free to create images that more accurately reflect the realities of some situations as well as images that reflect your imagination and subjective experiences. Experiment and have fun!

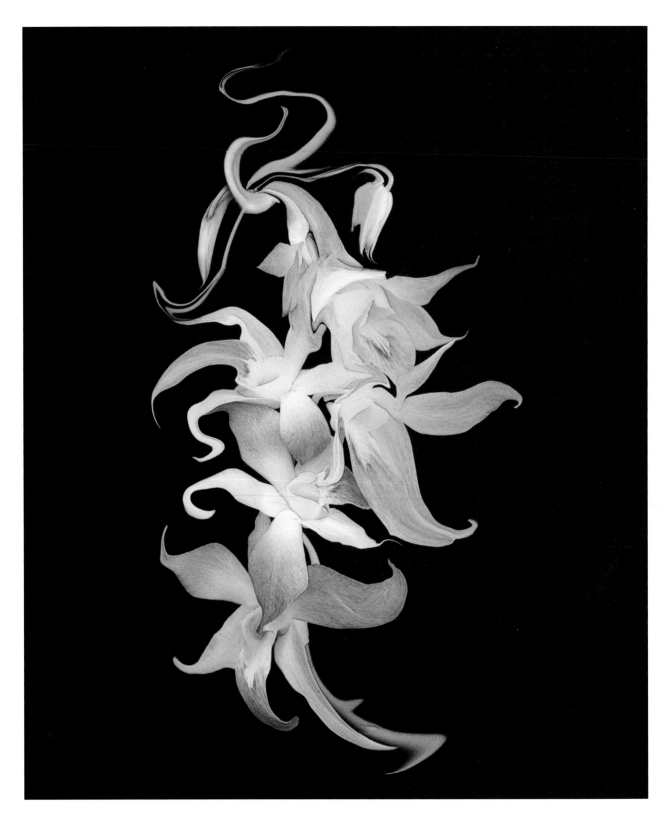

Creative Effects

For some nature photographers, the goal is simply to take the best shot they can to document what they see and then to optimize it in Adobe Photoshop. That's fine. Other photographers are latent artists at heart but may believe (rightly or wrongly) that they have no inherent ability to create art from a blank canvas. But given a camera as the starting point and a digital darkroom, they can make magic.

Of course, creativity is an artistic form; not every technique appeals to every photographer, and some images are more suited for one approach than another. As you read through this chapter, consider each technique as a jumping-off point for your own ideas rather than a cookbook approach to creative imagery.

9

Chapter Contents
Black and White
Filters
Digital Montages
Digital Multiple Exposures
The Evolution of an Image

Black and White

Some images lend themselves to black and white, to say nothing of the fact that right now black-and-white images are very popular. In fact, there is a timeless quality to many black-and-white prints.

Converting to Black and White

Digital cameras capture images in color, but there are a variety of ways that you can easily convert them into black and white. While some folks may opt to simply desaturate their images by creating a Hue/Saturation adjustment layer and sliding the Saturation slider all the way to the left, or by choosing Image > Mode > Grayscale, we don't recommend those approaches because the results are often very flat and bland (see Figure 9.1). Instead, we recommend using the new Black & White adjustment layer or a Channel Mixer adjustment layer. We find that with some images we prefer the Channel Mixer and others, the new Black & White tool.

Figure 9.1
Simply desaturating, or just changing the mode to grayscale, often converts an image to a rather bland black-and-white version. (Photo by Ellen Anon.)

Converting to Black and White via the Channel Mixer

Recall from Chapter 8, "Composites," that when you wanted to make a selection of part of an image, you could look at the red, green, and blue channels and see what information was in each. You can use this same information to help convert to black and white. The Channel Mixer allows you to specify how much information you want each channel to contribute to the final image. It's a good idea to begin by opening the Channels panel and clicking each channel individually to see what detail is present in each (see Figure 9.2). That will give you an idea of where to begin in the Channel Mixer.

Red channel

Blue channel

Green channel

Figure 9.2
Check each channel to see what information it is contributing to the final image. (Photo by Ellen Anon.)

To convert an image to black and white, take the following steps:

1. Return to the Layers panel, and create a Channel Mixer adjustment layer (see Figure 9.3) by clicking the same adjustment layer icon at the bottom of the panel and choosing Channel Mixer from the drop-down menu.

Figure 9.3
Create a Channel Mixer adjustment layer to use for converting the image to black and white.

2. Check the Monochrome box.

3. You can use the default settings or click in the Preset drop-down menu to try the various presets.

4. Modify the percentages from each channel to create a more dramatic black-and-white version of your file. You can choose settings from –200% to +200% for each channel. As you adjust one, you're likely to need to tweak the other settings. Usually it's best to have the percentages from the three channels total close to 100%. Sometimes we go a little beyond 100% for a more contrasty image with a lot of punch, but you have to make sure you're not sacrificing image detail for increased contrast (see Figure 9.4). When you go above 100% a warning triangle with an exclamation point appears by the Total percent.

Figure 9.4
Experiment with the settings for each channel to create a black-and-white image with considerable impact. (Photo by Ellen Anon.)

5. Usually we leave the Constant option at its default of 0, but moving it to the left darkens the image, and moving it to the right lightens it.

When you first open a Channel Mixer adjustment layer and check the Monochrome box, the default values are red = 40, green = 40, and blue = 20. While this is a good starting place for many images, most of the time you will want to further adjust the sliders. Often, the red channel provides the most contrast, but it's likely you may find some information in the green or blue channels that you want to emphasize; if so, you may increase those channels somewhat. When you increase one channel, you may need to decrease the other channels. You may even choose to increase one channel dramatically and then use a negative value for the other channels. Make these decisions based on your taste and the characteristics of the individual image. Often, noise is more prominent in the blue channel, so if noise is a problem in your image, you may opt to use a negative value there. There really are no typical values that apply to most images. After a little experimentation with the settings for each channel, you'll have a dramatic black-and-white image.

With the new presets that are available in Photoshop CS3, we often find it helpful to consider several versions of an image. If you're not certain that the values you have selected are the best possible combination, click the Snapshot button in the History panel to take a snapshot of the image this way. Then, reopen the Channel Mixer adjustment layer (by double-clicking its icon in the Layers panel), and try a new combination of values or one of the presets. You can repeat this process as many times as you desire. To go back to an earlier snapshot, return to the top of the History panel, and click the desired snapshot, as shown in Figure 9.5. Note that snapshots disappear when you close the image.

Figure 9.5

By taking snapshots of previous combinations of settings in the Channel Mixer, you can try a variety of settings and choose which one you prefer.

Note: Because you used an adjustment layer to convert the image to black and white, as long as you save the image with the layers intact, you can go back and modify the settings.

Converting Using the Black & White Adjustment

Photoshop CS3 has a new Black & White adjustment layer. At first glance there are a lot of sliders to adjust. But what we've found is that this new tool is very powerful and simultaneously very easy to use. It is now our preferred method of converting to black and white.

We normally begin by hitting the Auto button. We can honestly say it's one of the few times we check out an "auto" anything routinely! But Adobe did a good job figuring out the Auto algorithms.

The Auto settings tend to be a little conservative for our taste, so we often proceed to tweak the sliders. At first glance, the order of the sliders may seem to be a bit random (see Figure 9.6), but if you envision a color wheel, then it's easy to see that each slider represents a portion of the color wheel, and neighboring sliders are adjacent on the color wheel. When you adjust these sliders, you think in terms of the amounts of the individual colors. If you want a color to be lighter in the black-and-white image, you increase the setting for the corresponding slider, and if you want it to be darker, you decrease it. The sliders can range from –200 to +300. Using extreme settings can sometimes lead to clipping, so be sure to check the histogram.

Figure 9.6
Each of the sliders works on a particular range of colors to lighten or darken the tonality of those pixels.

Note: The sliders in the Black & White tool do *not* work in conjunction with their opposites, as do some types of adjustments. So to darken a blue sky, you would decrease the settings for the blue and possibly the cyan sliders, but you would not need to change the yellow or red sliders (the opposites of blue and cyan).

The Black & White adjustment also offers a choice of presets to create certain effects. You can select any of these presets and then continue to adjust the individual sliders to suit the particular image.

In addition to controlling the tonality of each color range, the Black and White tool makes it easy to tint the image by checking the Tint option box. This automatically applies a sepia tint to the image (see Figure 9.7). We often prefer to decrease the saturation of this tint slightly using the Saturation slider. If you prefer a different hue for the tint, adjust the Hue slider as desired.

Figure 9.7
We converted this image to black and white (and colorized the pistils, which we'll describe in the next section), and then we created a sepia-toned version.

Comparing the Results Using the Channel Mixer and the Black & White Adjustment

To give you an idea of the differences possible using the various tools and settings, we began with an image and converted it using several presets in the Channel Mixer including the infrared setting, the Auto setting in the Black & White adjustment and finally a composite (see Figure 9.8). The results will vary by image, and the ideal approach for your particular image is up to you.

Figure 9.8

Comparison of the original
image and several black-
and-white conversions

Original image

Black and White tool auto conversion

Black and White tool custom settings

Continues

Figure 9.8 (*Continued*)

Channel Mixer Infrared preset

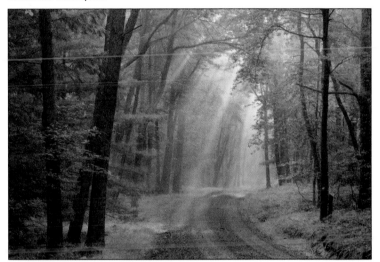

Channel Mixer with Orange Filter preset

Composite using Infrared preset version and custom settings in Black and White tool version

Colorizing Black-and-White Images

You may be quite content with the black-and-white rendition of your image, or you may want to experiment with adding color back into your image, depending on the effect you're after.

For example, you may decide that you'd like to emphasize one particular aspect of the picture by having it in the original color while the rest of the picture remains black and white. This look—popular in greeting cards—is incredibly easy. All you need to do is select the Brush tool, set it to black, make sure the Channel Mixer or Black & White adjustment layer is active (highlighted), and paint over the areas you want to be in color (see Figure 9.9). It's that simple!

Figure 9.9 By painting with black on the layer mask in the Channel Mixer or Black & White adjustment layer, we returned color just to the man. (Photo by Ellen Anon.)

Hopefully by now you recognize that you're using the layer mask that came with the adjustment layer to mask out the monochromatic effects. If you'd prefer the color to be more subdued, reduce the opacity of the brush by going to the Options bar and setting it accordingly.

If you want to have a *different* color in that one area than what was originally there, create a Hue/Saturation layer on top of the Channel Mixer layer, and adjust the Hue slider (as well as the Saturation and Lightness sliders if desired) until the target item is the shade you prefer. That's what we did earlier in Figure 9.7.

Some people prefer a more hand-tinted look. An easy way to create such a look is to take the following steps:

1. Create your black-and-white file using the Channel Mixer or Black & White adjustment as described in the preceding sections.

2. Reduce the opacity of the adjustment layer to achieve the desired look, using the Opacity slider in the Layers panel (see Figure 9.10). The final opacity is a matter of individual preference.

Figure 9.10 By reducing the opacity of the Channel Mixer or Black & White adjustment layer, you can create a hand-tinted look. (Photo by Ellen Anon.)

3.   If you want to change the hue of the colors, add a Hue/Saturation adjustment layer, and adjust the Hue slider to taste. The Hue/Saturation adjustment layer changes the color of the entire image, albeit with reduced saturation because of the Channel Mixer layer.

4.   If you want to change the color of only part of your image and leave the remainder with the look created in step 3, add another Hue/Saturation layer and create a layer mask so that only the areas of the mask corresponding to the areas you want to change are white and the rest of the mask is black. Adjust the Hue slider to taste.

An alternate approach to adding color to a black-and-white image is to create a Stamp Visible layer after using the Black & White adjustment layer or the Channel Mixer. Set the Brush tool to Color mode in the options bar, and select the desired color in the Color Picker. Reduce the opacity of the brush to subdue the colors. Paint each area as appropriate.

Sepia-toned images have an aged look that is also quite popular and is easy to create. It's another approach to colorizing a monochromatic image. We already described using the Black & White adjustment layer to create a sepia-toned image. If you used the Channel Mixer to convert your image to black and white, take these steps:

1.   After you have converted your image to black and white, open a new Black & White adjustment layer.

2.   Check the Tint box.

3.   Adjust the Hue and Saturation sliders to taste.

Try It! Open the image called BlackAndWhite on the accompanying CD or one of your own color images. Try converting it to black and white using the Black & White and Channel Mixer adjustment layers. Experiment with restoring color in part of it or giving it a hand-tinted or sepia look.

Filters

Photoshop includes a huge array of filters that make it easy to distort your picture in all sorts of ways. It's beyond the scope of this book to cover them all, but we'll describe a few that we find useful. However, the best way to get familiar with the filters is to open an image and begin experimenting. We'll begin by describing how to use Smart Filters and regular filters.

Note: If you opt for the "experimental" approach, it's a good idea to turn on the History Log in your General Preferences (refer to Chapter 4, "Foundations," for details) so that you can remember what you did if you stumble across something wonderful! In fact, any time you are being "creative" with your image, it's smart to turn on the History Log. You may think you'll remember exactly what you did, but if you're anything like us, at some later date you'll be frustrated because you can't recall how to replicate the effect.

Using Smart Filters on Smart Objects

CS3 has added Smart Filters, meaning that filter effects can be readjusted repeatedly, even if you close and reopen the image. This is a welcome addition, very similar to the flexibility of the adjustments in adjustment layers. By using Smart Filters, you can create different combinations of filter effects that you can dynamically adjust as desired. Unfortunately, Smart Filters are available only for certain filter effects with 16-bit images but are available for all filters with 8-bit images. (For more explanation of Smart Filters and Smart Objects, refer to Chapter 5, "Workflows and First Steps.")

Note: The following filters can be used as Smart Filters with 16-bit images: all Blur filters except Smart Blur; Lens Correction (from the Distort group); all Noise filters; all Render filters except Lighting Effects; all Sharpen filters; and Emboss, Find Edges and Solarize from the Stylize group.

The ultimate in flexibility is to have a raw image placed as a Smart Object at the beginning of your workflow with Smart Filters applied to the raw image. Currently, there are some limitations that will sometimes cause you to have to make some workflow choices. For example, a cleanup or cloning layer will not update to reflect any further changes you make to the Smart Object raw file. If you do your dust cleanup in ACR, or the cleanup layer contains only a few pixels to cover some very small dust spots and the Smart Filters you want to use are for sharpening, you'll be fine. But if you readjust the color or tonality of the raw file in any way or use a filter that causes a dramatic effect, the clone layer will be outdated and need to be redone.

We recommend that when you want to experiment with creative filter effects you create a duplicate version of your optimized image and then flatten it by choosing Layer > Flatten Image. By doing this you can save your optimized file as a 16-bit file.

Note: An alternative approach is to create a Stamp Visible layer at the top of your workflow by holding down the Alt/Option key and choosing Layer > Merge Visible. Make certain to continue to hold down the Alt/Option key while clicking Merge Visible. This will create a new composite layer at the top of your workflow to use for your creative filter effects. The advantage of this approach is that the entire file is stored together. The downside is that you may have to convert the entire file to an 8-bit image. If you have no use for the file without the creative filter effects, then this approach may be preferable.

To use most of the creative filters, you'll need to convert the image to an 8-bit file by choosing Image > Mode > 8-Bit. Then choose Filter > Convert for Smart Filters. This will change the layer into a Smart Object, and the filters you apply will be editable.

When you want all the filter effects to apply to certain areas of the image, you can use the Smart Filter Layer mask and paint the mask white or black to show or reveal the effects, just as you did with adjustment layer masks (see Figure 9.11).

Figure 9.11
Use the mask on the Smart Filter layer to control what parts of the image are affected by the Smart Filters.

If you want one filter to affect part of the image and another filter to affect a different area, it gets a little more complicated. In Figure 9.12 we added a pastel paintbrush effect to lend a painterly feel to the image. We used the layer mask to slightly subdue the effect.

1. Begin by applying the Smart Filter to the image and masking out any areas you don't want to be affected.

2. Duplicate this layer.

3. Go to Layer > Smart Object > Rasterize. This will apply the effects of the filters on the previous layer.

4. Go to Filter > Convert for Smart Filter. This will turn this layer back into a Smart Object that includes the effects of the previous layer. That way you can apply additional filters and use the layer mask to apply the effects differently than you did in the previous layer. Use the layer mask to reveal only the portion of the image you want to be affected by this filter or to subdue the effects of the filter beyond what's available in the filter settings.

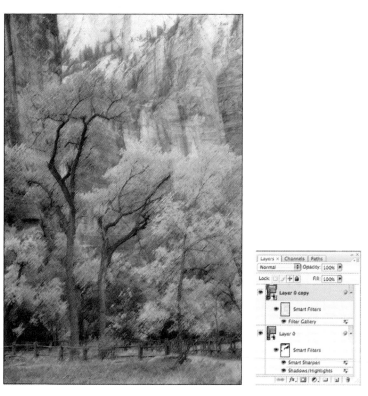

Figure 9.12 Add a layer mask to a Smart Object layer to further control the effects of the filter and where it is applied.

Using Filters Without Smart Objects

Just as with Smart Filters, since most of the creative filters work on 8-bit images only, we recommend that you duplicate your optimized master file and create a separate file to do your creative work. That way the master file remains a 16-bit file, and the creative file is 8-bit.

If you have no use for the original file without the creative effects, then you may prefer to create a Merge Visible layer at the top of the workflow by holding down the Alt/Option key and choosing Layer > Merge Visible. Make certain to continue to hold down the Alt/Option key while clicking Merge Visible. Apply the filter effects to this layer. Then you can reduce the effect later by adjusting the opacity of the layer, or you can add a layer mask to apply the filter to specific parts of the layer only.

If the filter effect you want to apply is grayed out, it means that you'll need to convert the file to 8-bit. To do so, select Image > Mode > 8-Bits/Channel.

Many of the filters take considerable time to process. If you are going to experiment with different effects, a useful trick is to duplicate your image by choosing Image >

Duplicate and significantly reduce the size of the duplicate file. Then experiment with the filters on the smaller file. When you have established a combination of filters and settings that you are satisfied with, apply the same combination to your original file.

Note: Some filters are processed only using RAM. If a filter requires all your available RAM to process an effect, you may get an error message.

Blurs

Photoshop CS3 has an impressively long list of blurs, but we'll cover only a few of them that are particularly applicable to nature photographs. We find that Gaussian blurs, and occasionally lens blurs are the main ones we use. You may want to explore other blurs such as smart blurs, motion blurs, and zoom blurs as well.

Gaussian Blurs

Gaussian blurs produce a hazy effect and blur the image by an adjustable amount. They're quite useful when you want to blur a section of your image. However, it's important to remember that if you make a selection of the area you want to blur, a Gaussian blur considers that selection a general guideline, but not an absolute mandate, for the boundaries of the blur. This transition area between blurred and not blurred sections is more apparent the more blur you apply. At times it can create a glow around your subject, as it does in the photo in Figure 9.13.

Figure 9.13
Although the background was selected when the Gaussian blur was applied, it included some of the pink from the spoonbill, resulting in a pleasant glow around the bird. (Photo by Ellen Anon.)

To apply a Gaussian blur, take the following steps:

1. Make a copy of your Background layer.
2. You may choose to first select the area to apply the blur to using any of the selection tools, or you may prefer to rely completely on a layer mask.
3. Apply the blur to the copy layer, if you have made a selection first, by choosing Filter > Blur > Gaussian Blur. If you prefer to rely on a layer mask, it will be

easier to apply the blur to the Background layer and then add a layer mask to the Background copy layer that will be the sharp layer. You will be using the layer mask to reveal blur wherever desired.

4. Using the preview as a guide, set the radius to determine how much blur you want.

5. Add a layer mask, if desired, by clicking the Add Layer Mask icon at the bottom of the Layers panel to further hide or reveal the blur effect.

Lens Blur

The Lens Blur filter mimics the appearance of a reduced depth of field so that your subject remains in focus while the background fades away. With this filter, you specify part of the image as your subject that you want to remain in sharp focus and then set it to progressively blur other areas. You can also control the creation and appearance of specular highlights.

Note: Although the Lens Blur filter can be helpful at times, it's still more efficient to use the correct aperture setting in the field.

1. Duplicate the Background layer (by dragging it to the Create A New Layer icon in the Layers panel).

The key to the Lens Blur filter is creating a *depth map*. Don't let the name intimidate you. This is where you define what parts of the image you want sharp and what parts to blur, as well as how much blur you want to add. The depth map is essentially a layer mask.

There are two ways to create a depth map; one way is to use an alpha channel, and the other is to use a selection. The easiest way, and one that works well with scenics, is to create it from an alpha channel. Figure 9.14 shows an image in which the Lens Blur filter is being used to blur the trees in the background. An alpha channel with a gradient was created to tell the filter which parts of the image to keep sharp and which parts to blur.

Figure 9.14

The Lens Blur filter was used to blur the trees in the background. The depth map was based on a gradient on an alpha channel. (Photo by Ellen Anon.)

2. To create a depth map based on a selection, skip to step 3. To create a depth map using an alpha channel, follow these steps:

a. Open the Channels panel, and create a new alpha channel by clicking the Create New Channel icon . Your preview becomes entirely black.

b. Select the Gradient tool from the Tools panel. The gradient is used to define a gradual transition from black to white so that the blur tapers off gradually.

c. On the options bar, open the Gradient picker (click the arrow next to the first field), and then click the third option in the drop-down panel (see Figure 9.15). This produces a gradient from the black to white. Set the gradient type to Linear by clicking the first icon to the right of the Gradient picker in the Options bar.

Figure 9.15
Choose the black-to-white gradient to use as the basis of your depth map.

> **Note:** You can use any style gradient that works for your particular image. For example, a radial gradient may be effective if you want to have everything blur around your subject.

d. After you apply the blur, *wherever the gradient is black, the image will be sharp; where the gradient is white, the image will be blurred.* So if you begin near the bottom of your image and drag the gradient toward the top, the blur affects the top of your image but not the bottom. Note that you can create this gradient anywhere in your image or invert it if desired. Later—in the Lens Blur Filter dialog box—you can also refine where it begins.

e. Your alpha channel is now ready, containing the gradient that determines where the blur is strongest and weakest. Click the RGB channel, and then return to the Background copy layer in the Layers panel. *Skip to step 4.*

3. An alternate approach to creating the depth map is to create a selection first and use this selection as the basis for the depth map. This approach is frequently useful with a discrete subject such as an animal or bird that you want to separate from the background:

a. Create a selection using any of the selection methods to define the area you want to blur.

b. Save the selection by choosing Select > Save Selection. Do *not* feather the selection.

c. In the Save Selection dialog box (shown in Figure 9.16), do the following:

- Leave the channel set to New.

- Enter a name that will allow you to easily recognize your selection. In this example we used "whitepeacock."

- Under Operation, leave New Channel selected.
- Once you've done this, click OK.

Figure 9.16
Save your selection with an easily recognizable name as a new channel.

d. Deselect the selection by choosing Select > Deselect.

e. To feather the selection, go to the Channels panel, and click the channel you saved to make it visible. It appears as a black-and-white version of your image.

f. Choose Blur > Gaussian Blur, and using your mask as a preview, determine how soft the edge of the mask should be.

g. Click the RGB channel, and return to your Background copy. Proceed as follows.

4. Now, regardless of how you created your blur depth map, choose Filter > Blur > Lens Blur.

5. At the right of the Lens Blur dialog box, under Depth Map, set the source for the depth map to Alpha Channel 1 (shown in Figure 9.17) or to the selection, depending on which method you have followed.

Figure 9.17
Choose the alpha channel to use as the basis for your depth map (if you created a depth map using a gradient on an alpha channel) or the name of the selection (if you made a selection to serve as the basis of the map).

6. Set the preview to Faster initially to generate previews to help you select your settings. Then change it to More Accurate when you have made your final choices to preview the effect.

7. The Blur Focal Distance slider allows you to fine-tune where the blur begins. (It's similar to setting your camera at a certain focal distance.) To use it, click the part of the image you want to remain sharp. Photoshop sets the Blur Focal Distance automatically for you.

8. Drag the Radius slider to define how much blur to add, checking the preview (see Figure 9.18).

Figure 9.18
Preview the amount and placement of the blur. Note that this image uses a saved selection in the alpha channel as the basis of the depth map. (Photo by Ellen Anon.)

9. Once you've set your Source and Blur Focal Distance settings, adjust the other options to get the look you want, using the preview to see how the settings interact:

- The Iris settings allow you to specify the shape and size of specular highlights. Some readers will appreciate the fine control this offers, while others may prefer to use the default settings. If your image doesn't have any specular highlights, then don't worry about setting the Iris values.

- The Specular Highlights settings enable you to determine which values should be used as specular highlights. The Brightness setting allows you to specify how bright to make the specular highlights, while the Threshold setting specifies which values are to be used as specular highlights. (You can choose from 0 to 255.) True specular highlights should have a value of 255, but you may want to create specular highlights by using a slightly lower setting. Many images have no specular highlights.

Some people choose to add some noise to simulate the appearance of film grain. If you choose to add noise, check the box to make it monochromatic. (Adding color noise will look like digital noise, which we try to eliminate!) Usually the Gaussian distribution appears more natural than uniform.

10. When you are satisfied with your settings, click OK to perform the blur.

11. If you find that you blurred areas you didn't intend to, you can modify them by adding a layer mask to your blurred image layer. Make sure to use as soft a brush as possible on the layer mask.

Smart Blur

The Smart Blur filter (Filter > Blur > Smart Blur) blurs pixels throughout the entire image based on how similar or dissimilar they are and the settings you specify. Of course, you can use a Smart Blur filter in conjunction with a layer mask to apply the blur only to specific portions of your image. Smart Blur offers several options, as shown in Figure 9.19.

Figure 9.19
The Smart Blur filters offer several controls, including Radius, Threshold, Quality, and Mode, which determine not only the strength of the blur but also the appearance.

- The Radius setting refers to how large an area Photoshop checks for dissimilar pixels. The larger the area, the more chance of finding dissimilar pixels and so the more likely blur will be applied.

- The Threshold value refers to how different two pixels must be before Photoshop recognizes them as different enough to blur. The lower the value, the more blur that will be applied.

- Quality refers to the quality of the preview. Initially, to save time, you may prefer to use the Low setting and change it to High when you are close to your desired values.

  Smart Blur also offers three modes, which are illustrated in Figure 9.20.

Normal mode

Figure 9.20
Depending on the mode and settings used in Smart Blur, you can create a gentle blur or some unusual painterly effects. (Photo by Ellen Anon.)

Continues

Edge Only mode with Filter faded to 45 percent

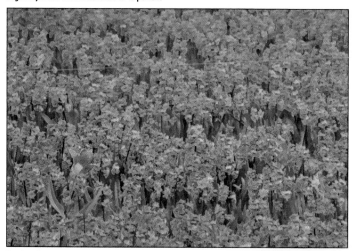

Overlay Edge mode with Filter reduced to about 25 percent

Figure 9.20
(Continued)

- In Normal mode the blur is applied to the entire selection and works as anticipated. In some images it can create a painterly effect, while in Edge Only or Overlay Edge, you can get some very creative outlined effects.

- Edge Only applies black-and-white edges and may convert your entire image to a maze of black and white lines and shapes. This can be useful if you want to create an outlined version of your image.

- Overlay Edge retains the general colors of your image but applies white lines and shapes to edges where significant contrast occurs.

The effects generated using the three mode settings are quite different and fun to explore. We find it helpful to use them in conjunction with reduced opacity of the Background copy layer to obtain unique versions of our images.

Note: To reduce the effect of any filter immediately after applying it, choose Edit > Fade, and reduce the effect by adjusting the slider. This option exists only immediately after applying the filter.

The Liquify Filter

The Liquify filter can be a lot of fun. It's a lot like finger painting with the pixels but with a lot more control and much cleaner hands! You can stretch, push, pull, pucker, or bloat any area to create subtle or dramatic distortions. This is one of Ellen's favorite filters to use to create artistic effects with flowers (see Figure 9.21).

Figure 9.21 Using the Liquify filter transforms a bland picture of orchids into a striking fine art image. (Photo by Ellen Anon.)

Liquify can be used with 16-bit or 8-bit images, but not on a Smart Object layer. Unfortunately, it's not available as a Smart Filter. If your image already has other filter effects on a Smart Object layer, duplicate the Smart Object layer by dragging it to the Create a new layer icon at the bottom of the Layers panel. Then choose Image > Smart Object > Rasterize. This will convert the Smart Object layer to a regular pixel layer.

Be aware that unless you have a fast computer with a lot of memory, processing the Liquify effects may be slow. For that reason, you may want to convert a copy of your image to 8-bit and use the filter on that version. Once you have established effective settings for your image, you can save them and then apply them to a 16-bit version if you prefer. Don't forget to work on a copy of your Background layer, both for safety and so you can apply a layer mask or reduce the opacity of the layer.

Perhaps more than any other filter in Photoshop, this is one you have to play with to use effectively. Let's look at the Liquify dialog box, which you open by choosing Filter > Liquify. There are a variety of tools in the toolbox column on the left, as shown in Figure 9.22. Some of these tools apply the distortions, while others, such as the Freeze tool, enable you to apply a quick mask to certain areas to "freeze" the effects. The Hand and Zoom tools work as usual. The primary tool we tend to use is the Warp tool, although it's worth experimenting with the others.

| | Forward Warp tool |
| Reconstruct tool |
	Twirl Clockwise (Alt/Option-click to twirl counterclockwise)
	Pucker tool
	Bloat tool
	Push Left tool
	Mirror tool
	Turbulence
	Freeze Mask
	Thaw Mask
	Hand tool
	Zoom tool

Figure 9.22 The Liquify dialog box offers several tools. ((Photo by Ellen Anon.)

On the right side of the Liquify dialog box (shown in Figure 9.23) are options for using the tools:

Figure 9.23
On the right side of the Liquify dialog box are the controls for the various tools.

Brush Size   Is as expected: it refers to the size of the brush and can be controlled by the bracket keys on your keyboard or via the setting in the dialog box.

Brush Density   Controls how the brush is feathered at the edges. The effect is strongest in the center of the brush and lighter at the edges.

Brush Pressure   Controls how quickly the distortions are applied when you drag a tool across your preview image. Using too large a pressure may make it difficult to stop exactly where you want.

Brush Rate   Controls how quickly distortions are applied when you use a tool that can be held stationary, such as bloat or twirl.

Turbulence Jitter   Sets how tightly the Turbulence tool scrambles the pixels.

Reconstruction Options   Allow you, with the Reconstruct tool selected, to specify a mode for the reconstruction, which can either create further distortions or revert to the original image.

When you have achieved the desired effect, if you're working on a full-resolution image, you can simply click OK to apply your work to the picture. If you are using a small file version of your image as we suggested at the start of this section, click Save

Mesh. Another dialog box appears in which you can name the effect and specify where to save it (see Figure 9.24).

Once the mesh is saved, open your full-sized file, choose Filter > Liquify, and click Load Mesh. Choose the mesh you just saved, and click OK to perform the distortion. If you are feeling adventurous, apply a saved mesh to an unrelated image—sometimes serendipity comes into play, and you create something unexpected but wonderful!

Note: Although the Liquify tool is most commonly used to create distortions, it can also be used to correct distortions. It can even be used as a form of digital plastic surgery on photos of people.

Try It! Open the image called Liquify on the accompanying CD or open one of your own images, and see what you can create with it. Be sure to vary the settings and tools to get different effects.

Using the Filter Gallery

Recent versions of Photoshop (CS and newer) contain a filter gallery (Filter > Filter Gallery) rather than just a simple list of individual filters. This gallery enables you to preview the effects of a variety of filters, as well as to preview the effects of combining them and reordering them. This saves a lot of time as you experiment with different effects, but unfortunately, it works only on 8-bit images. The good news is that you can use it as a regular filter or as a Smart Filter on a Smart Object layer. When used as a Smart Filter, you can go back and modify the filter settings and order and even add and remove effects.

We often find that when using filters, one thing leads to another, and pretty soon you may have created something you love but perhaps couldn't have imagined ahead of time. The more you experiment with these filters, the more predictable they will become for you.

The Filter Gallery contains thumbnails that give you an idea of each effect. As shown in Figure 9.25, this dialog box also previews the various effects and settings on your image. You can vary the settings, combine filters, vary the order (which can substantially change their effect), and even repeat filters. The filters are applied in the order you select them, but you can drag the filter name to a different position to reorder them. To select an effect, click the corresponding thumbnail. If you want to add an additional effect, Alt/Option+click each additional filter. Clicking the eyeball icon toggles the visibility of the effect.

Figure 9.25
We used the Filter Gallery to create a painterly effect by combining the Dry Brush and Diffuse Glow filters.

Before beginning with the Filter Gallery, you should take several preparatory steps:

1. Usually when we experiment with filters, we're using files that have already been optimized. To avoid accidentally mucking up an image you've already put effort into, work on a copy of the master file by choosing Image > Duplicate.

2. Close the original file. This ensures you won't accidentally save changes to your master file such as flattening it.

3. Flatten the image by choosing Layer > Flatten Image.

4. Choose Image > Mode > 8-Bits/Channel.

5. Duplicate the Background layer by dragging it to the Create A New Layer icon at the bottom of the Layers panel. Now you'll be adding your creative effects on a layer so that not only are you not damaging your pixels, you can also later reduce the opacity of the layer or add a layer mask to it to control where the effects are applied.

6. If you are using Photoshop CS3, choose Filter > Convert for Smart Filters. This changes the layer into a Smart Object layer.

7. Choose Filter > Filter Gallery.

Some of the filters we frequently try are Glass (Distort grouping), Dry Brush, Poster Edges and Rough Pastels (which are in the Artistic group), and Water Paper (Sketch group). You will find your own favorites the more you experiment with the filters. However, don't forget to use the filters that are not part of the Filter Gallery as well. They are available from the Filter menu on the main menu bar.

Sometimes the distortion filters can lead to some exciting results, as shown in Figure 9.26. This poppy was distorted using polar remapping, then copied, liquefied, and a bit of the original image returned to complete the effect. Pretty wild, but that's what happens when you let your imagination go along with the filters in Photoshop!

Figure 9.26 This rather boring picture of a poppy was transformed into a fantasy image using a variety of the filters found in Photoshop, along with a little imagination. (Photo by Ellen Anon.)

Additional Filter Effects

Quite a few software companies have produced filter effect plug-ins for Photoshop. Many of these can lead to interesting effects as well. Often, you can download a free sample to see whether it's something you might want to use.

Photos courtesy of Fabiola Alcazar.

Flaming Pear (www.flamingpear.com) has a variety of filters that lead to some fun and dramatic effects. Fabiola Alcazar is particularly talented with using these filters. In this image she copied the background layer of her original image and then applied Flexify, using modes Equirectangular and Mirror Ball, while setting Multiply as Glue. She then experimented with the Latitude, Longitude, and Spin settings until she liked the results.

Continues

Additional Filter Effects *(Continued)*

Fabiola created this second picture almost entirely using filters. The boat and the moon are the natural elements she began with. To create the image, she opened a new canvas and then dragged in the boat silhouette, scaling it as needed. She flattened the layers and applied the Flood filter, barely touching the boat. To add the stars, she opened a new layer and applied Glitterato. She reduced the opacity of this layer and then added a layer mask to remove the stars from the boat. She then dragged in a moon and scaled it to taste, reducing the opacity to match the image.

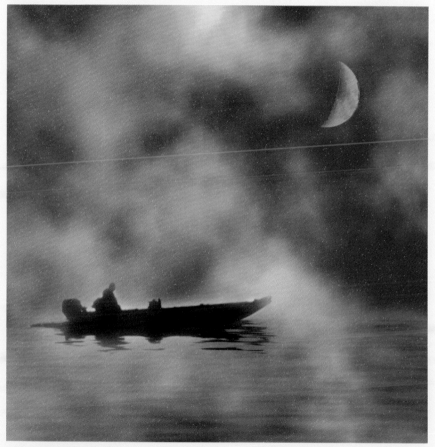

Photos courtesy of Fabiola Alcazar.

Try It! Open the image called FilterGallery on the accompanying CD or open one of your own images, and experiment with a variety of filters. Try different combinations and orders of filters while varying the settings.

Digital Montages

Combining shots, or creating "slide sandwiches," has been a popular film technique for years. Traditionally, one slide had to be overexposed by about two stops and the other by a single stop to yield an acceptable exposure. At best, it's an approach that requires a lot of trial and error and bracketing.

Freeman Patterson, Tony Sweet, and André Gallant's slide sandwiches are among the most impressive and inspiring. André creates several types of montages, including surreal, mirror, and cross montages, which he describes in his book *Dreamscapes*.

It's not only possible to emulate these same effects in Photoshop, it's actually easier to do so! One reason is that we have the flexibility to alter exposures as needed. Another reason is that if you didn't think of using a particular image as part of a montage while you were in the field, it doesn't matter. You can make several versions of the same file in Photoshop. And in Photoshop, you can go further and combine numerous images in a variety of ways.

Before you begin to make your montages, remove any dust in your images. After all, double the dust means double the cleanup required later! Final exposure and color changes are usually best made after creating the montage.

Mirror Montages in Photoshop

by André Gallant

Whether working with transparency film or using Photoshop, I'm fascinated by photo montages. *Dreamscapes*, a book I wrote and illustrated on the subject, is a result of my obsession. Although mirror montages are not for everyone, I particularly like their symmetry and the intricate designs they create. Your imagination is your only boundary.

Continues

Mirror Montages in Photoshop *(Continued)*

The mirror montages illustrated here were created in Photoshop using one of the two identical slides that render a similar result on film. Here is how I achieve this:

1. First, I choose File > New and produce a file the same size as the final mirror montage (for example, a width of 12" and height of 8" for a full-frame 35mm horizontal image). This is where I'll be inputting the two images that will create the mirror montage.

2. I scan my slide (or negative) and then crop the image to 8"×12".

3. I then sharpen, adjust the levels, and brighten the image if it's dark in tone.

4. I drag the image to the new file.

5. I then go back to the original scan (still on my desktop) and choose Image > Rotate Canvas > Flip Canvas Horizontal.

6. I drag the reversed image over the original one in the new file.

7. In the Layers panel blending mode list, I choose Multiply. This merges the images and creates the mirror montage.

8. The final photograph often needs to be brightened. You can do so by brightening the images individually, or you can choose Layer > Flatten Image and then brighten your final creation.

There are other combinations to mirror montages. You can also invert one image over the other (rotate canvas 180°), or you can reverse and invert an image over the other (flip canvas vertically). There is a substantial difference in the possible combinations.

© André Gallant, www.andregallant.com

Blending Modes

Before proceeding with ways to combine images, you need to have some understanding of blending modes.

Back in Chapter 5, you learned about layers. Recall that in many ways, pixel layers in Normal blending mode—which is what we've been using—act like prints. Whatever is on top is what you see. If you "cut a hole" in the top layer by using a layer mask to partially hide that layer, you see what's underneath. If you reduce the opacity of the top pixel layer, you see some of the top layer and some of the layer beneath it. In Normal mode, the layers blend together in an intuitive way.

Figure 9.27
Photoshop CS3 offers 25 different blending modes to combine layers.

However, Photoshop at its core is a series of mathematical algorithms, and there can be (and are) other instructions (algorithms) for how to blend two layers. These are called *blending modes*. Photoshop CS and CS2 have 23 blending modes; CS3 added two more modes. Don't panic! The good news is that you don't have to memorize what each one does. Instead, you can simply scroll through the drop-down list in the Layers panel (see Figure 9.27). You'll soon realize that the most useful blending modes for photographers are Normal, Multiply, Screen, Overlay, Soft Light, Difference, and Luminosity.

But sometimes, one of the other modes will create magic for you, so don't hesitate to try them all.

Each blending mode is a different set of instructions for how to combine two layers. For those of you who are more intuitive, don't worry about fully grasping each algorithm. Feel free to skip ahead and experiment with actually using the blending modes. For those of you who are more analytical, we're providing this explanation.

The different blending modes are grouped together in the drop-down list according to those with somewhat similar functions:

Normal Every pixel in the top active layer is displayed normally, regardless of the colors of the underlying layer.

Dissolve If the active top layer is 100% opaque with hard edges, this mode has no effect. It affects feathered edges only and layers using reduced opacity. Instead of giving a translucent appearance with reduced opacity settings, it simply turns some pixels on and others off.

Darken This mode uses pixels from the top layer only if they are darker than those in the layer below. However, it compares the pixels on a channel-by-channel basis and may use channels from both layers for any particular pixel.

Multiply This provides an effect similar to holding two slides together and looking through them.

Color Burn and Linear Burn Both of these blending modes use colors in the active layer to reduce brightness, often resulting in extreme color changes with darkened edges.

Lighten This is the opposite of Darken. Photoshop uses the pixels in the active layer only if they are lighter than those in the layer below. Again, lightness is determined on a channel-by-channel basis in each layer.

Screen This is the opposite of Multiply and lightens the image as if you had overexposed it.

Color Dodge and Linear Dodge   Both of these use colors to increase brightness. Light colors have the greatest effect and can simulate intensely bright effects.

Overlay, Soft Light, and Hard Light   These are three of the blending modes that darken the dark colors and lighten the light colors. Note that Overlay and Soft Light can be used for nondestructive dodge and burn techniques.

> **Overlay**   Multiplies or screens the colors depending on the background color. The base color is mixed with the blend color to reflect the lightness or darkness of the original color.

> **Soft Light**   Works similarly but gives an effect similar to shining a diffused spotlight on the image.

> **Hard Light**   Also multiplies or screens the colors depending on the base color, but the effect is more similar to shining a harsh spotlight on the image.

Vivid Light and Linear Light   These are useful for increasing contrast. Vivid Light is akin to combining Color Dodge and Color Burn; Linear Light gives an effect similar to combining Linear Dodge and Linear Burn.

Pin Light   This is an extreme effect that keeps only the darkest blacks and lightest whites and makes everything else invisible.

Hard Mix   Hard Mix produces a posterized image consisting of up to eight colors, including red, green, blue, cyan, magenta, yellow, black, and white. The blend color is a product of the base color and the luminosity of the blend layer. It can be used to sharpen by blending a blurred layer using Hard Mix and then decreasing the Fill to about 10% or less.

Difference and Exclusion   These modes either subtract the colors of the top active layer from the underlying layer or vice versa, according to which layer has the greatest brightness value. Blending with whites inverts the base colors, while black produces no change. Exclusion is slightly lower in contrast than the Difference mode. These modes can lead to striking creative effects when combining two images.

Hue   This mode creates a blend color with the luminance and saturation of the base color and the hue of the blend color.

Saturation   Saturation retains the values from the active layer and mixes them with the hue and luminosity values of the underlying layer.

Color   This mode creates a color with the hue and saturation values from the active layer combined with the luminosity values of the underlying layer. This is useful if you want to replace the color in part of your image and have it maintain the expected variations in tonal value.

Luminosity   This blending mode retains the lightness values from the active layer and mixes them with the hue and saturation values from the underlying layer. This can be useful when applying Curves or Unsharp Mask to avoid unexpected color shifts.

Lighter Color (New to CS3)   Lighter Color uses the lighter color of the two layers. It's similar to Lighten but operates on all channels at once rather than per channel.

Darker Color (New to CS3)   Darker Color makes the darker color of the two layers visible and operates on all channels at once. It's similar to the Darken blending mode, which bases the calculations per channel.

Figure 9.28 shows the results when a Background layer of an image is copied and flipped horizontally upon itself in six different blending modes. Note that for this image, Exclusion and Hue provided interesting results, so they were included in this illustration.

Normal

Multiply

Screen

Overlay

Difference

Exclusion

Hue

Figure 9.28

Compare the results obtained by copying the background, flipping the image, and then varying the blending mode. (Photo by Ellen Anon.)

Note: On a Windows system, to preview the effects of the various blending modes, scroll through them by highlighting the top pixel layer and clicking Shift++ (plus) or Shift+- (minus).

Surreal Montages

A very common effect photographers seek is a dreamy blur. You've seen it in many artistic photos: a kind of glow or soft focus around the subject that we call a *surreal montage* (see an example in Figure 9.29). Even the most mundane subjects can become evocative when done in this way.

Figure 9.29
Surreal montages seem
to have an ethereal glow
around them that makes
them quite evocative.
(Photo by Ellen Anon.)

Note: The surreal montage in Figure 9.29 would not be possible using film because of the amount of white and nearly white in the image. This is a distinct advantage of digital photography.

The traditional way to capture a surreal dream montage is to take two shots with your camera on a tripod, not moving it between shots. Take one image two stops overexposed at f22 or comparable, and sharply focused, and the other one stop overexposed with a wide open aperture and blurred. Defocus in the direction that makes the blur get larger than the subject rather than smaller, because the blurred version is going to provide the glow around your subject. The first image is going to provide the detail.

When done with a film camera, you couldn't use a wide-angle lens because the blur would be insufficient. You were also limited to subjects that were close to middle toned. If you wanted to do a surreal montage of a light subject, it was often impossible because you would lose all detail in the overexposed versions.

Photoshop enables you to go beyond these restrictions and create surreal montages using any lens, since you can use a Gaussian blur to blur the image as much as needed. Also, you can capture light images while retaining detail and adjust the exposure after the fact as necessary.

Note: For slightly different effects, experiment with some of the other Blur tools.

If you know you want to make a surreal montage, go ahead and capture two versions of the image as described in the preceding paragraphs. However, if it wasn't until editing your pictures that you realized an image would be great as a surreal montage, convert the same image twice, making one considerably lighter than the other. You can try plus two and plus one exposures in the raw converter, but we often try to avoid clipping any data, so adjust the exposures accordingly. Since some of the glow results from areas without detail, you may choose to allow some clipping. This is a matter of experimenting and seeing what effects you personally prefer. You can always lighten the exposure of the composite using Levels or Curves.

Note: If you are using a version of Photoshop prior to CS2, you need to save and rename the first conversion before converting the image a second time.

To create the surreal montage, take the following steps:

1. Open your two images, as shown in Figure 9.30.

Figure 9.30
Open a light, but detailed, image as well as a slightly darker, but blurred, version of the same image. (Photo by Ellen Anon.)

2. Select the Move tool ⊕, and while holding down the Shift key, drag the darker, blurred image on top of the lighter one.

3. Change the blending mode of this layer (in the Layers panel) to Multiply.

4. If the blurred layer is not as blurred as you would like, select that layer, and make it a Smart Object by choosing Layer > Smart Object.

5. Next choose Filter > Blur > Gaussian Blur. If you are working from an in-focus original, you may need a blur ranging from 15 to 40, depending on the amount of detail in the original image. The advantage of working this way is you can judge the necessary amount of blur in real time.

6. Adjust the overall exposure as needed with a Curves or Levels adjustment layer.

You can create a similar but slightly different effect by combining two images that are underexposed by one to two stops. Instead of using the Multiply blending mode, choose Screen. Figure 9.31 shows the original image and a version created using Multiply and another by using Screen. Which approach is better will vary by image and whether the detail you want to retain is primarily in the lighter or darker tonalities.

Original

Screen Mode

Multiply Mode

Figure 9.31
Creating surreal montages using the Multiply or Screen blending modes yields slightly different results. In this case, we prefer the Screen results, but in other cases Multiply will do a better job. (Photo by Ellen Anon.)

Note: You may want to experiment with using the Overlay or Soft Light blending modes instead of Multiply. The effect is a little different, and depending on your individual taste as well as on the particular image, you may prefer one over the other. With these blending modes you may not need the images to be quite as light as with Multiply. You'll notice an increase in contrast and saturation.

Cross and Flip Montages

Another approach to combining images is to take the same image and combine it with a second identical shot that is rotated 90° or flipped 180°; André Gallant calls these *mirror montages*. This can yield some amazing abstract designs. One of the keys is to experiment with the different blending modes. Often, Multiply, Overlay, Difference, Exclusion, Luminosity, or Color yields some interesting results.

Usually, you begin with well-exposed images and lighten the montage as needed after you combine the layers. Depending on the choice of blending mode, you may or may not need to adjust the exposure.

To create mirror or flip montages, take these steps:

1. Open an image, and duplicate the Background layer by dragging it to the Create A New Layer icon.
2. Ctrl+click/⌘+click the icon for the Background copy layer to select it.
3. Choose Edit > Transform > Rotate, and select 90° in either direction or flip horizontal or vertical. The choice depends upon the particular image and what you think might look good.
4. Scroll through the different blending modes to see what looks good. Sometimes nothing works, and sometimes you hit a winner, as you can see in Figure 9.32.

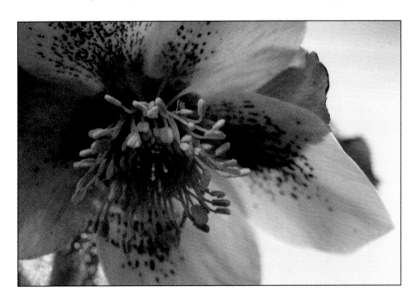

Figure 9.32
Flipping this image horizontally and selecting the Difference blending mode resulted in a dramatic abstract design. (Photo by Ellen Anon.)

Continues

Figure 9.32
(Continued)

5. If you have elected to rotate your image 90°, chances are you will want to crop and use the center square formed by the overlap of the two images.

6. Sometimes you can repeat the process and copy the montage, rotate, or flip it and blend it to create a virtual kaleidoscope, as shown in Figure 9.33.

Figure 9.33
Duplicating the montage, flipping it, and blending it upon itself resulted in a kaleidoscope. (Photo by Ellen Anon.)

Try It! Open the image called Flip on the accompanying CD, or open one of your own. Duplicate it, and then rotate or flip it to create various effects. Be sure to scroll through the blending modes to see how they affect the montage.

Mirror Images

Mirror images are very similar to flip montages, except that the two images are side by side rather than on top of each other. This creates an obvious dramatic symmetry that can be quite compelling. Natural phenomena that have strong design components, such as sand dunes, rock formations, waves, and even trees, lend themselves to this approach. Remember that the center of your image is formed by what is on the edges of your file, so your subject may need to be placed toward the edges of the original rather than your typical composition.

To create a mirror montage, take the following steps:

1. Open your file (see Figure 9.34), and duplicate it by choosing Image > Duplicate. This is easier for this technique than simply copying the Background layer, as you did earlier.

Figure 9.34 Open a file you think will work as a mirror. (Photo by Ellen Anon.)

2. Select your original file, and choose Image > Canvas Size to determine the size of your image.

3. If you are going to create a horizontal montage, double the width of the canvas, but leave the height alone (see Figure 9.35). Anchor the original to the right or left as desired by clicking the anchor arrow ▦. (If you are creating a vertical montage, then double the height, and leave the width alone. Anchor the image at the top or bottom as desired.) Click OK.

Figure 9.35
Double the canvas size in width if you are creating a horizontal mirror, or double it in height if you are creating a vertical mirror.

4. Select the copy of the image, and drag it onto the original using the Move tool.

5. Select the Background copy layer, and choose Edit > Transform > Flip Horizontal (or Vertical).

6. Use the Move tool to align the flipped layer next to the original.

7. When you get close, it's easier to use the arrow keys on your keyboard to nudge the layer into place.

Using this technique creates symmetry that sometimes creates what appears to be odd creatures or faces (see Figure 9.36). These often add to the intrigue of images created this way.

Figure 9.36 The symmetry of mirror montages often creates what appears to be creatures in unexpected places. (Photo by Ellen Anon.)

Multiple Subject Montages

So far, we've been describing a variety of ways to combine two versions of the same image, but it's also possible to combine two different images. One approach to combine two different images to have one image provide the texture and to have the other provide the subject matter. You can stack one on top of the other, rotate, or flip one as desired. And of course, the effect is going to vary dramatically depending on the way you combine the two images. You could simply reduce the opacity of the top image and leave it in Normal blending mode, or you could choose any of the other blending modes.

> **Note:** Shots of wood, tree bark, textured glass, frost, rocks, snow, rain, and lots more can be used as texture.

Figure 9.37 shows a flower image and a shot of the rain on the greenhouse wall. The greenhouse wall file was dragged on top of the flower using the Move tool. Scrolling through the blending modes, the image jumped to life in the Difference mode. However, the flower was a little too unrecognizable, so we added a layer mask to the second layer and used it to reveal the center of the original flower in the layer below.

Figure 9.37
Combining two very different shots in
the Difference mode led to this striking
image. (Photo by Ellen Anon.)

There are no simple rules and absolutes to follow when creating montages. You
are the artist, and you have to decide what works and what doesn't. It's your chance to
apply all the knowledge you've gained in the previous chapters!

For example, you could add texture to a surreal montage created from the steps
in an earlier section:

1. Open two versions of an image that you want to use to create a surreal montage, and follow the steps described earlier. We'll use the surreal montage shown
in Figure 9.38.

Figure 9.38
We'll combine this surreal montage with a texture shot of wood siding. (Photo by Ellen Anon.)

2. Open a shot that you want to use as texture.

3. Drag the texture shot on top of the other layers by using the Move tool.

4. Reduce the opacity of this layer in the Layers panel so that it provides a subtle, but not overpowering, texture. Often, you may be in the range of 10% to 20% opacity, but of course, this varies depending upon the particular images you're using.

> **Note:** Beyond relying on reducing the opacity, experiment with changing the blending mode of the texture layer as well.

The final result (see Figure 9.39) should be subtly different than a straight shot, and it is this unexpected texture that captures your viewer's attention.

Figure 9.39
Combining a texture with a surreal montage can give a subtle soft feel to the image. (Photo by Ellen Anon.)

On occasion, we have combined all of the techniques discussed so far into one image. Figure 9.40 is the result of two totally different images of sand dunes montaged together and then mirrored horizontally. Note that unlike in the previous examples, two different images were combined equally as the foundation for the montage. That entire montage was then duplicated and mirrored vertically, and the image was cropped.

 Note: Montages can also consist of two totally different images combined using blending modes or opacity.

Figure 9.40
Almost all the techniques described so far in this section were combined to create this dramatic image. (Photo by Ellen Anon.)

The ways to combine images in Photoshop is infinite. The only limit is your imagination!

 Try It! Open the images called Texture and Flower on the accompanying CD, or open two of your own images, and practice combining them using various blending modes. Remember to reduce the opacity of the texture layer so it doesn't overpower the image.

Digital Multiple Exposures

Ever since Ellen was exposed to some of Freeman Patterson's creative multiple exposures, she decided there *had* to be a way to create the same effect digitally. Although some methods were available on the Internet, none worked reliably and well. It took some time and experimentation, but at last she figured out how to create multiple exposures of as many images as desired in Photoshop. Since then Nikon has offered the ability to create multiple exposures in some of its cameras, but other camera manufacturers have yet to follow suit.

For those not familiar with Freeman's techniques, he uses film and takes multiple images (9, 16, or 25), slightly moving his camera between shots. Sometimes he moves the camera in a vertical or horizontal direction, depending on what would be a natural movement for the subject. Sometimes he zooms the camera between shots, and at other times he combines zooming the camera with rotating it slightly between shots. The results are artistic, soft-abstract renditions of familiar subjects (see Figure 9.41).

Figure 9.41
Multiple exposures can render familiar subjects in pleasing artistic abstract ways. (Photo by Ellen Anon.)

Note: To learn more about the in-camera and artistic techniques for taking multiple exposures, see *Photo Impressionism* by Freeman Patterson and André Gallant (Key Porter Books Limited, 2002).

To use a digital camera to create multiple exposures, you can still shoot the original files in RAW. Then batch process the images in ACR so that all are adjusted the same way (as described in Chapter 3). Be sure to remove dust when possible. Although normally you could go ahead and open the files, there is a potential problem. The issue is memory. For example, with a 1DsMKII camera, each 16-bit converted file is roughly 95 megabytes. If you have 9 or 10 images to combine, your multiple exposure file is going to be close to one gigabyte in size before you do anything else to it. You're going to need a lot of RAM and hard drive space to deal with files that large. If you don't have enough memory, you can convert the raw files to JPEGs first by choosing Save in the raw converter. Create the composite using the JPEGs and then save the composite as a TIFF. That way you'll maintain image quality and maximize the use of your computer's resources.

Note: Sometimes Photoshop is a little disbelieving that you'd want to open 10 images at once and asks you whether you're sure you really want to open that many. If you don't have a lot of memory on your machine, you may need to resize the files or use them as JPEGs out of necessity.

The key to combining multiple images within Photoshop is as follows:

1. Open all the images.
2. Select the first image, and move it slightly on your monitor.
3. Open the second image.
4. Shift+drag the second image on top of the first (hold the Shift key while clicking the second image, and drag it on top of the first image, still holding the Shift key). Using the Shift key automatically centers the new image on top of the original.

5. Reduce the opacity of the second image to 50% in the Layers panel.

6. If you have a third image to add, drag it on top of the others, but reduce its opacity to 34%.

7. For a fourth layer, reduce the opacity to 25%; a fifth layer is 20%, a sixth layer is 17%, a seventh layer is 15%, an eighth layer is 13%, and a ninth or tenth layer is 10% (see Figure 9.42).

Figure 9.42
Reduce the opacity of each layer according to how many layers you are combining to create abstract expressive images.

Note: The trick is to set the opacity for each layer according to the number of images you are using. If you are using two images, the first is 100%, and the second is 50%—that is, 100 divided by 2. The third layer's opacity is 100 divided by 3, the fourth is 100 divided by 4, and so on.

8. Leave the blending mode for these layers set to Normal except for the final layer, which you may want to set at Overlay or Soft Light to add a little punch to the image.

9. You can adjust the exposure using a Levels or Curves adjustment layer, and you can adjust the color using any of the color adjustment layers.

The ability to create digital multiple exposures opens up entire worlds of creativity. The only downside is the need for a lot of memory, both compact flash card space as well as computer memory. Often it's a good idea when shooting a multiple exposure to do it more than once; subtle differences in the amount you moved the camera can make a huge difference in the success of the image.

When shooting multiple exposures, make sure to shoot a blank shot between groupings so that you'll know where each series begins and ends.

The Evolution of an Image

To give you an idea of the mental process as well as the specific technique that can be followed when attempting to become more expressive with an image, here are the various steps that Ellen took with a rather unimpressive photo (Figure 9.43). Note that she could have decided to stop with any of the versions of this photo.

Figure 9.43 This is the original image, which was not as interesting as Ellen had hoped. (Photo by Ellen Anon.)

1. First she duplicated the optimized image, flattened it, and closed the original.

2. She made a copy of the Background layer by dragging it to the Create a new layer icon. That way, when she applied a filter, she could later modify the strength of the filter effect by changing the opacity of the layer. She could also use a layer mask if she wanted to limit the areas affected by the filter.

3. She chose Adjustment > Black & White and used the layer mask to return color to the three leaves, but she didn't like the result (Figure 9.44).

Figure 9.44 Applying a Black and White adjustment and using the layer mask led to this version of the picture. (Photo by Ellen Anon.)

4. Next, she turned off the visibility icon for the Black & White adjustment and opened a Curves adjustment layer and selected the Negative (RGB) preset. This dramatically changed the picture, as you can see in Figure 9.45.

Figure 9.45 Turning off the Black&White layer and creating a Curves layer using the Negative (RGB) preset made a dramatic change in the image. (Photo by Ellen Anon.)

5. Although she liked the effect she had achieved, the colors felt too unnatural. She opened a Hue Saturation adjustment layer and dramatically changed the hue. This resulted in more natural colors that some may prefer (Figure 9.46).

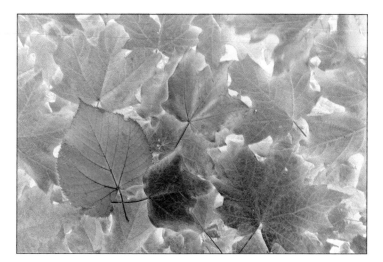

Figure 9.46 By making a drastic change to the hue, Ellen restored somewhat more natural, but still different, colors. (Photo by Ellen Anon.)

Creative Vision and Extreme Color

by Tony Sweet

Being a big fan of "extreme color," I'm always on the lookout for various ways to intensify color in image situations. This scene was shot in the fall in New Hampshire. There was a small patch of birch trees, orange fall color, and a surprising foreground patch of purple flowers. This is a tremendous scene for color interpretation.

A straight shot of the image was OK but didn't render the color I was seeing in my imagination. Smoothly panning this scene for one second was an excellent way to fill the frame with color more than a straight shot. I was able to "paint" over the picture space by panning the camera in an up-and-down fashion, keeping in line with the birch trees as much as possible, creating a colorful abstract of line and color.

Post-processing in Photoshop, I used three adjustment layers:

Curves adjustment layer #1   I placed the point in the middle of the graph and used the arrow key to slightly move the point downward to darken the image a little.

Curves adjustment layer #2   I created and saved a small S curve to slightly increase contrast and loaded the curve for this adjustment layer.

Hue/Saturation layer   Because this is an abstract image, I felt free to boost saturation to achieve the image I see in my imagination. Here, I increased the saturation in the Master window to 25.

© Tony Sweet, www.tonysweet.com

Note: The key to any creative endeavor is to wonder "what if . . ." and then find out.

This chapter has only touched the tip of the iceberg in terms of what you can do with your images. We hope you'll use these ideas as a starting point to create imaginative versions of some of your own photographs.

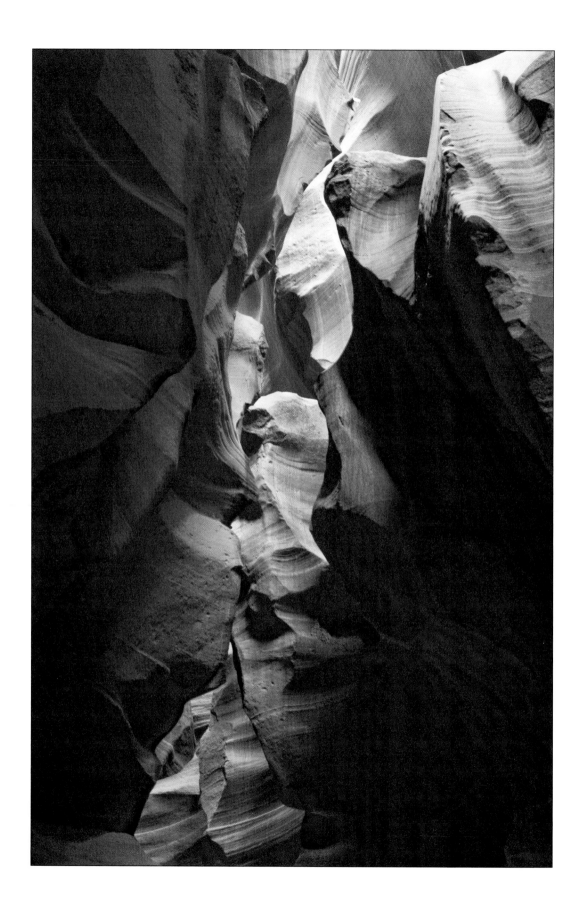

Output

Spending time outdoors in nature capturing beautiful images is often inspirational, and it's a driving force for many of us, but creating lasting output to share with others, and to view time and time again, is also special. In earlier chapters, we focused on optimizing the images, and in this chapter, we'll take a look at how to produce the best output. We'll talk about printing your images, creating slide shows, and creating a web gallery to share your images with an even broader audience.

10

Chapter Contents
Output Workflow
Printing Your Images
Creating Business and Greeting Cards
Creating Slide Shows
Creating a Web Gallery

Output Workflow

The output workflow actually starts very early in the process of optimizing your photographic images in Photoshop. Of course, we could go so far as to say that every optimization step is part of the output workflow, since you're generally trying to make the image look its best in order to produce the best output. However, what we're referring to here is saving the image. Although we tend to talk about saving the image near the end of the workflow, in actual practice you should be saving from early in the workflow. As a general rule, every time you perform any significant optimization step on your image, you should resave so you won't lose any changes should something go wrong.

The idea is to save a master image (in addition to archiving your original capture) that contains all of the image and adjustment layers in a single file, which becomes your master image, to be used as the basis for all future output (see Figure 10.1). After you've saved the final result safely, you're ready to move on to actually preparing that image for output.

Figure 10.1
Your master image file should contain all of the image and adjustment layers used to create the optimal output. (Photo by Ellen Anon.)

Try It! To get a feel for the best output workflow, open the image PrintWorkflow.psd on the accompanying CD, and follow the steps in the next few sections to prepare that image for an 8"×10" print.

Duplicating the Image

By this time, you can well imagine how important your master image is. As you'll see in the next few sections, the process of preparing your image for output can result in changes to the number of pixels in your image as well as to the actual color and tonal values for those images. Therefore, if you are using our *traditional workflow*, we recommend using a working copy of your image while preparing it for output. This ensures that the original master image remains safely saved without risking a permanent loss of pixels.

> **Note:** Although technically using our traditional workflow you could use your master image to prepare for output and then do a Save As, it's risky because it's far too easy to accidentally do a Save on the image and override your master file. That's why in our standard workflow we recommend getting in the habit of working on a duplicate copy.

As a result, the first step in the *traditional output workflow* is to create a duplicate copy of the image by choosing Image > Duplicate. The Duplicate Image dialog box (shown in Figure 10.2) appears, allowing you to enter a name for the new image document. The name in the text box is simply the name of the document you are duplicating with the word *copy* appended to it. You can enter a different name if you want, which becomes the filename if you save this duplicate image later.

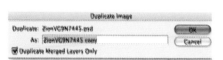

Figure 10.2
The Duplicate Image dialog box allows you to specify a name for the image, as well as to specify whether you want to flatten the image through the Duplicate Merged Layers Only checkbox.

The Duplicate Image dialog box also contains a checkbox labeled Duplicate Merged Layers Only. This checkbox is enabled only if the image you're duplicating contains multiple layers. If you check it, the duplicate image is a flattened version of the original image. We recommend checking this box for two main reasons. First, it flattens the image into a single layer, reducing the amount of memory required by the image. (Remember, the master image with all layers intact has already been saved, and you're working on a duplicate copy.) This can speed up the process of preparing the image for output and sending the data to the printer. Second, sharpening can be applied only to a single layer, so if you have multiple image layers in the image, this streamlines the sharpening process.

When you have established the desired settings, click OK to actually create the working copy of your image file, and then close the original master image.

If you are using our *flexible workflow* and you don't have a separate Clone/Healing brush layer, you don't need to duplicate your master file because you can apply sharpening and other output adjustments as Smart Filters directly on the background Smart Object layer. Since the Smart Object layer references the original file, you won't lose quality as you repeatedly resize the image for each different type of output. However, you will still need to adjust the sharpening settings each time you resize the image because the amount of sharpening necessary will vary according to the file size, resolution, and amount of detail. The advantages to applying the sharpening as a Smart Filter are that you will have one file with all the adjustments, including the sharpening, and that you can readjust the amount of sharpening at any time. However, if you do have a clone layer, then you will need to duplicate the master file and follow the steps for the standard output workflow.

Note: If you are using our *traditional workflow*, we also recommend applying sharpening and noise reduction as Smart Filters so that you can adjust the settings as necessary. Sometimes after you see the final output, you'll realize your settings need tweaking. By using Smart Filters, that's easy to do.

Resizing

Chances are the native size of your image doesn't match the final output size you're targeting so you need to resize it. This involves setting both the resolution and the actual output size. To change the size of the image, choose Image > Image Size, which brings up the Image Size dialog box (shown in Figure 10.3).

Figure 10.3
The Image Size dialog box allows you to resize your image for the final output.

Although you would normally start at the top of a dialog box and work your way down, in the case of the Image Size dialog box, it makes more sense to start at the bottom and work your way up. At the bottom, be sure the Resample Image checkbox is checked, which enables Photoshop to resize the image using interpolation, changing the number of pixels within the image. The drop-down list to the right of the Resample Image checkbox provides options for the algorithm to use for interpolating the data in your image, as shown in Figure 10.4.

Figure 10.4
You can choose from five options for the interpolation algorithm in the Image Size dialog box, but you generally use only Bicubic or Bicubic Smoother.

Bicubic is an all-purpose option. If you're creating a particularly large enlargement from your original, the Bicubic Smoother option is a better choice, and you can use it any time you're enlarging. Bicubic Sharper is designed to maintain sharpness when reducing the size of an image, but we prefer to control the sharpening ourselves and therefore don't usually use this option, although some people use it to save time when preparing images for display on the Web.

Note: The other two options—Nearest Neighbor and Bilinear—are not appropriate for producing high-quality photographic output and should not be used.

The Constrain Proportions checkbox ensures that you maintain the aspect ratio for the image. If you clear this checkbox, it's possible to stretch the image in one direction or the other. Although this might not be a problem when done to a very small degree, it can produce a distorted result if taken too far, and we recommend eliminating the possibility altogether by keeping this checkbox selected.

The Scale Styles checkbox box determines whether layer styles are scaled when you resize the image or whether layer styles are kept at their same size. This isn't an issue at this point since you have already flattened the image. However, you generally want to scale any layer styles, so if you are resizing an unflattened image, keep this checkbox box selected.

The Resolution box in the Document Size section of the Image Size dialog box determines how the pixels are distributed when the image is output, and it plays a role in determining how many pixels are required in the final image. For digital display (monitors and digital projectors, for example), this number is actually irrelevant. However, because some software applications where you may import your images do indeed look at this number, we recommend setting it to about 96 pixels per inch (ppi) for those situations. For printing, the best resolution depends on the output method being used, but 300 ppi is a good standard value.

Note: If you're working with film scans, it's particularly important to keep an eye on the Resolution setting. If you've scanned at 4000 dpi, you don't want to resize to a 20"×30" print without changing the resolution to a more appropriate value, or you'll produce an absolutely huge file that takes forever to resize and likely crashes your computer.

The next step is to set the actual output size. For images that will be printed, this should be done in the Document Size section, setting either the Width or the Height. You can change the unit of measure with the drop-down list to the right, and if you have the Constrain Proportions checkbox box selected (as we recommend), then setting the Width or the Height causes the other to be adjusted automatically.

Note: When you make adjustments that affect the actual pixel dimensions of the image in the Image Size dialog box, the current size is displayed after the Pixel Dimensions label, with an indication of the starting size shown in parentheses.

For images that will be displayed digitally on a monitor or digital projector, the size should be adjusted using the Width or Height text boxes in the Pixel Dimensions section. This allows you to set the specific pixel sizing for your intended purpose. For a digital slide show, for example, you might set these dimensions to fit within the resolution of your digital projector. For a website, you might set them to a standard output size you deem appropriate for your specific site design.

Note: Check the resolution of your projector, and use those values to set the height or width to resize images that you'll use in a slide show. Many projectors have a native resolution of 1024×768, while others may be 1400×1050, and so on. Your images must fit within those specifications.

Once you've established the sizing parameters in the Image Size dialog box, click OK, and Photoshop resizes the image accordingly.

Note: Some people are tempted to wait and resize in the Print dialog box. We don't recommend that because for best results you need to sharpen your image based on its final size. If you wait to resize in the Print dialog box, you have to do the sharpening before resizing. You'd be surprised how different the results can be.

Reducing Noise

Although you could certainly insert steps to reduce noise earlier in your workflow, it often becomes more apparent as you are preparing your image for output. We recommend applying any noise reduction before sharpening to make sure the process of sharpening won't exaggerate the noise, so this is a good time to apply such a correction, if you haven't done so already.

Photoshop CS2 added a noise reduction filter called Reduce Noise (found under the Filter > Noise submenu). If noise exists in your image, it's most likely found in the dark shadow areas, both because it contrasts better there and because that is where the digital camera or film scanner has the most difficulty reading accurate values. Zoom in on the dark shadow areas looking for pixels with random colors that don't match their surroundings, as shown in Figure 10.5. If you find noise that is problematic in the image, try using Reduce Noise to minimize it.

If you have opted to use our *flexible workflow* beginning with a raw file placed as a Smart Object, you can click the Smart Object layer and use the Reduce Noise filter as a Smart Filter directly on that layer. However, if you have used other Smart Filters in conjunction with a layer mask, then you will need to duplicate the background Smart Object layer by dragging it to the New Layer button at the bottom of the Layers panel. This will create a new Smart Object layer. In fact, we recommend duplicating the background layer anyway so that you can add a mask to the noise reduction filter and apply it only where necessary. If you have a separate Clone/Healing brush layer in your workflow, you will need to follow our standard workflow.

If you are using our *traditional workflow*, you'll also need to create a new separate layer for this correction. Begin by creating a copy of your background image layer by dragging it to the New Layer button at the bottom of the Layers panel. This ensures that you are preserving the original image data, as well as gaining the opportunity to mask out any areas of this layer if the noise reduction isn't needed or introduces color problems.

To use the Reduce Noise filter, choose Filter > Convert For Smart Filters, and then choose Filter > Noise > Reduce Noise from the menu. This first changes the layer into a Smart Object so that you can apply the noise reduction as a Smart Filter. The Reduce Noise dialog box opens (see Figure 10.6), which includes a number of parameters that allow you to adjust its behavior.

Figure 10.5 Noise is most often found in the dark shadow areas of an image when high ISO settings or long exposures are used with a digital camera. (Photo by Tim Grey.)

Figure 10.6
The Reduce Noise dialog box allows you to control the behavior of this filter to reduce the effect of noise in your photographic images. (Photo by Tim Grey.)

Make sure to zoom in on the preview image in the Reduce Noise dialog box so you can see detail in the image clearly. We often zoom in to 200 or even 300% magnification. You can adjust the zoom percentage for the preview using the plus and minus buttons below the preview image. You can click the preview image to see the "before" version without the effect of the Reduce Noise filter, releasing the mouse to see the "after" version again.

Note: It's a good idea to set all of the settings in Reduce Noise to 0 before starting so you'll be able to see the effect of each individually as you work to find the best settings.

The most important setting in the Reduce Noise dialog box is the Reduce Color Noise slider. This setting determines how aggressively color noise, exhibited by random color variations (as opposed to luminance noise exhibited by tonal variations), should be reduced in the image (see Figure 10.7). The potential risk is that you'll reduce the overall color in the image by using a setting that is too high, because it causes an averaging of pixel values within the image. To help ensure you're getting the best results with a minimum of unintended effects, we recommend starting with a very low setting and then gradually increasing the value until you have effectively minimized the noise.

CHAPTER 10: OUTPUT ■

Figure 10.7

The Reduce Color Noise slider, as the name implies, allows you to reduce the effect of noise exhibited by color variations in your images. (Photo by Tim Grey.)

The Strength setting controls the amount of noise reduction you'd like to have applied to luminosity noise in the image—that is, noise exhibited by tonal rather than color variations. This is noise that is exhibited by tonal variations at the pixel level; generally, this isn't a significant issue in digital images, and increasing the Strength setting too much effectively blurs the detail out of your image. However, we still recommend adjusting this setting for images that have significant noise to see whether it provides a benefit.

The Preserve Details slider controls the amount of edge detail you want to maintain. Adjusting this too high reduces the effect of luminosity noise reduction controlled by the Strength setting (and in fact, this setting is available only if the Strength is set higher than 0). However, generally you want to use a relatively high setting here, such as 50% to 60%, to ensure you are maximizing the amount of detail in the image (see Figure 10.8).

Figure 10.8
You can use the Preserve Details slider to ensure that maximum detail is maintained in the image despite the changes being applied by Reduce Noise. (Photo by Tim Grey.)

After you've reduced the noise in your image, you may want to enhance detail slightly to compensate for the slight loss caused by the noise reduction process. The Sharpen Details setting allows you to enhance edges within the image (see Figure 10.9). We recommend starting with a low setting and gradually increasing the value until you have achieved the desired level of edge enhancement, without creating any quality problems within the image.

Figure 10.9

Use the Sharpen Details setting to enhance edges in your image after applying noise reduction, starting with a low value and gradually increasing it until you have achieved the desired result. (Photo by Tim Grey.)

Advanced Settings

If you discover that you have significant luminosity noise in an image, we recommend returning the Strength setting to 0 and selecting the Advanced option. When you select the Advanced option, the area with the settings controls is divided into tabs, as shown in Figure 10.10. The settings discussed in the previous section appear on the Overall tab, while new settings become available on the Per Channel tab.

The Per Channel tab allows you to adjust the noise reduction individually for each color channel in your image. When you select one of the color channels from the drop-down list below the smaller preview on the Per Channel tab, that preview is updated to reflect that channel, and you can adjust the Strength and Preserve Details settings individually for the channel, as shown in Figure 10.11.

Figure 10.10
When you select the Advanced option in the Reduce Noise dialog box, the settings will be divided into tabs. (Photo by Tim Grey.)

Figure 10.11
The Per Channel tab allows you to adjust the Strength and Preserve Details adjustments individually for each channel in your image.

The greatest benefit of these advanced settings is the ability to target additional noise reduction to a single channel, such as the blue channel, which is typically where the most noise exists within digital images. If you have an image with strong noise, it's helpful to examine each of the channels and set individual settings for each to minimize the amount of noise each channel contributes to the overall image, while simultaneously minimizing the amount of noise reduction that's applied to each channel. You can use much higher settings in one particular channel and lower settings in the other channels. This will help preserve details while at the same time reducing the luminosity noise. Then when you have selected the best settings for each channel, return to the initial part of the dialog box, and set any additional overall luminosity noise reduction that's needed.

Once you have applied appropriate noise reduction to your image (if necessary), click OK in the Reduce Noise dialog box to apply the settings to your image.

When applying any noise reduction to an image, no matter how carefully done, there is a risk of some loss of image detail. One way to limit the amount of detail lost is to limit the application of the filter to just those areas of the image where noise is an issue. For example, you may not notice the noise in busy parts of your image, but many nature images have large out-of-focus backgrounds where noise may be more obvious. To apply noise reduction selectively, add a layer mask to the Noise Reduction filter layer by clicking the Add Layer mask button at the bottom of the Layers panel. Then paint with black to remove the noise reduction from areas; or conversely, as you learned in earlier chapters, begin by filling the layer mask with black (Edit > Fill > Use: Black), and then paint with white to selectively apply the noise reduction to parts of the image. Of course, you can reduce the opacity of the brush to partially reveal the noise reduction in other areas of the picture.

CHAPTER 10: OUTPUT ■

Note: As with most tasks in Photoshop, there are other ways to go about noise reduction. Some people find it helpful to duplicate the image layer, blur it, and then reduce the opacity of the layer to taste. This option may work well with a particularly high noise image, but you'll also need to add a layer mask to remove the blurred effect from your subject. Another good way of reducing bothersome noise is to duplicate the background layer, blur it, and change the blending mode to Color.

Note: There are a number of third party noise reduction plug-ins available that can help with unusually severe noise problems. One that we have had particularly good results with is Noiseware Pro available at www.imagenomic.com.

Removing JPEG Artifacts

Although we highly recommend capturing in RAW whenever possible, we recognize that some nature photographers are still going to utilize JPEG capture at times. The Reduce Noise filter includes an option that helps reduce the appearance of JPEG artifacts in the image, which are a by-product of how the JPEG file format compresses the image data. To help compensate for visible JPEG artifacts, select the Remove JPEG Artifact checkbox (shown in Figure 10.12).

Try It! Practice removing noise from your photos by opening the image Noise.tif on the accompanying CD and applying the Reduce Noise filter to it.

Figure 10.12

The Remove JPEG Artifact checkbox in Reduce Noise allows you to minimize the effect of JPEG compression in your images. In this image, you can see the artifacts above the thorn in the center of the image. (Photo by Tim Grey.)

Sharpening

Sharpening is an important aspect of preparing your image for output and is of particular importance for nature photographers who are often concerned with maintaining maximum detail in their images. It's not a way to make up for poor in-camera techniques, and you can't make a blurry picture tack sharp. However, you can compensate for the small amount of softening that occurs in the digital process by applying a sharpening filter. The sharpening filters enhance edge contrast, which helps improve the overall perceived detail in your images. In other words, they create an illusion of increased sharpness.

Though it's important to evaluate the effect of your sharpening settings based on a view of the actual pixels in your image, we don't work with the image set to 100% scale while applying sharpening. Doing so allows you to view only a portion of your image (in most cases). Instead, we prefer to set the image to fit the screen (View > Fit On Screen) and use the 100% preview in the dialog box for the sharpening filter being used to make judgments about the settings. This allows you to then click any area of your actual image to set the preview to show that area.

At this point in the *traditional output workflow*, we're working on a flattened version of our master image file that may or may not contain a noise reduction layer. The initial flattening of the original image is important so we can apply sharpening—which affects only one layer at a time—to the entire image in the event that we have additional pixel layers for tasks such as image cleanup or object removal. When preparing nature images for print, particularly for large prints, we recommend creating a copy of the background layer for the sharpening. That way you can add a layer mask and apply the sharpening just to the subject and not to the background. Many nature images have out-of-focus backgrounds that should be blurry. Furthermore, by sharpening the subject and not the background, you can help the subject to stand out from the background.

If you've created a noise reduction layer, duplicate that layer rather than the background layer. If you used a layer mask on the noise reduction layer, click the layer mask on the new layer, and drag it to the trash can. In the event you opt to use a layer mask on your sharpening layer, you'll need a different mask than the one you used for the noise reduction. We'll talk more about targeted sharpening later in this chapter.

If you are using the *flexible workflow* and have done all your cleanup in the raw converter and do not have a clone layer, then you can apply your sharpening as a Smart Filter to the background layer. If you have used other Smart Filters on the background layer using a mask, duplicate the background layer for the sharpening. As with the traditional workflow, if you are preparing an image for a large print, we recommend that you duplicate the background layer, create a new Smart Object layer, and apply the sharpening as a Smart Filter. That way you can add a mask to apply sharpening to selected areas only.

Since sharpening is so important to the final appearance of your image, you may wonder why it comes so late in the process. One reason is that the sharpening settings you use vary based on the output size and should be optimized for the output size and printing process you're using. Another is that sharpening, while beneficial to the image, is a destructive process in the standard workflow in that it alters pixel values, so we want to apply it as part of our output workflow rather than to the master image.

The Unsharp Mask Filter

It used to be that the most common tool for sharpening images was the Unsharp Mask filter. Since Photoshop CS2, Smart Sharpen has become the sharpening tool of choice for most nature photographers. Nonetheless, we begin by talking about Unsharp Mask, because understanding how it works will help you use the Smart Sharpen filter.

The Unsharp Mask filter provides excellent control over the sharpening process, enabling you to improve the overall appearance of the image without introducing quality problems in the process. To use Unsharp Mask, first choose Filter > Convert for Smart Filters to change the layer into a Smart Object, and then choose Filter > Sharpen > Unsharp Mask from the menu. The Unsharp Mask dialog box appears (see Figure 10.13), which contains three settings you can adjust to modify the sharpening effect: Amount, Radius, and Threshold. Because you're using it as a Smart Filter, you can readjust the settings at any time.

Figure 10.13
The Unsharp Mask dialog box allows you to control the sharpening effect on your image with three individual sliders called Amount, Radius, and Threshold. (Photo by Tim Grey.)

Unsharp Mask operates by enhancing contrast along the edges of objects within your image. In other words, it's enhancing contrast where contrast already exists. Adjusting the controls in the Unsharp Mask dialog box allows you to change how this contrast enhancement is applied.

The Amount setting determines how much the contrast is enhanced along edges. Think of this as an intensity control. The higher the setting, the more intense the edge contrast is in your image.

The Radius setting allows you to determine the size of the area to be affected by the boost in contrast along the edges. For images with high detail, you generally want to have the impact affect only a small area for each edge.

The Threshold setting determines how much difference must exist between two pixels for the sharpening to be applied. With a minimum Threshold setting of 0, virtually all pixels are affected by sharpening. As you increase the value, fewer areas are sharpened because they must exhibit a certain amount of contrast before they're considered to be an edge. This helps you maintain smooth textures in areas of the image where that is important.

The most common question photographers ask is what settings they should use. And the response is generally different no matter who they ask! In fact, there are a variety of ways to get good results from the sharpen filters, so we feel that rather than give you a priori values to use, it's better if you develop an understanding of how the different settings work. That way you can choose what works best for your image. Ellen, along with Rick Holt, has developed a demo that is useful for understanding the different settings.

Figure 10.14 demonstrates how the sharpening works. Contrast is added to every edge. If a pixel is white, then the contrast is black; if it's black, the additional contrast is white; if it's yellow, the contrast is blue; if it's red, the contrast is cyan; and so on. The contrast is the opposite of the pixel. You control the intensity of the contrast with the Amount slider, how far out the contrast extends with the radius slider, and whether the contrast is applied by the threshold slider.

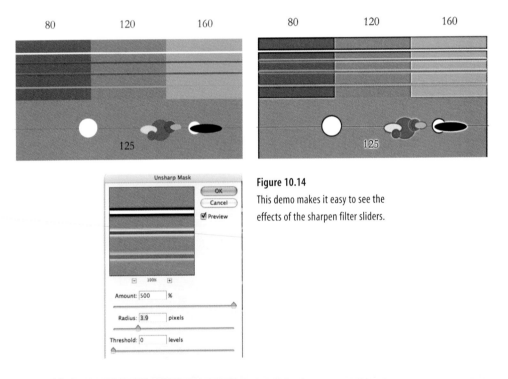

Figure 10.14
This demo makes it easy to see the effects of the sharpen filter sliders.

Try It! Download the file named SharpenDemo, and experiment with a variety of different settings. Adjust the sliders to extremes to see the effects.

Having said that, we will offer the following as some guidelines. Generally, you can combine a very low (0.2–0.8 depending on file size and detail) Radius with a very high Amount (300–500) and get good results. That is often Ellen's preferred method when using Unsharp Mask (see Table 10.1). Alternatively, you can use a smaller Amount (7–150) and a larger Radius (0.8–2.0) and also achieve very good results. For high-detail images, such as most nature images, you should use a Threshold setting of 0. That way you can enhance small differences so that details like feathers appear more distinct. Conversely, if you're sharpening a portrait of your significant other, a Threshold setting of

8–12 is probably appropriate. (You won't win points from anyone if you sharpen every wrinkle and imperfection in their face!)

Table 10.1 Typical Unsharp Mask Settings for High-Detail Nature Images

	Amount	Radius	Threshold
Low-res image	300% to 500%	0.2 to 0.8	0
High-res image	300% to 500%	0.8 to 2.0	0

Note: As digital cameras continue the megapixel race, newer cameras may appear with even higher resolutions that can use higher Unsharp Mask settings.

It's important that you evaluate the effect of Unsharp Mask on a 100% preview of your image. When your image is set to Fit on Screen, it's often at an odd magnification that causes temporary artifacts to appear on the monitor. These artifacts make it difficult to judge the sharpening amounts. When you change the magnification to 100%, those artifacts disappear. You can change the zoom percentage for the image to 100% by choosing View > Actual Pixels from the menu. This enables you to evaluate the sharpening effect looking at the actual effect in the image on which you're working. If you prefer to see the entire image while you're working so you can choose which areas you want to evaluate for the best sharpening effect, set the zoom to fit the image on screen by choosing View > Fit On Screen from the menu. Then click anywhere in your image to set that as the preview area in the Unsharp Mask dialog box. It's important to realize, however, that when you work this way, you must use the preview within Unsharp Mask to evaluate the results, not the actual image.

Once you've established your settings for Unsharp Mask, click OK to apply the effect.

The Smart Sharpen Filter

As we mentioned earlier, Photoshop CS2 introduced a filter called Smart Sharpen that quickly became the sharpen tool of choice for most nature photographers. The Smart Sharpen filter includes the ability to mitigate the sharpening in highlights and shadows in your images individually, which can be very helpful especially when you have artifacts or noise in shadow areas of the image. That way you can decrease the sharpening applied to the noisier parts of the image. In addition, it provides a much larger preview window for viewing the effects at 100%, and it offers the ability to change the type of blur algorithms it uses to create the sharpening. Tim wishes it included a specific Threshold control to maintain smooth textures throughout the image. Despite this limitation, Ellen has found that it does an outstanding job with about 98% of her nature images and uses it as her sharpening method of choice.

To use Smart Sharpen, create duplicate layers as described at the beginning of the Sharpening section, and choose Filter > Sharpen > Smart Sharpen from the menu. The Smart Sharpen dialog box (shown in Figure 10.15) appears, with the large preview area set to the default of 100%.

Figure 10.15
The Smart Sharpen dialog box includes a large preview and settings to help you control how sharpening is applied to your images. (Photo by Tim Grey.)

Note: The key setting in the Smart Sharpen dialog box is the Remove drop-down list, where you choose a blur type. Be patient; we'll explain that in just a second.

As with the Unsharp Mask filter, you can click and hold on the preview image to see what the image looks like without sharpening applied, and you can release to see it with the effect. You can also drag within this preview area to change your view to a different area of the image. Clicking the actual image centers the preview on that position, just like you're able to do with Unsharp Mask. The Preview checkbox controls whether the effect is visible in the actual image, as opposed to being visible only in the preview area within the Smart Sharpen dialog box.

Below the Preview checkbox are options for Basic and Advanced. With Basic selected (which is the default), only the Sharpen settings are available. When you select Advanced, tabs appear for Shadow and Highlight, as you can see in Figure 10.16. Although these settings are worth considering, in many nature photographs it's often more important to distinguish between applying the sharpening to the subject or the background rather than the highlights or shadows. Nonetheless, the Advanced settings enable you to apply sharpening to most of your subject while reducing how much is applied to any shadow or highlight areas. This can be particularly helpful with photographs of dark furry mammals such as bison or bears.

Figure 10.16
When you select the Advanced option in Smart Sharpen, tabs are added enabling you to reduce the sharpening in the shadows and/or highlights.

The Basic settings in Smart Sharpen include the Amount and Radius settings you're familiar with from Unsharp Mask, as described in "The Unsharp Mask Filter" section previously. The settings function in the same way, with Amount controlling the intensity of the halos created along edges in your image and Radius controlling the size of those halos. As a general starting point, the default values of 100% for Amount and 1.0 for Radius are good. Refer to the settings recommended in the previous section for more details on how you might adjust these basic controls.

At the bottom of the Basic sharpening section is a More Accurate checkbox. This is in effect the Threshold command. More Accurate actually results in selecting more "edges," while leaving the box unchecked results in less areas being categorized as edges. Although this option requires additional processing time, it also produces better results for most nature images and enables you to use lower Amount and Radius settings. We recommend keeping this checkbox selected for most images you are sharpening with Smart Sharpen.

The blur removal settings are the key controls in the basic settings for Smart Sharpen and in fact are what differentiates this section the most from the features available in Unsharp Mask. Instead of applying simple edge contrast with a fixed approach (with the specific application varying based on settings used) as with Unsharp Mask, the Smart Sharpen filter takes an intelligent approach based on the settings you establish. The primary control here is the Remove drop-down list, which controls the algorithm used to process the image when it comes to reducing the appearance of specific types of blur in the image (see Figure 10.17). We'll describe these options in more detail in a moment, but the point is that instead of just applying added contrast to the image as Unsharp Mask does, Smart Sharpen can counter specific causes of blur in your images to help you produce the best results possible. We recommend leaving this at Lens Blur for most images.

Figure 10.17
The Remove drop-down list provides various options for reducing the effect of blur in your image to improve the perceived sharpness.

The default setting of Gaussian Blur causes the Smart Sharpen filter to process the image with the same algorithm used by Unsharp Mask. With this setting used, the results achieved with Smart Sharpen are very similar to the results achieved with Unsharp Mask with the same settings.

The next option for blur removal is Lens Blur. This option adds another element to the "smart" aspect of the Smart Sharpen filter. It causes the filter to detect edges and texture detail within the image. The sharpening effect is adjusted in those areas to maintain fine detail and reduce the size of halos. This is the setting we recommend using for most images because it does the most to achieve the typical goals of the photographer applying a sharpening effect to an image.

The final option for blur removal is Motion Blur. This option is designed to compensate for blur caused by motion of either the camera or the subject during the capture. Of course, these are generally the type of images you would discard in favor of better ones, but when you have an important image that exhibits such blur, this option in Smart Sharpen helps you compensate for it.

When you select the Motion Blur option from the Remove drop-down list, the additional Angle control becomes active (see Figure 10.18). This is the same Angle control found in the Motion Blur filter used to create rather than remove such an effect. You can click anywhere in the circle to identify a point you'd like the angle control to intersect with, or you can click and drag to move the line representing the angle to be used around the circle. Type a specific value in the text box, or use the up and down keys on your keyboard to increase or decrease the value by one degree at a time. If you hold the Shift key while using the up and down arrow keys, the value changes by 10 degrees at a time. It can be quite tricky to find just the right angle for a given image, so we recommend starting with a setting that seems to be in line with the direction of motion within the image and then use the up and down arrow keys on your keyboard to fine-tune the value until you achieve the best effect.

Figure 10.18
When you select Remove Motion Blur, an Angle control becomes available for you to adjust the direction of the visible blur in your image.

When you select the Advanced option in the Smart Sharpen dialog box, two additional tabs appear: Shadow and Highlight. These tabs contain additional settings that allow you to reduce the sharpening effect in these particular areas (see Figure 10.19).

Figure 10.19
Among the Advanced options are settings that allow you to control the mitigation of sharpening in the shadow and highlight areas of your images.

Although there are separate tabs for limiting sharpening for both shadow and highlight areas within the image, the controls and behavior of each are identical. Both tabs allow you to adjust how much you want to reduce the sharpening effect in each area, as well as contain controls for determining how broad a range of shadow and highlight values should be affected. We discuss the controls here collectively. You simply need to apply the settings as needed on the Shadow or Highlight tab (or both of them) to apply the desired adjustment in the particular tonal areas of the image where you need it.

When adjusting the settings on the Shadow tab, we recommend zooming in to the darkest areas of the image and, for the Highlight tab, zooming in on the brightest areas. This allows you to better evaluate the settings as you adjust them on each of the tabs.

Here are the settings available on the Shadow and Highlight tabs:

Fade Amount   The Fade Amount setting controls how much the sharpening effect should be reduced within the shadow or highlight areas of the image. A value of 0% means the sharpening effect is not reduced at all, and the maximum value of 100% means the sharpening effect should be completely removed from the affected area of the image. Start with a value of 0%, and gradually increase the value until the sharpening effect is reduced in the target areas to the extent desired.

Tonal Width   The Tonal Width setting allows you to specify how broad a range of tonal values should be affected by the reduction in sharpening effect. Very low values mean sharpening is removed only from the very dark pixels in shadow areas, and a high value causes the effect to be removed from a broader range of tonal values, extending into the midtone values. We usually use a value in a range from about 10 to 50 so the reduction in sharpening affects only the true shadow areas of the image but evaluate all shadow areas to determine the best value for your particular image. Since noise is often worse in shadow areas, you may want to focus your attention there.

Radius   The Radius setting provides control over how far out from each pixel Photoshop should look when deciding whether a particular pixel is contained within a shadow area. Frankly, even large adjustments of this control have a minimal effect on the final results achieved, so we recommend just leaving it at the default value of 1 pixel.

Beware that the settings you establish on the Shadow and Highlight tabs are "sticky," which means that whatever settings you use for one image will remain selected the next time you use Smart Sharpen. So if you use the Advanced features at times, it's a good idea to get in the habit of checking and returning the Fade Amount settings to zero while setting the rest of your sharpening. Otherwise, you may be reducing the amount of sharpening in the highlights or shadows without realizing it.

Targeted Sharpening

Although at times it can be useful and efficient to sharpen the whole image at once, in many nature images it's advantageous to sharpen only portions of your image. Localized sharpening is particularly helpful when there is a specific subject against an out-of-focus background, such as often occurs with bird or flower photography. In such situations, it can be nearly impossible to find a Threshold setting in the Unsharp Mask filter that adequately sharpens the subject and does not affect the background. The Smart Sharpen filter using the Lens Blur setting often does a good enough job, particularly with small images, that you may not feel the need to block the sharpening from background areas. However, when you are creating a large print, you will still want to control which areas are sharpened.

The best method in such cases is to sharpen on a separate layer and use a layer mask to precisely control which areas are affected. The mask allows for various gradations of the sharpening within the image as well as eliminates the sharpening effects from areas, such as sky or water, that sometimes show increased noise when sharpened.

This approach is extremely precise, quick, and easy. If you are using the *traditional output workflow*, you must do the sharpening on a copy of the background layer.

If you are using the *flexible workflow*, you may be on the background layer if there are no other Smart Filters being used or on a copy of the background layer if there are. Then to selectively apply the sharpening, take the following steps:

1. Choose Filter > Sharpen > Smart Sharpen, setting the values as described earlier in this chapter.

2. While holding the Alt/Option key, click the Create Layer Mask icon to add a black layer mask to the sharpening layer. This temporarily hides the effect of the sharpening from the entire image.

3. Select the Brush tool by pressing the B key, and select the default colors of black and white by pressing the D key. Make certain that white is the foreground color, pressing X to swap foreground and background colors if necessary. Use a soft-edged brush at 100% opacity to reveal the sharpening in your primary subject. If there are areas that need some sharpening but not full sharpening, paint those areas with a reduced opacity. By using a soft-edged brush, you don't have to worry about precisely following the edges of your subject. This should be a quick mask to create, not a painstaking one.

 Note: You can also use this layered method with the Unsharp Mask filter in place of the Smart Sharpen filter. In addition, you can use layer masks with Smart Filters.

Prepping a File for Output

by Lewis Kemper

Let's start with some assumptions:

- There are many ways to do anything correctly in Photoshop, and there is no one right way. I'll discuss my methods, and I have never had anyone reject a print for quality reasons—and I have made prints that measure several feet in width by up to seven feet in length.

- You have completed your "master file," where you have already done all your exposure and color correction, plus whatever other Photoshop wizardry you have applied. Create the master file from the largest original digital file you can get without interpolating data. I save all my master files as PSD files, with the layers intact and unsharpened.

- Your monitor is hardware calibrated, and you've applied the correct paper/printer profile in the printer dialog box to assure consistent and reliable results.

Now let's get on to the process of prepping a file for output:

1. The first step I take is to flatten my file. I do this because I am going to sharpen the image based on file size, and if the image has multiple layers, it is easier to sharpen if it is flattened.

2. Once the file is flattened, I size the image for the output use. If I am sending a file to my Epson ink-jet printer, I size it to output size at 180 pixels per inch (ppi). I have done numerous tests and have found that 180 ppi works fine for all my needs, and because it is a relatively low resolution, I can get larger prints from smaller files. (When saving for output on other devices, I consult with the operator of these devices to determine the optimum resolution.)

Ghost Trees in Fog, Yellowstone National Park, WY   *Lewis Kemper*

3. So if I have an approximately 50MB (8-bit) file from my Canon 1Ds MII camera and I want to make a print that will fit on 16×20 paper, I resize the image to approximately 19"×12.5" at 180 ppi, using Bicubic Sharper interpolation. (If I were enlarging a file, I would use the Bicubic Smoother algorithm.)

4. Once the file is sized, then I apply sharpening. The reason I wait until the image is sized is because the amount of sharpening an image needs is based on the image's size: a smaller image needs less sharpening than a large one. I use a 3-step action that I wrote that does three levels of sharpening on the image: one level to sharpen the edges only, one level to sharpen texture, and one level to sharpen contrast.

If you are using the sharpening filters found in Photoshop directly, I recommend Smart Sharpen or the old standby Unsharp Mask.

5. Since sharpening can accentuate any small dust I may have missed in my original spotting of my master file, I reexamine the image for dust. To do this, I enlarge the image to 100% or the Actual Pixels view. Then, using the Ctrl/⌘ key in conjunction with the Page Up and Page Down keys, I go through the entire image, from the upper-left corner to the lower-right corner. If I find any new dust, I remove it using either the Healing Brush or the Clone Stamp tool, depending on the situation.

6. My image is ready to be sent to the printer. When the printer dialog box comes up, I make sure the printer driver is set to No Color Adjustment and that the proper Paper Type, Print Quality, and Ink Type options are set. Then, using the color management options in the dialog box, I apply the proper ICC profile for the paper and printer combination I am using for my output.

If you follow these steps and have a calibrated monitor and accurate profiles for your printing devices, you no longer have to waste time and money doing test prints. What you see on your monitor should match (as close as possible) what comes out of your printer.

© Lewis Kemper, www.lewiskemper.com

Printing Your Images

Once you've prepared the image through the output workflow, you're ready to produce a print, which is typically the ultimate goal for nature photographers. When sending the image to the printer, it's important that you use the appropriate settings to ensure accurate color and optimal quality.

Note: Remember that getting an accurate print depends on a calibrated monitor display. If your monitor isn't calibrated, you can't trust the colors displayed to be accurate, and therefore you can't be assured of a matching print.

Soft Proofing

An optional additional step that can be helpful before actually sending your image to the printer is *soft-proofing*, which enables an on-screen preview of what the print will look like. A printed image often looks slightly different from what you see on the monitor, even when using the correct printer/paper profiles in a color managed workflow because of the particular qualities of the paper and ink. There may be some loss of contrast, brightness, and/or color saturation. Soft-proofing offers you a chance to preview those differences and make some adjustments so that the print looks the way you expect.

To soft-proof an image, first create a duplicate copy of the image by choosing Image > Duplicate. That way you can compare the file the way you've been viewing it to the way it will appear when printed. You can configure and enable a soft-proofing display by choosing View > Proof Setup > Custom from the menu and configuring your output print settings. When you click OK, the image simulates the final printed output, and you can tweak the soft-proof by making a few small adjustments to make it more similar to the original. You then make the print from the soft-proof version.

Configuring the Print Settings

To get started, choose File > Print from the File menu. The Print dialog box shown in Figure 10.20 appears.

Note: You must choose File > Print rather than File > Print One Copy in order to access the necessary options even if you intend to print only one copy.

Note: The same process applies for black-and-white images as for color images. However, some printers are better than others when it comes to producing accurate grayscale output, as discussed in Peter K. Burian's "Ideal Printers for Black-and-White Outputs" sidebar later in this chapter.

Figure 10.20
The Print dialog box, accessed by choosing the Print option from the File menu, allows you to control the basic color management settings for output. (Photo by Ellen Anon.)

If you are using a Mac, you must begin by clicking the Page Setup button. As shown in Figure 10.21, this elicits an additional dialog box where you choose your printer, paper size, and format. Windows users access similar options later in the Printer Properties dialog box.

Figure 10.21
On a Mac you must use the Page Setup dialog box to specify your printer, paper size, and orientation.

Note: The printing dialog boxes are one of the few places where there are significant differences between the Mac and Windows versions.

Make sure the Color Management option is selected from the drop-down list at the top right of the dialog box. In the Print section, set the option to Document so the working space or embedded profile is used to determine the color values from your image being sent to the printer.

Beneath that are the key settings related to color management. For the Color Handling drop-down list, select Photoshop Manages Colors. The Printer Profile drop-down list is where you need to select the profile appropriate for the printer, ink, and paper you're using to produce the print. Many printers now include "canned" custom profiles, which are designed for the printer, ink, and paper combination their name implies, but were not created specifically for the printer sitting on your desk.

For Rendering Intent, which deals with how colors that your printer can't produce are changed to colors it is able to print, we recommend that for most images you select Relative Colorimetric, which ensures that colors your printer can produce are rendered accurately, while any color it can't produce is shifted to the closest in-gamut color. However, some images, often those with very saturated reds, may look better if you use the Perceptual rendering intent. Perceptual compresses the entire color gamut of your image into the printer's gamut, rather than adjusting only the colors that are actually out of gamut, but in some cases, as was the case with the example used in Figure 10.20, this can result in a more natural-looking result.

Photoshop CS3 has added an excellent soft-proofing feature into the Print dialog box. That helps you determine which rendering intent is best for your image. To use it, check Colormatch Preview in the bottom middle of the dialog box. That way you can experiment with the different rendering intents from the drop-down box and see the differences it makes to your output

Beneath the Rendering Intent drop-down list, select the Black Point Compensation checkbox so that black in your image is mapped to black in the output.

When you have set the appropriate settings in the Print dialog box, click the Print button to bring up another Print dialog box (shown in Figure 10.22). The dialog boxes differ between the Mac and Windows platforms. In Windows, select the printer you're sending the image to in this dialog box, and then click Properties. The Properties dialog box for the particular printer you are using appears (see the example in Figure 10.23). The settings you use in the printer Properties dialog box depend on your particular printer model, but in general, you need to set the appropriate paper type and size, quality settings, and color management settings. *Find the least invasive color management choice—such as a "no color adjustment" or similar option—to ensure that the printer doesn't try to alter the color values in the printing process.* As unintuitive as this may be, it enables Photoshop to handle the color management for the print, which is what you want. Otherwise, your print will have some unusual colors and tonalities.

Figure 10.22 The Print dialog box allows you to select the specific printer you want to use for printed output.

Figure 10.23

On Windows, clicking the Properties button in the Print dialog box opens the Properties dialog box for the printer you selected.

On a Mac you will need to specify your printer from the next Print dialog box (see Figure 10.24) and then select Print Settings from the Copies & Pages drop-down menu. You will need to reselect your printer and specify your media type. We recommend you choose Advanced Settings under Mode and select SuperFine1440dpi for Print Quality. The precise options that are available vary by printer and paper type. We recommend choosing Finest Detail when possible.

Figure 10.24

Although the specific settings may vary by printer and paper, set the media type and quality settings in the Print Settings dialog box.

Note: Although many printers offer an option to print at 2880dpi, we don't recommend this because visually we haven't seen any difference in the quality of the prints and because it uses more ink. In addition for some printers, it takes longer.

Next, select Printer Color Management from the drop-down menu, and choose Off (No Color Adjustment) (see Figure 10.25). As mentioned previously for Windows, you must choose No Color Management in order to have Photoshop manage your colors so that your output appears as you expect it to appear. Otherwise, you will get unpredictable results and waste time, paper, and ink…to say nothing of feeling very frustrated!

Figure 10.25

Choosing No Color Management is essential for having your print match your monitor

With all settings established for the print, click OK in the printer Properties dialog box and then OK in the Print dialog box to send the job to the printer.

Peter K. Burian is a stock photographer, the author of *Mastering Digital Photography and Imaging* (Sybex, 2004), and the coauthor of *Photoshop Elements 5 Workflow* (Sybex, 2006). As a regular contributor to several photo magazines, including *Shutterbug*, *Here's How*, *Photo Life*, and *Australian Photography*, he frequently tests digital cameras, lenses, scanners, and printers. We asked him to give us his picks for black-and-white printers.

Ideal Printers for Black-and-White Outputs

by Peter K. Burian

Photographers who love black-and-white prints are often disappointed with their ink-jet outputs. Although it should be possible to make a truly neutral monochrome print with color inks, few machines are designed to do a competent job without a frustrating process that involves constant fine-tuning in the printer driver and making test prints until one is very close to neutral.

At one time, there was another issue, especially with printers using pigmented inks, such as the now-discontinued Epson Stylus Photo 2200. This problem was *metamerism*: the tendency for inks to change color under different types of illumination. A print may look quite different under incandescent light, fluorescent light, and sunlight, for example.

Epson, Canon, and Hewlett-Packard have solved the technical problems, and all three now market certain ink-jet printers that are optimized for making monochrome outputs. As a bonus, all those machines also accept fine-art media, including thick papers such as "canvas." The most popular of these, the 13×19"-format Epson Stylus Pro R2400 employs the eight-color UltraChrome K3 pigmented inkset, including three blacks. (The K3 inks are also used in the current wide-format Epsson models, including the Stylus Pro 3800, 4800, and 7800.)

My tests of the R2400 confirmed significantly reduced metamerism. The color prints show a very wide range of color and great vibrancy, while the monochrome outputs matched the best silver halide prints that I had seen in the past; the improvement was partly due to a remarkable increase in maximum density. The Display Permanence Rating provided by Wilhelm Imaging Research (WIR) ranges from 61 years to 118 years, depending on the Epson media used, and even longer when the prints are displayed under glass with a UV filter.

This Epson machine also features a remarkably versatile driver option—Advanced Black & White printing mode. When selected, only the three black inks are used for prints without any apparent color cast. The new driver provides many of the features that previously required the purchase of a separate raster image processor (RIP), an advanced printer driver that provides maximum control over the entire printing process. With simple adjustments, you can replicate warm or cool tone prints such as sepia or platinum, expanding the range of options available to the monochrome fine-art print maker.

HP was actually the first of the companies to employ a pigmented inkset that virtually eliminated metamerism and also satisfied dedicated black-and-white print makers. Its latest 13×19"-format machine, the Photosmart Pro B9180, employs seven colors of Vivera pigments, including a gray plus photo black or matte black. (HP's newest wide-format Designjet Z2100 series employs the same inks and gains a built-in spectrophotometer for creating custom color profiles for virtually any media.) Although designed to make vividly saturated color outputs, the Photosmart Pro B9180 also generates excellent monochrome prints. The WIR Display Permanence Rating is impressive too: more than two centuries when using certain premium-grade HP or Hahnemühle papers.

Continues

Ideal Printers for Black-and-White Outputs *(Continued)*

This HP machine provides advanced color management options, including a Black & White Printing mode that's optimized for making prints without a color cast. However, black-and-white toning options are not available. The printer driver includes an option for printing with black and gray ink only as well as a "composite gray" mode that employs additional inks. In my view, the Pro B9180 is an ideal choice for monochrome printing because it produces a snappy effect with rich darker tones and pure whites, good shadow detail, a pleasing tonal gradation, and a high apparent sharpness for a very striking effect.

At the time of this writing, Canon had announced the 13×19"-format PiXMA Pro9500 that employs ten new Lucia pigments, including "a three-ink mono system for enhanced black-and-white output, low metamerism, and reduced graininess." This model was not yet available but will include a new printer driver with advanced color controls, RAW file printing, and a Photoshop plug-in with "professional features." According to WIR, the estimated Display Permanence Rating is "in excess of 100 years for color images and significantly beyond that for monochrome" when using certain media.

Several wide-format Canon imagePROGRAF models are available, including the iPF5000, employing a full 12 Lucia pigments, including two gray and two black, for making stunning color outputs or truly neutral monochrome prints. This 17"-format desktop model includes a driver with features such as Neutral, Cool, and Warm black-and-white effects and, like all imagePROGRAF models, a 16-bit driver for prints with a wider dynamic range.

Regardless of your size requirements and personal preferences, it's no longer difficult to find a suitable ink-jet printer that can generate pro-caliber black-and-white and color prints that will last for generations. Before making a final decision as to the one that would best suit all your needs, read some reviews on all models on the Internet, and visit a retailer to evaluate the quality of prints made by each machine in your price range.

© 2007 Peter K. Burian, www.peterkburian.com

Choosing the Best Paper

The choice of paper when producing a print is a very subjective decision. When we're asked by nature photographers what paper should be used, our typical response is that you really need to try various papers for yourself to find what you like best. However, as subjective as this decision is, here are some general guidelines to help you decide.

A big part of the decision has to do with the type of effect you want to produce in the print. The first consideration is the surface type. For images where you want to have maximum detail, contrast, and vibrancy of colors, a semi-gloss paper is a popular choice. For example, a crisp high-detail image of highly saturated flowers or a strong landscape image with a silhouetted foreground subject generally works well on a semi-gloss paper such as Epson's Premium Luster and similar papers from other manufacturers. Full-gloss papers are less popular because they tend to produce strong reflections, so it's difficult to actually see all the detail in the image.

Many professional nature photographers use matte papers for their prints. Velvet papers, available from a variety of companies, often provide a rich look to the prints with full detail readily visible. However, if you're accustomed to the type prints you get from a photo lab, it may take you a while to adjust to the look and feel of a print on matte paper.

For images that are more artsy, such as more delicate flowers with subtle colors or a photo captured under very diffuse lighting on an overcast day, or abstracts, you may want to maintain the subtle mood by choosing an art-style paper such as a water-color paper. These are usually matte papers formulated for ink-jet printers with various textures. Art papers often tone down the colors, contrast, and details in your image to produce a print that looks more like a painting.

Decisions about what texture paper to use depend on personal style and on the content in the image. When in doubt, most people opt for a smooth paper surface. However, many other textures are available that add to the aesthetics of an image. Images with deep, rich colors, such as the greens of a rain forest, can produce beautiful results with a canvas surface that lends a painterly look to the image. Images that have smooth or subtle textures can be enhanced by a textured paper that adds a certain random aspect to the surface.

We strongly recommend that you test a wide variety of papers to find the ones you feel work best for your images. Many third-party paper manufacturers offer "sampler" packs that provide an economical way for you to test many papers as you discover your new favorites. Above all, experiment with many different papers so that you can find options that enhance the qualities of your images and that help define an individual style for you.

Note: The website www.Inkjetart.com/samples.html offers a variety of inexpensive sampler packs so you can experiment to see which papers you prefer. The site www.redriverpaper.com/samples/index.htm also offers sample packs including greeting card kits.

Adding Borders

Although your images are no doubt beautiful all by themselves, as you gain more knowledge of optimizing those images with Photoshop, you may want to find ways to add expressive touches to your images. One way to add a creative effect without altering the basic content of the image is to add an artistic border around your image.

There are a variety of methods you can use to add such a border to your image. One of these is a plug-in from Extensis (www.extensis.com) called PhotoFrame. This software includes thousands of photo edges you can apply to your images, making the process very easy.

However, you can produce similar effects within Photoshop with no special software. Rather than removing pixels from your image to create the edge effect, we recommend adding a new layer above the image layer to serve as the artistic border around the image. So, start by creating a new layer above your image layer by clicking the New Layer button at the bottom of the Layers panel. Then select Edit > Fill from the menu, choose white from the Use drop-down list, and click OK to fill this layer with white (see Figure 10.26). Of course, you don't really want to cover up the entire image with white, but this provides the foundation for this technique.

Figure 10.26

The first step in creating an artistic border around the edge of your image is to create a new pixel layer and fill it with white.

To help you better identify the area you want to apply the border effect to, turn off the visibility of the new layer you filled with white by clicking the eye icon to the left of its thumbnail on the Layers panel. Next, choose the Rectangular Marquee selection tool, and drag from *near* the top-left corner of the image to *near* the bottom-right corner (as shown in Figure 10.27). This becomes the area along which the edge effect is added, with anything outside the selection hidden and anything inside the selection retained, so be sure to position this selection accordingly. When you're finished, turn the visibility of the white layer you created back on by clicking in the box where the eye icon was.

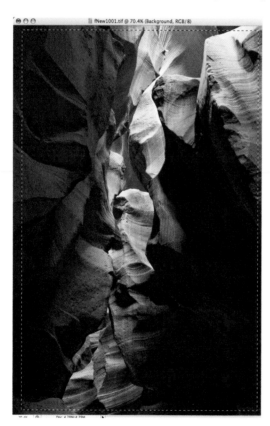

Figure 10.27

Create a selection with the Rectangular Marquee tool to define the area where the border will be created. (Photo by Ellen Anon.)

The next step is to switch into Quick Mask mode, which allows you to modify the selection with a bit more flexibility. To switch to Quick Mask mode, press Q on your keyboard, or click the button on the right side directly below the Color Picker on the Tools panel. The selection is now displayed using a mask display, with a color (red by default) showing the area that was not selected and no color (which therefore allows the white layer to appear) in the selected area (see Figure 10.28).

Figure 10.28
Switching to Quick Mask mode causes the selection to be displayed as a color overlay, with the overlay representing areas of the image that are not selected.

To apply a creative shape to this edge, apply a filter to the Quick Mask display. Choose Filter > Filter Gallery from the menu (see Figure 10.29). Start by selecting an initial filter to work with from the sections in the center of the dialog box. We prefer the filters in the Brush Strokes and Distort sections for this purpose, but anything is fair game if you like the final result. Ellen's favorite is Spatter, which is in Brush Strokes. As you're adjusting the settings for this filter along the right side, keep in mind when you're looking at the preview that white areas are where the image will be visible and black areas are where the image will be blocked in the final result.

Figure 10.29 Use the Filter Gallery to apply filters that distort the edge of the selection on your image.

After you've established settings for the filter you've selected, you can actually add other filters to create a more complex pattern. To do so, click the New Effect Layer button at the bottom right of the dialog box. This initially duplicates the first filter you added, but you can then select a different filter to change it, adjusting the settings as desired.

Once you have a basic shape for the border you want to apply to your image, click OK in the Filter Gallery dialog box. The shape of the Quick Mask display is altered based on your filter selections. Switch back to normal mode for the selection by again pressing Q or by clicking the button on the left below the Color Picker on the Tools panel. The selection reflects the edge shape you created by applying filters in Quick Mask mode.

Note: The selection shape may not perfectly reflect the result of filtering in Quick Mask, because the "marching ants" border of the selection follows the line along the division only between pixels that are at least 50% selected and those that are less than 50% selected.

Because you want to retain only the outer portion of the white layer that was added to this document, the selection needs to be inverted to include only the outer border area. Choose Select > Inverse from the menu to invert the selection. You can then use this selection as the basis of a layer mask to block out the white layer where it isn't selected. To do so, simply click the Add Layer Mask button at the bottom of the Layers panel. The result is a white border around your image that blocks the outer edge, but with an artistic shape to that edge that can help enhance the textures and mood of the image (see Figure 10.30).

Figure 10.30
When you add a layer mask with an active selection you have modified with the application of one or more filters, the image is masked based on that selection to hide areas outside the selection, resulting in an artistic edge effect. (Photo by Ellen Anon.)

Creating Business and Greeting Cards

A great way to share your work with others is to create cards that feature your favorite images. You can create business cards to hand out or greeting cards for personal use or to sell.

Creating a business card is in many ways similar to creating a greeting card. In some ways, it's easier since you don't have the issue of folding the final print and the related layout issues to contend with. We'll begin with designing business cards, and we'll divide this into two basic tasks—creating an individual business card and creating the print layout—to make it more manageable.

Creating a Business Card

To create the card layout, start by making a new document for this purpose. Select File > New from the menu, and create a document that is 3.5" wide and 2" tall (the standard dimensions for business cards) at 300 dpi (see Figure 10.31). Be sure the Color Mode is set to RGB, and leave the bit depth at 8-bit. Use White for Background Contents. Click OK to create your new document.

Figure 10.31
Create a new document with the dimensions of your individual business card to get started.

Note: If you prefer to make a vertical business card, simply switch the Width and Height settings when creating your new document for the business card layout.

The next step is to add an image to the layout. To do this, follow these steps:

1. Open the image you want to include, and create a duplicate copy, flattening it in the process.

2. Resize it to fit the dimensions of your business card.

3. Use the Move tool to drag the image into the business card layout, as shown in Figure 10.32.

You have these options:

- If you want to rotate the image, select Edit > Transform > Rotate from the menu, move the mouse outside the bounding box, and drag to rotate. When you're happy with the rotation, press Enter/Return, or double-click inside the bounding box.

- You can also resize the image by selecting Edit > Transform > Scale, holding the Shift key as you drag a corner to resize, and pressing Enter/Return or double-clicking inside the bounding box to apply. Use the Move tool to fine-tune the position of the image as needed.

- To include multiple images, simply repeat the process, making sure the correct image layer is selected in the Layers panel when you rotate, resize, or move the image.

Adding Text

Of course, although it may be tempting to consider the photograph the key component of the perfect business card, you'll need text for it to actually serve the intended purpose! Creating text layers in Photoshop is quite easy, and you can exercise tremendous flexibility in the appearance of the text. To add a text layer, select the Text tool from the Tools panel, and click the image close to where you want the text to appear. You can reposition the text later, so don't worry if it's not in the precise position you want. A flashing cursor appears, allowing you to start typing immediately. Make sure the text is set to an appropriate size before you start typing so you'll be able to see and manage the text. On the Options bar (shown in Figure 10.33), there is a drop-down list for text size with two Ts of different sizes to the left of it. We recommend starting with a point size of 12 initially.

Figure 10.33 The Options bar for the text tool contains a number of settings related to the overall appearance of your text.

As you type your initial text, don't worry about the font attributes, because you'll change those in a moment. Just type the text you want to appear. When you're finished, *don't* press the text keyboard's Enter/Return key as you may be inclined to do if you want to create multiple lines of text. In terms of adjusting the final layout of your text, it's much easier if each text element, or line of text, is created as a separate text layer. When you're finished typing that block of text, simply switch to the Move tool, and get yourself ready to fine-tune the position of the text.

Note: When you create a text layer, the name of the layer automatically changes whenever you change the text itself, with the name reflecting that text.

With the Move tool active, drag the text to the desired position, using the arrow keys on your keyboard to get the text into the perfect position. You're then ready to adjust the attributes of the text. To do so, double-click the thumbnail icon for the text layer on the Layers panel. This selects the text associated with that layer so that any changes you make to the attributes affect all of the text.

On the Options bar the first setting to consider is the font type. The Font drop-down list provides a WYSIWYG (What-You-See-Is-What-You-Get) sample preview, showing you what the font actually looks like to the right of the font name. To the right of the Font drop-down list is another drop-down list that allows you to select the style for the text. Your options are Regular, Italic, Bold, or Bold Italic. Keep in mind that some fonts do not support all of these style options directly.

To the right of the font and font style drop-down lists is where you choose the font size. This uses the same point size system you may be familiar with from using word processing software, with 12 points being the standard for most documents, but 10 or even 8 points often necessary for the reduced real estate of a business card.

To the right of the font size drop-down list is the anti-aliasing drop-down list. This controls how the lines within the text are refined to avoid a stair-step pattern along curved lines. Choose among the various settings to get a preview of the effect, but we generally find that the Sharp option provides excellent results.

The next set of buttons allows you to control the text alignment, with the standard choices of left, center, and right represented by icons on the buttons. Since you're not going to be creating paragraphs of text, the default setting of left alignment is probably adequate, but at times you may find it helpful to use a different option to help you align text properly.

The colored box to the right of the text alignment buttons defines the color of the text. It reflects the current color of the active text layer; click this colored box to open the Color Picker and select a new color. Note that the selected text appears inverted, so you don't see the final result until you apply the change to your text (for example, by selecting the Move tool as discussed earlier).

The Warp Text button brings up the Warp Text dialog box (shown in Figure 10.34), where you can adjust the shape of the path upon which the text is written. Normally, the text simply flows across a straight line. However, you can have it move across a curved line or have the text itself warped into a particular shape. The Warp Text dialog box includes a Style drop-down list, where you can specify the particular shape you'd like to use, along with settings to adjust the particular style you've chosen.

Figure 10.34
The Warp Text dialog box allows you to distort the text so it flows along a path that isn't straight.

Note: For advanced users, the last button on the Options bar for the Text tool opens the Character panel, which provides more options for fine-tuning the text appearance.

Applying Layer Styles

Once you've created the basic layout for your card, experiment with adding some layer styles to your text or image layers. These allow you to add dimension to the elements that compose your business card design. To add a layer style, first select the desired layer on the Layers panel. Then click the Layer Style button fx, at the bottom of the Layers panel. A list of available layer styles pops up (see Figure 10.35). Let's start with a simple drop shadow to add some depth to the current layer. When you select an option from the list, the Layer Style dialog box (shown in Figure 10.36) appears. Along the left side are the available styles, and in the center are the options for the currently selected style. You can add more than one style to the current layer by selecting it from the left. Be sure to click the text rather than the checkbox so the option is activated and the options for that style are shown at the same time.

Figure 10.35
When you click the Layer Style button, a pop-up list provides the available options for the effects you can apply to elements within your text or image layers.

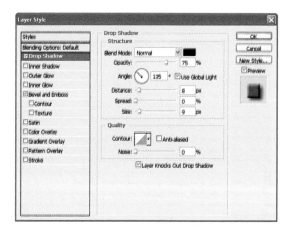

Figure 10.36
The Layer Style dialog box allows you to select the various effects to add to the current layer and adjust the settings for those effects.

Adjust the settings in the center section of the dialog box as desired. Remember that a subtle effect is generally best because it provides the impression of depth without overwhelming the viewer. The best settings are usually those you feel are a little too subtle. To get you started, add a Drop Shadow layer style and a Bevel and Emboss layer style to your text layers. When you've added the desired settings, click OK to apply them to the current layer.

Chances are you want to apply a consistent style to all the text elements in your business card layout. When you add a layer style to a layer, an icon that matches the button you clicked initially at the bottom of the Layers panel is added on the right side of that layer in the Layers panel. To copy the layer styles to other layers, hold down the Alt/Option key, and click and drag the Layer Style icon to the desired layers. You can copy the layer styles to as many layers as you need.

To adjust the Layer Style settings later, simply double-click the icon on the right side of the layer on the Layers panel. The Layer Style dialog box appears, where you can select the style on the left and adjust the settings in the center, clicking OK when you're finished making adjustments. You will have to drag the updated layer style icon to other layers using the same styles—they won't automatically update otherwise.

Note: If you create a combination of layer style settings that you particularly like, you can save them so you can easily use them on other projects. For example, you might create a combination of styles that you like for your business cards. To save them, click New Style while in the Layer Style dialog box. A new dialog will appear in which you can name the style and specify whether to Include the Layer Effects and/or Blending Options. You could call it "Business Card Styles." Then this new style will appear as the last icon in the Layer Styles panel. When you want to create a new business card, click Styles, at the top left of the Layer Style dialog and choose the Business Card style icon. That style will immediately be applied to the text. You can create customized styles for nearly any purpose. To remove a layer style, drag it to the trash can, or Alt/Option+click it, and use the little scissors that appear to click and remove the style.

Saving the Layout

Once you've added image and text layers to the layout, fine-tuned their settings and positions, and applied layer styles as desired, you should have a business card that you're proud to distribute. Be sure to save this document as a TIFF or PSD file with all layers intact so you can make revisions as desired at a later date. This master file will be the basis of the print layout we'll create in the next section.

Try It! Open the image BizCard on the accompanying CD, and create a business card layout..

Creating the Print Layout

With the business card layout created, the next step is to create a print layout that includes multiple business cards so you can print sheets of them at a time. Although prescored business card papers are available, most of these that we've seen don't provide a material that is adequate for photo-quality printing. In addition, when you separate them along the scored edges, the result does not look very professional. Therefore, we recommend using a paper designed specifically for producing photo-quality output on your photo ink-jet printer for this purpose. In general, you'll get the best results from coated matte papers.

For this example, we'll assume you're printing to an 8.5"×11" sheet of paper that produces good results on your photo ink-jet printer, but you could certainly use a larger paper size if you prefer. The first step is to create a new document with the dimensions of the paper. Select File > New from the menu, and in the New dialog box, enter dimensions of 8.5" for Width, 11" for Height, 300 dpi for Resolution, and make sure the document is set to RGB with a bit depth of 8-bit. Click OK to create the new document.

Add new vertical guides at 0.5" and 4.5" to mark the left edge of each business card by selecting View > New Guide from the menu (shown in Figure 10.37). Guides are nonprinting lines that you can place at any horizontal or vertical position within a document to provide layout guidance. Then add new horizontal guides at 0.5", 3", 5.5", and 8", marking the top of each business card (see Figure 10.38). This provides a framework for you to place each business card into this document.

Figure 10.37
The New Guide dialog box allows you to place a guide at a specific position within your page layout document.

Figure 10.38
Add guides to the page layout for your business cards to provide a reference for where each individual card should be placed.

If you don't still have the business card layout document open, open it now. Then create a working copy by selecting Image > Duplicate from the menu. Select the Duplicate Merged Layers Only checkbox to flatten the image in the process, and click OK. Then use the Move tool to drag this flattened duplicate into the new document you created for your print layout.

Drag this business card layer to the top-left position defined by the guides you added to the document (as shown in Figure 10.39). By default, the layer snaps into the corner identified by the guides you added as you get close; if it doesn't, choose View > Snap to turn on this feature.

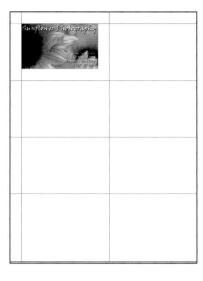

Figure 10.39
Move the first business card into the print layout in the first position at the top left of the document.

At this point, it's a good idea to add a Stroke layer style to this image layer, which makes it easier to cut out the individual business cards after printing. To do so, click the Add Layer Style button at the bottom of the Layers panel, and select Stroke from the pop-up menu. Set the size to about 2 pixels, with Position set to Outside (see Figure 10.40). Click the Color box to bring up the Color Picker and set a color for this stroke. (We recommend using black and cutting this area out of the final business cards, but you could also set a color you like and keep it as a frame for the cards.)

Figure 10.40
Add a stroke to the individual business card layer so you have a reference for cutting each card out later.

Once you have positioned the first business card layer, select the Move tool, then hold down the Alt/Option key, and drag a copy of your card to the next position on the page. Repeat this process to place a business card layer at every position you defined with the guides you added to the document, as shown in Figure 10.41.

When you have finished creating a complete page layout, save it as a TIFF or PSD file so you can always refine the layout later if desired. You're then ready to print this document as you would any other and then cut out the individual business cards.

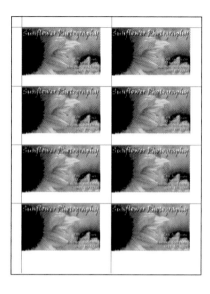

Figure 10.41
When you have placed a business card at each position within your page layout, save the file, and use it as the source for printing your cards.

Creating a Greeting Card

With the ability to make their own prints on a wide variety of papers, many nature photographers have started producing greeting cards featuring their images on the front. Whether these are used to send a message to family or friends or sold to generate a profit, creating greeting cards featuring your photography can be a fun and rewarding experience.

We've seen many photographers get frustrated trying to create greeting cards because they're not sure how to create the page layout. Often they'll try to print a single image in the normal way, attempting to change the page layout settings so that image appears in the correct position on the final printed card. Unless you're a master of spatial orientation, this can prove to be very difficult to get right on the first try or even on the tenth try. We'll show you an easier way!

Creating the Template

Start by creating a new blank document that matches the dimensions of the sheet of paper to which you'll actually be printing. For example, you can print to a standard 8.5"×11" sheet of stock and score the page yourself, or you can purchase prescored paper specifically designed for this purpose. We'll use the example of an 8.5"×11" sheet that will be folded in half for this demonstration.

To get started, choose File > New from the menu to open the New dialog box (Figure 10.42). Change the unit of measure for the dimensions to inches using the drop-down list to the right of the Width field. (When you change the unit of measure for either Width or Height, the other will also change automatically.) Enter dimensions for Width and Height based on the paper setting, but consider the orientation as you do so. If you want to produce a card with a vertical orientation, you need to create a document with a horizontal orientation because the page will be folded lengthwise. Similarly, if you want a card with a horizontal orientation, create the new document with a vertical orientation.

Figure 10.42
In the New dialog box, enter the settings for the page you'll use as the template for your greeting card.

Set the Resolution to the value you plan to use for printing, such as 300 dpi. Make sure the color mode is set to RGB, the bit depth is appropriate for the images you're using (since you're just preparing a print, using 8-bit is perfectly fine here), and set the Background Contents to White so you're working with a white page. Then click OK to create the new document you'll use for your greeting card layout.

To help you visualize the actual page layout and where you want to place the image or images to include on the greeting card, place guides on the document you've created. At the very least, put a guide marking the fold line for the page. You might also want to place guides to identify the margins of the page to keep the images you place within the printable area.

Let's assume a horizontal page that will result in a vertical image layout for our example greeting card. Therefore, the document you've created is 11" wide and 8.5" tall. You want to place a guide halfway along the width to mark the fold location, so select View > New Guide from the menu. This opens the New Guide dialog box, which allows you to specify a position and orientation for the new guide you're adding. In this example, you set the Orientation to Vertical and the Position to "5.5 in," with the abbreviation "in" representing inches. Click OK, and the guide is added. You can add other guides in a similar manner, for example, about a half inch from each edge of the "front" of the card to identify the printable area you want to use for images, as shown in Figure 10.43.

Figure 10.43
Place guides in the template document to help you visualize the page layout for your greeting card, making it easier to properly position images within the layout.

Note: Many printers don't actually print content perfectly centered on the page, leading to challenges in creating an effective template. Perform some test prints early in the process to confirm the behavior of your printer—being sure to use the appropriate settings to center the output on the page—and adjust the template layout accordingly.

Having the layout of the page clear in your head can be a challenge here. If you're at all unclear on how the page should be structured, take a sheet of paper, fold it in half, and draw a simple sketch on the front of the card. Then unfold the paper and hold it in front of you to match the page layout you're creating in Photoshop. This should help clarify where the front really is on the blank page you're working on. In this example, the front of the card is on the right side of the new page.

Note: You can use guides in any way that helps you create a page layout. For example, you might mark the center of the image area of the card or break the area into thirds to help you place pictures as desired.

Adding Images to the Layout

Once you've created your template document and have added guides to help you with the layout, you're ready to start placing images. Start by opening the image you want to add to your layout. You'll probably want to resize the image (for example, down to about a 4"×6" size for our sample card created from an 8.5"×11" sheet). In addition, it's easier to work with if you flatten it, so create a duplicate copy to protect your original. Select Image > Duplicate from the menu, check the Duplicate Merged Layers Only checkbox, and click OK. Then select Image > Image Size from the menu. Make sure the Resample Image checkbox is selected, and set the Resolution to the same value you used for the new document you created. Then set the size as appropriate for the size of the greeting card document. (You'll be able to fine-tune the sizing later.)

With the image prepared, select the Move tool from the Tools panel (or press the V shortcut key). Point the mouse at the image, click and hold the button, and drag all the way into your new document; make sure the image window isn't maximized and that you're able to see both documents at the same time. Don't release the mouse until the pointer is over this new document, with a plus sign showing on the pointer to indicate you're creating a copy of the image layer. When you release the mouse, the image is added as a separate layer to the new document, as shown in Figure 10.44.

Fine-tune the position of the image layer by dragging with the mouse or using the arrow keys on your keyboard. Each press of one of the arrow keys moves the image by 1 pixel. You can increase this to 10 pixels by holding the Shift key while pressing the arrow key.

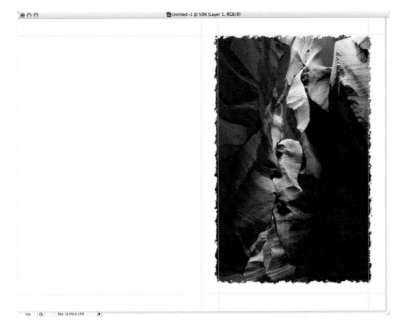

Figure 10.44
Drag the image into the card template and place it as desired.

To resize the image on the page, select Edit > Transform > Scale. This places a bounding box around your image layer. Hold the Shift key to constrain the proportions of this image layer, and drag one of the corners to resize the image. You can also click and drag the image itself while you're in the middle of the transform to adjust the position of the image layer. When you have applied the resizing as desired, press Enter/Return, or double-click inside the bounding box. Keep any increase in size to a minimum because repeatedly resizing can degrade image quality.

If you're adding multiple images to the greeting card, follow this same procedure for each of them. If the images will overlap, their order on the Layers panel determines whether individual layers appear above or below the others. The stack in the document is the same as shown on the Layers panel, with an image above another blocking part of any images below if they overlap.

Note: You can also add layer styles to the images you use in your greeting cards, which we covered earlier when showing how to create business cards.

Adding Text

You may decide that you'd like to add text to the card, either on the front of the card or on the back, to offer a little information about the subject or about you, as shown in Figure 10.45. Doing so is easy. Select the Text tool, and click where you'd like to add the text. Use the Options bar to choose the font, size, and color that you prefer, just as we described earlier for business cards. You can rotate the card by choosing Image > Rotate Canvas if necessary so you can add text in a different direction. This can be particularly helpful with horizontally oriented cards.

Slot Canyon   Page, Arizona

Figure 10.45
Add text to provide a
greeting, information
about the subject, or your
contact information.

Save and Print

Once you've created your document for your greeting card, save it so it can be printed
in the future. We recommend saving the document as a TIFF or Photoshop PSD file,
retaining all layers so you can fine-tune the layout in the future if desired.

To print the greeting card, try not to think of it as a special layout but rather as a
composite image that consumes an entire sheet of paper. Insert the appropriate size paper
in your printer, and then print the image as you normally would. In other words, even
though your example greeting card will ultimately be a vertical card created from a
folded sheet of paper, think of your example as an image in a horizontal format that
needs to be printed in Landscape mode to a normal sheet of paper. This helps simplify
the process in your mind and makes it easier to get to the final result of a printed card
that you can fold, sign, and send to the lucky recipient.

Try It! Open one of your favorite images, and create a greeting card.

Creating Slide Shows

There are many programs available for creating intricate digital slide shows. However,
since this is a book about Photoshop, we'll show you how to create a basic slide show
incredibly quickly directly within Photoshop. As we discussed in Chapter 2, "Bridge,"
you can quickly create a slide show in Bridge and even rate or delete images while viewing the slide show. Some photographers find that quite helpful while editing. In addition,
there is another type of slideshow you can create. It seems most photographers aren't
familiar with the fact that you can create basic slide shows within Photoshop, utilizing a
somewhat obscure capability offered by PDF documents.

Here's how to create a slide show in Photoshop as a PDF document:

1. Select File > Automate > PDF Presentation from the menu. The PDF Presentation dialog box appears (see Figure 10.46), which includes the basic settings for creating your slide show.

Figure 10.46
The PDF Presentation dialog box allows you to establish the settings for a basic slide show that can be played using the Adobe Reader software used to read PDF documents.

2. Click the Browse button, selecting the image files you want to include (you have to select all individual image files rather than being able to select a single folder), and click Open. The images you selected are added to the list of source files for the presentation. Alternatively, you could choose to use the open images.

> **Note:** It's a good idea to create copies of your master images to use for this purpose, resizing them down to about the display resolution you intend to use for the slide show. Otherwise, the PDF file used for the final presentation can become very large. It's also a good idea to convert the images to the sRGB color space (Edit > Convert to Profile) to ensure the best color possible for monitor or projector display.

3. In the Output Options section, select Presentation so the final result is an automatic presentation rather than a simple PDF document.
4. If you want the slide show to advance automatically rather than requiring the viewer to click the mouse for each image, select the Advance Every checkbox, and enter the number of seconds you want the presentation to delay between images in the Seconds text box.
5. Select the Loop After Last Page checkbox if you want the slide show to automatically loop indefinitely.
6. Select an effect from the Transition drop-down list if desired. The None option causes the images to switch without any effect. Some of the effects are relatively amateur in appearance. We consider the Wipe effects to be the most appropriate, but experiment with the various options to decide what you like best.

7. If you want any additional information to appear with each image, check the appropriate box.

8. Click the Save button to continue. The Save dialog box appears, allowing you to select a location and filename for your PDF presentation file.

When you click Save, the Save Adobe PDF dialog box appears. This is a rather complicated dialog box (see Figure 10.47), but you can avoid the complexity by simply selecting the Smallest File Size option from the Adobe PDF Preset drop-down list at the top of the dialog box. This ensures that the final PDF file remains at a reasonable file size while still ensuring excellent image quality for display on a monitor or digital projector. We recommend checking the Optimize for Fast Web Preview and View PDF After Saving boxes.

Figure 10.47
The Save Adobe PDF
dialog box

When you click the Save PDF button in the Save Adobe PDF dialog box, Photoshop processes your images to resize them for the slide show and then creates the final PDF file. The result is saved in the location you specified. You can then open that PDF file with Adobe Reader (in most cases, you can simply double-click the file to do so), and the slide show starts automatically. To return to a normal screen, use the Esc key.

Creating a PDF slide show can be helpful when you want to send your images to someone and have them view them as a slide show.

Creating a Web Gallery

Prints aren't the only form of output nature photographers want to produce. Displaying images on the Web is becoming more popular, providing a great way to share your images with a large audience easily and affordably. Although building a professional-quality website can require either many hours of learning and creating or a considerable budget, Photoshop makes it easy to create a basic gallery of your images to display on screen through the Web Photo Gallery automation tool.

To get started, choose File > Automate > Web Photo Gallery from the Photoshop menu. The Web Photo Gallery dialog box (shown in Figure 10.48) appears, where you can establish the various settings that define the appearance of the final gallery.

Figure 10.48
The Web Photo Gallery dialog box allows you to establish settings that enable Photoshop to create all the files necessary for a basic gallery for your images on the Web.

Note: If you're reviewing your images in the Bridge application, select the images you want to include in a web gallery, and then choose Tools > Photoshop > Web Photo Gallery from the Bridge menu to open the Web Photo Gallery dialog box with the selected images automatically set as the source for the gallery.

At the top of the dialog box is a Styles drop-down list where you can choose the overall appearance of the website. Because the names don't provide a completely clear indication of what the site layout will look like, we recommend that you select the first option from the drop-down list and then use the up and down arrow keys to cycle through the various options. A thumbnail display on the right side of the dialog box gives you an indication (though very small) of what the layout will look like.

In the E-mail box, enter your email address if you'd like it to be displayed in the contact information on the gallery you're creating. This provides a simple link for people to use if they want to contact you with questions about your images or (better yet) how to purchase an image.

In the Source Images section, specify both the source of images and the destination for the files to be created as part of your gallery. From the Use drop-down list, select Folder if you want to specify a particular folder containing image files you want to use in your gallery. If you have selected images in Bridge that you want to include in the gallery, choose the Selected Images From Bridge option.

Note: If you're going to be using a folder as the source of images, you may want to copy those images into a new folder so you can more easily manage the collection of images to be included in the gallery.

If you have set the source to Folder, click the Browse button to open a separate dialog box, where you can identify the folder where the images to be included in the gallery are stored. If there are additional folders within the source folder with images you want to include in the gallery, select the Include All Subfolders checkbox.

To select the folder where you want all of the files for your gallery to be saved, click the Destination button. As with the Browse button for setting the source, this opens a dialog box where you can specify a folder or create a new folder.

The Options section of the Web Photo Gallery dialog box contains a large number of settings, broken down into various sections that are accessed by choosing a category from the drop-down list at the top of this section:

General   The General options control some of the basic parameters of the website. You can specify whether you want the file extension for the HTML files that form the website to be .htm or .html, though this isn't a significant concern because all current servers and web browsers support both file extensions. The checkbox Use UTF8 Encoding For URL allows you to ensure that URLs containing international characters function properly. The Add Width and Height Attributes for Images checkbox causes sizing information to be included in the HTML files for images, so the layout of the page remains fixed as the images load. We recommend selecting this option. The Preserve All Metadata checkbox ensures that all metadata is retained within the image files being created for the web gallery.

Banner   The Banner options allow you to specify the text that appears on the page. Enter values for each field if you want that information displayed on your gallery. Leave any of them blank if you do not want particular text included.

Large Images   The Large Images section provides settings that determine how large the "full-sized" images appear in your gallery. Although it's possible to maintain the native size of your image files by clearing the Resize Images checkbox, we recommend checking this box so the images can be adjusted to a more appropriate size. The Small, Medium, and Large sizes provide basic values for you to use, and we usually recommend the Large setting unless file sizes are a particular concern. You can also select the Custom size and enter a maximum pixel size for your images. The JPEG Quality setting determines the quality setting used for the JPEG images that are saved, which has a direct effect on the size of the image files. We recommend using the High setting for JPEG Quality, although you could use a lower setting if file size is a serious concern for your site, such as if you expect many visitors to be using dial-up Internet connections. At the bottom of this section, set Border Size in pixels if you want to have a border around your images, and select the desired checkboxes below in the Titles Use section if you want to include additional text as titles for your images.

Thumbnails   The Thumbnails section provides similar settings to those used for the Large Images section, except that these settings relate to the small thumbnail versions of the images to be displayed in the gallery. We recommend using a Large setting for these so the thumbnails are large enough to be clearly visible and identifiable in the gallery.

Custom Colors   The Custom Colors section allows you to specify the color for text and links for those styles that support this option. We generally recommend leaving these to the defaults so visitors have the Internet-standard experience on your site, such as text links that have not yet been visited appearing in blue and those that have been visited appearing in purple. You can also select different colors for the background and the banner.

Security   The Security section contains various settings to place text over the top of your images. There are many options available that enable you to use specific attributes (such as filename) for this text. You can also choose Custom Text and enter your own text to be placed over your images as well as adjust the font attributes as desired.

We recommend that you use one of these options or apply a watermark to your images as we describe in Chapter 11; it's extremely common for images to be illegally downloaded from websites and used for all sorts of purposes even though the file size is relatively small.

Once you've established all the settings applicable to your gallery, click OK to have Photoshop process all the files, placing them into the folder you set as the destination. This includes a series of HTML files and resized images, divided into folders (see Figure 10.49). The entire contents of the destination folder can then be uploaded to your website server so the site can be accessed on the Internet.

Figure 10.49
After establishing the desired settings for your gallery in the Web Photo Gallery dialog box, a website is created for you automatically.

In this chapter we've explained methods for sharing your images after they have been optimized. This is only a starting point for producing great output, and we encourage you to be creative in how you prepare your images for display. In the next chapter, we'll demonstrate some additional time-saving techniques for optimizing your workflow.

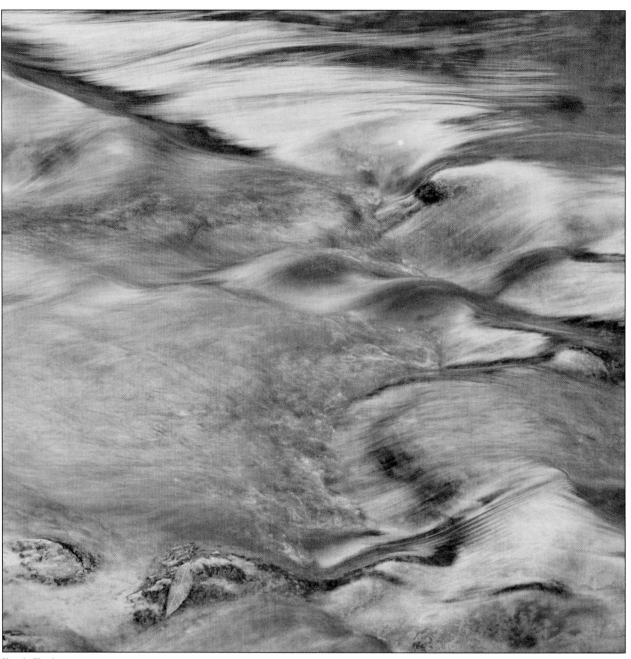

Photo by Ellen Anon.

Time-Savers

Throughout this book we've provided you with the best techniques for optimizing your images at every stage of the digital workflow. In this last chapter, we'll present some ways to help you save time and improve your efficiency. Adobe Photoshop has a variety of ways for you to automate many of the tasks that you perform repeatedly. That way you can spend less time optimizing images and more time being creative either in the field with your camera or in Photoshop!

11

Chapter Contents
Actions and Batch Processing
Using the Image Processor
Creating a Copyright Brush
Individualizing Keyboard Shortcuts

Actions and Batch Processing

Time is in short supply for most of us. And if we're offered a way to get a job done with equal quality but in far less time, most of us would eagerly choose the more efficient method…if for no other reason than ultimately it means we'll have more time to get back to the things we love, such as taking more photos!

When it comes to getting efficient with repetitive tasks in Photoshop, one of the keys is creating actions and applying those actions to a group of images in batch. Actions allow you to automate just about any series of steps you can perform in Photoshop. You can record a series of steps and then have those steps applied to additional images in exactly the same way. Batch processing allows you to apply the action to a group of images at once. The result can be a significant boost to your productivity.

Let's look at an example where your intent is to create an action to add the Safe Dodge and Burn layers that we covered in Chapter 6, "Exposure Adjustments."

Creating an Action

The Actions panel is "command central" for creating and managing your actions. So, start by selecting the Actions panel (shown in Figure 11.1). If it isn't visible, choose Window > Actions from the menu, or use the keyboard shortcut Alt+F9/Option+F9.

CHAPTER 11: TIME-SAVERS

Figure 11.1
The Actions panel is "command central" for creating and managing your actions.

On the panel, actions are organized into folders called *sets*. Photoshop includes a Default Actions set with a variety of included actions, but you should divide your actions into sets that define logical groups. For instance, in this example, you may create a new set called Adjustments to contain the various actions you may utilize when optimizing images. You may create other sets for actions you use for creative effects or for output—such as setting up the template for a business or greeting card as we discussed in Chapter 10, "Output." The important thing is to create sets that are logical to your particular workflow and that will enable you to quickly locate an action.

Note: Click the fly-out menu on the top right of the Actions panel to access some additional action sets that Adobe includes. Some of these may save you the time of creating an action yourself, and/or you may discover a fun effect to add to an image.

To create a new set, click the Create New Set button 🗀 at the bottom of the Actions panel. In the New Set dialog box (shown in Figure 11.2), enter a name, and click OK.

Figure 11.2

The New Set dialog box allows you to create a new set that helps you manage the various categories of actions you're creating.

Note: When creating an action, it's a good idea to work with a copy of one of your images. Copy one of your images to the desktop before you start creating the action, and use that as the file you adjust in the process of recording the action.

With this set active, the next step is to start recording your new action. Click the Create New Action button ![button] at the bottom of the Actions panel. In the New Action dialog box (see Figure 11.3), enter a descriptive name for this action. For this example, let's use "Dodge and Burn Layers." The Set option defaults to the one that was selected when you created the new action, but you can choose a different set from the drop-down list if desired. The Function Key option allows you to set a shortcut key for the new action you're creating, which can be convenient if you're applying this action individually to single images. Finally, the Color setting determines what color the action shows up as if you use Button mode for the Actions panel. This allows you to color-code the individual actions. Although some people find this very useful for categorizing certain types of actions, we prefer using the default system of grouping actions into sets, so we leave the Color setting at None.

Figure 11.3

In the New Action dialog box, specify a name for the new action, the folder you want it stored in, and a function key to use as a shortcut key to run the action.

Once you've established the panel characteristics for the new action, click Record, and you're actively recording the action. Don't worry, though—time isn't an issue. Photoshop doesn't record the time you take between your steps but instead records the final result of each step you perform so those steps can be repeated as quickly as possible when you apply the action to an image. You can perform any adjustment or command on an image as part of an action. However, keep in mind that any step that depends on specific positioning within the image can be problematic because image dimensions vary from one photo to the next. In those instances, you may have to include a Stop or Modal Control in the action. We'll cover how to do that later in this chapter.

Note: When recording an action, make sure to perform the steps in the order you want them repeated when you run the action. Sometimes it's helpful to write down the steps ahead of time. But you can revise the settings as often as you need to while recording the action; Photoshop will actually use only the final result of each step. In addition, the steps on the action can be edited, reordered, turned off, duplicated, or deleted later.

We'll record an action to create Safe Dodge and Burn layers as an example. This is a good one for you to try as well. To create a Safe Dodge and Burn Layers action, take these steps:

1. Open the image being used as the example for the action.
2. Select the Actions panel.
    a. (This step is optional.) Create a new set; we created one called Adjustments.
    b. Select the new action icon, and name the action. We called ours Dodge and Burn Layers.
    c. Click the Record button [●].
3. Open a Curves adjustment layer, but make no adjustments to the curve. Click OK so that the adjustment layer is added to the Layers panel.
4. Change the blending mode for the layer to Multiply. Initially the entire image will appear too dark.
5. Double-click directly on the word *Curves*, and type **Burn**.
6. Choose Edit > Fill > Black. This step fills the layer mask with black to completely hide the darkening effect we introduced in step 3.
7. Open another Curves adjustment layer, but make no adjustments to the curve. Click OK so that the adjustment layer is added to the Layers panel.
8. Change the blending mode for the layer to Screen. Initially the entire image will appear too light.
9. Double-click directly on the word *Curves*, and type **Dodge**.
10. Choose Edit > Fill > Black.
11. Click the Brush tool to select it.
12. Change the opacity of the brush in the toolbar to about 15%. Including steps 11 and 12 in the action will mean that you're all ready to start the actual dodging and burning on the image after you run the action.
13. Click the Stop button [■] to stop recording.

You've now created an action, which can then be applied to an individual image or to many images at once by using batch processing. Each step in the action can be viewed within the Actions panel, as shown in Figure 11.4. Anytime you want to run the action, have the image open, open the Actions panel, select the action, and click the Play icon [▶]. If you created a keyboard shortcut for the action, to run the action on an open image, just click the shortcut.

Figure 11.4
The Actions panel will show each of the steps in the action.

When you create an action that you're likely to use on a batch of images, we recommend saving the image and closing the file as the last steps in the action. Obviously this isn't practical in an action such as the one we just created—but that's an action geared primarily toward use on one image at a time. By saving and closing the file within the action, you help ensure that each processed image is saved and closed correctly.

Always save your action set after recording a new action. A system crash or improper shutdown will wipe out any new actions. To prevent accidentally losing the action, you must save the action set by using the panel menu in the Actions panel and choosing Save Actions.

Advanced Controls in Actions

Creating a basic action is pretty simple and straightforward, but at times you may need to do something a little fancier. For example, perhaps you want to be able to change the values used in some of the dialog boxes in the action. In that case, you need a modal control. A *modal control* pauses the action at the point where you need to fill in the appropriate settings. You can also use a modal control to enable you to use any of the tools, such as Crop or Transform, that require you to press Enter/Return to apply them. When the action comes to that step, it pauses and cues you to perform the necessary task. When you're done, you click OK in the dialog box or press Enter/Return, and the action resumes playing. Essentially, the modal control simply turns on any dialog box associated with the step.

To create a modal control for a specific step of an action, click the empty box to the left of that step (see Figure 11.5). Clicking the icon [...] toggles it on and off. If you toggle the modal control off, the action will use the settings you used while recording the action. An action that contains modal controls will have a red modal icon by its name.

Figure 11.5
New modal controls enable you to change settings in dialog boxes while running an action.

Although many tasks can be automated using actions, any task that requires something to be done at a specific position in the image may present a problem with images of different sizes, resolutions, or orientations. For example, creating a single action to apply a copyright to the lower-right corner of an image is more challenging than it would seem because of different image sizes and resolutions. Most tools can be recorded, but some—such as the painting tools—cannot.

One thing that can help is to insert a Stop into the action. A Stop lets you perform a task that cannot be recorded—such as creating a selection. To include a Stop in an action, click the command just prior to where you want the Stop to occur. Click the Actions panel drop-down menu (see Figure 11.6), and choose Insert Stop. This will cause a message box to appear in which you type instructions to yourself so you remember what you need to do. When you're done, click the Play button to continue the action. You can insert the Stop while recording the action or after you're done.

Figure 11.6 Choose Insert Stop from the panel menu in the Actions panel, and complete the message box.

Another use of Stops is to record a reminder or message as to what should be done at a particular step. To do this, you follow the same steps as we just described, but you must check the option Allow Continue. When the message box appears during the action, the user can read the message and then click Continue rather than stopping the action.

Inevitably there will be times you'll record an action with steps you no longer want included, or you'll realize that you left something out. Although you could start over and record a new action, sometimes it's easier to revise the existing action.

Removing a step from an action is easy. Choose the action in the Actions panel, and reveal the steps by clicking the expansion arrow. Choose the step you want to remove, and either drag it to the trash can icon or click the trash can icon.

To add one or more steps to the action, choose the action, and use the expansion arrow to reveal the steps. Choose the step just prior to where you want to begin the additional steps. Click the Record button, and record the missing steps. When you're done recording the additional steps, click the Stop button.

Batch Processing

As you can see, recording an action is relatively straightforward. Just start recording, perform the steps you want included in the action, and then stop recording. Where many photographers run into trouble is in attempting to apply the action in a batch to a series of images, which is ironically where you achieve the real benefit of actions. The problem is with the confusing choices that are offered to you in the Batch dialog box.

To get started, select the action you want to apply to a group of images from the Actions panel. Then choose File > Automate > Batch from the menu, which brings up the Batch dialog box (shown in Figure 11.7). Because you selected an action first, the Set and Action drop-down lists default to the one you want to apply to your images.

Note: When you're applying an action to a group of images in batch, we recommend copying the image files to a separate folder to protect the originals.

Figure 11.7
The Batch dialog box allows you to specify the action you want to run on a group of images, as well as other settings that determine which images should be processed and how they should be handled.

The Source section provides a number of options related to the images you'll be processing with the action. The Source drop-down list allows you to specify where the source images are located:

- We generally use the Folder option so we can specify a specific location where we've copied the images to be processed.

- The Import option applies to images being imported from a particular source at the time the action is run.

- The Opened Files option applies to all images currently open in Photoshop.

- Bridge applies the action to all images currently selected in Adobe's Bridge.

If you have included an Open step in your action, select the Override Action "Open" Commands check box so the action actually opens and processes the files you specified in the source folder, rather than having the same image you used to create the action opened repeatedly. If your action does not contain an Open command, then you must not check this box; otherwise, the Batch command won't open the files you've selected for batch processing. So, in other words, don't check this option if the action was recorded to work on an image that's already open or if the action contains Open commands for specific files that are used as part of the action.

If you have used the Folder option for Source and there are more images in subfolders below that folder, select the Include All Folders check box so those images are also processed.

The Suppress File Open Options Dialogs option causes all images to be opened with default values without bringing up any Options dialog boxes that may be associated with the particular open operation. The most common situation where this would be an issue is for raw files—normally the ACR dialog box is displayed when a raw file is opened. By checking this option in the Batch dialog box, the default or previously specified settings are used instead of opening the ACR box. As a general rule, keep this check box selected, since the point of using batch processing is to allow a group of images to be processed without any user intervention required.

Similarly, select the Suppress Color Profile Warnings check box so the action won't pause for missing profiles or profile mismatches in any of the images you are processing. When this option is selected, the default action specified in the Color Settings dialog box is performed when either of these situations occurs.

The next section of the Batch dialog box is the Destination section, which allows you to specify parameters for the output that is generated by the batch process. From the drop-down list, select the Folder option so that the processed images are saved into a specific folder and don't overwrite the original files. The other options are None (which leaves the file open unless the action recorded a Save command) and Save and Close (which causes each image to be saved as it is processed, replacing the existing files). If you use the Folder option, click the Choose button to bring up the Browse For Folder dialog box, where you can specify which folder you'd like to save the processed images in (including the ability to create a completely new folder for this purpose).

One of the biggest points of confusion for photographers using the Batch dialog box relates to the Override Action "Save As" Commands check box. You use this option so you can specify a Save As command in the action and then have the new files saved to whatever folder you specify in the Batch command, rather than the one you used when you created the action. It causes Photoshop to ignore the specific filename and folder you used when creating the action. If you don't use this option and you specify a filename in the Save As dialog box when you record in the action, then when you run the action, the new file will be renamed to the same name you used when creating the action.

If you want to save the processed images using their original filenames but in a different folder than you specify in the Batch command, you must save your image when recording the action. Then in the Batch processing dialog box, check Override Action "Save As" Commands, and specify the destination folder. If you don't check this option, then Photoshop will save the images in two places. One will be the folder that you specify as the destination, and the other will be in the folder you used while creating the action. Note that the action must contain a Save As command to use this option. If you try to use it with an action that doesn't contain a Save As command, the batch processing won't save the processed files.

In the File Naming section, you have considerable flexibility in naming the files that are created. You can type specific text into the option boxes or select a variable from the drop-down list. For example, if you want to save the images with a filename in the structure Slideshow_0001.jpg, enter **Slideshow_** in the first box, select 4 Digit Serial Number from the drop-down list in the second box, and then select the Extension option from the third drop-down list. The default values of Document Name and Extension cause the original filenames to be retained. If you're using a serial number option, specify the starting value in the Starting Serial # box, which defaults to 1.

In the Errors section, choose whether you want to Stop For Errors or simply have Photoshop Log Errors To a File without interrupting the batch processing. We prefer to use the Stop For Errors option so we know right away if there is a problem we need to correct.

When you've set all the settings you want to use for the action you are applying to a group of images, click OK, and Photoshop processes all of the images specified in the Source section with the action specified in the Play section, saving the resulting output based on the settings in the Destination section. This processing is done automatically at top speed, making the process very efficient.

Whenever you find yourself performing the same task on a group of images, consider making an action to automate that process. The small amount of time spent creating the action pays significant dividends when you apply that action in batch to a large group of images.

Al Ward, in addition to being the technical editor for this book, is the brain behind ActionFx.com, a website dedicated to Photoshop Presets (actions, shapes, brushes, layer styles, et al.), and has over 65,000 presets available for download at this writing. In the accompanying excellent sidebar, he provides tips for creating watermarks.

Creating Watermark Actions

by Al Ward

The ability of actions to record nearly every process in Photoshop sounds great, but few actually wrap their minds around these incredible handy tools and utilize them in their work. Not so many years ago there simply wasn't much documentation on actions, and a natural assumption was that they required some degree of programming skill. This could not be further from the truth. If you can navigate a Photoshop panel and have had experience with a tape recorder, VCR, DVD-R, or other media capturing device, then you already have the concept behind actions mastered...you just don't realize it yet. This chapter gives you an excellent start on working with actions, and I encourage you to go through the information carefully.

All that said, you may still be wondering what actions can do for you as a photographer. The answer is plenty, whether you're interested in photo correction, photo manipulation, simple productivity, or even web design and funky special effects.

One repetitive function an action can perform with ease over and over again so you don't have to, is the creation and placement of a watermark. Photographers who display their work online and don't want to suffer the thieves of this world running off with their livelihood can quickly set up an action that will place a watermark on a single image or on an entire folder of images when using the action with the Batch command.

Note that these types of actions are often dependent on an image's resolution and size. I recommend creating actions of this nature for specific image orientations and resolutions. For instance, the action outlined here works well on a portrait photo, 8×11, at 300 ppi. Although the action will work regardless of the image size and resolution, the text may spill off the edges on an image with a different resolution. Build an entire toolkit of watermark actions using variable image sizes in a single action set, and name each action in the set based on the photo orientation and resolution it is designed for. An example may be WM_Portrait_8x11_300ppi, placed in a set of actions called "My Watermarks."

Here's the process to create such an action:

1. Open the Actions panel. Create a new action set, and call it Watermarks.

2. Open an image. Create a new action in the set, and give it a name; something like Watermark-001 will do for this trial run. (It can be renamed as you see fit later). Click Record.

3. Anything you do in Photoshop is now recording. First, ensure the rulers are displayed (View > Rulers). Then, right-click the ruler bar on the top or side, and select Percent. This will ensure the watermark appears with the same positioning no matter the size of the image, the resolution, or the orientation (landscape or portrait).

4. Select the Type tool. Change the foreground color to whatever color you would like your watermark to be, and then select the font and font size you want to use. For instance, a light gray/white foreground color, a semi-bold font set to 14–20 pixels works well for most of my photos. Also, for watermarks I place in the middle of images, I set the justification to Center.

Continues

Creating Watermark Actions *(Continued)*

5. Move the mouse to the spot where you want to start typing. If you would like the watermark to be placed directly in the center of each photo, watch the top and side rulers as you move the mouse, and click when both the side and top ruler markers are at 50%. Type your watermark info (such as **Copyright 2007, mygenericwebsite.com**). Once typed, you may edit the text as needed (Transform > Rotate, Transform > Scale, and so on).

6. To make the text appear embossed rather than have a simple color fill, open the layer styles for the text layer, and apply a simple bevel. Accept the style by clicking OK, and then reduce the fill opacity for the layer to 0, or a slightly higher percentage if you want some color to remain yet remain transparent. You may also opt to add a drop shadow, outer glow, or other text enhancing setting with your style.

7. When you are happy with the new watermark, stop recording, and *save the action set* to a folder on your hard drive where you can easily find it later.

8. Open another image, preferably with a different orientation, and rerun the action. If you followed the directions in this sidebar, you'll see the watermark in the same position on the new image, despite orientation or resolution.

Now you are set to add a watermark to all your photos. Use the information in this chapter to set up a batch process using this action, and ensure the batch saves copies of the images and does not save over the originals. Again, the authors describe this process, so please take care in reading and practicing on "throwaway" files until you are sure you have it mastered.

On a parting note, you may want to create watermark actions using varied fonts, colors, and watermark positions. Save these to the same action set, and create an entire toolbox of Watermark actions. Trust me, your life will be a lot easier if you incorporate actions into your Photoshop mind-set. Enjoy!

© Al Ward, ActionFx.com

Creating a Droplet

A droplet provides a way to run an action on a single image, a group of images, or a folder of images, directly from your desktop (or elsewhere). You create a droplet icon for the action and then drag the images (or folder) onto it to run the action. Using a droplet can save you time since you don't have to bother with the Batch dialog box in order to run the action.

You must create the action first. Then to create a droplet, follow these steps:

1. Choose File > Automate > Create Droplet. This elicits a dialog box very similar to the Batch dialog box except that it begins with a Save Droplet In drop-down menu (see Figure 11.8).

Figure 11.8
The Create Droplet dialog box is quite similar to the Batch dialog box.

2. Specify where to save the droplet. Usually if you want the convenience of a droplet, you'll want it to be on your desktop, but you could create a special folder just for droplets or you could choose to store them elsewhere such as in Documents. You'll also need to name the droplet. We recommend using a name that readily identifies what the action does.

3. Choose the set and the action.

4. Complete the rest of the options, which are identical to those we described in detail in the section on batch processing.

5. Click OK, and the droplet will be saved wherever you specified.

To use the droplet, drag any image or folder containing images onto it. Photoshop will automatically launch if it's not already running, and you can be off taking more photos!

Using the Image Processor

The Image Processor was introduced into Photoshop in CS2 and is a major time-saver. It allows you to convert images into different sizes and formats that you specify and stores them wherever you specify. That's a huge time-saver as you prepare images for the Web, e-mails, a slide show, and so on. It's similar to a batch command except that you don't have to create an action to make it work.

The Image Processor can convert files to either JPEG, TIFF, or PSD formats or to two or more different formats simultaneously (see Figure 11.9). In addition, it can resize images to fit within specific dimensions for each format. It can also embed a color profile or convert the JPEGS to sRGB, run an action, and/or include copyright metadata in the converted images! That's a lot of convenience in one dialog box!

Figure 11.9

The Image Processor makes it easy to resize images for different outputs.

To use the Image Processor, follow these steps:

1. To access the Image Processor from Bridge, choose Tools > Photoshop > Image Processor. To access it from within Photoshop, choose File > Scripts > Image Processor.

2. Specify the images you want to process. You can use open files or select a folder of images.

3. If you are using raw files, you may want to check the option to Select Open First Image to Apply Settings. That way you can customize the raw settings to apply to the first image, and the Image Processor will apply those same settings to the remaining raw files. That can be very helpful if the images were shot under similar lighting conditions. If you don't check this option, the Image Processor will use the existing settings for each image. If you have customized the settings for each image in ACR, you should not check this option.

4. Select a location to store the processed images. If you choose Save in Same Location, the Image Processor will automatically create a separate folder within that folder for the processed images. Each file format will have its own folder.

5. Select the file types and options. The Resize to Fit option is particularly convenient. You can specify the maximum height and width in pixels for the image. The Image Processor will retain the aspect ratio of the original file but resize the image to fit within the dimensions you specify. For example, if you are processing images to use in a slide show and your projector has a resolution of 1024×768, you would set those dimensions.

6. Select an action to run if you choose. Some people create a sharpening action for their web sized or slide show images and have the Image Processor run it.

7. Fill in the copyright information, but remember that this is metadata. It will not appear as a copyright symbol and text on the image itself. (To do that, you can use the copyright brush that we'll cover later in this chapter or use a watermark action as Al Ward described.)

8. Keep the Include ICC Profile option checked.

9. Click Run. If the settings you have established are ones that you will use frequently, you can opt to save them for even more time efficiency. That way when you open the Image Processor, you'll just need to click Load, select the settings, and select the Source folder.

Creating a Copyright Brush

One of the tasks that most nature photographers wish they could automate is adding a copyright to an image. Although Al Ward showed you, in an earlier sidebar, how to create an embossed watermark, some people are more comfortable using a copyright brush. The effect is just slightly different. To create a brush that contains your copyright, follow these steps:

1. Go to File > New File, and create a new document. The exact size is not important, but it is helpful to make it with a transparent background, as shown in Figure 11.10. Set the resolution to 96 since the main use for the copyright is likely to be for email and web images.

Figure 11.10
Make certain to set the background to transparent when creating the new file to use for the copyright brush.

2. Select the Text tool and the font you want to use. Ellen uses Snell Roundhand, Crisp, but any font you like will work. We use an 18-point font size.

3. Select the color for the text in the Text tool Options bar at the top of the monitor (see Figure 11.11). This will become the default color for the brush. We suggest using either white or black. You'll adjust the opacity of the brush when you use it, so don't worry about it being too obvious and distracting.

Figure 11.11 Select the font, size and color for your copyright brush in the Text tool Options bar.

4.   Type © and your name. Include the year if you choose. To access the © symbol on a Mac, type Option+G. In Windows, it's a little more difficult; hold the Alt key while pressing 0169 on the number pad. You must use the number pad, not the numbers immediately above the keyboard. On a laptop you may have to use the function key as well to access the number pad numbers.

5.   Ctrl+click/⌘+click the text layer icon in the Layers panel to select the text (see Figure 11.12).

Figure 11.12 You must turn the text into a selection before converting it into a brush.

6.   Select the Brush tool. Make certain that the hardness setting is set to 100%.

7.   Choose Edit > Define New Brush Preset. We name the brush Copyright and include the name of the font (see Figure 11.13).

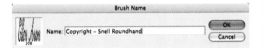

Figure 11.13 Make sure to name your copyright brush in a way that makes it easy to find.

8.   Click OK.

9.   You don't need to save the document; you can simply close it. You now have a brush that is your copyright.

To use your copyright brush on an image, follow these steps:

1.   Select the Brush tool, and then go to the Brush presets in the tool options bar (see Figure 11.14). Choose the copyright tool you just made.

Figure 11.14
Choose your copyright brush from the Brush presets.

2.   Create a new layer on your document (optional). By placing the copyright on a new layer, you can adjust the opacity of the copyright symbol after you make it by adjusting the opacity of the layer in the Layers panel. Alternatively, you can set the opacity of the brush to 60% although at times you may want it more or less opaque.

3. To change the color of the text, click the foreground Color Picker, and select the desired color.

4. To change the size of the copyright, use the bracket keys just as you do with any other brush tool.

5. Position the cursor, and with a single click, apply the copyright!

 Note: Placing a copyright on an image gives some protection against illegal use of the image, although for full protection you must register your images with the U.S. Copyright Office. For more information about how to register your images, see Carolyn Wright's excellent website and free blog, www .PhotoAttorney.com.

Individualizing Keyboard Shortcuts

As you've noticed, there are a lot of shortcuts in Photoshop. Some of them become second nature to almost everyone who uses Photoshop regularly and are major time-savers, while others are quite esoteric. People vary greatly as to their feelings about using shortcuts. We find that they are often useful to help us work more efficiently, and throughout the book we have tried to recommend our favorites to you.

Amazingly, even with the abundance of shortcuts in Photoshop, there isn't a shortcut for everything! You may decide that there's a step you perform repeatedly that you'd like to create a short for. For example, the adjustment shortcuts don't bring up an adjustment layer; instead, they access the adjustments that are performed directly on the pixels. Perhaps you'd like to have a shortcut to create a new Curves adjustment layer. The shortcut Ctrl+M/⌘+M is set by default to create a Curves adjustment. To change the shortcut to create a Curves adjustment layer, follow these steps:

1. In the menu, choose Edit > Keyboard Shortcuts. This will bring up a dialog box (see Figure 11.15).

Figure 11.15
You can create your own customized shortcuts for most steps that you regularly perform

2. Click the expansion arrow next to the word *Layer*, and choose New Adjustment Layer > Curves.

3. Click the Curves layer to cause a small white box to appear in that line.

4. If a shortcut already exists for the command, it will appear in the white box. Since creating a Curves adjustment layer doesn't have a default shortcut, the box is initially blank. Type the shortcut you want to use in the box. In this case we suggest using Ctrl+M/⌘+M so that the familiar shortcut for Curves brings up an adjustment layer for Curves.

5. Click OK. If the shortcut is already in use, a warning dialog will appear. If you click OK, the shortcut will be reassigned to your new command.

You'll find that most shortcuts are already taken, so you may have to reissue one that you don't tend to use. Of course, this means you'll get accustomed to using certain shortcuts on your home machine that won't work for others.

Another potential drawback (or advantage) of creating customized shortcuts for adjustment layers in particular is that the shortcut will first elicit a dialog box asking whether you want to name the layer, create a clipping group, and so on. Most of the time we don't want to do that, so there's an extra click to make the dialog box go away. Since the purpose of the shortcut was to save time, it's debatable whether it actually does. However, if you frequently use it to create a clipping group (make the adjustment so it affects only the layer immediately beneath it), then the shortcut may be a good time saver!

In this chapter we've presented some methods for you to improve the efficiency of your workflow and share your images in a variety of ways. As with all the chapters in this book, the underlying theme has been producing the very best results possible with your images and then sharing those images. Now that you have learned many techniques to help you achieve these goals, we hope you'll find an increased passion for your photography, an increased desire to share your images with the world, and a heightened level of skill in achieving exactly the results you envision for your photographs!

Index

Note to the Reader: Throughout this index **boldfaced** page numbers indicate primary discussions of a topic. *Italicized* page numbers indicate illustrations.

S

S curve, **198–199**, *199*
s/n (signal-to-noise) ratio, 19, **21**
sampling settings
    Clone Stamp tool, 160
    color cast, 220
    Color Replacement tool, 141
    composites, 269
    Eyedropper tool, 126–127
    greeting cards, 366
    Magic Wand tool, 129
    output, 326
Saturation blending mode, 305
saturation settings, **228–229**, *228–229*
    ACR, **79–80**, 83–85
    black-and-white image colorization, 285
    color casts, **212–213**, *212–213*
    extreme color, 321
Saturation tab, 83–84
Save Adobe PDF dialog box, 370, *370*
Save As dialog box, 382–383
Save button, 90, 93
Save Copies To option, 43
Save in Same Location option, 387
Save Log Items To option, 102
Save Selection dialog box
    Lens Blur filters, 291–292, *292*
    settings, 136, *136*
Save Settings option, 73
Save Workspace option, 113
saving
    ACR images, 90
    ACR settings, **72–73**, *73*
    business card layout, 361
    greeting cards, **368**
    selections, **135–137**, *136–137*,
        291–292, *292*
    slide shows, 370
    workspace, **50**, *50*, 113
Scale Styles option, 327
scaling
    business cards, 358
    greeting cards, 367
    layer styles, 327
Scratch Disks section, **106–107**, *106*
Screen blending mode, 304, 309, *309*
screen modes, **110–111**, *111*
scroll wheel, 102
Security section, 373
Select Images From Bridges option, 371
Select Open First Image to Apply Settings
    option, 387
selections
    composite elements, **263–268**, *264–268*
    feathering, **134**
    layer masks, **181–182**, *181–182*,
        232–233, *232–233*
    loading, **135–137**, *136–137*
    saving, **135–137**, *136–137*, 291–292, *292*
    tools, **118**
        combining, **134–135**
        Lasso, **118–123**, *119–122*
        Magic Wand, **126–130**, *128–129*
        Magnetic Lasso, **123–126**, *124*, *126*
        Quick Selection, **130**, *131*
        Refine Edge, **131–132**, *131*, *133*
Selective Color adjustment layer, **230–231**,
    230–231
Selective Color Options dialog box, 231
semi-gloss paper, 352
sensor elements, 21
sepia tint, 280, 285
Sessions Only log option, 102
Set Vanishing Point tool, 243
sets
    action, 376–377, *377*
    keyword, 59, *59*
shadows and highlights
    Smart Filters, 148
    Smart Sharpen filter, **342–343**
    working with, **202–207**, *203–204*, *207*
Shadows slider, 80
Sharpen Details setting, 331, *332*
sharpening, **335–336**
    ACR, **82–83**, *82*
    bird eyes, 236
    and noise, 326
    Smart Sharpen filter, **339–343**, *340–342*
    targeted, **343–344**
    Unsharp Mask filter, **336–339**, *337–338*
sharpness, evaluating, 115
Sharpness slider, 82
Shaw, John, **224–225**
Shield option, 155
shortcuts
    ACR, **66–67**
    keyboard, **390–391**, *390*
Show Amount of setting, 194, *194*
Show Background Drop Shadow option, 104
Show Channels in Color option, 104
Show Clipping option, 195–196
Show Crosshair In Brush Tip option, 109
Show Menu Colors option, 104
Show More Options option, 204, *204*
Show Overlay option
    Clone Stamp tool, 161, *161*
    Retouch tool, 70, *70*
Show Tool Tips option, 104
Show Tooltips option, 39
shutter speed
    in exposure, 19, 23
    Merge to HDR feature, 254
signal-to-noise (s/n) ratio, 19, **21**
silhouettes, **17–18**, *18*
silicon chip noise levels, 21
size
    business cards, 357–358
    canvas, 168, 312, *312*
    crop, **68**, *68*, 155
    files, **89**
    greeting card images, 367
    greeting cards, 364
    Image Processor for, 387, *387*
    output, **326–328**, *326*
    scroll wheel for, 102
    thumbnails, 48, *48*, 51, *51*
    Web Photo Gallery images, 372
    windows, **110**, *110*
skies
    libraries of, **26–27**, *27*
    replacing in composites, **271–273**,
        272–273
slide sandwiches, 302
slide shows
    Bridge, **60–61**, *60–61*
    creating, **368–370**, *369*
Slideshow Options dialog box, 60, *60*
sloppy cloning, 166
Smallest File Size option, 370
Smart Blur filter, **294–295**, *294–295*
Smart Filter Options dialog box, 149, *149*
Smart Filters, **147–148**
    example, **148–149**, *148–149*
    in output, 325–326
    on Smart Objects, **286–288**, *287–288*
Smart Objects, 8
    characteristics, **146–147**, *147*
    opening, **89**
    with Shadow/Highlight adjustment, 203
    Smart Filters on, **286–288**, *287–288*
Smart Sharpen filter, 336, **339–343**,
    340–342
smooth paper, 353
Smooth slider, 132
Soft Light blending mode, 305, 310
soft-proofing printing, 346
sorting images, **53–54**
    Filter panel, **57–58**, *57–58*
    keywords, **58–60**, *59*
    labeling, **56–57**, *56*
    rating, **55–56**, *56*
    zooming and comparing, 54, *54–55*
source
    batch processing, 381
    History Brush, 142
    Web Gallery images, 371
Space menu, **88**
Spatter option, 355
Specular Highlights settings, 293
split neutral-density filters, 2, **187–188**,
    187–188
Split Toning tab, **85**
Spot Healing Brush tool, 159–160, **162**, 165
Spyder2 monitor-calibrating package, 97
sRGB workspace, 88, **99–100**
stacking images, **51–53**
Stamp Visible layers, 250, *251*
    black-and-white image colorization, 285
    filters, 287
Standard option
    cursor, 108
    Refine Edge, 132, *133*
Standard Screen mode, 111
Startup Scripts preferences, 41, *41*
stitching images. *See* composites
Stop For Errors option, 383
Stops in actions, 380, *380*
storage
    RAW format vs. JPEG, 10
    strategies, **32–33**
straightening horizons, 69, *69*, **156–157**,
    156–157
Strength setting, 331–332